Assessment in Early Childhood Education

SIXTH EDITION

Sue C. Wortham

Professor Emerita
University of Texas at San Antonio

PEARSON

Boston   Columbus   Indianapolis   New York   San Francisco   Upper Saddle River
Amsterdam   Cape Town   Dubai   London   Madrid   Milan   Munich   Paris   Montreal   Toronto
Delhi   Mexico City   São Paulo   Sydney   Hong Kong   Seoul   Singapore   Taipei   Tokyo

Vice President and Editor in Chief: Jeffery W. Johnston
Senior Acquisitions Editor: Julie Peters
Vice President, Director of Marketing: Margaret Waples
Senior Marketing Manager: Christopher Barry
Senior Managing Editor: Pamela Bennett
Senior Project Manager: Mary M. Irvin
Senior Operations Supervisor: Central Publishing
Senior Operations Specialist: Laura Messerly
Senior Art Director: Jayne Conte
Cover Designer: Suzanne Duda
Cover Art: Jupiter Images
Composition: PreMediaGlobal
Printer/Binder: Courier Companies, Inc.
Cover Printer: Courier Companies, Inc.
Text Font: 10.5/12 Giovanni Book

Photo Credits: Image 100, p. 1; Anne Vega/Merrill, pp. 13, 28; Scott Cunningham/Merrill, pp. 40, 227, 249; Patrick White/Merrill, pp. 52, 214; David Mager/Pearson Learning Photo Studio, pp. 80, 143, 149; Katelyn Metzger/Merrill, p. 110; Krista Greco/Merrill, p. 136; Valerie Schultz/Merrill, pp. 166, 242; Ariel Skelley/Getty Images, Inc. – Blend Images, p. 186; Barbara Schwartz/Merrill, pp. 209, 221; George Dodson/PH College, p. 277; Anthony Magnacca/Merrill, p. 288.

NOTE: Every effort has been made to provide accurate and current Internet information in this book. However, the Internet and information posted on it are constantly changing, so it is inevitable that some of the Internet addresses in this textbook will change.

Library of Congress Cataloging-in-Publication Data

Wortham, Sue Clark
Assessment in early childhood education / Sue C. Wortham.—6th ed.
    p. cm.
  ISBN-13: 978-0-13-248122-9
  ISBN-10: 0-13-248122-7
  1. Educational tests and measurements—United States.   2. Psychological tests for children—
  United States.   3. Ability in children—United States—Testing.   4. Early childhood education—
  United States—Evaluation.   I. Title.
  LB3060.217.W67 2012
  372.126—dc22

                                                        2010054568

8 9 10 V092 16 15 14

www.pearsonhighered.com

ISBN-10:   0-13-248122-7
ISBN-13: 978-0-13-248122-9

Preface

Students preparing to become teachers of children from infancy through the primary grades must be prepared to measure or evaluate children who are in the period of development called *early childhood*. Tests and other types of assessments designed for young children are different from those intended for children in later grades in elementary school. Because infants and children under age 8 have developmental limitations different from those of older children, a textbook that includes discussion of assessment in the early childhood years must be written from a developmental perspective.

During the years since 2000, early childhood educators have been challenged in their efforts to assess very young children using the most important strategies for their ongoing development. As a result, it is especially important that future teachers and teachers who are struggling with these issues be fully informed about the range of assessment possibilities and where they are the most beneficial for young children.

Traditional and Authentic Assessment Strategies

This book is written for teachers and future teachers of young children. It includes information about standardized tests and, more important, other types of assessments that are appropriate for young children, such as observation, checklists, and rating scales. Assessments designed by teachers are explained both for preschool children and for kindergarten and primary-grade children who are transitioning into literacy. With the ever-growing trend toward performance assessment, portfolios, and other methods of reporting a child's performance, chapters describing these strategies have been expanded and enhanced. The approach of this edition is the development of an assessment system that includes traditional as well as authentic assessment strategies in a comprehensive plan. Thus, in this new edition, we seek to inform the reader about all types of assessments and their appropriate use.

New to This Edition

- Updated information on standardized tests and examples of standardized tests reports
- New information on children with disabilities throughout the text
- Additional information on environmental assessment
- New information on diagnostic tests for infants and toddlers
- Expanded information on high-stakes testing and issues with the No Child Left Behind Act
- Expanded information on play-based assessment
- Expanded information on the relationship between state standards and performance assessments

How to Assess Young Children

Earlier editions of this book were developed in response to the expressed needs of teachers and graduate students who must understand and use current trends in assessment and put them into perspective within the reality of public schools that are required to focus intensively on standardized tests. Fortunately, commercial publishers of curriculum kits and textbooks for public schools are increasingly including performance as well as traditional assessments in their guides for teachers. Portfolios are becoming common as well. Nevertheless, teachers still need help on how to maintain a balance between these new strategies and standardized testing.

An important factor in the assessment of young children is when and how they should be measured. This is a controversial issue. The strengths and weaknesses of each type of assessment presented are discussed, as is research on the problems surrounding testing and evaluation in early childhood. Because many sources in the literature and other textbooks do not include the limitations as well as the merits of assessment techniques, this text provides an objective perspective on issues surrounding the efficacy and effectiveness of assessment strategies.

Organization

The book is divided into four parts. Part I provides an introduction to assessment in early childhood in **chapters 1** and **2**. Part II is devoted to standardized tests and how they are designed, used, and reported in **chapters 3** and **4**. Classroom assessments are discussed in Part III. Observation, checklists, rating scales, and rubrics are covered in **chapters 5** and **6**, while teacher-designed strategies and performance-based strategies are described in **chapters 7** and **8**. Finally, Part IV is devoted to the use of assessment systems and how all the strategies discussed in the chapters leading

to Part IV can be incorporated into an assessment system or comprehensive assessment plan. **Chapter 9** focuses on the portfolio as an assessment system or part of an assessment system. **Chapter 10** addresses the relationship teachers should have with parents and how a partnership can be developed that will best serve the child's learning and assessment. Included in the relationship is how student progress can be reported to parents and how parents can contribute to the reporting process.

Acknowledgments

I would like to thank the reviewers who provided valuable suggestions and feedback for this sixth edition: Susan Churchill, University of Nebraska–Lincoln; Colleen Klein-Ezell, Southeastern Louisiana University; Julia A. Ray, Southeast Missouri State University; Jocelynn Smrekar, Clarion University of Pennsylvania; Janette C. Wetsel, University of Central Oklahoma; and Karl F. Wheatley, Cleveland State University. Their comments were perceptive and their suggestions constructive. The reviewers were thoughtful in their ideas for how the text could be improved.

It is also important to thank the staff at Pearson, who helped in the conceptualization of important revisions as well as in the production process: Julie Peters, senior acquisitions editor; Mary Irvin, senior project manager; and Nancy Holstein and Penny Burleson, editorial assistants.

About the Author

SUE CLARK WORTHAM is Professor Emerita of Early Childhood and Elementary Education at the University of Texas at San Antonio. Prior to beginning a teaching career in higher education in 1979, she taught prekindergarten through second grade in public schools, worked as a school district administrator, and was a consultant at an education service center.

She has authored numerous texts, including *Early Childhood Curriculum: Developmental Bases for Learning and Teaching* (5th ed., 2010), Pearson. She coauthored *Play and Child Development* (4th ed., 2012) with Joe Frost and Stuart Reifel, also published by Pearson. Organizational publications include *Childhood 1892–2002*, published by the Association for Childhood Education International, and *Playgrounds for Young Children: National Survey and Perspectives*, coauthored with Joe Frost, published by the American Alliance for Health, Physical Education, Recreation, and Dance (AAHPERD).

In 1992, she served as a Fulbright Scholar in Chile. She was president of the Association for Childhood Education International (ACEI) from 1995 to 1997. Since retirement, she has been very active in the development of the Global Guidelines for Early Childhood Education and Care that resulted from an international symposium held in Ruschlikon, Switzerland, in 1999. Subsequently, she has a leadership role in the development, validation, and implementation of the ACEI Global Guidelines Self-Assessment Tool adapted from the original guidelines. To date it has been used in twenty countries and has been translated into Spanish, French, Chinese, and Portuguese.

Dr. Wortham has served as director of educational programs for World Children's Relief and Volunteer Organization, a small nongovernmental organization (NGO), for the past 8 years. She engaged in training teachers and principals in Haiti, Senegal, Burkina Faso, and Sierra Leone. The teacher-training program developed for World Children's Relief is now sponsored by the ACEI.

Brief Contents

Contents

CHAPTER 2

How Infants and Young Children Should Be Assessed   28

PART II   Standardized Tests

CHAPTER 3

How Standardized Tests Are Used, Designed, and Selected   52

CHAPTER 4

Using and Reporting Standardized Test Results   80

PART III   Classroom Assessments

CHAPTER 5

Observation   *110*

CHAPTER 7

Teacher-Designed Strategies   186

PART IV   Using Assessment Systems

CHAPTER 9

Portfolio Assessment   *242*

Communicating With Families   277

*C*HAPTER 1

An Overview of Assessment in Early Childhood

Chapter Objectives

As a result of reading this chapter, you will be able to

1. Understand the purposes of assessment in early childhood
2. Understand different meanings of the term *assessment*
3. Understand the history of tests and measurements in early childhood
4. Develop an awareness of issues in testing young children

Understanding Assessment in Infancy and Early Childhood

Not too long ago, resources on early childhood assessment were limited to occasional articles in journals, chapters in textbooks on teaching in early childhood programs, and a few small textbooks that were used as secondary texts in an early childhood education course. Very few teacher preparation programs offered a course devoted to assessment in early childhood. Now, in the 21st century, assessment of very young children has experienced a period of very rapid growth and expansion. In fact, it has been described as a "virtual explosion of testing in public schools" (Meisels & Atkins-Burnett, 2005, p. 1).

There has also been an explosion in the numbers of infants, toddlers, and preschoolers in early childhood programs and the types of programs that serve them. Moreover, the diversity among these young children increases each year. Currently, Head Start programs serve children and families who speak at least 140 different languages. In some Head Start classrooms, ten different languages might be used. Head Start teaching teams may also be multilingual, also representing diversity (David, 2005).

What Is Assessment?

What do we need to know about all these diverse children with all kinds of families, cultures, and languages? The study of individuals for measurement purposes begins before birth with assessment of fetal growth and development. At birth and throughout infancy and early childhood, various methods of measurement are used to evaluate the child's growth and development. Before a young child enters a preschool program, he or she is measured through medical examinations. Children are also measured through *observations* of developmental milestones, such as saying the first word or walking independently, by parents and other family members. Children might also be screened or evaluated for an early childhood program or service. Assessment is really a *process*. A current definition describes the assessment process: "Assessment is the process of gathering information about children from several forms of evidence, then organizing and interpreting that information" (McAfee, Leong, & Bodrova, 2004, p. 3).

Assessment of children from birth through the preschool years is different from assessment of older people. Not only can young children not write or read, but also the young developing child presents different challenges that influence the choice of measurement strategy, or how to measure or assess the child. Assessment methods must be matched with the level of mental, social, and physical development at each stage. Developmental change in young children is rapid, and there is a need to assess whether development is progressing normally. If development is not normal, the measurement and evaluation procedures used are important in making decisions regarding appropriate intervention services during infancy and the preschool years.

Purposes of Assessment

Assessment is used for various purposes. We may want to learn about individual children. We may conduct an *evaluation* to assess a young child's development in language or mathematics. When we need to learn more, we may assess the child by asking her or him to describe what she or he has achieved. For example, a first-grade teacher may use measurement techniques to determine what reading skills have been mastered and what weaknesses exist that indicate a need for additional instruction.

Assessment strategies may be used for *diagnosis.* Just as a medical doctor conducts a physical examination of a child to diagnose an illness, psychologists, teachers, and other adults who work with children can conduct an informal or formal assessment to diagnose a developmental delay or identify causes for poor performance in learning.

If medical problems, birth defects, or developmental delays in motor, language, cognitive, or social development are discovered during the early, critical periods of development, steps can be taken to correct, minimize, or remediate them before the child enters school. For many developmental deficits or differences, the earlier they are detected and the earlier intervention is planned, the more likely the child will be able to overcome them or compensate for them. For example, if a serious hearing deficit is identified early, the child can learn other methods of communicating and acquiring information.

Assessment of young children is also used for *placement*—to place them in infant or early childhood programs or to provide special services. To ensure that a child receives the best services, careful screening and more extensive testing may be conducted before selecting the combination of intervention programs and other services that will best serve the child.

Program planning is another purpose of assessment. After children have been identified and evaluated for an intervention program or service, assessment results can be used in planning the programs that will serve them. These programs, in turn, can be evaluated to determine their effectiveness.

Besides identifying and correcting developmental problems, assessment of very young children is conducted for other purposes. One purpose is *research.* Researchers study young children to better understand their behavior or to measure the appropriateness of the experiences that are provided for them.

The National Early Childhood Assessment Resource Group summarized the purposes for appropriate uses of assessment in the early childhood years as follows:

Purpose 1: Assessing to promote children's learning and development

Purpose 2: Identifying children for health and social services

Purpose 3: Monitoring trends and evaluating programs and services

Purpose 4: Assessing academic achievement to hold individual students, teachers, and schools accountable (Shepard, Kagan, Lynn, & Wurtz, 1998). (See Figure 2-1.)

How were these assessment strategies developed? In the next section, I describe how certain movements or factors, especially during the past century, have affected the development of testing instruments, procedures, and other measurement techniques that are used with infants and young children.

Early Intervention for a Child with
Hearing Impairment

....

ulio, who is 2 years old, was born prematurely. He did not have regular checkups
during his first year, but his mother took him to a community clinic when he had a
cold and fever at about 9 months of age. When the doctor noticed that Julio did not
react to normal sounds in the examining room, she stood behind him and clapped her
hands near each ear. Because Julio did not turn toward the clapping sounds, the doctor
suspected that he had a hearing loss. She arranged for Julio to be examined by an
audiologist at an eye, ear, nose, and throat clinic.

Julio was found to have a significant hearing loss in both ears. He was fitted with
hearing aids and is attending a special program twice a week for children with hearing
deficits. Therapists in the program are teaching Julio to speak. They are also teaching
his mother how to make Julio aware of his surroundings and help him to develop a
vocabulary. Had Julio not received intervention services at an early age, he might have
entered school with severe cognitive and learning deficits that would have put him at a
higher risk for failing to learn.

The Evolution of Assessment
of Young Children

Interest in studying young children to understand their growth and development
dates back to the initial recognition of childhood as a separate period in the life
cycle. Johann Pestalozzi, a pioneer in developing educational programs specifically
for children, wrote about the development of his $3^1/_2$-year-old son in 1774 (Irwin &
Bushnell, 1980). Early publications also reflected concern for the proper upbringing
and education of young children. *Some Thoughts Concerning Education* by John
Locke (1699), *Emile* (Rousseau, 1762/1911), and Frederick Froebel's *Education of
Man* (1896) were influential in focusing attention on the characteristics and needs
of children in the 18th and 19th centuries. Rousseau believed that human nature
was essentially good and that education must allow that goodness to unfold.
He stated that more attention should be given to studying the child so that
education could be adapted to meet individual needs (Weber, 1984). The study
of children, as advocated by Rousseau, did not begin until the late 19th and early
20th centuries.

Scientists throughout the world used observation to measure human behaviors.
Ivan Pavlov proposed a theory of conditioning to change behaviors. Alfred Binet developed the concept of a normal mental age by studying memory, attention, and intelligence in children. Binet and Theophile Simon developed an intelligence scale to
determine mental age that made it possible to differentiate the abilities of individual

children (Weber, 1984). American psychologists expanded these early efforts, developing instruments for various types of measurement.

The study and measurement of young children today has evolved from the child study movement, the development of standardized tests, Head Start and other federal programs first funded in the 1960s, and the passage of Public Law 94-142 (the Individuals with Disabilities Education Act) and Public Law 99-457 (an expansion of PL 94-142 to include infants). Currently, there is a movement toward more meaningful learning or authentic achievement and assessment (Newmann, 1996; Wiggins, 1993). At the same time, continuing progress is being made in identifying, diagnosing, and providing more appropriate intervention for infants and young children with disabilities (Meisels & Fenichel, 1996).

The Child Study Movement

G. Stanley Hall, Charles Darwin, and Lawrence Frank were leaders in the development of the child study movement that emerged at the beginning of the 20th century. Darwin, in suggesting that by studying the development of the infant one could glimpse the development of the human species, initiated the scientific study of the child (Kessen, 1965). Hall developed and extended methods of studying children. After he became president of Clark University in Worcester, Massachusetts, he established a major center for child study. Hall's students—John Dewey, Arnold Gesell, and Lewis Terman—all made major contributions to the study and measurement of children. Dewey advocated educational reform that affected the development of educational programs for young children. Gesell first described the behaviors that emerged in children at each chronological age. Terman became a leader in the development of mental tests (Irwin & Bushnell, 1980; Wortham, 2002).

Research in child rearing and child care was furthered by the establishment of the Laura Spelman Rockefeller Memorial child development grants. Under the leadership of Lawrence Frank, institutes for child development were funded by the Rockefeller grants at Columbia University Teacher's College (New York), the University of Minnesota, the University of California at Berkeley, Arnold Gesell's Clinic of Child Development at Yale University, the Iowa Child Welfare Station, and other locations.

With the establishment of child study at academic centers, preschool children could be observed in group settings, rather than as individuals in the home. With the development of laboratory schools and nursery schools in the home economics departments of colleges and universities, child study research could also include the family in broadening the understanding of child development. Researchers from many disciplines joined in an ongoing child study movement that originated strategies for observing and measuring development. The results of their research led to an abundant literature. Between the 1890s and the 1950s, hundreds of children were studied in academic settings throughout the United States (Weber, 1984). Thus, the child study movement has taught us to use observation and other strategies to assess the child. Investigators today continue to add new knowledge about child development and learning that aids parents, preschool teachers and staff members, and professionals in institutions and agencies that provide services to children and families. In the last decade of the 20th century and in the 21st century, brain research has opened up a whole new perspective of the nature of cognitive development and the importance of the early years for optimum development and later learning (Begley, 1997; Shore, 1997). These new findings have caused early childhood educators to reflect on the factors that affect early development and the implications for programming for children in infancy and early childhood.

Standardized Tests

Standardized testing also began around 1900. When colleges and universities in the East sought applicants from other areas of the nation in the 1920s, they found the high school transcripts of these students difficult to evaluate. The *Scholastic Aptitude Test (SAT)* was established to permit fairer comparisons of applicants seeking admission (Cronbach, 1990).

As public schools expanded to offer 12 years of education, a similar phenomenon occurred. To determine the level and pace of instruction and the grouping of students without regard for socioeconomic class, objective tests were developed (Gardner, 1961). These tests grew out of the need to sort, select, or otherwise make decisions about both children and adults.

The first efforts to design tests were informal. When a psychologist, researcher, or physician needed a method to observe a behavior, he or she developed a procedure to meet those needs. The procedure was often adopted by others with the same needs. When many people wanted to use a particular measurement strategy or test, the developer prepared printed copies for sale. As the demand for tests grew, textbook publishers and firms specializing in test development and production also began to create and sell tests (Cronbach, 1990).

American psychologists built on the work of Binet and Simon in developing the intelligence measures described earlier. Binet's instrument, revised by Terman at Stanford University, came to be known as the *Stanford–Binet Intelligence Scale.* Other Americans, particularly educators, welcomed the opportunity to use precise measurements to evaluate learning. Edward Thorndike and his students designed measures to evaluate achievement in reading, mathematics, spelling, and language ability (Weber, 1984). Because of the work of Terman and Thorndike, testing soon became a science (Scherer, 1999). By 1918, more than 100 standardized tests had been designed to measure school achievement (Monroe, 1918).

After World War II, the demand for dependable and technically refined tests grew, and people of all ages came to be tested. As individuals and institutions selected and developed their own tests, the use of testing became more centralized. Statewide tests were administered in schools, and tests were increasingly used at the national level.

The expanded use of tests resulted in the establishment of giant corporations that could assemble the resources to develop, publish, score, and report the results of testing to a large clientele. Centralization improved the quality of tests and the establishment of standards for test design. As individual researchers and teams of psychologists continue to design instruments to meet current needs, the high quality of these newer tests can be attributed to the improvements and refinements made over the years and to the increased knowledge of test design and validation (Cronbach, 1990).

Head Start and the War on Poverty

Prior to the 1960s, medical doctors, psychologists, and other professionals serving children developed tests for use with preschool children. Developmental measures, IQ tests, and specialized tests to measure developmental deficits were generally used for noneducational purposes. Child study researchers tended to use observational or unobtrusive methods to study the individual child or groups of children. School-age children were tested to measure school achievement, but this type of test was rarely used with preschool children.

After the federal government decided to improve the academic performance of children from low-income homes and those from non-English-speaking backgrounds, test developers moved quickly to design new measurement and evaluation instruments for these preschool and school-age populations.

In the late 1950s, there was concern about the consistently low academic performance of children from poor homes. As researchers investigated the problem, national interest in improving education led to massive funding for many programs designed to reduce the disparity in achievement between poor and middle-class children. The major program that involved preschool children was Head Start. Models of early childhood programs ranging from highly structured academic, child-centered developmental to more traditional nursery school models were designed and implemented throughout the United States (White, 1973; Zigler & Valentine, 1979).

All programs funded by the federal government had to be evaluated for effectiveness. As a result, new measures were developed to assess individual progress and the programs' effectiveness (Laosa, 1982). The quality of these measures was uneven, as was comparative research designed to compare the overall effectiveness of Head Start. Nevertheless, the measures and strategies developed for use with Head Start projects added valuable resources for the assessment and evaluation of young children (Hoepfner, Stern, & Nummedal, 1971).

Other federally funded programs developed in the 1960s, such as bilingual programs, Title I, the Emergency School Aid Act, Follow Through, and Home Start, were similar in effect to Head Start. The need for measurement strategies and tests to evaluate these programs led to the improvement of existing tests and the development of new tests to evaluate their success accurately.

Legislation for Young Children With Disabilities

PL 94-142

Perhaps the most significant law affecting the measurement of children was Public Law (PL) 94-142, the Education for All Handicapped Children Act, passed in 1975. This law, later amended and renamed the Individuals with Disabilities Education Act (IDEA), guaranteed all children with disabilities the right to an appropriate education in a free public school and placement in the least restrictive learning environment. The law further required the use of nondiscriminatory testing and evaluation of these children (McCollum & Maude, 1993).

The implications of the law were far reaching. Testing, identification, and placement of students with mental retardation and those with other disabilities were difficult. Existing tests were no longer considered adequate for children with special

8
....

CHAPTER 1

An Overview
of Assessment
in Early
Childhood

One Family's Experience with Head Start

....

Rosa is a graduate of the Head Start program. For 2 years, she participated in a class housed in James Brown School, a former inner-city school that had been closed and remodeled for other community services. Two Head Start classrooms were in the building, which was shared with several other community agencies serving low-income families. In addition to learning at James Brown School, Rosa went on many field trips, including trips to the zoo, the botanical garden, the public library, and a nearby McDonald's restaurant.

This year Rosa is a kindergarten student at West Oaks Elementary School with her older brothers, who also attended Head Start. Next year, Rosa's younger sister, Luisa, will begin the program. Luisa looks forward to Head Start. She has good memories of the things she observed Rosa doing in the Head Start classroom while visiting the school with her mother.

Luisa's parents are also happy that she will be attending the Head Start program. Luisa's older brothers are good students, which they attribute to the background they received in Head Start. From her work in kindergarten, it appears that Rosa will also do well when she enters first grade.

needs. Classroom teachers had to learn the techniques used to identify students with disabilities and determine how to meet their educational needs (Kaplan & Saccuzzo, 1989).

The law required that a team of teachers, parents, diagnosticians, school psychologists, medical personnel, and perhaps social workers or representatives of government agencies or institutions be used to identify and place students with disabilities. When appropriate, the child must also be included in the decision-making process. The team screens, tests, and develops an Individual Education Programme (IEP) for each child. Not all team members are involved in every step of the process, but they can influence the decisions made.

The term **mainstreaming** came to define the requirement that the child be placed in the least restrictive environment. This meant that as often as possible, the child would be placed with children developing normally, rather than in a segregated classroom for students in special education. How much mainstreaming was beneficial for the individual student? The question was difficult to answer. In addition, the ability of teachers to meet the needs of students with and without disabilities simultaneously in the same classroom is still debated. Nevertheless, classroom teachers were expected to develop and monitor the educational program prescribed for students with disabilities (Clark, 1976).

The identification and diagnosis of students with disabilities is the most complex aspect of PL 94-142. Many types of children need special education, including students with mental retardation, physical and visual disabilities, speech impairments, auditory disabilities, learning disabilities, and emotional disturbances, and students who are gifted. Children may have a combination of disabilities. The identification and comprehensive testing of children to determine what types of disabilities they have and how best to educate them requires a vast array of assessment techniques and instruments. Teachers, school nurses, and other staff members can be involved in initial screening and referral, but the extensive testing used for diagnosis and prescription requires professionals who have been trained to administer psychological tests (Mehrens & Lehmann, 1991).

Under PL 94-142, all children with disabilities between ages 3 and 21 are entitled to free public education. This means that preschool programs must also be provided for children under age 6. Public schools have implemented early childhood programs for children with disabilities, and Head Start programs are required to include them (Guralnick, 1982; Spodek & Saracho, 1994). Other institutions and agencies also provide programs for children with and without disabilities.

PL 99-457

Many of the shortcomings of PL 94-142 were addressed in PL 99-457 (Education of the Handicapped Act Amendments), passed in 1986. The newer law authorized two new programs: the Federal Preschool Program and the Early Intervention Program. Under PL 94-142, the state could choose whether to provide services to children with disabilities between ages 3 and 5. Under PL 99-457, states must prove that they are meeting the needs of all these children if they wish to receive federal funds under PL 94-142. The Federal Preschool Program extends the right of children with disabilities under PL 94-142 to all children with disabilities between ages 3 and 5.

The Early Intervention Program established early intervention services for all children between birth and age 2 who are developmentally delayed. All participating states must now provide intervention services for all infants and toddlers with disabilities (McCollum & Maude, 1993; Meisels & Shonkoff, 1990).

How to measure and evaluate young children with disabilities and the programs that serve them are a continuing challenge (Cicchetti & Wagner, 1990). The design of measures to screen, identify, and place preschool children in intervention programs began with the passage of PL 94-142 and was extended under PL 99-457. Many of these instruments and strategies, particularly those dealing with developmental delay, were also used with preschool programs serving children developing normally, as well as those with developmental delays or disabilities.

As children with disabilities were served in a larger variety of settings, such as preschools, Head Start programs, child-care settings, infant intervention programs, and hospitals, early childhood educators from diverse backgrounds were involved in determining whether infants and young children were eligible for services for special needs. Early childhood educators and other practitioners in the field were challenged to be knowledgeable in measurement and evaluation strategies for effective identification, placement, and assessment of young children in integrated early childhood settings (Goodwin & Goodwin, 1993).

Many questions were raised about appropriately serving young children with diverse abilities. Meeting the developmental and educational needs of infants and preschool children with disabilities and at the same time providing mainstreaming were a complex task. How should these children be grouped for the best intervention services? When children with and without disabilities were grouped together, what were the effects when all of them were progressing through critical periods of development? Not only was identification of young children with disabilities more complex, but evaluation of the infant and preschool programs providing intervention services was also difficult.

PL 101-576

The Americans with Disabilities Act (ADA), passed in 1990 (Stein, 1993), and the amendments to PL 94-142 (IDEA) have had an additional impact on the education of young children with disabilities. Under the ADA, all early childhood programs must be prepared to serve children with special needs. Facilities and accommodations for young children, including outdoor play environments, must be designed, constructed, and altered appropriately to meet the needs of young children with disabilities. The PL 94-142 amendments, passed in 1991, require that the individual educational needs of young children with disabilities must be met in all early childhood programs (Deiner, 1993; McCollum & Maude, 1993; Wolery, Strain, & Bailey, 1992). These laws advance the civil rights of young children and have resulted in the inclusion of young children in preschool and school-age programs. As a result, the concept of mainstreaming is being replaced by **integration**, or **inclusion**, whereby all young children learn together with the goal that the individual needs of all children will be met (Krick, 1992; Wolery & Wilbers, 1994). The efforts of these programs and their services must be assessed and evaluated to determine whether the needs of children are being met effectively.

Individuals with Disabilities Education Improvement Act of 2004

The Congress reauthorized the Education for All Children Act of 1975 in 1997 (IDEA). The reauthorization of the 1997 law required special education students to participate in state tests, and states were to report results of those tests to the public. Many states were slow to comply with the law and there were no consequences for states that did not comply.

The No Child Left Behind Act of 2001 (NCLB) required states to test at least 95% of their students with disabilities. Subsequently, the Individuals with Disabilities Education Improvement Act of 2004 was aligned with the requirements of NCLB. Final regulations of the law were officially published in August 2006. Three important rules addressed the impact of NCLB. A provision of NCLB was that highly qualified teachers must be hired. The regulations clarified this rule for special education teachers: states could create a state standard of evaluation for special education teachers.

NCLB specified that states could still use other methods of diagnosing children with learning disabilities. The response-to-intervention process involved providing intervention services for students. Students who did not respond could be referred for special education services. This process was clarified in the regulations, which stated that states could still use other methods of diagnosing children with learning disabilities. A third provision caused some controversy. This required that students in private schools would be provided services through the public schools. School districts were required to set aside a certain percentage of their federal funds for services to private school students (*Education Week*, n.d; Samuels, 2006; U.S. Department of Education, 2006).

Current Issues and Trends in Assessment in Early Childhood Education

The 1980s brought a new reform movement in education, accompanied by a new emphasis on testing. The effort to improve education at all levels included the use of standardized tests to provide accountability for what students are learning. Minimum competency tests, achievement tests, and screening instruments were used to ensure that students from preschool through college reached the desired educational goals and achieved the minimum standards of education that were established locally or by the state education agency. As we continue in a new century, these concerns have increased.

Trends in a New Century

In the 1990s many schools improved the learning environment and achievement for all children; nevertheless, a large percentage of schools were still low performing in 2000 and 2001. Inadequate funding, teacher shortages, teachers with inadequate training, aging schools, and poor leadership affected quality education (Wortham, 2002).

During the 2000 presidential campaign, candidate George W. Bush named quality education as one of the goals of his presidency. After his election, President Bush worked for legislation that would improve education for all children. After months of dialogue and debate, Congress passed a new education act in December 2001. The No Child Left Behind Act (NCLB), signed into law on January 8, 2002, had an impact on testing required by individual states. In addition to other provisions, all states were required to administer tests developed by the state and to set and monitor adequate yearly progress (Moscosco, 2001; Wortham, 2002).

President Bush was also committed to strengthening early childhood programs. In 2002, several projects were conducted to support early childhood programs. Under the Sunshine Schools program, the U.S. Department of Education focused on what is working in early childhood education and gave attention to highly effective state, district, city, county, and campus programs (Grissom, personal communication, April 4, 2002).

Another Bush initiative, Good Start, Grow Smart, was intended to strengthen Head Start and improve the quality of experiences for children. The initiative provided the following:

- Training for nearly 50,000 Head Start teachers on the best techniques
- Assurance that preschool programs are more closely coordinated with K–12 educational programs
- A research effort to identify effective early literacy programs and practices (Grissom, personal communication, April 4, 2002).

In July 2001, the White House hosted the White House Summit on Early Childhood Cognitive Development. The Early Childhood–Head Start Task Force formed following the summit published a new guide, *Teaching Our Youngest* (Grissom, personal communication, April 4, 2002).

The early childhood education projects initiated by the Bush administration to improve education stressed the importance of improving early childhood programs;

The No Child Left Behind Act of 2001

NCLB requires states to do the following (U.S. Department of Education, 2001):

- Provide public school choice and supplemental services for students in failing schools as early as fall 2002.
- Integrate scientifically based reading research into comprehensive instruction for young children.
- Set and monitor adequate yearly progress, based on baseline 2001–2002 data.
- Issue annual report cards on school performance and statewide test results by 2002–2003.
- Implement annual, standards-based assessments in reading and math for grades 3 to 8 by 2005–2006.
- Assure that all classes are taught by a qualified teacher by 2005–2006.

U.S. Department of Education (2001). Retrieved February 14, 2007, from http://www.ed.gov/aclb/overview/intro/factsheet/html.

nevertheless, there is no doubt that mandates for increased standards-based testing will continue in the future in spite of concerns of their relevancy, especially for young children. Fortunately, child-outcome standards have also been developed by professional organizations in addition to state education agencies. The National Council for the Social Studies issued *Curriculum Standards for the Social Studies* (National Council for the Social Studies, 1994). Improved Head Start Performance Standards published in 1996 included children from birth to age 5 (Early Head Start, 2000). These standards and others provide guidelines for early childhood educators as they strive to improve programs and experiences for young children. By 2005, standards that included early childhood were available in many states. Some were in response to NCLB, but others were part of the emerging efforts to establish state and national standards for development and learning (Seefeldt, 2005).

Individual states are continuing to develop, implement, and review early learning guidelines as the set standards for preschool curriculum. All states except for Hawaii were engaged in or had completed the process in 2009 (National Child Care Information and Technical Assistance Center [NCCIC], 2009).

The Accountability Era

The major issue in education today is the idea of accountability. Even before the rules and regulations surrounding the legislation for No Child Left Behind (NCLB) were issued, there were growing concerns about accountability. The interest in developing more responsibility for student results evolved from a perception that states had been evaluating school systems on the basis of available resources rather than student performance. NCLB addressed student performance, public reporting of achievement results, consequences for poor student performance, and continuous improvement (Edweek, 2004). Individual states were also responding to the need for accountability by moving from a focus on curriculum offerings and funding levels to standards-based accountability. States now have set standards, developed assessment systems, and assigned responsibilities for meeting the goals and designating rewards and sanctions to achievement levels. If states want to continue getting benefits under NCLB, they have to follow the new policies for accountability (National Council of State Legislatures, 2009).

Emerging Issues With NCLB

The requirements of NCLB were to be implemented by 2006. In the summer of 2006 it was evident that there were difficulties in complying with the law.

An early issue was the requirement that schools report test scores by racial subgroup. Nearly two dozen states had been granted waivers in reporting by subgroups. Other schools avoided the problem by determining that numbers of students in racial subgroups were too small to be statistically significant. Their scores were not included (Rebora, 2006).

The law also provided that states would implement standards-based assessments in reading and math by 2006. Ten states were notified in 2006 that a portion of state administrative funds would be withheld for failing to comply fully with NCLB. Twenty-five states might also lose a portion of their aid if they didn't comply fully with NCLB and comply with the testing requirement by the end of the school year. The monetary penalties caught many states by surprise. In addition, states had difficulty providing the extensive documentation required to demonstrate that the tests met that state's academic standards (Olson, 2006). Further, states had to

Assessments can be conducted while young children engage in independent work.

14

....

CHAPTER 1

*An Overview
of Assessment
in Early
Childhood*

demonstrate how they were including students with disabilities and English language learners (ELLs) in their testing system. This included developing alternative assessments when needed. When combined with concerns about testing young children in the early childhood years, NCLB had an impact on all populations of students, including those in the preschool years.

The reauthorization of NCLB was due in 2007. Congress had already blocked action on the reauthorization until after the 2008 election. The Obama administration indicated in 2009 that the rewriting of the law would focus on teacher quality, academic standards, and more attention given to help failing schools and students. The Commission on No Child Left Behind (2009) urged Secretary of Education Arne Duncan to retain some core elements of NCLB. Regardless of the direction of continuing reform in education, the federal government would continue to expand its influence on accountability and would also encourage the movement from individual state standards to national standards (Dillon, 2009; *The New York Times*, 2009).

Concerns About Testing Young Children in Early Childhood Settings

The increased use of testing at all levels has been an issue in American education, but the testing of young children is of particular concern. Standardized tests and other assessment measures are now being used in preschool, kindergarten, and primary grades to determine whether children will be admitted to preschool programs, promoted to the next grade, or retained. During the late 1980s and early 1990s, tests were used to determine whether students should be promoted from kindergarten to first grade or placed in a "transitional" first grade. Although this practice is now less popular, it persists in some school districts and states (Smith, 1999). In 2000, the National Association of Early Childhood Specialists in State Departments of Education (NAECS/SDE) was concerned about the continuing trend to deny children's entry to kindergarten and first grade. They issued a position statement, "Still! Unacceptable Trends in Kindergarten Entry and Placement" (National Association of Early Childhood Specialists in State Departments of Education [NAECS/SDE], 2000). This continuing effort to advocate appropriate assessment of very young children was endorsed by the Governing Board of the National Association for the Education of Young Children (NAEYC, 2001).

By 2006, states used a wide range of types of assessments with young children entering public school. Screening tests were in use in many states for hearing and vision as well as developmental assessments and readiness tests. Many states conducted screening to identify children at risk for failing to succeed in school and/or developmental disorders or disabilities. Some states met the criteria for developmentally appropriate assessments, while others did not. For example, California required observation and portfolio materials in preschool assessments. On the other hand, Georgia students were tested for first-grade readiness at the end of the kindergarten year to determine grade placement (Education Commission of the States, 2006). More information on these topics will be provided in later chapters.

The announcement by President Bush in 2003 that all Head Start students would be given a national standardized test assessment raised new concerns. At issue were validity and reliability of tests for preschool children (Nagle, 2000) and whether such "high-stakes" testing should be used to evaluate the quality of Head Start programs (Shepard et al., 1998). Policy makers had to address these and other concerns about appropriate assessment of young children in their decisions about how to evaluate preschool programs that receive federal funding (McMaken, 2003).

In February 2003, a large group of early childhood experts wrote to their congressional representatives to express their concerns about the impending test. They made the following points:

1. The test is too narrow.
2. The test may reduce the comprehensive services that ensure the success of Head Start.
3. The test is shifting resources away from other needs within Head Start.
4. Testing should be used to strengthen teaching practices, not evaluate a program, and should in no way be linked to program funding (Fair Test, 2003; NAEYC, 2004).

In September 2003, the new test, the *National Reporting System* (NRS) (U.S. Department of Health and Human Services [HHS] Head Start Bureau, 2003), was administered by the Head Start Bureau in the Department of Health and Human Services (HHS) Administration for Children and Families to more than 400,000 children ages 4 and 5, and continues to be administered each year. In 2005, when Head Start funding was being considered, the Government Accountability Office (GAO) issued a report on the NRS. The report said that the NRS had not shown that it provided reliable information on children's progress during the Head Start program year, especially for Spanish-speaking children. Moreover, the NRS had not shown that its results were valid measures of the learning that took place in the program. In its recommendations, the GAO required that the Head Start Bureau establish validity and reliability for the NRS. As a result the NRS was not to be used for accountability purposes related to program funding (Crawford, 2005; Government Accountability Office [GAO], 2005). Because the Bush administration reportedly intended to use the NRS to establish accountability requirements similar to NCLB, this GAO finding essentially halted the use of the test for that purpose.

Concerns About Testing Young Children With Cultural and Language Differences

A concurrent concern related to current trends and practices in the assessment of young children is the question of how appropriate our tests and assessment strategies are in terms of the diversity of young children attending early childhood programs. Socioeconomic groups are changing dramatically and rapidly in our society, with an expansion of the poorer class and a corresponding shrinking of the middle class (Raymond & McIntosh, 1992). At the same time, an increase in minority citizens has occurred as the result of the continuing influx of people from other countries, especially Southeast Asia and Central and South America. Moreover, Hispanic families are no longer concentrated in the Southwest; their growth in many parts of the country has caused new communities to have unprecedented high percentages of Hispanic children. Seventy-nine percent of young ELLs in public schools speak Spanish. In addition, approximately 460 languages are represented in schools and programs in the United States, including Spanish, Chinese, Arabic, Armenian, and Hmong (Biggar, 2005; Lopez, Salas, & Flores, 2005). Assessment of the developmental progress of children from these groups is particularly important if their learning needs are to be identified and addressed.

Evidence shows that standardized test scores have had a high correlation to parents' occupations, level of education, the location of the student's elementary school, and the family's income bracket. Moreover, students from limited English backgrounds tend to score lower on reading and language fluency tests in English. They typically perform better on computational portions of mathematics tests (Wesson, 2001). The fairness of existing tests for children who are school disadvantaged and linguistically and culturally diverse indicates the need for alternative assessment strategies for young children (Biggar, 2005; Goodwin & Goodwin, 1993, 1997). A major issue in the 21st century is appropriate measurement and evaluation strategies that will enhance, rather than diminish, the potential for achievement.

The history of assessment of minorities who are bilingual students or learning English as a second language is one of potential bias. Children have been and continue to be tested in their nondominant language (English) or with instruments that were validated on an Anglo, middle-class sample of children. As a result, many Hispanic preschool children were and are still regularly diagnosed as developmentally delayed and placed in special education (Lopez et al., 2005). The issue of appropriate assessment of these children was addressed by court cases such as *Diana v. California State Board of Education* (1968) and *Lau v. Nichols* (1974). More recently, NCLB and the Head Start NRS have addressed the issue of testing ELLs (Crawford, 2005; David, 2005; GAO, 2005).

The overidentification of minority students for special education is often related to language and cultural differences. Some of the issues addressed in the rising numbers of minority children being referred to special education were traced in one study to inconsistent methods of determining home language and English proficiency, confusion as to the purpose of language screening instruments, and a need for more training for teachers in meeting the needs of culturally and linguistically diverse children and families (Abebe & Hailemariam, 2008; Hardin, Roach-Scott, & Peisner-Feinberg, 2007).

Increasing concerns about overidentification of minority children is addressed in two significant books. *Why Are So Many Minority Students in Special Education? Understanding Race and Disability in Schools* (Harry & Klingner, 2005) is one effort to explain the problem. The authors address the issue of the disproportionate representation of minorities in special education. *Racial Inequity in Education* (Loren & Orfield, 2002) addresses many factors that include language, high-stakes testing, inappropriate and inadequate special education for minority children, and the role of the federal government.

Another concern about testing children with cultural and language differences is the process of screening preschool children who fit into this category. A problem of correctly screening young children who are learning English may lead to the underidentification of children who have special needs or overidentification of special needs because English language delays are misdiagnosed as a disability (NAEYC, 2005a). Recommendations were made for appropriate screening and assessment and program accountability for correctly serving young children in English.

The impact of NCLB on testing ELLs has resulted in the development of new English language proficiency tests based on new standards adopted by each state. More importantly, the tests measure the reading, writing, speaking, and listening skills of ELLs (Zehr, 2006). In summer 2006, five states had failed to meet the Department of Education's deadline to have tests in place. While some states designed their own tests, other states adopted tests designed by consortia or testing corporations. Nevertheless, because test development and implementation were still in the beginning stages, little was known about the validity and reliability of the tests and whether the tests met the requirements of the law. The New York example reveals the complexity of the assessment of ELLs. The New York State test was designed to measure language acquisition, while the tests meeting NCLB measured English language skills. This was true for bilingual and ELL programs throughout the United States prior to NCLB. It would take many years to develop and validate tests that would resolve how to assess the language skills of limited-English speakers that were comparable with tests for English-speaking students.

Assessment of young children who are from families that are culturally and linguistically diverse must include many dimensions of diversity. It is not useful to proceed with assessment that is culturally fair for Hispanic or Asian populations generally. The many variations within communities and cultures must be considered, among them the educational background of the parents and the culture of the immediate community of the family. Congruence between the individual cultural perceptions of the assessors and the children being assessed, even when both are from the same culture or language population, must also be considered (Barrera, 1996). Many types of information, including the child's background and the use of assessments, must be combined to determine a picture of the child that reflects individual, group, and family cultural characteristics (Lopez et al., 2005).

Concerns About Testing Young Children With Disabilities

The use of testing for infants and young children with disabilities cannot be avoided. Indeed, Meisels, Steele, and Quinn-Leering (1993) reflected that not all tests used are bad. Nevertheless, Greenspan, Meisels, and others (1996) believe that assessments used with infants and young children have been borrowed from assessment methodology used with older children and do not represent meaningful information about their developmental achievements and capacities. Misleading test scores are being used for decisions about services, educational placements, and intervention programs. These developmental psychologists propose that assessment should be based on current understanding of development and use structured tests as one part of an integrated approach that includes observing the child's interactions with trusted caregivers. Assessment should be based on multiple sources of information that reflect the child's capacities and competencies and better indicate what learning environments will best provide intervention services for the child's optimal development.

Play-based assessment is one major source of information among the multiple sources recommended. Play assessment is nonthreatening and can be done unobtrusively. Moreover, during play, children can demonstrate skills and abilities that might not be apparent in other forms of assessment. Children's ability to initiate and carry out play schemes and use play materials can add significant information (Fewell & Rich, 1987; Segal & Webber, 1996). In transdisciplinary play-based assessment, a team that includes parents observes a child at play. Each member of the team observes an area of development. During the assessment the child's developmental level, learning styles, patterns of interaction, and other behaviors are observed (Linder, 1993).

NCLB has had an impact on curriculum and assessment of children with disabilities. While identification of children can begin very early in life, the needs of the children as they enter public education are not usually identified until first grade. However, during the last 10 years, the nature and objectives of kindergarten have changed because of advances in knowledge about what young children are capable of learning and the advent of the standards-based accountability movement. Kindergarteners are taught and tested on the mastery of academic standards. This change in expectations has affected the kindergarten year for children at risk for learning disabilities. The kindergarten year formerly was used to work with at-risk children and refer them for testing at the end of the year. When they reached first grade they would be referred for identification and possible special education services. Children with disabilities or who are at risk for learning problems now need identification and services earlier than first grade. Identification of disabilities and referral for services should now be considered for the kindergarten year, even if some disabilities are difficult to identify in early childhood (Litty & Hatch, 2006).

NCLB also added accountability measures to IDEA, as described earlier in the chapter. School districts must test at least 95% of students with disabilities and incorporate their test scores into school ratings. There has been strong public reaction to the inclusion of special education students in state testing and reporting. Some policy makers see this provision as an important step in every child receiving a high-quality education. Critics worry that the law is not flexible enough to meet individual needs of students with disabilities. Many teachers felt that special education students should not be expected to meet the same set of academic content standards as regular education students. These issues were yet to be resolved when the final regulations were published in August 2006 for the Individuals with Disabilities Education Improvement Act of 2004 (*Education Week*, n.d.; U.S. Department of Education, 2006).

Since 2006, work has continued to address the issue of identifying and serving students with learning disabilities. The focus of this effort has been to find more flexible and research-based strategies for both identifying students who need intervention services and better serving students with quality instruction and evaluation (Division for Early Childhood of the Council for Exceptional Children, 2007). Two models for a more inclusive instructional process for all students are Response to Intervention (RTI) and Universal Design for Learning (UDL).

Response to Intervention addresses all student needs whether or not they have been identified as learning disabled. RTI is implemented through a three-tiered process of responding to the needs of all children (Burns & Coolong-Chaffin, 2006; Millard, 2004). All students begin at the first tier. Students who need more targeted education are served in the second tier. Students who need intensive intervention are served in the third tier. This tier can include special education services.

The RTI model seeks to match students with the most effective instruction. The core features of RTI are high-quality classroom instruction, research-based instruction, classroom performance, universal screening, continuous progress monitoring during interventions, and fidelity measures (Millard, 2004).

Universal Design for Learning (UDL) also seeks to include all kinds of students, including students with learning disabilities, English language barriers, emotional or behavior problems, lack of interest or engagement, or sensory and physical disabilities. UDL is based on the need for multiple approaches to instruction that meet the needs of diverse students (Center for Applied Special Technology [CAST], 2009). It applies recent research on neuroscience and uses technology to make learning more effective for all students. The curriculum includes customized teaching that includes multiple means of representation, multiple means of action and expression, and multiple means of engagement (CAST, 2009).

Authentic and Performance Assessment

Assessment is in a period of transition. Teachers of young children are moving from more traditional strategies of assessing for knowledge and facts to assessing the students' ability to reason and solve problems. Despite the demands for accountability for addressing early childhood standards, assessments provide a variety of methods for children to demonstrate what they understand and can do.

A broader view of assessment has incorporated a multidimensional approach to measurement, as described earlier in the sections on concerns for assessment of children from diverse populations and children with disabilities. It is now felt that too much attention has been given to the use of standardized tests, rather than a multidimensional approach that uses many sources of information. The more inclusive practice of assessment, which includes work samples, observation results, and teaching report forms, is called **alternative assessment**. These alternatives to standardized tests measure how students can apply the knowledge they have learned (Blum & Arter, 1996; Maeroff, 1991). Within this evolution in the purposes for assessment and interpretation of assessments is the move to authentic and performance assessments. **Authentic assessments** must have some connection to the real world; that is, they must have a meaningful context. They are contextual in that they emerge from the child's accomplishments. **Performance assessments** permit the child to demonstrate what is understood through the performance of a task or activity (Wortham, 1998).

Performance assessment as applied through the use of portfolios provides a multifaceted view of what the young child can understand and use. Performance assessment is used because teachers in early childhood programs seek information about the child's development and accomplishments in all domains. Performance assessment combined with other assessments provides a longitudinal record of change in development, rather than an assessment of a limited range of skills at a particular time. It is appropriately used with infants, young children, school-age children, children from diverse populations, and children with disabilities (Barrera, 1996; Meisels, 1996; Wortham, 1998).

Documentation is another form of performance assessment. First developed in Reggio Emilia schools in Italy and now widely used in the United States, documentation is a process of collecting and displaying children's work on projects (Wurm, 2005). More about documentation will be discussed in chapter 8.

This broader view of assessment in early childhood programs is echoed by the organizations that endorsed and supported the *Guidelines for Appropriate Curriculum Content and Assessment in Programs Serving Children Ages 3 Through 8*, a position statement of the NAEYC and the NAECS/SDE adopted in 1990 and renewed in 2000 and 2001 (NAEYC, 1992; NAECS/SDE, 2000). These guidelines proposed that the purpose of assessment is to benefit individual children and to improve early childhood programs. Appropriate assessment should help enhance curriculum choices, help teachers collaborate with parents, and help ensure that the needs of children are addressed appropriately. Rather than being narrowly defined as testing, assessment should link curriculum and instruction with program objectives for young children (Hills, 1992). Authentic and performance assessments provide dynamic assessment approaches that benefit the child, parents, caregivers, and teachers.

Standards for Beginning Teachers

The era of accountability includes expectations for the appropriate preparation of teachers. Just as states set standards for student curriculum and assessment for diverse children, there are standards for preparing and assessing whether beginning teachers are qualified to teach young children.

The Interstate New Teacher Assessment and Support Consortium (INTASC) includes state education agencies and national education organizations. The consortium believes that each state's education system should have a teacher licensing policy that requires teachers to know and be able to effectively help all students achieve the state standards for students (Council of State School Officers, 2007, 2009).

The Mission of INTASC

The mission of INTASC is to provide a forum for its member states to learn and collaborate in the development of

- Compatible educational policy on teaching among the states.
- New accountability requirements for teacher preparation programs.
- New techniques to assess the performance of teachers for licensing and evaluation.
- New programs to enhance the professional development of teachers (Council of Chief State School Officers, 2007, p. 1).

The licensing standards for early childhood teachers has been addressed by three organizations: the Association of Teacher Education (ATE), the National Association for the Education of Young Children (NAEYC), and the Association for Childhood Education International (ACEI). A position statement on early childhood teachers was issued by ATE and NAEYC in 1991 (ATE & NAEYC, 1991). The position statement also calls for state early childhood organizations and agencies to develop policies leading to certification that is distinct from policies related to elementary and secondary certification. In addition, policies for early childhood teachers should be congruent across the 50 states.

The *Position Paper on the Preparation of Early Childhood Education Teachers* was issued by ACEI in 1998 (Association for Childhood Education International [ACEI], 1998). It calls for early childhood specialization to be developed within broader policies for teacher preparation. Early childhood teachers should have a broad and liberal education. Experiences should also include foundations of early childhood education, child development, the teaching and learning process, and provisions for professional laboratory experiences.

NAEYC also developed a position statement on ethical conduct (NAEYC, 2005). Standards of ethical behavior by early childhood care and education teachers are based on a commitment to

- Appreciate childhood as a unique and valuable stage of the human life cycle.
- Base our work on knowledge of how children develop and learn.
- Appreciate and support the bond between child and family.
- Recognize that children are best understood and supported in the context of family, culture, community, and society.
- Respect the dignity, worth, and uniqueness of each individual (child, family member, and colleague).
- Respect diversity in children, families, and colleagues.
- Recognize that children and adults achieve their full potential in the context of relationships that are based on trust and respect (NAEYC, 2005b, p. 1).

Summary

The measurement and assessment of children begins very early in the life span. Newborns are tested for their neonatal status, and infant tests designed to assess development begin the trend for testing and assessment in the early childhood years. Assessments in the early childhood years have many purposes; some are beneficial for young children, and others are detrimental.

The advent of measures to assess and evaluate young children's development and learning occurred at the beginning of the 20th century. As the decades passed, significant trends in the study of young children and services and programs implemented for young children have driven the need to develop standardized tests and other measures to evaluate children's progress and program effectiveness.

Many issues surround the testing of young children. Some educators question the validity and reliability of standardized tests used with young children, as well as the purposes for administering tests to children who are culturally and linguistically diverse. At the same time, the use of individual testing and evaluation to identify children with disabilities and provide services for them continues to serve a valuable purpose.

REVIEW QUESTIONS

1. Why are very young children measured in infancy and in the preschool years? Give examples.
2. Explain developmental deficits. How are developmental deficits identified and treated?
3. Why is research conducted on the development of very young children? How can such research be used?
4. How were Pestalozzi and Rousseau pivotal in the origins of understanding and measuring young children?
5. Why has the child study movement been the major resource for understanding child development?
6. How does the history of standardized testing include testing with infants and young children? What kinds of standardized tests are beneficial for children under age 6?

7. Why were standardized tests developed for Head Start? How were they used?
8. Why were standardized tests developed as a result of legislation for young children with disabilities? How are they used?
9. Why is it difficult to develop assessments for children who are culturally and linguistically different? What factors must be addressed in their assessment?
10. What are some of the weaknesses in assessments of young children with disabilities? How can these difficulties be overcome?
11. How is authentic assessment different from assessment using standardized tests?

SUGGESTED ACTIVITIES

1. Review a recent journal article on a topic related to current issues in the testing and assessment of young children. The article should have been published within the past 5 years. Describe the major points in the article and your response. Be prepared to share in small groups.
2. What are the policies followed in your state regarding the use of standardized tests? What

tests are administered in the primary grades? How are they chosen? How are the results used?
3. How does the school district in your community screen preschool children for possible disabilities? What types of assessments are used? If children need further testing to identify specific needs, what process is used? Who conducts the tests with the child?

KEY TERMS

alternative assessment
authentic assessment
documentation
inclusion

integration
mainstreaming
performance assessment

$\mathcal{S}$ELECTED WEB SITES

National Child Care Information and Technical
Assistance Center
http://nccic.acf.hhs.gov

National Conference of State Legislatures
http://www.ncsl.org

Association for Childhood Education International
http://www.acei.org

National Association for the Education of Young
Children
http://www.naeyc.org

Council of Chief State School Officers
http://www.ccsso.org

$\mathcal{R}$EFERENCES

Abebe, S., & Hailemariam, A. (2008). Factors influencing teachers' decisions to refer students for special education evaluation. Retrieved July 15, 2009, from http://ERICWebPortal/custom/portlets/recordED503139

Association of Childhood Education International. (1998). ACEI position paper. Preparation of early childhood education teachers. Retrieved July 16, 2009, from http://www.acei.org/prepec.htm

Association of Teacher Educators & National Association for the Education of Young Children (1991, July/August). Early childhood teacher certification. A position statement of the Association of Teacher Educators and the National Association for the Education of Young Children. Washington, DC: NAEYC.

Barrera, I. (1996). Thoughts on the assessment of young children whose sociocultural background is unfamiliar to the assessor. In S. J. Meisels & E. Fenichel (Eds.), *New visions for the developmental assessment of infants and young children* (pp. 69–84). Washington, DC: Zero to Three: National Center for Infants, Toddlers, and Families.

Begley, S. (1997, Spring/Summer). How to build a baby's brain. *Newsweek Special Edition*, 28–32.

Biggar, H. (2005). NAEYC recommendations on screening and assessment of young English-language learners. *Young Children, 60*(6), 44–47.

Blum, R. E., & Arter, J. A. (1996). Setting the stage. In R. E. Blum & J. A. Arter (Eds.), *A handbook for student performance assessment in an era of restructuring* (pp. I:1–I:2). Alexandria, VA: Association for Supervision and Curriculum Development.

Burns, M. K., & Coolong-Chaffin, M. (2006, November). Response to intervention: The rate of and effect on school psychology. *School Psychology Forum: Research in Practice, 1*, 3–15.

Center for Applied Special Technology (CAST). (2009). What is Universal Design for Learning? Retrieved July 15, 2009, from http://www.cast.org/research/wd/index.html.

Cicchetti, D., & Wagner, S. (1990). Alternative assessment strategies for the evaluation of infants and toddlers: An organizational perspective. In S. J. Meisels & J. P. Shonkoff (Eds.), *Handbook of early childhood intervention* (pp. 246–277). New York: Cambridge University Press.

Clark, E. A. (1976). Teacher attitudes toward integration of children with handicaps. *Education and Training of the Mentally Retarded, 11*, 333–335.

Commission on No Child Left Behind. The Aspen Institute. (2009, July 13). Commission urges Duncan to uphold core NCLB elements in the law. Retrieved July 21, 2009, from http://www.aspeninstitute.org/2009/07/13/commission

Council of Chief State School Officers. (2007). Interstate New Teacher Assessment and Support Consortium (INTASC). Retrieved July 16, 2009, from http://www.ccsso.org/Projects/interstate_new_teacher_assessment

Council of Chief State School Officers. (2009). INTASC Standards Development. Retrieved July 16, 2009, from http://www.ccsso.org/ projects/Interstate_new_teacher_assessment

Crawford, J. (2005, May/June). Test driven. *NABE News, 28*, 1.

Cronbach, L. J. (1990). *Essentials of psychological testing* (5th ed.). New York: Harper & Row.

David, J. (2005). Head Start embraces language diversity. *Young Children, 60*(6), 40–43.

Deiner, P. L. (1993). *Resources for teaching children with diverse abilities.* Fort Worth, TX: Harcourt Brace Jovanovich.

Dillon, S. (2009, April 14). Education standards likely to see toughening. *The New York Times.com* (1–4). Retrieved July 2, 2009, from http://www.nytimes.com/2009/04/15/education

Division for Early Childhood of the Council for Exceptional Children. (2007). Promoting positive outcomes for children with disabilities. Missoula, MT: Author

Early Head Start. (2000, December). What Is Early Head Start? Retrieved January 29, 2007, from http://www.ehsnrc.org/Aboutus/ehs.htm

Education Commission of the States. (2006). Kindergarten screening and assessment requirements. Retrieved January 29, 2007, from http://mb2.ecs.org/reports/Report.aspx?id=31

Education Week. (2009, July 15). Accountability. Retrieved July 15, 2009, from http://www.edweek.org/re/issues/accountability/

Education Week. (n.d.) *Special education.* Retrieved January 29, 2007, from http://www.edweek.org/rc/issues/special_education

Fair Test. (2003). Head Start Letter. Retrieved January 29, 2007, from http://www.fairtest.org/nattest/Head_Start_Letter.html

Fewell, R. R., & Rich, J. (1987). Play assessment as a procedure for examining cognitive, communication, and social skills in multihandicapped children. *Journal of Psychoeducational Assessment, 2,* 107–118.

Froebel, F. (1896). *Education of man.* New York: Appleton.

Gardner, J. W. (1961). *Excellence: Can we be equal and excellent too?* New York: Harper & Row.

Goodwin, W. L., & Goodwin, L. D. (1993). Young children and measurement: Standardized and nonstandardized instruments in early childhood education. In B. Spodek (Ed.), *Handbook of research on the education of young children* (pp. 441–463). New York: Macmillan.

Goodwin, W. L., & Goodwin, L. D. (1997). Using standardized measures for evaluating young children's learning. In B. Spodek & O. N. Saracho (Eds.), *Issues in early childhood educational assessment and evaluation* (pp. 92–107). New York: Teachers College Press.

Government Accountability Office. (2005, May). Further development could allow results of new test to be used for decision making. Retrieved January 29, 2007, from http://www.gao.gov/new.items/d05343.pdf

Greenspan, S. I., Meisels, S. J., & the Zero to Three Work Group on Developmental Assessment. (1996). Toward a new vision for the developmental assessment of infants and young children. In S. J. Meisels & E. Fenichel (Eds.), *New visions for the developmental assessment of infants and young children* (pp. 11–26). Washington, DC: Zero to Three: National Center for Infants, Toddlers, and Families.

Guralnick, M. J. (1982). Mainstreaming young handicapped children: A public policy and ecological systems analysis. In B. Spodek (Ed.), *Handbook of research in early childhood education* (pp. 456–500). New York: Free Press.

Hardin, B. J., Roach-Scott, M., & Peisner-Feinberg, E. S. (2007). Special education referral evaluation and placement practices for preschool English language learners. *Journal of Research in Childhood Education, 22,* 39–54.

Harry, B., & Klingner, J. (2005). *Why are so many minority students in special education? Understanding race and disability in schools.* New York: Teachers College Press.

Hills, T. W. (1992). Reaching potentials through appropriate assessment. In S. Bredekamp & T. Rosegrant (Eds.), *Reaching potentials: Appropriate curriculum and assessment for young children* (pp. 43–64). Washington, DC: National Association for the Education of Young Children.

Hoepfner, R., Stern, C., & Nummedal, S. (Eds.). (1971). *CSE-ECRC preschool/kindergarten test evaluations.* Los Angeles: University of California, Graduate School of Education.

Irwin, D. M., & Bushnell, M. M. (1980). *Observational strategies for child study.* New York: Holt, Rinehart & Winston.

Kaplan, R. M., & Saccuzzo, D. P. (1989). *Psychological testing: Principles, applications, and issues* (2nd ed.). Belmont, CA: Brooks/Cole.

Kessen, W. (1965). *The child*. New York: Wiley.

Krick, J. C. (1992). All children are special. In B. Neugebauer (Ed.), *Alike and different: Exploring our humanity with young children* (Rev. ed., pp. 152–158). Washington, DC: National Association for the Education of Young Children.

Laosa, L. M. (1982). The sociocultural context of evaluation. In B. Spodek (Ed.), *Handbook of research in early childhood education* (pp. 501–520). New York: Free Press.

Linder, T. W. (1993). *Transdisciplinary play-based assessment (TPBA): A functional approach to working with young children* (Rev. ed.). Baltimore: Brookes.

Litty, C. G., & Hatch, A. (2006, February). Hurry up and wait: Rethinking special education identification in kindergarten. *Early Childhood Education Journal, 33*, 203–208.

Locke, J. (1699). *Some thoughts concerning education* (4th ed.). London: Churchill.

Lopez, E. J., Salas, L., & Flores, J. P. (2005). Hispanic preschool children: What about assessment and intervention? *Young Children, 60*(6), 48–54.

Losen, D. J., & Orfield, J. *Racial inequality in special education*. Retrieved July 15, 2009, from https://www.gse.harvard.edu

Maeroff, G. I. (1991, December). Assessing alternative assessment. *Phi Delta Kappan*, 272–281.

McAfee, A., Leong, D. J., & Bodrova, E. (2004). *Basics of assessment. A primer for early childhood education*. Washington, DC: National Association for the Education of Young Children.

McCollum, J. A., & Maude, S. P. (1993). Portrait of a changing field: Policy and practice in early childhood special education. In B. Spodek (Ed.), *Handbook of research on the education of young children* (pp. 352–371). New York: Macmillan.

McMaken, J. (2003, March). *Early childhood assessment*. Denver, CO: Education Commission of the States. Retrieved January 29, 2007, from https://www.ecs.org/html/Document.asp?chouseid=4319

Mehrens, W. A., & Lehmann, I. J. (1991). *Measurement and evaluation in education and psychology* (4th ed.). New York: Harcourt Brace.

Meisels, S. J. (1996). Charting the continuum of assessment and intervention. In S. J. Meisels & E. Fenichel (Eds.), *New visions for the developmental assessment of infants and young children* (pp. 27–52). Washington, DC: Zero to Three: National Center for Infants, Toddlers, and Families.

Meisels, S. J., & Atkins-Burnett, S. A. (2005). *Developmental screening in early childhood: A guide* (5th ed.). Washington, DC: National Association for the Education of Young Children.

Meisels, S. J., & Fenichel, E. (Eds.). (1996). *New visions for the developmental assessment of infants and young children*. Washington, DC: Zero to Three: National Center for Infants, Toddlers, and Families.

Meisels, S. J., & Shonkoff, J. P. (Eds.). (1990). *Handbook of early childhood intervention*. New York: Cambridge University Press.

Meisels, S. J., Steele, D. M., & Quinn-Leering, K. (1993). Testing, tracking, and retaining young children: An analysis of research and social policy. In B. Spodek (Ed.), *Handbook of research on the education of young children* (pp. 279–292). New York: Macmillan.

Millard, D. (2004). Understanding responsiveness to intervention in learning disabilities determination. Retrieved July 15, 2009, from http://www.wrightslaw.com/infor/rti.index.htm

Monroe, W. S. (1918). Existing tests and standards. In G. W. Whipple (Ed.), *The measurement of educational products. 14th yearbook of the National Society for the Study of Education, Part II* (pp. 71–104). Bloomington, IL: Public School.

Moscosco, E. (2001, December, 14). New federal education law passes. *Austin American-Statesman*, p. A4.

Nagle, R. J. (2000). Issues in preschool assessment. In B. Bracken (ed.), *Principles and recommendations for early childhood assessments*. Washington, DC: National Goals Panel.

National Association for the Education of Young Children. (2001). Still! Unacceptable trends for kindergarten entry and placement. *Young Children, 56*, 59–61.

National Association for the Education of Young Children. (2004, February 26). Early education experts highlight concerns about new nationwide test of four-year-olds in Head Start. Retrieved January 29, 2007, from http://www.naeyc.org/about/releases/20040226.asp

National Association for the Education of Young Children. (2005a, Summer). *Screening and assessment of young English-language learners*. Washington, DC: Author.

National Association for the Education of Young Children. (2005b). *NAEYC code of ethical conduct and statement of commitment (revised)*. Washington, DC: Author.

National Association for the Education of Young Children and the National Association of Early Childhood Specialists in State Departments of Education. (1992). Guidelines for appropriate curriculum content and assessment in programs serving children ages 3 through 8. In S. Bredekamp & T. Rosegrant (Eds.), *Reaching potentials: Appropriate curriculum and assessment for young children* (pp. 9–27). Washington, DC: Authors.

National Association of Early Childhood Specialists in State Departments of Education. (2000). *Still! Unacceptable trends in kindergarten entry and placement*. Washington, DC: Author.

National Child Care Information and Technical Assistance Center (NCCIC). (2000). State early learning guidelines on the web. Retrieved July 21, 2009, from http://nccic.acf.hhs.gov/pubs/goodstart/elgwebsites.html

National Council for the Social Studies. (1994). *Curriculum standards for social studies*. Silver Spring, MD: Author.

National Council of State Legislatures. (2009). Testing, standards, and accountability: Overview. Retrieved July 9, 2009, from http://www.ncsl.org/IssuesResearch/Education/Testing.Standard

The New York Times. (2009, July 21). The No Child Left Behind Act news. Retrieved July 21, 2009, from http://topics.nytimes.com/top/reference/timestopics/subjects

Newmann, F. M. (1996). Introduction: The school restructuring study. In F. M. Newmann & Associates, *Authentic achievement: Restructuring schools for intellectual quality* (pp. 1–16). San Francisco: Jossey-Bass.

Olson, L. (2006, July 12). Department raps states on testing. *Education Week, 25*(42), 1, 36–37.

Raymond, G., & McIntosh, D. K. (1992). The impact of current changes in social structure on early childhood education programs. In B. Neugebauer (Ed.), *Alike and different: Exploring our humanity with young children* (Rev. ed., pp. 116–126). Washington, DC: National Association for the Education of Young Children.

Rebora, A. (2006, April 19). NCLB's counting problems, textual artifacts, and going nuclear. *Teacher Magazine*.

Rousseau, J. J. (1911). *Emile, or On education* (B. Foxley, Trans.). London: Dent. (Original work published 1762)

Samuels, C. A. (2006, August 9). Final IDEA regulations clarify key issues. *Education Week*. Retrieved August 9, 2006, from http://www.edweek.org

Scherer, M. (1999). Perspectives/measures and mismeasures. *Educational Leadership, 56*, 5.

Seefeldt, C. (2005). *How to work with standards in the early childhood classroom*. New York: Teachers College Press.

Segal, M., & Webber, N. T. (1996). Nonstructured play observations: Guidelines, benefits, and caveats. In S. J. Meisels & E. Fenichel (Eds.), *New visions for the developmental assessment of infants and young children* (pp. 207–230). Washington, DC: Zero to Three: National Center for Infants, Toddlers, and Families.

Shepard, L., Kagan, S. L., Lynn, S., & Wurtz, E. (1998). *Principles and recommendations for early childhood assessments*. Washington, DC: National Goals Panel.

Shore, R. (1997). *Rethinking the brain*. New York: Families and Work Institute.

Smith, S. S. (1999). Reforming the kindergarten round-up. *Educational Leadership, 56*, 39–44.

Spodek, B., & Saracho, O. N. (1994). *Dealing with individual differences in the early childhood classroom*. New York: Longman.

Stein, J. U. (1993). Critical issues: Mismanagement, informed consent, and participant safety. In S. J. Grosse & D. Thompson (Eds.), *Leisure opportunities for individuals with disabilities: Legal issues* (pp. 37–54). Reston, VA: American Alliance for Health, Physical Education, Recreation, and Dance.

U.S. Department of Education (2001). Fact sheet on the major provisions of the conference report to H.R.I., the No Child Left Behind Act. Retrieved February 14, 2007, from http://www.ed.gov/nelb/overview/intro/factsheet.html

U.S. Department of Education. (2006, August 3). *IDEA 2004 news, information, resources*. Washington, DC: Author.

U.S. Department of Health and Human Resources Head Start Bureau. (2003). *National Reporting System*. Washington, DC: Author.

Weber, E. (1984). *Ideas influencing early childhood education. A theoretical analysis*. New York: Teachers College Press.

Wesson, K. A. (2001). The "Volvo effect"—Questioning standardized tests. *Young Children, 56*(2), 16–18.

White, S. H. (1973). *Federal programs for young children: Review and recommendations* (Vol. 13). Washington, DC: U.S. Government Printing Office.

Wiggins, G. P. (1993). *Assessing student performance*. San Francisco: Jossey-Bass.

Wolery, M., Strain, P. S., & Bailey, D. B. (1992). Reaching potentials of children with special needs. In S. Bredekamp & T. Rosegrant (Eds.), *Reaching potentials: Appropriate curriculum and assessment for young children* (pp. 92–112). Washington, DC: National Association for the Education of Young Children.

Wolery, M., & Wilbers, J. S. (Eds.). (1994). *Including children with special needs in early childhood programs*. Washington, DC: National Association for the Education of Young Children.

Wortham, S. C. (1998). Introduction. In S. C. Wortham, A. Barbour, & B. Desjean-Perrotta, *Portfolio assessment: A handbook for preschool and elementary educators* (pp. 7–13). Olney, MD: Association for Childhood Education International.

Wortham, S. C. (2002). *Childhood 1892–2002* (2nd ed.). Olney, MD: Association for Childhood Education International.

Wurm, J. P. (2005). *Working in the Reggio way*. St. Paul, MN: Redleaf Press.

Zehr, M. A. (2006, July 12). New era for testing English-learners begins. Federal officials to review exams developed to meet requirements of NCLB. *Education Week*. Retrieved July 12, 2006, from http://www.edweek.org

Zigler, E., & Valentine, J. (Eds.). (1979). *Project Head Start: A legacy of the War on Poverty*. New York: Free Press.

CHAPTER 2

How Infants and Young Children Should Be Assessed

Chapter Objectives

As a result of reading this chapter, you will be able to

1. Discuss how assessment should be improved for the 21st century
2. Describe how assessment should be used in early childhood
3. Describe how measurement and evaluation are used with infants, preschoolers, and school-age children
4. Understand the differences between formal and informal assessments
5. Describe different types of informal assessments
6. Explain how performance assessments reflect authentic learning

The topic of assessing young children was introduced in chapter 1. The fact that infants and preschool children are measured differently from older children and adults was discussed, as was the evolution of testing and assessment in the United States. Also discussed were issues and trends in assessment in early childhood education in a new century. Much attention was given to concerns about testing young children, particularly preschool children. The National Reporting System, implemented with Head Start, is a good example of how demands for accountability have displaced decades of research on the appropriate assessment of young children. The National Education Goals Panel reported that standardized achievement tests should not be administered before age 8 (see Figure 2-1). The conflict of expectations for achievement in NCLB and the reality of assessing children in bilingual and ELL programs and children with disabilities have resulted in confusion over testing requirements and results.

In this chapter, appropriate methods of assessing infants and children will be described. The focus will be on the future and what assessment should do, as well as how assessment should specifically serve children in the early childhood years. Principles for quality assessments describe how assessments should be conducted and used. They also include the characteristics of quality assessments. These varied assessments can be organized to provide a comprehensive plan for evaluation, also called an assessment system. The components of a comprehensive assessment system will be described, followed by how assessment results are used in preschool and school settings.

What Assessment Should Do

The history of assessment is cumulative. This means that each era in the history of measuring children has provided methods for assessment that are still in use today. Although there are issues as to when and how some of the methods are used, as discussed in chapter 1, all contributions are still relevant in some context to learn about children's development and learning. The goal of the discussion in this part of the chapter is to address the concerns and issues raised about the testing and evaluation of young children and to set criteria for higher goals of the process. The objective is not to eliminate established methods and replace them with new ones, but to formulate how to use each most effectively to serve the needs of the child. First, criteria for optimal approaches to assessment will be described generally, followed by how assessment should be used for the benefit of young children specifically.

Principles for Assessment

Assessment Should Use Multiple Sources of Information

No matter what strategy is used for assessment, a single application for evaluation is insufficient (Greenspan, Meisels, & the Zero to Three Work Group on Developmental Assessment, 1996). Each assessment strategy has strengths and limitations; moreover, a single method provides only one portion of what needs to be known about a child. A variety of strategies provides a comprehensive picture of the

Appropriate Uses and Technical Accuracy of Assessments Change Across

Birth	1	2	3	4

Purpose 1: Assessing to promote children's learning and development

Parents and caregivers observe and respond as children develop language and physical skills.

Parents, caregivers, and preschool teachers use direct measures, including observations of what children are learning to decide what to teach next.

Purpose 2: Identifying children for health and special services

All children should be screened regularly for health needs, including hearing and vision checks, as part of routine health care services.

Children entering Head Start and other preschool programs should be screened for health needs, including hearing and vision checks.

Many serious cognitive and physical disabilities are evident at birth or soon thereafter. As soon as developmental delays or potential disabilities are suspected, parents and physicians should seek in-depth assessments.

Individual children with possible developmental delays should be referred for in-depth assessment.

Purpose 3: Monitoring trends and evaluating programs and services

Because direct measures of children's language and cognitive functioning are difficult to aggregate accurately for ages from birth to 2, state reporting systems should focus on living and social conditions that affect learning and the adequacy of services.

Assessments, including direct and indirect measures of children's physical, social, emotional, and cognitive development, could be constructed and used to evaluate prekindergarten programs, but such measures would not be accurate enough to make high-stakes decisions about individual children.

Purpose 4: Assessing academic achievement to hold individual students,

FIGURE 2-1   Purposes for early childhood assessments

Source: Shepard, L., Kagan, S. L., Lynn, S., & Wurtz, E. (Eds.) (1998). *Principles and recommendations for early childhood assessments.* Report submitted to the National Education Goals Panel. Washington, DC: National Education Goals Panel, pp. 20–21. Washington, DC: U.S. Government Printing Office.

the Early Childhood Age Continuum (Birth to Age 8).

Kindergarten	1st grade	2nd grade	3rd grade	
5	6	7	8 years	Beyond age 8

Teachers use both formal and informal assessments to plan and guide instruction.

All children should be screened at school entry for vision and hearing needs and checked for immunizations.

Some mild disabilities may become apparent only in the school context. Districts and states must by law have sound teacher and parent referral policies so that children with potential disabilities are referred for in-depth assessment.

Beginning at age 5, it is possible to use direct measures, including measures of children's early learning, as part of a comprehensive early childhood assessment for monitoring trends. Matrix sampling should be used to ensure technical accuracy and to provide safeguards for individual children. Because of the cost of such an assessment, states or the nation should pick one grade level for monitoring trends in early childhood, most likely kindergarten or first grade.

teachers, and school accountable

Before age 8, standardized achievement measures are not sufficiently accurate to be used for high-stakes decisions about individual children and schools. Therefore, high-stakes assessments intended for accountability purposes should be delayed until the end of third grade (or preferably fourth grade).

Mara Larson—Kindergarten

The children in Mara's classroom enjoy the center activities that follow each day's math lesson. They don't know that when they are playing counting and number games, Mara is assessing their progress. For example, when they are learning about numerals, Mara might have a lesson in which children use counters to place the correct number of objects under numeral cards up to ten. In another activity, children take turns throwing dice, counting the total, and selecting the correct numeral. A third game is a game board with a spinner. The child spins the wheel and counts out the correct number to match the numeral where the spinner lands. If the answer is correct, the child advances one square on the game board. At first, Mara guides small groups of children in the math activities. When she observes children who have mastered the math objective of the game, she allows them to play the game independently. Mara continues to guide the children she observes having difficulties with the skills used in the activities. Mara also observes children as they participate in math lessons and also assigns tasks that serve as assessments.

child's development and learning from different perspectives (Feld & Bergan, 2002). For infants and toddlers, several observations are better than a single observation, and other inputs into development, such as parents' and caregivers' views of the child, provide a more complete picture of the child's progress. For older children who have entered school, achievement of learning becomes important. The kindergarten and school-age child should be able to demonstrate learning in more than one way and on more than one occasion. Use of a variety of measures of learning ensures an accurate view of the child's accomplishments (Greenspan et al., 1996; McAfee, Leong, & Bodrova, 2004; National Education Association, 1994; Shepard, 1989; Wiggins, 1993).

Assessment Should Benefit the Child and Improve Learning

The purpose of evaluating infants and toddlers is generally to determine whether the child is developing normally or exhibits delay and needs assistance or intervention. The purposes of assessment are to benefit the child. When young children enter school, however, assessments can have negative purposes that are not related to the needs and interests of the child. As is discussed elsewhere in this text, tests are sometimes administered to young children to determine whether they can be admitted to a preschool program or promoted in grade. In the primary grades, tests are administered to determine the child's achievement during a school year. When such tests are given to determine the child's progress and to plan appropriate instruction based on what the child has accomplished, the purpose will benefit the child and improve learning. On the other hand, when such tests are used merely for evaluation of the school program and have no implications for how the child will be

Gloria Fuentes—Toddler Class

$\mathcal{S}$everal weeks into the school year, two children in Gloria's class still speak very little in school. Gloria has questions about their language development. She schedules conferences with parents to get their help in assessing their child's language ability. As a result of the conversations with parents, she discovers that one of the children readily speaks at home but is still shy and uncertain about school. Another child comes from a home where English is not spoken. From her discussions with these parents, Gloria knows more about the children's language needs. Different approaches will be used with each child to help him or her use more language. One will need much attention and emotional support each day to ensure that he or she is confident and secure enough to talk in class. The other will need daily opportunities to learn and use new English words in classroom activities.

served, they do not benefit the child and should not be used. Whatever assessment strategies are used, the information should be used to guide the child and enhance learning (Copple & Bredekamp, 2009; Wiggins, 1993, 1998).

Assessment Should Involve the Child and Family

The family should have an important role in assessment. Infants and toddlers are unable to understand their developmental progress; however, their parents and caregivers are primary sources of information. Although tests can be administered to measure development, a parent's knowledge about the child is essential for a true understanding of the child's developmental characteristics (Darragh, 2009; Popper, 1996; Rocco, 1996).

Preschool, kindergarten, and primary-grade children are more able to understand what they know and what they are able to do. This ability increases with the child's age and maturity. However, parental input is still very important. By the time the child is in the primary grades, self-assessment improves. Students can evaluate their progress and have a voice in how they can best succeed in mastering learning objectives. Assessment is not just administered to students, but accomplished with active participation by the students.

Assessment Should Be Fair for All Children

Chapter 1 pointed out that many tests are inappropriate for children who are culturally or linguistically diverse. In addition, educators must evaluate children with disabilities accurately and fairly. Because tests may not reflect a child's culture or language, other, more effective methods must be employed. As was mentioned earlier, a variety of strategies can overcome the limitations of a single method or test. The person administering the evaluation must be alert to limitations and have other strategies to acquire the needed information. This is especially important in the case

Margie Phillips—First Grade

Two boys in Margie's first-grade class are having trouble copying information from the board. As a result, they are not having success in completing board assignments. Margie feels that the boys are not paying attention; however, she talks to the parents and suggests that the parents seek professional help to determine whether there is a problem. The parents of the boys take them to a local university to be tested by an early childhood diagnostician. After the assessment, the specialist calls Margie and explains that the boys have difficulty transferring information from the board to paper. They are unable to remember the written material between seeing it on the board and then looking down to their paper. Both boys need to have the written information written out and placed on their desks for easy referral. Although Margie feels that changing her methods for the two boys is unnecessary and shows favoritism, she follows the specialist's recommendations. When she tries placing the information on the boys' desks, she is surprised to see that they improve in completing assignments.

of children who are culturally and linguistically diverse or whose abilities are outside normal developmental ranges (Barrera, 1996; Genishi & Dyson, 2009; Goodwin & Goodwin, 1993).

Principles for Early Childhood Assessments

The previous section described principles for assessing all children. As a follow-up to that information, we can address how those principles are applied to young children. Principles for early childhood assessments are not just relevant for the assessment of children, but have implications for program evaluation and quality (Epstein, Schweinhart, DeBruin-Parecki, & Robin, 2004). In the early childhood years, assessment of development is the primary focus. The NAEYC position statement calls for sound assessment that reflects how young children grow and learn. Sound assessment is described through a series of statements of principles (Copple & Bredekamp, 2009, pp. 21–22):

A. Assessment of young children's progress and achievements is ongoing, strategic, and purposeful. The results of assessment are used to inform the planning and implementation of experiences, to communicate with the child's family, and to evaluate and improve teachers' and the program's effectiveness.

B. Assessment focuses on children's progress toward goals that are developmentally and educationally significant.

C. There is a system in place to collect, make sense of, and use the assessment information to guide what goes on in the classroom (formative assessment). Teachers use this information in planning curriculum and learning experiences and in moment-to-moment interactions with children—that is, teachers continually engage in assessment for the purpose of improving teaching and learning.

D. The methods of assessment are appropriate to the developmental status and experiences of young children, and these methods recognize individual variation in learners and allow children to demonstrate their competence in different ways. Methods appropriate to the classroom assessment of young children, therefore, include results of teachers' observations of children's work samples, and their performance on authentic activities.

E. Assessment looks not only at what children can do independently but also at what they can do with assistance from other children or adults. Therefore, teachers assess children as they participate in groups and other situations that are providing scaffolding.

F. In addition to this assessment by teachers, input from families as well as children's own evaluations of their work are part of the program's overall assessment strategy.

G. Assessments are tailored to a specific purpose and used only for the purpose for which they have been demonstrated to produce reliable, valid information.

H. Decisions that have a major impact on children, such as enrollment or placement, are never made on the basis of results from a single developmental assessment or screening instrument/device but are based on multiple sources of relevant information, including that obtained from observations of and interactions with children by teachers and parents (and specialists as needed).

I. When a screening or other assessment identifies children who may have special learning or developmental needs, there is appropriate follow-up, evaluation, and if indicated, referral. Diagnosis or labeling is never the result of a brief screening or one-time assessment. Families should be involved as important sources of information.

The NAEYC position statement demonstrates how appropriate assessment is tailored to the changing developmental needs of young children. As children go through developmental differences, assessments that best measure the variations in development are employed. Figure 2-1 shows how four purposes of assessment in early childhood development change as children progress from birth until the primary grades.

How Infants and Young Children Are Assessed

As exemplified in the *Principles and Recommendations for Early Childhood Assessments* (National Education Goals Panel, 1998) just discussed, there are many reasons for measuring and evaluating young children, and various methods are available to accomplish our goals. Sometimes we measure the child informally. We might look for characteristics by watching the child's behaviors at play or in a setting arranged for that purpose. A pediatrician may watch a baby walk during an examination to determine whether he or she is progressing normally. In a similar fashion, a teacher may observe a child playing to determine how he or she is using language.

A second-grade teacher who constructs a set of subtraction problems to evaluate whether his or her students have mastered a mathematics objective is also using an **informal test.**

Formal methods, or standardized instruments, are also used for measurement and evaluation. These are more extensive and proven measures for evaluation. Specialists in tests and measurements design and then try out, with a large number of children, instruments that evaluate the characteristics that have been targeted. This process ensures that educators can use the information gained each time the test is given to another child or group of children. This type of test is called a **standardized test** because a standard has been set from the results achieved by using the test with children who are representative of the population.

Why do we measure infants and young children? The most common purpose is to assess development. Soon after a child's birth, the **obstetrician** or **pediatrician** evaluates the newborn by using the *Apgar scale* (Apgar, 1975) to determine whether he or she is in good health. Thereafter, at regular intervals, parents, doctors, and teachers follow the baby's development by using tests and informal evaluation strategies (Greenspan et al., 1996; Wodrich, 1984). The screening test for phenylketonuria (PKU) may also be administered to detect the presence of the enzyme phenylalanine, which can cause mental retardation if not managed through diet. In addition, there are newborn screening tests for cystic fibrosis and congenital hypothyroidism (Widerstrom, Mowder, & Sandall, 1991).

But what if development is not progressing normally? How can evaluation measures be used to help the young child? In recent years, researchers, medical specialists, and educators have learned how to work with children at increasingly younger ages to minimize the effects of delays in growth or other problems that retard the child's developmental progress. Various strategies and instruments are now available. A **neonatologist** conducts a comprehensive evaluation on a premature baby to determine what therapy should be initiated to improve the infant's chances for survival and optimal development. A young child can be tested for hearing loss or mental retardation. The child who does not speak normally or who is late in speaking is referred to a speech pathologist, who assesses the child's language and prescribes activities to facilitate improved language development.

During a child's infancy and toddler years, child development specialists follow the child's progress and initiate therapy when development is not normal (Meisels, 1996). During the preschool years, this effort includes evaluating and predicting whether the child is likely to experience difficulties in learning. Tests and other measures are used to help to determine whether the child will develop a **learning disability** and how that disability will affect his or her success in school. Again, when problems are detected, plans are made to work with the child in a timely manner to help him or her to overcome as much of the disability as possible before entering school. The child may have a vision problem, difficulty in hearing, or a disability that may interfere with learning to read. The evaluation measures used will help identify the exact nature of the problem. In addition, test results will be used to help determine what kind of intervention will be most successful (Greenspan et al., 1996; Wodrich, 1984).

Assessment for Risk in Developmental Status

When Sarah was 6 months old, her teenage mother gave her up for adoption. Because Sarah's father could not be located to agree to release her for adoption, Sarah was placed temporarily in a foster home.

Prior to placement with the foster family, Sarah had lived with her mother in her maternal grandparents' home. In addition to Sarah's mother, six other children were in the family. Both grandparents were employed. Sarah's primary caregiver had been an aunt with mental retardation who was 12 years old.

For the first few days after Sarah was placed in the foster home, she cried when the foster parents tried to feed her. She sat for long periods of time and stared vacantly, without reacting to toys or people. She had no established patterns for sleeping and usually fretted off and on during the night.

When a pediatrician examined Sarah, she was found to be malnourished, with sores in her mouth from vitamin deficiencies. As determined by the *Denver Developmental Screening Test,* she was developing much more slowly than normal.

A special diet and multivitamins were prescribed for Sarah. Members of the foster family patiently taught her to enjoy eating a varied diet beyond the chocolate milk and cereal that she had been fed previously. Regular times for sleeping at night gradually replaced her erratic sleeping habits. Her foster family spent many hours playing with her, talking with her, and introducing her to various toys.

By age 11 months, Sarah had improved greatly. She was alert, ate well, began to walk, and said a few words. Her development was within the normal range, and she was ready for adoption.

Sarah had benefited from being placed in a home where she received good nutrition, guidance in living patterns, and stimulation for cognitive, physical, and social development. Without early intervention, Sarah's delay in development might have become more serious over time. Adaptability to an adoptive home might have been difficult for her and her adoptive parents. If she had been unable to adjust successfully with an adoptive family, she might have spent her childhood years in a series of foster homes, rather than with her adoptive family. She also would have been at risk for not learning successfully beginning in the first years of schooling.

During the preschool period or even earlier, a different kind of developmental difference may emerge. Parents or other adults who deal with the child may observe that the child demonstrates a learning ability or potential that is much higher than the normal range. A more formal evaluation using a standardized test may confirm these informal observations. Plans then can be made to facilitate the child's development to help him or her to achieve full potential for learning.

Combating Limitations in Vocabulary and Concept Development

Micah, who is 4 years old, is the sixth child in a family of seven children. Both of his parents work, and he and his younger brother are cared for by a grandmother during the day. Although Micah's parents are warm and loving, their combined income is barely enough to provide the basic necessities for the family. They are unable to buy books and toys that will enhance Micah's development. Because the family rarely travels outside the immediate neighborhood, Micah has had few experiences that would broaden his knowledge of the larger community.

Fortunately, Micah's family lives in a state that provides a program for 4-year-old children who can benefit from a prekindergarten class that stresses language and cognitive development. The program serves all children who come from low-income homes or who exhibit language or cognitive delay.

In response to a letter sent by the school district, Micah's grandmother took him to the school to be tested for the program. Micah's performance on the test showed that he uses a limited expressive vocabulary and lacks many basic concepts. When school begins in late August, Micah will start school with his older brothers and sisters and will be enrolled in the prekindergarten class.

Micah will have the opportunity to play with puzzles, construction toys, and other manipulative objects that will facilitate his cognitive development. Stories will be read and discussed each day, and Micah will be able to look at a variety of books. Micah's teacher will introduce learning experiences that will allow Micah to learn about shapes, colors, numbers, and many other concepts that will provide a foundation for learning in the elementary school grades.

Micah will also travel with his classmates to visit places that will help him learn about the community. They may visit a furniture or grocery store or a bread factory. Visitors to the classroom will add to the students' knowledge about occupations and cultures represented in the community. The children will have opportunities to paint, participate in cooking experiences, and talk about the new things they are learning. They will dictate stories about their experiences and learn many songs and games. When Micah enters kindergarten the following year, he will use the knowledge and language he learned in prekindergarten to help him to learn successfully along with his 5-year-old peers.

Although potential for learning may be assessed at a very early age in the child who is gifted or talented, learning aptitude may also be evaluated in the general population during the preschool and primary school years. Educators wish to determine children's learning abilities and needs, as well as the types of programs that will be most beneficial for them. Informal strategies and formal tests are used with individual children and groups of children to assess what and how much they have already learned and to evaluate weak areas that can be given special attention. Informal and formal strategies are also used to evaluate the success of programs that serve children, as well as provide indicators for how programs can be improved.

Developing a Comprehensive System of Assessment

If measurement and evaluation of infants and young children were to follow the criteria for assessment in a new century, a system for assessment should be developed. The combination of measurement methods used will depend on the uses for the system, but, overall, many of the components to be described will be included in any plan for evaluation. Using a comprehensive system of assessment involves planning. Not only do teachers need to understand what strategies and tools are available and how to use them, but they also need to have a plan for conducting assessments (Bowers, 2008; National Association for the Education of Young Children, 2005). There are many types of assessment systems. Chapters 9 and 10 describe some systems that are currently used in early childhood programs. All systems use most of the options described next.

Components of an Assessment System

Standardized Tests

Standardized tests are designed to measure individual characteristics. The tests may be administered to an individual or to a group. The purpose of standardized tests is to measure abilities, achievements, aptitudes, interests, attitudes, values, and personality characteristics. The results can be used to plan instruction, to study differences between individuals and groups, and for counseling and guidance.

Classroom Assessment Strategies

Standardized tests are not the only tools available for evaluation and assessment. Various types of informal instruments and strategies to determine development and learning are available as well.

School districts often use informal tests or evaluation strategies developed by local teachers or staff members. In early childhood programs, an informal screening test may be administered to preschool children at registration to determine their instructional needs. Likewise, the speech teacher may use a simple screening instrument to evaluate the child's language development or possible speech difficulties.

Observation. One of the most valuable ways to become aware of the individual characteristics of young children is through observation. Developmental indicators in early childhood are more likely to be noted from children's behavior in natural circumstances than from a designed assessment or instrument. Adults who observe children as they play and work in individual or group activities are able to determine progress in all categories of development (Segal & Webber, 1996). The child who

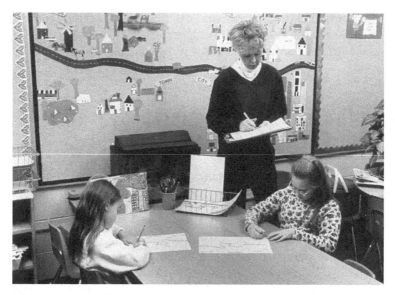

Observation is part of an assessment system.

shows evidence of emerging prosocial skills by playing successfully in the playground is demonstrating significant growth in social development. Children who struggle to balance materials on both sides of a balance scale demonstrate visible signs of cognitive growth. Physical development can be evaluated by observing children using playground equipment. Because young children learn best through active involvement with their environment, evaluation of learning may be assessed most appropriately by observing the child during periods of activity. Observation records can be used to plan instruction, to report progress in various areas of development, and to track progress in mastery of preschool curriculum objectives.

Teacher-Designed Measures. Teachers have always used tests that they have devised to measure the level of learning after instruction. Early childhood teachers are more likely to use concrete tasks or oral questions for informal assessment with young children. Teachers frequently incorporate evaluation with instruction or learning experiences. Activities and games can be used both to teach and to evaluate what the child has learned. Evaluation can also be conducted through learning centers or as part of a teacher-directed lesson. Although pencil-and-paper tests are also a teacher-designed measure, they should not be used until children are comfortable with reading and writing.

Checklists. **Developmental checklists** or other forms of learning objective sequences are used at all levels of preschool, elementary, and secondary schools. Often referred to as a **scope,** or **sequence of skills,** a checklist is a list of the learning objectives established for areas of learning and development at a particular age, grade level, or content area. Many checklists are standardized, while others are locally developed by a teacher or school district and are not standardized.

Skills continuums are available from many sources. The teacher may construct one, or a school district may distribute checklists for each grade level. Educational textbook publishers frequently include a skills continuum for teachers to use as an instructional guide with the textbook they have selected. State education agencies now publish objectives to be used by all school districts in the state.

Rating Scales. **Rating scales** are similar to checklists. They contain criteria for measurement that can be based on learning objectives or other factors. The major difference between checklists and rating scales is that rating scales provide for measurement on a continuum. Checklist items are rated with a negative or positive response. Rating scales can be used for many purposes when a range of criteria is needed to acquire accurate information.

Rubrics. **Rubrics** have been developed to evaluate authentic and performance assessments. They include a range of criteria like rating scales, but have indicators that can be used to determine quality of performance or to assign a grade. Rubrics are used most frequently with portfolio assessment, but are appropriate for performance assessment that is not part of a portfolio.

Performance and Portfolio Assessments. Additional forms of informal assessments focus on more meaningful types of evaluation of student learning. Sometimes called **performance assessments** or **authentic assessments** (Goodwin & Goodwin, 1993; Wiggins, 1993), these evaluation measures use strategies that permit the child to demonstrate his or her understanding of a concept or mastery of a skill. The evaluation might take the form of a teacher-directed **interview** in which a dialogue with the child would reveal the child's thinking and understanding. Other procedures might include games, **directed assignments**, or activities related to a project.

Processes for reporting student progress related to outcome-based or authentic assessments are also intended to communicate learning and development from a meaningful perspective. Traditional report cards and standardized test results do not necessarily reflect the student's progress accurately. **Portfolios** with samples of the student's work are one type of reporting of progress that is compatible with outcome-based assessment. A detailed narrative or **narrative report** of the student's progress developed by the teacher is another process that enables the teacher to describe the nature of the child's activities that have resulted in achievement and learning.

Technology-Based Assessments. Early childhood educators in the 21st century have access to computers and assessments that are available through technology. One source of technological assessment is **assessment software.** Assessments from computer software can be an adaptation of paper-based assessments, such as reading or mathematics checklists, or assessments that are linked to a specific curriculum. Other software can be acquired that permits the design of activities and lesson plans or continuous revision of assessment tools.

Assessment resources are also available on the Internet. **Electronic management of learning (EML)** makes it possible to collect, analyze, and report progress in children's learning that can then be used to document learning outcomes and plan for subsequent learning objectives and activities. This type of assessment management uses Web pages. Through EML, parents, teachers, and administrators can access information about children's learning and assessment-based curriculum planning (Feld & Bergan, 2002).

Using Assessment Results

Earlier in the chapter, we discussed the kinds of assessments that are needed for a new century. Components of a comprehensive system of evaluation were described. Now we can summarize how and when the system of assessment should be used. The discussion will relate to preschool and primary-grade children rather than infants and toddlers. In keeping with the premise that assessment should benefit the child and improve learning, three primary purposes for comprehensive assessment throughout the year can be reviewed: planning for instruction, reporting progress, and evaluating the instructional program continuously from the beginning until the end of the school term.

Using Assessment Results to Plan for Instruction

If assessments should benefit the child, then assessments in preschool and primary-grade settings should be linked to learning experiences and instruction. If they are to be fair for all children and authentic, they include all types of strategies that provide a comprehensive picture of each child's progress and needs. The teacher selects the assessment methods that are relevant to the information needed and uses the results in planning for curriculum and instruction. This assumes that the teacher is concerned with individual rates of development and learning and is prepared to address individual differences. The learning activities that are available in the classroom and through teacher instruction reflect not only curriculum goals established by the school, but also how each child can best achieve these goals.

Using Assessment Results to Report Progress

The limitations of report cards were discussed earlier in relationship to the broader information provided by performance assessments. Just as we need multiple assessment strategies to assess young children, these assessment strategies should be used to report how the child has developed and what has been learned. If the assessment system is comprehensive, the method to report the child's progress should also be comprehensive and provide many examples of how the child demonstrated growth and achievement. Parents receive limited information from reports that rate a child average, above average, or below average in preschool settings. Likewise, a report that indicates that the child's progress is satisfactory or unsatisfactory tells little about the child's learning experiences and accomplishments. Rather than a snapshot of progress, a comprehensive picture of the child should be conveyed in the progress report, regardless of whether the child is in preschool or in the primary grades.

Using Assessment Results to Evaluate the Instructional Program

The assessment process includes evaluation of the effectiveness of the teacher's instruction and the activities and materials used with children. The teacher uses assessment information to determine whether instructional strategies were successful for children to learn new concepts and skills or whether new approaches are needed. The teacher might ask the following questions about the success of instruction: Were the children interested and engaged in the materials or activities? Did the children demonstrate a deeper understanding of concepts as a result of an instructional activity? Was the activity the right length of time? Too short? Too long? What changes might be made to improve the effectiveness of the activity?

With this type of evaluative reflection, the teacher demonstrates that assessment should focus not on student achievement but rather on how well students are progressing and the role that the quality of instruction has on this progress. If some students need additional opportunities to learn information and skills, the teacher considers how more varied activities might accomplish the goal. Should the concepts be incorporated into different types of activities, or should they become a part of a continuum that includes a new direction or focus? Young children need many opportunities to learn new skills, and encountering concepts in new contexts provides meaningful routes to understanding and the ability to use what is being learned.

Environmental Assessment

When assessment of the instructional program is discussed, child progress is part of the purpose; nevertheless, the teacher is also being evaluated. Assessment of the environment also informs how well the instructional program serves young children. Both the indoor and outdoor environments can be evaluated. The *Environmental Rating Scales (ECERS)* are used to assess elements of the indoor environment as well as how teachers function in the environment. *The Early Childhood Rating Scale, Revised Edition* (Harms, Clifford, & Cryer, 2005) and *Infant/Toddler Environment Rating Scale, Revised Edition* (Harms, Cryer, & Clifford, 2006) are representative of appropriate environmental assessments. Teachers College Press has print copies of the scales, while Branagh Information Group holds the electronic rights to the scales (ERS Data System, 2009).

The Playground Checklist (Frost, 2007) provides for the evaluation of the outdoor environment. The checklist contains sections that address what the playground contains, the condition of the playground, how the playground and playground leader function, and how the playground and/or playground leader should function. The Playground Checklist can be located in *Play and Child Development* (Frost, Wortham, & Reifel, 2008).

Assessment of Young Children: The Process

We proposed earlier that assessment occurs throughout the school year. In this section, we will describe how a process of assessment proceeds from the beginning of the school year until the final evaluation at the end of the year. Ongoing assessment is complemented by periodic assessment for reporting periods.

Preassessment

At the Beginning of the Year

Each year, when a teacher receives a new group of students, the first task is to learn about individual differences and determine each child's current developmental level. Young children have uneven rates of development. Each domain in development—physical, social, cognitive, and language—develops differently within and between children. Development occurs in spurts and may lag for a period of time. The teacher might use observation, checklists, and discussions with the child and parents to determine each child's current status. This initial evaluation provides the teacher with a starting place for planning learning experiences and activities. This step in the assessment process is also called **preassessment** because the teacher is conducting assessment prior to planning curriculum based on individual needs.

Throughout the Year

The teacher uses preassessment whenever a new cycle of learning is initiated. For example, if a teacher is planning for a new unit of study with students, a preassessment might be conducted to find out what children already know about the topic. If the teacher has taught all of the shapes and now wants to use them all together, a group preassessment might be conducted to determine if the children are still familiar with the individual shapes.

Ongoing Assessment

Ongoing assessment is conducted almost continuously throughout the year. In the course of group lessons, activities in learning centers, and observation of play, the teacher notes the child's progress or difficulties that might be impeding progress. Notation of this information is made in anecdotal records or some other type of record-keeping system so that the information can be used for planning.

The process of ongoing evaluation can also use **formative assessment** and **summative assessment.** Formative assessments are the strategies the teacher uses to monitor a child's progress in mastery of information or skills during a series of learning activities. Summative assessment is used at the end of a cycle of instructional experiences to confirm mastery of information or skills.

Formative assessment is used during instructional periods to monitor how children are progressing and serves as a planning tool based on individual children's needs. Summative assessment assures the teacher that the children understand the concept being taught and can move on to the next stage of instruction. These two types of assessments will be explained further in chapter 7.

Assessment at the End of Reporting Periods

Generally, at the end of a period of several weeks, teachers are asked to evaluate a child's progress and accomplishments. At this time, the teacher might record the child's progress for the period of time, as well as plans for the child in the next reporting period. Because some type of report, either oral or written, is made to parents at the end of the reporting period, the teacher might include documentation of the child's work and/or a written summary of progress. In addition to observing the child, the teacher might use specific tasks to document acquisition of a concept or skill. The teacher might interview the child to determine how the child perceives and uses information introduced in classroom activities. In addition, the child might have the opportunity to self-evaluate, and parents can describe their observations of the child's progress.

Assessment at the End of the School Year

The most complete assessment and reporting of progress is conducted at the end of the school year. At this time, the teacher needs to summarize the child's progress for all the reporting periods. In some settings, this summarization occurs at a midpoint in the year, as well as at the end of the year. A variety of strategies might be used to determine progress, including teacher-designed assessments in different content areas, standardized achievement tests, student self-evaluation, and a written narrative of the student's accomplishments. As will be discussed in later chapters, a variety of possibilities exists to document what the student has accomplished during the year. In many school districts, this summative information is passed on to the next teacher to help in the initial assessment at the beginning of the next school year.

Addressing and Assessing for Standards

Chapter 1 included information on the impact of NCLB on early childhood education and the controversy between early childhood specialists and standardized testing requirements for Head Start programs. This chapter has focused on how infants and young children should be assessed and for what purposes. In this section of the chapter we will examine the impact of organizational, state, and national standards of the assessment of children in the early childhood years, particularly in the preschool years.

Evolution of Early Education Standards

Until the last 10 years, the focus on learning and assessment with young children has been on appropriate kinds of assessment. The movement to establish standards was part of a national effort to improve American public schools in the latter decades of the 20th century. The first standards were developed by content-area organizations such as the National Council of Teachers of Mathematics (NCTM), the National Center for History in the Schools (NCHS), and the National Council of Teachers of English (NCTE) (see chapter 1). By the mid-1990s, standards had been published for all of the fields of education taught in elementary and secondary schools (Gronlund, 2006; Seefeldt, 2005). The purpose of the standards is to provide clarity for curriculum content, to raise expectations for student learning, and to ensure accountability, as required by NCLB.

When states entered the work of establishing standards, kindergarten and other school-based pre-primary programs were included. Because each state developed its own standards, each is different. In addition, the quality of the standards varies from state to state (Scott-Little, Kagan, & Frelow, 2006). The state standards became the structure for accountability required by NCLB.

In the early years of standards development, educators of preschool children were not included in the standards movement. Standards were considered difficult to establish because of the wide age range and diversity of preschool programs. In addition, early childhood programs were sponsored by different types of organizations and functioned differently from public schools. The philosophy of learning can be different between early childhood teachers and elementary school teachers (Seefeldt, 2005).

Most states have developed standards for preschool children. A few states have developed standards for infant and toddler programs. The standards have become the curriculum framework for preschool programs, particularly publicly funded programs. There are important benefits to having and addressing early learning standards. First, they encourage educators to understand the learning potential in the infant, toddler, and preschool child and help develop quality early childhood programs. Second, they establish definite expectations for preschool children of different ages and provide guidelines for communication of children's accomplishments. Third, they provide for the requirements for accountability for the children's development and achievement as well as program quality (Gronlund, 2006).

Challenges When Assessing Young Children to Meet Standards

How do early educators address the assessment of young children to meet expectations and accountability in state standards? Are the principles for appropriate assessment described in this chapter compatible with the assessments needed for early learning standards? They can be, but teachers face challenges in answering the call for greater accountability and the emphasis on achievement of skills (Oliver & Klugman, 2006). Standards require teachers to be more intentional in how they assess young children. In their planning for teaching and assessment, they need to make the link between the learning experiences and the standards

Assessing for Standards in Indiana

A university professor in Indiana was prepared to teach a graduate class in authentic assessment. She had planned to talk with the students about how authentic assessment could be incorporated into assessments for meeting state standards. The students responded eagerly to the exchange of ideas for assessment; however, they informed the professor that they had been given worksheet-formatted tests on which the students could fill in a circle next to the correct answer. These were the primary tools to assess reading and math standards in kindergarten.

Source: Cress, S. W. (2004, October). Assessing standards in the "real" kindergarten classroom. *Early Childhood Education Journal, 32,* 95–99.

very clear. Standards will need to be integrated into the existing curriculum and assessments that are proven to be of high quality for young children. Otherwise, they might find themselves narrowing the curriculum, depending on direct teaching, and using inappropriate testing methods (Cress, 2004; Gronlund, 2006; Oliver & Klugman, 2006).

Guidelines for Working With Young Children in an Assessment Setting

When teachers and other professionals conduct assessments with infants and young children, they need to be sensitive to the special requirements of working with very young children. They also need to be constantly aware of professional ethics that are necessary when conducting assessments with all children. Confidentiality of information acquired through assessment should be used when working with assessment results. Parents should be included in understanding assessment results and should understand the reasons for the assessment (Darragh, 2009). Young children have very short attention spans and are easily distracted. Administrators of assessment instruments and other strategies will benefit from the following guidelines:

1. Contact the home for parental permission to conduct the assessment.

2. Have all materials ready before the assessment session and review procedures for administering the assessment before the child arrives.

3. If possible, be sure that the child is familiar with the environment when conducting an assessment. For very young children, the session might need to be conducted in their homes. For assessments administered to children entering a group setting, results will be more accurate if the child has been given time to adjust to the school setting. The test administrator should also be familiar to the child.

4. Before beginning the assessment session, develop rapport with the child. Engage the child in a conversation or introduce a toy before the session begins. Once the child seems comfortable, the first assessment tasks can begin.

5. Be alert to signs of fatigue or behaviors that indicate that the child is no longer responding to assessment tasks. Take a brief break or remind the child how to respond to tasks before resuming the session.

6. Use assessment time efficiently. The child should not be hurried, but assessment tasks should be administered with little lag in time while the child is alert and attentive.

7. Consider adaptations that might be needed for children with disabilities. Be knowledgeable about how tasks might be adapted within requirements for how standardized tests should be administered. If alternative procedures can be used, permit the child to respond differently to a test item. Caution must be used, however, not to change the intent of the item or the type of response that is appropriate as well as correct.

Assessing Aggie's Knowledge of Concepts

*A*ggie is 6 years old and entering first grade in an inclusion class. All the children are administered a test of basic concepts that requires the child to mark the correct answer for three pictures given to identify the concept asked for by the teacher. Because Aggie's physical limitations have affected her fine-motor development, she is unable to hold a pencil or crayon or to make a mark on the test. Instead, her teacher conducts the test orally and asks Aggie to indicate which of the three pictures is the correct answer. Aggie can point with some difficulty, so the teacher exposes only one row of pictures at a time and asks Aggie to point to the picture that matches the concept she has described.

Summary

We need to be able to evaluate the growth and development of young children for various purposes. Specialists who work with children from various perspectives have devised formal and informal assessments that can be used with newborns, as well as later in the early childhood years. Members of the medical profession, psychologists, educators, and parents all want to know whether the young child is developing at a normal rate. If development deviates from acceptable progress in some way, tests and other evaluation strategies are available to study the child and to help devise early intervention measures that can minimize or eliminate the developmental problem.

As we work with young children in a new century, we need to consider how the available assessment methods are best used. In view of the many concerns and issues about testing young children, assessment should focus on meeting the child's developmental and learning needs. We should take advantage of the many assessment strategies available but, at the same time, be sure that we understand the purposes, strengths, and limitations of each type when including them in a system for comprehensive evaluation and reporting. All assessments should have a meaningful purpose and method and be related to the child's development and learning. The assessments used to report progress should also be meaningful to parents and other adults who need to understand the child's profile of progress and learning needs. The assessment process should include the child and the child's parents if the process is to be the most comprehensive and informative.

In the next eight chapters, each component of a comprehensive evaluation system will be discussed, beginning with standardized tests. Informal methods will then be discussed, with portfolio assessment serving as a model for the desired comprehensive assessment plan that will best benefit the young child.

REVIEW QUESTIONS

1. What should be the purposes for assessing young children?
2. Who are the professionals who test young children?
3. How can a young child's development be atypical? Give examples.
4. Why are infant neonatal scales administered? Infant development scales?
5. What is the purpose of preschool intelligence tests?
6. How are adaptive scales used? Give examples.
7. Why do schools administer tests to preschool children? Describe the purposes.
8. How do schools use group achievement tests? State education agencies? National agencies?
9. How are informal measures different from psychological or standardized tests?
10. Why is observation an important evaluation method to use with young children?
11. How do performance assessments differ from other types of informal assessment? What should performance assessments reflect?
12. What is a comprehensive assessment system? How is it used for instruction and reporting progress?
13. Why is a comprehensive assessment system better than more traditional reporting methods?
14. How is assessment used throughout the school year? Describe different purposes for assessment at the beginning of the school year, at the end of reporting periods, and at the end of the school year.

SUGGESTED ACTIVITIES

1. Examine a test for infants and a test for primary-grade children discussed in this chapter. Describe the similarities and differences between the two measures. Discuss how the tests reflect the developmental level of the children. What are the unique characteristics of each test?
2. Conduct an interview with a preschool teacher and a primary-grade teacher. Find out what kinds of standardized tests are administered in the classroom and what types of informal assessment strategies the teacher uses. Write a report summarizing the types of assessments used by the two teachers.
3. Study the purposes of assessment presented in Figure 2-1. Four purposes are listed. Discuss how the assessments change from preschool to primary school. Contrast the differences you find for each purpose.

KEY TERMS

assessment software
authentic assessment
developmental checklist
directed assignment
electronic management of learning (EML)
formative assessment
informal test
interview
learning disability
narrative report
neonatologist
obstetrician
pediatrician
performance assessment
portfolio
preassessment
rating scale
rubric
scope (sequence of skills)
standardized test
summative assessment

Selected Web Sites

National Institute for Early Education Research
http://www.nieer.org

Child Care Exchange
http://www.ChildCareExchange.com

Education Week
http://www.educationweek.org

References

Apgar, V. (1975). A proposal for a new method of evaluation of a newborn infant. *Anesthesia and Analgesia, 32,* 260–267.

Barrera, I. (1996). Thoughts on the assessment of young children whose sociocultural background is unfamiliar to the assessor. In S. J. Meisels & E. Fenichel (Eds.), *New visions for the developmental assessment of infants and young children* (pp. 69–84). Washington, DC: Zero to Three: National Center for Infants, Toddlers, and Families.

Bowers, F. B. (2008, November/December). Developing a child assessment plan: An integral part of program quality. *Exchange,* pp. 51–55.

Copple, C, & Bredekamp, S. (Eds.). (2009). *Developmentally appropriate practices in early childhood programs* (3rd ed.). Washington, DC: National Association for the Education of Young Children.

Cress, S. W. (2004, October). Assessing standards in the "real" kindergarten classroom. *Early Childhood Education Journal, 32,* 95–99.

Darragh, J. (2009, May/June). Informal assessment as a tool for supporting parent partnerships. *Exchange,* pp. 91–93.

Epstein, A. S., Schweinhart, L. J., DeBruin-Parecki, & Robin, K. B. (2004, July). *Preschool assessment: A guide to developing a balanced approach.* National Institute for Early Education Research. Retrieved August 11, 2009, from http://nieer.org/resources/policybriefs/7.pdf

ERS Data System. (2009). *Software for the Environment Rating Scales.* Retrieved August 11, 2009, from http://www.ersdata.com/?source=google-adwords&gelid=CNS

Feld, J. K., & Bergan, K. S. (2002). Assessment tools in the 21st century. *Child Care Information Exchange, 146,* 62–66.

Frost, J. L., Wortham, S. C., & Reifel, S. (2008). *Play and child development* (3rd ed.). Upper Saddle River, NJ: Pearson Merrill Prentice Hall.

Genishi, C., & Dyson, A. H. (2009). *Children, language, and literacy.* New York: Teachers College Press.

Goodwin, W. L., & Goodwin, L. D. (1993). Young children and measurement: Standardized and nonstandardized instruments in early childhood education. In B. Spodek (Ed.), *Handbook of research on the education of young children* (pp. 441–463). New York: Macmillan.

Greenspan, S. I., Meisels, S. J., & the Zero to Three Work Group on Developmental Assessment. (1996). Toward a new vision for the developmental assessment of infants and young children. In S. J. Meisels & E. Fenichel (Eds.), *New visions for the developmental assessment of infants and young children* (pp. 11–26). Washington, DC: Zero to Three: National Center for Infants, Toddlers, and Families.

Gronlund, G. (2006). *Make early learning standards come alive: Connecting your practice and curriculum to state guidelines.* St. Paul, MN: Redleaf Press.

Harms, T., Clifford, R. M., & Cryer, D. (2005). *Early Childhood Environment Rating Scale, Revised edition (ECERS-R).* New York: Teachers College Press.

Harms, T., Cryer, D., & Clifford, R. M. (2006). *Infant–Toddler Environment Rating Scale, Revised Edition (ITERS).* New York: Teachers College Press.

McAfee, A., Leong, D. J., & Bodrova, E. (2004). *Basics of assessment. A primer for early childhood education.*

Washington, DC: National Association for the Education of Young Children.

Meisels, S. J. (1996). Charting the continuum of assessment and intervention. In S. J. Meisels & E. Fenichel (Eds.), *New visions for the developmental assessment of infants and young children* (pp. 27–52). Washington, DC: Zero to Three: National Center for Infants, Toddlers, and Families.

National Association for the Education of Young Children. (2005). *NAEYC early childhood program standards and accreditation criteria.* Washington, DC: Author.

National Education Association. (1994). *Assessing learning in the classroom.* Washington, DC: Author.

Oliver, S. J., & Klugman, E. (2006, July/August). Play and standards-driven curricula: Can they work together in preschool? *Exchange, 170,* 12–16.

Popper, B. K. (1996). Achieving change in assessment practices: A parent's perspective. In S. J. Meisels & E. Fenichel (Eds.), *New visions for the developmental assessment of infants and young children* (pp. 59–66). Washington, DC: Zero to Three: National Center for Infants, Toddlers, and Families.

Rocco, S. (1996). Toward shared commitment and shared responsibility: A parent's vision of developmental assessment. In S. J. Meisels & E. Fenichel (Eds.), *New visions for the developmental assessment of infants and young children* (pp. 55–58). Washington,

DC: Zero to Three: National Center for Infants, Toddlers, and Families.

Scott-Little, C., Kagan, S. L., & Frelow, V. S. (2006, March/April). State standards for children's learning. *Exchange, 168,* 27–34.

Seefeldt, C. (2005). *How to work with standards in the early childhood classroom.* New York: Teachers College Press.

Segal, M., & Webber, N. T. (1996). Nonstructured play observations: Guidelines, benefits, and caveats. In S. J. Meisels & E. Fenichel (Eds.), *New visions for the developmental assessment of infants and young children* (pp. 207–230). Washington, DC: Zero to Three: National Center for Infants, Toddlers, and Families.

Shepard, L. A. (1989). Why we need better assessments. *Educational Leadership, 46,* 4–9.

Shepard, L., Kagan, S. L., Lynn, S., & Wurtz, E. (1998). *Principles and recommendations for early childhood assessments.* Washington, DC: National Goals Panel.

Widerstrom, A. H., Mowder, B. A., & Sandall, S. R. (1991). *At-risk and handicapped newborns and infants.* Upper Saddle River, NJ: Prentice Hall.

Wiggins, G. P. (1993). *Assessing student performance.* San Francisco: Jossey-Bass.

Wiggins, G. P. (1998). *Educative assessment.* San Francisco: Jossey-Bass.

Wodrich, D. (1984). *Children's psychological testing.* Baltimore: Brookes.

How Standardized Tests Are Used, Designed, and Selected

Chapter Objectives

As a result of reading this chapter, you will be able to

1. Understand how standardized tests are used with infants and young children
2. Understand the process of standardized test design
3. Understand the differences between test validity and test reliability
4. Use resources and strategies for selecting and evaluating standardized tests
5. Understand issues in selecting and using standardized tests

Various methods and purposes for measuring and evaluating infants and young children were discussed in chapter 2. We differentiated between formal measures and informal measures of measurement. Psychological tests and some educational tests are considered formal instruments because they have been standardized.

In this chapter, we will look at some ways that standardized tests are used with infants and young children. Specific examples of tests and their purposes will be discussed.

How are standardized tests different from other kinds of measures? We will discuss how standardized tests are designed and tested to measure the desired characteristics. Test validity and reliability are explained, as well as their effects on the dependability of the test.

How Standardized Tests Are Used With Infants and Young Children

Types of Standardized Tests

Many types of standardized tests are available for use with infants and young children. All are psychological tests, whether they measure abilities, achievements, aptitudes, interests, attitudes, values, or personality characteristics. In the following sections, we will discuss each of these types of tests.

Ability refers to the current level of knowledge or skill in a particular area. Three types of psychological tests—**intelligence tests**, **achievement tests**, and **aptitude tests**—are categorized as ability tests because they measure facets of ability. Young children are often measured to determine the progress of their development. A measure used with such children may assess ability in motor, language, social, or cognitive skills. *McCarthy's Scales of Children's Abilities* (McCarthy, 1983), for example, has indexes for verbal, perceptual–performance, quantitative, cognitive, memory, and motor abilities.

Achievement is related to the extent to which a person has acquired certain information or has mastered identified skills. An achievement test measures ability in that it evaluates the child's achievement related to specific prior instruction. The *Peabody Individual Achievement Test—Revised* (American Guidance Service, 1997) is a measure of achievement in mathematics, reading recognition, reading comprehension, spelling, and general information.

Aptitude is the potential to learn or develop proficiency in some area, provided that certain conditions exist or training is available. An individual may have a high aptitude for music or art. Like achievement tests, aptitude tests also measure learned abilities. An aptitude test measures the results of both general and incidental learning and predicts future learning.

Intelligence tests are ability tests in that they assess overall intellectual functioning. They are also aptitude tests because they assess aptitude for learning and problem solving. The *Stanford–Binet Intelligence Scale* (Thorndike, Hagen, & Sattler, 1989) is an example of an intelligence scale that also measures individual aptitude.

Personality tests measure a person's tendency to behave in a particular way. Such tests are used to diagnose children's emotional problems. Because an inventory

54
....

CHAPTER 3

*How
Standardized
Tests are Used,
Designed, and
Selected*

is used to assess personality characteristics, the test is quite lengthy, usually containing several hundred items in a true–false format. Test items are answered by the parent or child or by both together and are analyzed to determine whether the child has certain personality traits.

Interest inventories are used to determine a person's interest in a certain area or vocation and are not used with very young children. A school-age child may be given a reading interest inventory to provide the teacher with information that will serve as a guide when helping the child select reading material.

Attitudes are also measured in older children and adults, rather than in young children. An **attitude measure** determines how a person is predisposed to think about or behave toward an object, event, institution, type of behavior, or person or group of people. Politicians frequently use such measures to determine the attitudes of voters on controversial issues.

Tests for Infants

Various psychological tests have been constructed for infants and young children. Such tests are challenging because of the child's developmental limitations. Babies are particularly difficult to evaluate because of their short attention span. Their periods of alertness are brief, and they have their own schedules of opportune moments for testing. In addition, developmental changes occur rapidly, making test results unreliable for more than a short time. Generally, because of these limitations, the validity and reliability of infant scales are questionable. The tests are difficult to administer and interpret. Nevertheless, they are useful in evaluating the status of newborns and infants (Wodrich, 1997).

The status of a newborn can be determined using various measures. The *Apgar scale* (Apgar, 1975), administered 1 minute and 5 minutes after birth, assesses the health of the newborn by evaluating the heart rate, respiratory effort, muscle tone, body color, and reflex irritability. Each characteristic is scored on a scale of 0 to 2. A score of 7 to 10 indicates the infant is in good condition; a score of 5 may indicate developmental difficulties. A score of 3 or below is very serious and indicates an emergency concerning the infant's survival. The *Brazelton Neonatal Behavioral Assessment Scale*, another neonatal measure (Als, Tronick, Lester, & Brazelton, 1979), measures temperamental differences, nervous system functions, and the capacity of the neonate to interact. Its purpose is to locate mild neurological dysfunctions and variations in temperament. A newer scale, the *Neonatal Behavioral Assessment Scale-Third Edition (NBAS-III)* (Brazelton, 1996; Brazelton, Berry, & Nugent, 1995), is used with newborns from the first day of life through the end of the first month. In this test, the infant's competence is measured through behavioral items. In addition to identifying the infant's performance, if administered with the parents present, it can be used to help parents understand their infant's signals and skills. This knowledge of child development generally and their baby's competence specifically can facilitate improvement in parenting skills (Widerstrom, Mowder, & Sandall, 1991). An adaptation of the NBAS to assess preterm infants came through the design of the *Assessment of Preterm Infants' Behavior (APIB)* (Als, Lester, Tronick, & Brazelton, 1982). It includes many of the items in the NBAS, but refined them to be able to observe the preterm infant's functioning (Als, 1986). The *Ounce Scale* (Meisels, Marsden, Dombro, Weston, & Jewkes, 2003) is another developmental scale suitable for parents, childcare personnel, and Early Head Start Teachers. Used with children from birth to 3.6 years old, the *Ounce Scale* is organized around six developmental domains and helps parents observe developmental milestones.

Infant development scales go beyond measuring neonatal status to focusing on development from 1 month to 2 years. The *Gesell Developmental Schedules* (Ball, 1977) were the first scales devised to measure infant development. Gesell designed them to detect infants who were delayed in development and might need special services. The *Bayley Scales of Infant Development (Third Edition) (BSID-III)* (Bayley, 2005) were designed to learn about the infant's intelligence, rather than overall development, while the *Communication and Symbolic Behavior Scales (CSBS)* (Wetherley & Prizant, 1993) are used to assess communicative and symbolic development, including symbolic play and constructive play. The *Mullen Scales of Early Learning* (Mullen, 1995) measure cognitive functioning in infants and toddlers from birth to 68 months. The assessment measures intellectual development through the child's response to prepared activities. The Gesell and Bayley instruments are difficult to administer because of their length; however, they are supposed to provide diagnostic information.

The *Denver II* (Frankenburg, Dodds, Archer, Shapiro, & Bresnick, 1990) is a simple screening instrument designed to identify children who are likely to have significant delays and need early identification and intervention, while the *Adaptive Behavior Assessment System (Second Edition) (ABAS-II)* (Harrison & Oakland, 2003) assesses the strengths and weaknesses in adaptive skills. The *Early Coping Inventory (ECI)* (Zeitlin et al., 1988) assesses how well the infant and toddler react and cope with different situations; in addition, the *Infant/Toddler Symptom Checklist (ITSC)* (DeGangi, Poisson, Sickel, & Wiener, 1995) screens infants and toddlers who show disturbances in sleep, feeding, and self-calming. Used with children from 7 to 30 months old, it can be administered by a parent or caregiver. Figure 3-1 presents information about some neonatal and infant tests.

Diagnostic Tests. There are diagnostic tests for infants to identify developmental or physical disorders. As with developmental and screening tests for infants and toddlers, it is very difficult to accurately acquire the needed information. The strategies for measuring lung function, for example, can be considered to be intrusive for infants (Panitch, 2004). Likewise, babies who have experienced a life-threatening event (ALTE) present challenges in what tests should be used, how to interpret the results, and how well the tests or assessment procedures will contribute to the many factors that can cause ALTE (Brand, Altman, Purtill, & Edwards, 2005). Observational measures to assess children with spinal cord injury can result in lack of agreement in the observers (Calhoun, Gaughan, Chafetz, & Mulcahey, 2005). Regardless, specialists in infant screening and diagnosis continue to research methods that provide the desired results with minimal invasive methods and more dependable results.

Tests for Preschool Children

Psychologists have designed a variety of tests to evaluate development and to detect developmental problems during the preschool years. Just as the testing of infants and toddlers presents challenges to test administrators, because of the children's developmental limitations, the evaluation of preschool children under age 6 must also be conducted with their developmental characteristics in mind. Instruments that assess

56
....

CHAPTER 3

*How
Standardized
Tests are Used,
Designed, and
Selected*

characteristics used to identify developmental delays or to diagnose sources of disabilities that affect the child's potential for learning are administered to one child at a time. Test items are concrete tasks or activities that match the child's ability to respond; nevertheless, validity and reliability are affected by such factors as the child's limited attention span and willingness to attempt to respond to the examiner. As children enter the preschool years, more instruments are available for evaluating development and developmental delay. To better understand the various types of tests, preschool tests are organized into screening, diagnostic, language, and achievement tests.

Screening Tests. Screening tests are administered to detect indicators that a child might have a developmental problem that needs to be further investigated. Screening

NAME	LEVEL	TYPE	PURPOSE
Apgar Scale	Neonate	Birth status	Assess health of the newborn infant
Brazelton Neonatal Behavioral Assessment Scale	Neonate	Neonatal status	Locate mild neurological dysfunctions and variations in temperament
Neonatal Behavioral Assessment Scale (NBAS)	First month		Identify the Infant's ability to modulate its behavioral systems in response to external stimuli
Adaptive Behavior Assessment System– Infant and Preschool	Infant and preschool	Adaptive skills	Assess strengths and weaknesses in adaptive skills
Assessment of Preterm Infant' Behavior (APIB)	Preterm infants	Preterm development	Identify current status and intervention targets
Bayley Scales of Infant Development–II (BSID-II)	Infant	Intelligence	Diagnose developmental delays in infants
Gesell Developmental Schedules	Infant	Development	Detect developmental delays
Denver II	1 month to 6 years	Developmental screening	Identify significant developmental delays
Communication and Symbolic Behavior Scales (CSBS)	Infants, toddlers, preschoolers	Language development	Assess communication and symbolic development
Mullen Scales of Early Learning	Birth to 68 months	Intellectual development	Assess cognitive functioning

FIGURE 3-1 Neonatal and infant tests

57
....

CHAPTER 3
*How
Standardized
Tests are Used,
Designed, and
Selected*

tests can be contrasted with diagnostic tests that examine the possible difficulties in depth to determine what measures need to be taken to correct the problems.

The *Denver II* (Frankenburg et al., 1990) was discussed earlier as a measure that can be used with infants and older children. It is administered by an examiner. In contrast, the *Ages and Stages Questionnaire (Third Edition) (ASQ-3)* (Squires & Bricker, 2009) uses parental reporting. The parent can complete the questionnaire or participate in an interview with an examiner. It is administered from age 4 months to 60 months and is also applicable for infants and toddlers.

The *AGS Early Screening Profiles* (Harrison, Kaufman, & Kaufman, 1990) can be administered from ages 2 years to 6 years 11 months. They include parent–teacher questionnaires as well as profiles in cognitive language, motor, and social development. The *Developmental Indicators for the Assessment of Learning (DIAL III)* (Mardell-Czundowski & Goldenberg, 1998) is also used for overall developmental delay. Administered to children ages 3 to 6 years, it includes direct observation and tasks presented to the child. The *Early Screening Inventory—Revised (ESI-R)*, 2008 edition (Meisels, Marsden, Wiske, & Henderson, 2008) has two forms: one for ages 3 to 4.4 years, and one for ages 4.5 to 6 years. It screens developmental domains and uses cutoff scores to determine whether the child needs to be referred for further evaluation. A parental questionnaire is used to provide supplementary information. The *Brigance Screens* (*Infant & Toddler Screen, Early Preschool Screen-II*, and *Preschool Screen-II*) (Brigance, 2002) is used with children from birth to 5 years. It is available in five languages. Finally, the *First Step Screening Test for Evaluating Preschoolers (First Step)* (Miller, 1993) has twelve subtests grouped into cognitive, communicative, and motor categories. There is also an optional social-emotional scale and adaptive behavior checklist. *First Step* is administered to children from ages 2 years 9 months to 6 years 2 months.

The screening tests just discussed cover various categories of development. The tests discussed next focus on social-emotional development. These screening instruments look at social behaviors and require sensitive and careful collaboration between the home and school because children's behaviors are affected by

Baker School for Early Learning
....

*B*aker School is a community school that targets services for toddlers and preschool children from a nearby public housing development. The children in the housing development represent a variety of ethnic groups and languages. Some are from families that recently emigrated from another country. Teachers in the program need input from parents on their child's current stage of development prior to entering the program. Parents can fill out the ***Ages and Stages Questionnaire*** with information about their child. The form includes questions about behaviors, speaking abilities, and physical skills as well as other indicators of development. Because the teachers are sensitive to possible language and literacy limitations, they are available if the parents need help filling in the information. In many cases they read the questions to the parents and record their responses on the test form.

58
....

CHAPTER 3

How
Standardized
Tests are Used,
Designed, and
Selected

environmental differences. While this type of screening is difficult to do accurately, social-emotional competence is very important and should be monitored (Meisels & Atkins-Burnett, 2005).

The *Devereux Early Childhood Assessment (DECA)* (Le Buffe & Naglieri, 1999) is designed to be administered through classroom observations. It has items that examine positive and negative behaviors such as attention problems, aggression, depression, and emotional control. The *Early Screening Project (ESP)* (Walker, Severson, & Feil, 1995) is administered to children ages 3 to 6 years and is administered in three stages. Children are ranked in social interaction, adaptive behavior, maladaption behaviors, aggressive behaviors, and reactions to critical events. A parent questionnaire looks at how the child plays with other children, how the child interacts with caregivers, and social problems such as difficulties with self-esteem or social avoidance. An instrument that uses parent ratings is the *Preschool and Kindergarten Behavior Scales (PKBS-2)* (Merrell, 2002). Administered to children ages 3 to 6 years, it examines positive and problem behaviors. (Figure 3-2 provides examples of items on screening tests.)

Diagnostic Tests. After a child has been screened and there are indicators that further evaluation is needed, tests for diagnostic assessment can be administered. Measures of adaptive behavior assess possible developmental problems related to learning disabilities. Adaptive behavior instruments attempt to measure how well the young child has mastered everyday living tasks such as toileting and feeding. The *Vineland Adaptive Behavior Scale (Second Edition)* (Sparrow, Balla, & Cicchetti, 2005)

Motor Skills

Gross Motor
  Jumping, skipping, hopping, catching, walking a straight line
Fine Motor
  Building with cubes, cutting, copying forms, writing name and copying words,
    drawing shapes

Cognitive Development

Pointing to body parts
Rote counting
Counting objects
Sorting and classifying pictures
Identifying and naming colors and shapes
Answering simple questions about concepts

Language Development

Identifying correct item in an array of pictures
Answering personal questions
Identifying objects and pictures
Placing object using positional words (*under, over, in,* etc.)

FIGURE 3-2 Examples of items on screening tests

59

CHAPTER 3

*How
Standardized
Tests are Used,
Designed, and
Selected*

assesses the everyday behaviors of the child that indicate level of development. The scale determines areas of weakness and strength in communication, daily living, socialization, and motor skills. Another instrument, the *AAMR* (American Association on Mental Retardation) *Adaptive Behavior Scale—School (ABS-S:2)* (Nihira & Lambert, 1993) assesses adaptive behavior in sixteen domains for social competence and independence. Figure 3-3 describes categories of adaptive behaviors.

Preschool intelligence tests and adaptive behavior scales are used to diagnose mental retardation. Although intelligence measures during the preschool years are generally unreliable because children's IQs can change enormously between early childhood and adolescence, they are used with young children to measure learning potential.

The *Stanford–Binet Intelligence Scale (Fifth Edition)*(Roid, 2003), the original IQ test, was designed to assess general thinking or problem-solving ability. It is valuable in answering questions about developmental delay and retardation. Conversely, *McCarthy's Scales of Children's Abilities* (McCarthy, 1983) is useful in identifying mild retardation and learning disabilities. Another instrument, the *Wechsler Preschool and Primary Scale of Intelligence (WPPSI-III)* (Wechsler, 2002), is useful in identifying signs of uneven development.

Other instruments address all domains of development. The *Kaufman Assessment Battery for Children (Second Edition) (K-ABC-II)* (Kaufman & Kaufman, 2005), *Battelle Developmental Inventory—II (BDI-II)* (Newborg, 2004), and *Bracken Basic Concept Scale—Revised* (Bracken, 1998), have comprehensive assessments of development.

Language Tests. The category of language tests for preschool children is very important because many children who are at risk for not learning successfully because they are poor or their first language is not English are frequently served prior to kindergarten. While some language tests for at-risk children are in English, others are available in both English and Spanish. The *Preschool Language Scale (PLS-4)* (Zimmerman, Steiner, & Pond, 2007) and *Peabody Picture Vocabulary Test (Fourth Edition)(PPVT-4)* (Dunn & Dunn, 1997) provide information on a child's language ability, which can help determine whether a child will benefit from a language enrichment program.

With the expanding numbers of limited English proficiency (LEP), children who are living in many states, language assessment tests are growing in importance.

Independent Living Categories	**Social Behavior Categories**
Physical development	Social engagement
Language development	Conformity
Independent functioning	Trustworthiness
	Disturbing interpersonal behavior
	Hyperactive behavior
	Self-abusive behavior
	Stereotyped behavior

FIGURE 3-3 Some categories assessed in adaptive behaviors

60

CHAPTER 3

*How
Standardized
Tests are Used,
Designed, and
Selected*

Children who have limited English proficiency may be served in a bilingual program or ELL program. The *Pre-LAS, Pre-IPT,* and *Woodcock-Muñoz Language Survey* (discussed shortly) are available in English and Spanish editions. There are also forms of these tests for school-age children.

The *Pre-Language Assessment Survey (Pre-LAS)* (CTB/McGraw-Hill, 2000) measures oral language proficiency. It is also used to make placement decisions, monitor progress over time, and identify learner needs. The *IDEA Proficiency Tests (Pre-IPT)* (Ballard & Tighe, 1989) were designed to help districts identify LEP children. The *Pre-IPT* is administered to 3 to 5 year olds and can later be used to release children from the LEP program. The *Woodcock-Muñoz Language Survey-Revised (WMLS-R)* (Woodcock & Muñoz-Sandoval, 2005) can be administered to children as young as age 2.

Achievement Tests. The *National Reporting System* (NRS) (U.S. Department of Health and Human Services Head Start Bureau, 2003) was designed for children in the Head Start program. This test was introduced in response to a policy established by the George W. Bush administration requiring a measure similar to those used for NCLB in public schools. The controversy over the use of the NRS was discussed in chapter 1. Figure 3-4 presents the categories and characteristics of preschool tests.

Tests for School-Age Children

For the child old enough to attend preschool and elementary school, many tests are available for use by teachers, school psychologists, program evaluators, and other personnel with responsibilities for students and the early childhood curriculum. In addition to preschool programs for children with disabilities, many states conduct programs for 4-year-old and kindergarten children as well. Descriptions of

St. Pius Preschool

*A*reas of southwest Arkansas are experiencing an influx of people from Mexico and Central America who work at a large local paper factory. Many of these families in one community attend St. Pius Catholic Church, and parishioners have seen the need to provide English classes and other services for the parents as they adjust to a new country and language. As the parents found work, church members also recognized a need for child care. They decided to include a concentrated English language development program when they added a child-care center to their outreach activities.

As they began the program, the parishioners realized they needed to find a test that would indicate the children's progress in learning English as well as provide a language assessment to send to local Head Start, preschool, and kindergarten programs when the children were transitioning out of the St. Pius school. They learned about the *Pre-Language Assessment Survey (Pre-LAS)* from public school colleagues. After learning how to use the instrument, they were ready to start implementing the test to better help their very young students learn English.

NAME	LEVEL	TYPE	PURPOSE
Screening Tests			
Ages and Stages Questionnaire	4–60 months	Developmental screening	Measure cognitive, language, motor, and social development
AGS Early Screening Profiles	2–6 years	Developmental screening	Measure cognitive, language, motor, self-help, social acculturation, and health development
Developmental Indicators for the Assessment of Learning (DIAL-III)	2–6 years	Developmental screening	Assess motor, language, and cognitive development
Early Screening Inventory–Revised (ESI-R)	3–6 years	Developmental screening	Assess developmental domains with cutoff scores for referrals
First Step Screening Test for Evaluating Preschoolers	2 years 9 months to 6 years 2 months	Developmental screening	Assess five developmental domains to identify preschoolers at risk for developmental delay
Social Emotional Screening			
Devereux Early Childhood Assessment (DECA)	2–5 years	Social-emotional screening	Examine positive and negative social-emotional behaviors
Early Screening Project (ESP)	3–6 years	Social-emotional screening	Rank children in social interaction, adaptive behavior, maladaptive behaviors, and aggressive behaviors
Preschool and Kindergarten Behavior Scales (PKBS-2)	3–6 years	Social-emotional screening	Examine positive and problem behaviors through parent ratings
Diagnostic Tests			
Vineland Adaptive Behavior Scale	3–16 years	Adaptive behavior	Measure weaknesses and strengths in everyday-living tasks
AAMR Adaptive Behavior Scale–School (ABS-S: 2)	3–16 years	Adaptive behavior	Assess adaptive behavior in terms of personal independence and development; can be compared to norms for children developing normally, with retardation, and with severe retardation
Stanford–Binet Intelligence Scale	2 years to adult	Global intelligence	Detect delays and mental retardation
McCarthy's Scales of Children's Abilities	2 years 5 months to 8 years	Intelligence	Identify and diagnose delay in cognitive and noncognitive areas through subtests; identify learning problems

FIGURE 3-4 Categories and characteristics of preschool tests

NAME	LEVEL	TYPE	PURPOSE
Diagnostic Tests			
Wechsler Preschool and Primary Scale of Intelligence (WPPSI-III)	4–6 years	Intelligence	Identify signs of uneven development, detect overall delay
Kaufman Assessment Battery for Children (K-ABC)		Comprehensive developmental assessment	Assess developmental delay and plan for instruction
Battelle Developmental Inventory	Birth to 8 years	Comprehensive developmental assessment	Identify child's strengths and weaknesses and plan for intervention or instruction
Bracken Basic Concept Scale–Revised	2 years 5 months to 7 years 11 months	Basic concept development	Quickly identify or comprehensively diagnose basic concept development
Language Tests			
Preschool Language Scale (PLS-4)	Birth to 6 years 11 months	Language	Measure receptive and expressive language z
Peabody Picture Vocabulary Test	2 years 5 months to 18 years	Vocabulary	Measure receptive vocabulary for Standard American English
Pre-Language Assessment Survey (Pre-LAS) (English and Spanish)	4–6 years	Language	Measure oral language proficiency and assess learner needs
IDEA Proficiency Tests (Pre-IPT) (English and Spanish)	3–5 years	Language	Identify children for placement in LED programs
Woodcock-Muñoz Language Survey (English and Spanish)	2 years to adult	Language	Measure language proficiency in English or Spanish; determine eligibility for bilingual programs or readiness for English instruction
Achievement Test			
National Reporting System (NRS)	5–6 years	Achievement	Measure achievement in preschool skills and effectiveness of Head Start program

FIGURE 3-4 (*Continued*)

some of these assessments were included in the previous section on preschool tests. Likewise, some of the assessments in this section include prekindergarten and kindergarten children. Although individual tests are available for some purposes in school-age programs, group testing is also used. Group tests require the child to use paper and pencil; therefore, test results may be affected by the child's ability to respond in this manner. Test validity and reliability may be affected by the child's ability both to respond in a group setting and to use a pencil to find and mark responses on the test. As students move into the primary grades, these factors become less important. The tests discussed in this section do not include the many tests designed by individual states to meet the requirements of NCLB. Instead, they address tests for delay in language, cognitive, and physical development and disabilities as children move into the primary grades.

Many public school programs are designed for children at high risk for learning disabilities. A number of programs are available, including bilingual and English language programs for children whose first language is not English, intervention programs for children with a physical or mental disability, and preschool programs for children from low-income homes who lack the early childhood experiences that predict successful learning. These programs may include a screening instrument to determine which children are eligible. In addition to the language tests discussed earlier, the *Bilingual Syntax Measure II* (Burt, Dulay, Hernandez-Chavez, & Taleporos, 1980) is a standardized test that can be used to screen children for language ability and dominance. The *Wechsler Intelligence Scale for Children (WISC-IV)* (Wechsler, 2003) and the *Bender Visual Motor Gestalt Test for Children (Second Edition) (Bender Gestalt-II)* (Bender, 2003) may be administered to a preschool or school-age child by a school psychologist or school diagnostician to determine whether the child needs educational services for children with disabilities. Poor performance on the *Bender Visual Motor Gestalt Test* by a school-age child indicates the need for further study of the child (Cronbach, 1990). The *Test of Visual-Motor Integration* (Hammill, Pearson, & Voress, 1996) is a similar test.

Achievement tests are useful when making decisions about instruction. If a child is exhibiting learning difficulties, a psychologist might administer the *Peabody Individual Achievement Test—Revised* (American Guidance Service, 1997) or the *Wide Range Achievement Test 3 (WRAT 3)* (Stone, Jastak, & Wilkinson, 1995) to gain information about specific learning disabilities. The teacher might administer the *Early School Inventory* (Nurss & McGauvran, 1976) or the *Boehm Test of Basic Concepts* (Boehm, 2000) to young children to determine their need for instruction in basic concepts or to assess successful learning of concepts previously taught.

Primary-grade teachers may also need specific information about a child having difficulties in the classroom. Diagnostic tests such as the *Spache Diagnostic Reading Skills* (Spache, 1981) can be administered by classroom teachers to pinpoint skills in which students need additional instruction. The *Child Observation Record (COR)* developed by the High/Scope Educational Research Foundation (2003) can be used in preschool through fifth grade in six developmental domains, including social development. Figure 3-5 includes examples of initiative items relating to adults, other children, and social problem solving. The checklists can also be used in Head Start programs and child-care centers and with children who speak English as a second language. Figure 3-6 presents information about tests used with school-age children.

Group achievement tests are used to evaluate individual achievement, group achievement, and program effectiveness. All of the new tests developed by individual states to provide accountability for student achievement are group achievement tests. A school district may administer achievement tests every year to determine each student's progress, as well as to gain diagnostic information on the child's need for future instruction. The same test results can be used at the district level to give

I. Initiative

A. Making choices and plans

1. Child indicates a choice by pointing or some other action.
2. Child expresses a choice in one or two words.
3. Child expresses a choice with a short sentence.
4. Child makes a plan with one or two details.
5. Child makes a plan with three or more details.

B. Solving problems with materials

1. Child expresses frustration when encountering a problem with materials.
2. Child identifies a problem with materials and asks for help.
3. Child tries one way to solve a problem with materials.
4. Child tries two ways to solve a problem with materials.
5. Child tries three or more ways to solve a problem with materials.

C. Initiating play

1. Child engages in exploratory play.
2. Child makes something with materials.
3. Child engages in pretend play.
4. During play with other children, child adds an idea that modifies the play.
5. Child joins with other children in playing a game with rules.

D. Taking care of personal needs

1. Child observes as others do a self-care activity.
2. Child accomplishes some parts of a self-care activity.
3. Child accomplishes all parts of a self-care activity.
4. Child identifies the need for a tool and uses it independently to accomplish a personal goal.
5. Child helps another child in a self-care activity or program routine.

II. Social Relations

E. Relating to adults

1. Child participates in a conversation initiated by a familiar adult.
2. Child participates in a conversation initiated by an unfamiliar adult.
3. Child initiates an interaction with an adult.
4. Child sustains an interaction with an adult.
5. Child involves an adult in an activity and sustains the involvement.

F. Relating to other children

1. Child responds when another child initiates an interaction.
2. Child initiates an interaction with another child.
3. Child sustains an interaction with another child.
4. Child invites another child to play.
5. Child shows loyalty to another child.

G. Resolving interpersonal conflict

1. In a conflict with another child, child responds with yelling or physical action.
2. Child requests adult help in resolving a conflict with another child.
3. Child identifies the problem in a conflict with another child.
4. With adult help, child offers a solution to a conflict.
5. Child negotiates the resolution of a conflict with another child.

H. Understanding and expressing feelings

1. Child expresses an emotion.
2. Child comforts another child.
3. Child talks about an emotion.
4. Child represents an emotion through pretend play or art.
5. Child identifies an emotion and gives a reason for it.

FIGURE 3-5   Examples from the Preschool Child Observation Record

Source: *Preschool Child Observation Record* (COR). (2003). Ypsilanti, MI: High/Scope Educational Research Foundation, 2003, Used with permission.

NAME	LEVEL	TYPE	PURPOSE
Bilingual Syntax Measure II	Kindergarten to grade 2	Language	Determine language dominance
Wechsler Intelligence Scale for Children (WISC-III)	$6\frac{1}{2}$–$16\frac{1}{2}$ years	Intelligence	Diagnose mental retardation and learning disability; includes verbal and performance subscales
Bender Visual Motor Gestalt Test for Children	4–10 years	Visual-motor functioning	Assess perceptual skills and hand–eye coordination, identify learning disabilities
Test of Visual-Motor Integration	4–17 years	Visual-motor functioning	Assess visual-motor ability
Peabody Individual Achievement Test–Revised	Kindergarten to grade 12	Individual achievement	Assess achievement in mathematics, reading, spelling, and general information
Early School Inventory	Kindergarten	Development	Assess physical, cognitive, language, and social-emotional development
Boehm Test of Basic Concepts	Kindergarten to grade 2	Cognitive ability	Screen for beginning school concepts
Brigance Diagnostic Inventory of Basic Skills	Kindergarten to grade 6	Academic achievement	Assess academic skills and diagnose learning difficulties in language, math, and reading
Spache Diagnostic Reading Skills	Grades 1 to 8 reading levels	Diagnostic reading test	Locate reading problems and plan remedial instruction
Child Observation Record (COR)	Prekindergarten to grade 5	Comprehensive developmental assessment	Provide appropriate assessment using developmental checklist

FIGURE 3-6 School-age tests

information on student's progress between and within schools and to determine the effectiveness of the district's instructional program.

Instructional effectiveness may also be evaluated at the state or national level. A state agency may administer statewide achievement tests to work toward establishing

66

....

CHAPTER 3

*How
Standardized
Tests are Used,
Designed, and
Selected*

a standard of instructional effectiveness in all schools within the state. Test results can identify school districts that both exceed and fall below the set standard. Indicators of poor instructional areas in many school districts pinpoint weaknesses in the state's instructional program and facilitate specific types of improvement. As was discussed in chapter 1, the No Child Left Behind Act, passed in 2001, required all states to develop and administer tests to measure achievement in public schools. For the first time, effectiveness of student achievement would be compared on a national basis across states to ensure higher standards for education. National assessments are made periodically to pinpoint strengths and weaknesses in the educational progress of U.S. children in different subject areas. These findings are frequently compared with achievement results of students in other countries.

In this section, we discussed how standardized tests are used. Although the tests described include various types with different purposes, the process used for their development is essentially the same. The next part of the chapter will focus on how standardized tests are designed, that is, the steps followed in the development of all standardized tests.

Steps in Standardized Test Design

Test designers follow a series of steps when constructing a new test. These steps ensure that the test achieves its goals and purposes. In planning a test, the developers first specify the purpose of the test. Next, they determine the test format. As actual test design begins, they formulate objectives; write, try out, and analyze test items; and assemble the final test form. After the final test form is administered, the developers establish norms and determine the validity and reliability of the test. As a final step, they develop a test manual containing procedures for administering the test and statistical information on standardization results.

Specifying the Purpose of the Test

Every standardized test should have a clearly defined purpose. The description of the test's purpose is the framework for the construction of the test. It also allows evaluation of the instrument when design and construction steps are completed. The *Standards for Educational and Psychological Testing* (American Psychological Association [APA], 1999) has established guidelines for including the test's purpose in the test manual. The standards are as follows:

> B2. The test manual should state explicitly the purpose and applications for which the test is recommended.
>
> B3. The test manual should describe clearly the psychological, educational and other reasoning underlying the test and the nature of the characteristic it is intended to measure. (p. 15)

Test designers should be able to explain what construct or characteristics the test will measure, how the test results will be used, and who will take the test or to whom it will be administered.

The population for whom the test is intended is a major factor in test design. Tests constructed for infants and young children are very different from tests designed for adults. As test developers consider the composition and characteristics of the children for whom they are designing the test, they must include variables such as age, intellectual or educational level, socioeconomic background, cultural background, and whether the young child can read.

Determining Test Format

Test format decisions are based on determinations made about the purpose of the test and the characteristics of the test takers. The test format results from the developer's decision on how test items will be presented and how the test taker will respond (Brown, 1983). One consideration is whether the test will be verbal or written. Although adults are most familiar with written tests, infants and young children are unable to read or write. Tests designed for very young children are usually presented orally by a test administrator. An alternative is to use a psychomotor response; the child is given an object to manipulate or is asked to perform a physical task.

For older children, high school students, and adults, other test formats are possible. Test takers may respond to an alternative-choice written test such as one with true–false, **multiple-choice**, or matching items. The test may be given as a **group test** rather than administered as an **individual test** to one person at a time. Short-answer and essay items are also possibilities.

After the test designers have selected the format most appropriate for the test's purpose and for the group to be tested, actual test construction begins. Experimental test forms are assembled after defining test objectives and writing test items for each objective.

Developing Experimental Forms

In preparing preliminary test forms, developers use the test purpose description as their guide. Test content is then delimited. If an achievement test for schoolchildren is to be written, for example, curriculum is analyzed to ensure that the test will reflect the instructional program. If the achievement test is to be designed for national use, then textbook series, syllabi, and curricular materials are studied to check that test objectives accurately reflect curriculum trends. Teachers and curriculum experts are consulted to review the content outlines and behavioral objectives that serve as reference points for test items.

The process of developing good test items involves writing, editing, trying out, and rewriting or revising test items. Before being tried out, each item for an achievement test may be reviewed and rewritten by test writers, teachers, and other experts in the field. Many more items than will be used are written because many will be eliminated in the editing and rewriting stages (Burrill, 1980).

A preliminary test is assembled so that the selected test items can be tried out with a sample of students. The experimental test forms resemble the final form. Instructions are written for administering the test. The test may have more questions than will be used in the final form because many questions will be revised or eliminated after the tryout. The sample of people selected to take the preliminary test is similar to the population that will take the final form of the test.

68

CHAPTER 3

*How
Standardized
Tests are Used,
Designed, and
Selected*

Purpose of and Rationale for Selected Tests

*T*he statement of purpose of a test describes the framework that will be used in designing the test. Information about the expected uses of the *Peabody Picture Vocabulary Test* (Dunn & Dunn, 1997) includes school, clinical, vocational, and research uses. Part of the school use description follows:

> Since the PPVT-R is a reasonably good measure of scholastic aptitude for subjects where the language of the home is Standard English, it should also be useful as an initial *screening device* in scanning for bright, low ability, and language impaired children who may need special attention. Too, it should be helpful in identifying underachievers, when used in conjunction with a measure of school achievement. (p. 3)

The *Bracken Basic Concept Scale–Revised* (Bracken, 1998) measures concepts in the early childhood years. A partial description follows:

> Divided into two separate instruments for quick identification or comprehensive diagnosis of basic concept development in children, the diagnostic full-scale instrument measures 258 concepts and is appropriate for use with children from ages 2.5 years through 7 years 11 months. The 30-item screening tests (forms A and B) are used to screen small groups of children to determine if further diagnosis is necessary. The screening tests are intended for children in kindergarten and first grade.

The tryout of the preliminary test form is described as *item tryout and analysis*. **Item analysis** involves studying three characteristics of each test question: difficulty level, discrimination, and grade progression of difficulty. The *difficulty level* of a question refers to how many test takers in the tryout group answered the question correctly. *Discrimination* of each question involves the extent to which the question distinguishes between test takers who did well or poorly on the test. Test takers who did well should have been more successful in responding to an item than test takers who did poorly. The item differentiates between people who have more or less knowledge or ability. The *grade progression of difficulty* refers to tests that are taken by students in different grades in school. If a test question has good grade progression of difficulty, a greater percentage of students should answer it correctly in each successively higher grade (Burrill, 1980).

Assembling the Test

After item analysis is completed, the final form of the test is assembled. As a result of item analysis, test items have been reexamined, rewritten, or eliminated. Test questions or required behaviors to measure each test objective are selected for the test.

If more than one test form is to be used, developers must ensure that alternative forms are **equivalent** in content and difficulty. Test directions are made final with instructions for both test takers and test administrators. In addition, information for test administrators includes details about the testing environment and testing procedures.

Standardizing the Test

Although test construction is complete when the final form is assembled and printed, the test has not yet been standardized. The final test form must be administered to another, larger sample of test takers to acquire norm data. **Norms** provide the tool whereby children's test performance can be compared with the performance of a reference group.

A reference group that represents the children for whom the test has been designed is selected to take the test for the purpose of establishing norms. The performance of the reference or sample group on the final test form during the standardization process will be used to evaluate the test scores of individuals or groups who take the test in the future.

The norming group is chosen to reflect the makeup of the population for whom the test is designed. If a national school achievement test is being developed, the standardization sample consists of children from all sections of the country to include such variables as gender, age, community size, geographic area, and socioeconomic and ethnic factors. For other types of tests, different characteristics may be used to match the norming sample with future populations to be tested.

Various kinds of norms can be established during the standardization process. Raw scores of sample test takers are converted into derived scores or standard scores for purposes of comparison. Standard scores are achieved by calculating the **raw score**, or the number of items answered correctly, into a score that can be used to establish a norm. Various types of standard scores can be used to compare the people selected to standardize the test with future populations who will be given the test. Each type of **grade norm** allows test users to interpret a child's test scores in comparison with the scores of children used to norm the test (Burrill, 1980). For example, an age score is established by determining the norms for age groups when the test is given to the norming sample. The age norms describe the average performance of children of various ages. Likewise, grade norms or grade-equivalent norms are established by determining the average scores made by children at different grade levels in the norming group (Brown, 1983).

Developing the Test Manual

The final step in test design is development of the test manual. The test developer describes the purpose of the test, the development of the test, and the standardization procedures. Information on test validity and reliability is also included to give test users information on the dependability of the test. When explaining standardization information in the user's manual, test developers describe the method used to select the norming group. The number of individuals included in standardizing the test is reported, as well as the geographic areas, types of communities, socioeconomic groups, and ethnic groups that they represent.

70

CHAPTER 3

*How
Standardized
Tests are Used,
Designed, and
Selected*

Validity and Reliability

Norm information is important for establishing confidence in analyzing and interpreting the significance of test scores. Test users also need information demonstrating that the test will be valuable for the intended purposes. Therefore, the test manual must provide information on validity and reliability. Both types of dependability indicators are equally important in determining the quality of the test. **Validity** is the degree to which the test serves the purpose for which it will be used; **reliability** is the extent to which a test is stable or consistent. Test validity can be determined through content validity, criterion-related validity, or construct validity.

When first designing a test, the developers describe its purpose. Test objectives or the test outlines provide the framework for the content of the test. When a manual provides information on **content validity**, the test developers are defining the degree to which the test items measured the test objectives and fulfilled the purpose of the test. Thus, for example, on an achievement test, content validity is the extent to which the content of the test represents an adequate sampling of the instructional program it is intended to cover. The content validity of a reading test would be based on how well the test items measured the reading skills examined in the test. The content validity of a mathematics test would look at the content of the objectives on the test and assess how well the test items measured that content.

Criterion-related validity is concerned with the validity of an aptitude test. Rather than analyzing course content, test items focus on skills or tasks that predict future success in some area. The estimates of predictive validity are concerned with stability over time. For example, an **intelligence quotient (IQ)** test might be predictive of school achievement. Likewise, Scholastic Aptitude Test scores may predict whether high school students will be successful in college. Validity is predictive because the criteria for success are the future grades the student will earn in college or the student's future grade-point average.

Criterion-related validity may be **concurrent validity**, rather than predictive validity. Instead of using a future measure to determine validity, current measures are used. The outside criterion is assessed when the test is standardized. The developer of an intelligence test may cite an existing intelligence test as the criterion to measure validity. The developer administers both intelligence tests to the sample group. If the new test scores correlate highly with scores on the existing test, they may be used to establish concurrent validity.

If a test measures an abstract psychological trait, the user's manual will describe how the sample group was tested to establish construct validity. **Construct validity** is the extent to which a test measures a relatively abstract psychological trait such as personality, verbal ability, or mechanical aptitude. Rather than examining test items developed from test objectives, one examines construct validity by comparing test results with the variables that explain the behaviors. For example, suppose the construct is believed to include certain behavioral characteristics, such as sociability or honesty. An instrument's construct validity can be checked by analyzing how the trait is affected by changing conditions. Alternatively, an instrument may measure level of anxiety; its construct validity is determined by creating experiments to find out what conditions affect anxiety (Linn & Gronlund, 2000).

71

CHAPTER 3

*How
Standardized
Tests are Used,
Designed, and
Selected*

Construct validity is necessary when measuring creativity. To have construct validity, a test designed to measure creativity must differentiate the behavior of creative people from that of uncreative people (Mehrens & Lehmann, 1991).

The validity of a test is the extent to which the test measures what it is designed to measure. Test users, however, are also interested in a test's dependability or stability in measuring behaviors. Test developers, therefore, also establish and report on the reliability of the instrument as part of the standardization process.

Test reliability is related to test item discrimination. When test items are analyzed after the initial item tryout, they are examined for discrimination power. After the final test form is administered to a norming sample, the items are analyzed again to ensure that the instrument is fairly reliable. The whole test is analyzed, rather than individual test items. The test manual reports the test's reliability as determined by using alternative-form, split-half, or test–retest reliability measures. A test's *reliability coefficient* describes the degree to which a test is free from error of measurement. If **alternative-form reliability** strategies are used, test developers construct two equivalent forms of the final test. Both forms are administered to the norming group within a short period. The correlation between the results on the two different forms measures the coefficient of reliability. For example, standardized achievement tests are published using several different forms of the test. To measure reliability, the norming group takes two forms of the test and then the results are compared to see if the performance on each of the tests was the same or very similar.

If a **split-half reliability** coefficient is used to establish reliability, the norming group is administered a single test, and scores on half of the test are correlated with scores on the other half of the test. Split-half reliability is determined from the contents of a single test. A test with split-half reliability is also considered to have **internal consistency**; that is, the items on each half of the test are positively correlated in measuring the same characteristics.

Test–retest reliability is also derived from the administration of a single test form. In this case, however, the test is administered to the norming group and then is administered again after a short interval. The two sets of scores are compared to determine whether they were consistent in measuring the test objectives.

Factors That Affect Validity and Reliability

Despite the measures and procedures that are used to ensure validity and reliability in standardized tests, other factors can affect test outcomes. Some common factors are reading ability, the physical condition of the testing room, memory, and the physical condition of the individual taking the test. Thus, if the testing room is uncomfortably warm or a student had inadequate rest the night before the test, scores will be affected.

Lack of adherence to time limits and lack of consistency in test instructions affect test scores. Other factors are inconsistency in the rating of essays from individual to individual and student guessing of test answers (Payne, 1997).

Validity is affected by such factors as unclear directions, difficulty of reading vocabulary on the test, and test items that are not appropriate for the test objectives (Linn & Gronlund, 2000). Reliability is affected by the number of test items or the length of the test, lack of interrater reliability, and extraneous events that affect the testing situation (Linn & Gronlund, 2000; McMillan, 2007).

72

CHAPTER 3

*How
Standardized
Tests are Used,
Designed, and
Selected*

These and other factors affect the possible errors on a test and the quality of the test. This variation in testing quality is accounted for in the **standard error of measurement**, discussed next.

Standard Error of Measurement

No matter how well designed, no test is completely free from error. Although there is a hypothetical **true score**, in reality it does not exist. The reliability of the test depends on how large the standard error of measurement is after analysis of the chosen method of determining reliability. If the reliability correlations are poor, the standard error of measurement will be large. The larger the standard error of measurement, the less reliable the test. Standard error of measurement is the estimate of the amount of variation that can be expected in test scores as a result of reliability correlations.

Several variables that are present during standardization affect test reliability as discussed earlier. First is the size of the population sample. Generally, the larger the population sample, the more reliable the test will be. Second is the length of the test. Longer tests are usually more reliable than shorter tests. Longer tests have more test items, resulting in a better sample of behaviors. The more items that measure a behavior, the better the estimate of the true score and the greater the reliability. Strict adherence to test directions by test administrators contributes to higher reliability, whereas variations in test instructions or coaching students can distort the reliability of test results.

The third variable that can affect standard error of measurement is the range of test scores obtained from the norming group. The wider the spread of scores, the more reliably the test can distinguish among them. Thus, the range of scores demonstrates how well the test discriminates between good and poor students (Gronlund, 1990). The spread of test scores can be related to the number of students taking the test. The larger the testing sample, the more likely there will be a wider spread of test scores.

Considerations In Choosing
and Evaluating Tests

Whenever a private school, public school district, preschool, or child-care center decides to use a test to evaluate children, educators must decide how to select the best test for that purpose. Those who select the test must determine the relevant questions to ask about the test. Brown (1983) identifies various factors that test users must considered: (1) the purpose of the testing, (2) the characteristics to be measured, (3) how the test results will be used, (4) the qualifications of the people who will interpret the scores and use the results, and (5) any practical constraints. All these factors are important in selecting tests for young children. Because of the developmental limitations of young test takers, test formats must be compatible with their ability to respond. Developmental limitations include short attention span, undeveloped fine-motor skills, inability to use reading skills for test responses, and poor performance on group tests. Limitations in training and experience in those who administer the test are also factors in test selection.

Other relevant concerns, particularly in selecting tests for young children, are the costs involved, testing time, and ease of scoring and using test results (Cronbach, 1990). The test must be reasonable in cost, and the time needed to administer the test should be suitable for young children.

A major issue is whether the test has quality. Is it a good test to use with the children? The person searching for an appropriate test will want to examine the test manual for indications of how well the test was designed and normed. The test manual should include information on the following:

1. *Purpose of the test.* The statement of purpose should include the rationale for the test, the characteristics the test is designed to measure, and the uses for the test.

2. *Test design.* The procedures and rationale for selecting test items and the development and trial of test forms should be explained.

3. *Establishment of validity and reliability.* The description should describe the procedures used to establish validity and reliability to include sufficient data on validity, reliability, and norms.

4. *Test administration and scoring.* Specific information should be given on how to administer and score the test and to interpret test results. Information should be adequate for users to determine whether the test is practical and suitable for their purposes. Potential problems should be pointed out that can be encountered when administering and scoring the test (Kaplan & Saccuzzo, 1989). See Figure 3-7 for questions that should be answered in a test manual, including an acceptable coefficient of reliability.

Test users need extensive training in tests and measurements to interpret a test manual adequately. For many users, the explanations and data reported in test manuals are complex and difficult to understand. A reader may have difficulty in deciding whether the reliability coefficient is adequate, whether the size and demographic characteristics of the norming population are appropriate, or whether test content and format are suitable for the intended uses. To obtain additional help in understanding the suitability of the test, test users will want to consult resources for test standards and reviews. The *Standards for Educational and Psychological Testing* (APA, 1999) includes standards for tests, manuals, and reports. It also includes standards for reliability and validity, as well as information that should be included on the use of tests.

The Buros Institute of Mental Measurements is perhaps the most important source in identifying, describing, and evaluating published tests. The series of *Tests in Print* is a comprehensive bibliography of thousands of tests in five volumes. The most recent, *Tests in Print VII* (Murphy, Spies, & Plake, 2006) consists of two volumes. The tests are listed by type, and basic information is given about each test.

The *Mental Measurements Yearbooks* include descriptive information about tests plus professional reviews. Information includes sources of information about test construction, validation, and use. Critical reviews of the tests are included. For example, the *Stanford–Binet Intelligence Scale* (Terman & Merrill, 1973) is the oldest and most highly regarded IQ test used in the United States. However, the fourth edition of the test (Thorndike, Hagen, & Sattler, 1986) was found to be significantly different

74

CHAPTER 3

*How
Standardized
Tests are Used,
Designed, and
Selected*

Reliability

1. How was reliability determined for the test? What were the methods used?
2. Does the reliability achieve recommended levels (0.90 or above for tests used to make decisions about individuals or 0.70 or above for research studies)?

Validity

1. Does the test actually measure what it purports to measure?
2. Is the test meaningful for your purposes?
3. How was the test validated? What specific criteria were used?

Standardization Sample

1. Was the number of subjects used to establish reliability, validity, and norms adequate?
2. What kinds of demographic and personal characteristics were included in the group of subjects? Are they similar to the population you will be testing?

Scoring

1. Are scoring keys available?
2. Is the time needed to score reasonable?
3. If the test is machine scored, is the cost reasonable? What sort of report is available? How long does it take for test results to be available?

Other Considerations

1. How long does is take to administer the test?
2. Are the test content and length appropriate for the developmental level if used with young children?
3. Does the test require reading? Is the reading level appropriate for students who will take the test?
4. How much training is required for the test administrator? Can the test be administered by classroom teachers?

FIGURE 3-7   Questions about test manuals about the quality of tests

from the earlier editions. Reviewers pointed out that users are given poor information on the accuracy of reliability scores, the test is less gamelike and therefore likely to be less appealing to children, and it overrepresents parents from high occupational and educational levels in the sample of children used for norming (Anastasi, 1989; Cronbach, 1989). Educators choosing a test need to be informed of the quality of the test being considered for selection. The most recent yearbook is the *Seventeenth Mental Measurements Yearbook* (Geisinger, Spies, Carlson, & Plake, 2007).

A resource that is particularly helpful to people without a background in test design at a technical level is *Test Critiques*, Volumes I–X (Keyser & Sweetland, 1984–1994). It includes information about test design and use, as well as a critique of the tests. Other resources for test evaluation and selection are particularly suitable for users of early childhood tests.

Test reviews can be accessed online. The Buros Center for Testing provides search engines for *Test Reviews Online* (http://www.unl.edu/buros). Another online source is *Psychware Sourcebook* (Krug, 1993). It identifies and describes computer products available for assessment in education, psychology, and business.

Brown (1983) summarized the steps in selecting and evaluating tests as follows:

75

CHAPTER 3

*How
Standardized
Tests are Used,
Designed, and
Selected*

1. Outline your general requirements: the purpose of testing, the characteristics to be measured, and the nature of the group to be tested. Consider also the qualifications of test users and practical considerations.
2. Identify what tests are available that appear to meet your needs. Here sources such as *Tests in Print, the Mental Measurement Yearbooks,* test publishers' catalogs, and test compilations will be most helpful.
3. Obtain further information about these tests from texts, journals, reference books, and consultation with people who have used this type of test.
4. Select the most promising tests. Obtain samples (specimen sets) of these tests.
5. Make a detailed evaluation of these tests, keeping in mind the unique requirements of your situation. On the basis of these evaluations, select the test(s) to be used.
6. If possible, conduct an experimental tryout of the test before putting it to use.
7. Use the test. Constantly monitor and evaluate its usefulness and effectiveness. (p. 463)

Summary

Standardized tests, despite their shortcomings, are useful for test users. Because they have been carefully developed through a series of steps that ensure their dependability, educational institutions, in particular, use them to measure students' characteristics. Good standardized tests are normed by using many individuals from various backgrounds who live in different parts of the United States. As a result, the tests also accurately measure the population to whom the tests are given.

Although the process of developing a standardized test may seem to be unnecessarily tedious, good test design requires careful planning and attention to each step. The ultimate validity and reliability of the test result from attention to design details, beginning with the definition of the test's purpose and ending with the description of technical data about the test's construction in the users' manual.

$\mathcal{R}$EVIEW QUESTIONS

1. What is a standardized test? Describe different types of standardized tests.
2. What is meant by *quantifiable scores?*
3. Describe norm referencing.
4. Why does a test need to have validity? Reliability? Can you have one without the other?

5. Why is the description of a test's purpose important? How does test purpose affect test design?
6. List some factors that test developers must consider before starting to develop a test.
7. What are the best test formats to use with preschool children?

8. How are experimental test forms used?
9. What is meant by *item tryout and analysis*? What is accomplished during this procedure?
10. Discuss three types of item analysis.
11. What kinds of information are acquired when a test is standardized?
12. How is a norming population selected?
13. Explain *content validity, criterion-related validity,* and *construct validity.*
14. Explain *alternative-form reliability, split-half reliability,* and *test–retest reliability.*
15. Why does every test have a standard error of measurement?

$\mathcal{S}$UGGESTED ACTIVITIES

1. Interview a kindergarten teacher in a public school to determine whether standardized tests are administered to kindergarten children. If tests are used, find out what tests are given and the purpose for test results. If standardized tests are not administered, find out the school's position on the use of standardized tests with young children under age 8.
2. Learn how to administer a standardized test such as the *Peabody Picture Vocabulary Test—Revised* and administer it to two preschool children. Be sure you use a test that is suitable to be given by teachers without extensive training. Evaluate the test results and write a report describing what you learned, including the following: (1) the process of test administration, (2) the similarities and differences between the two children tested, and (3) the difficulties you had in administering the test.
3. Review the steps in developing a standardized test. Discuss each step and its importance. Discuss how a final test might be less effective if a step is conducted inappropriately. What problems would be encountered later when the test design is completed?

$\mathcal{K}$EY TERMS

achievement test
alternative-form reliability
aptitude test
attitude measure
concurrent validity
construct validity
content validity
criterion-related validity
equivalent
grade norm
group test
individual test
intelligence quotient (IQ)
intelligence test

interest inventory
internal consistency
item analysis
multiple choice
norm
personality test
raw score
reliability
split-half reliability
standard error of measurement
test–retest reliability
true score
validity

Selected Web Sites

Child Care Exchange
http://www.childcareexchange.com

Buros Institute of Mental Measurements
http://www.unl.edu/buros

Test Reviews Online
http://www.buros.unl.edu/buros/jsp/search/jsp

References

Als, H. (1986). Assessing the neurobehavioral development of the premature infant in the environment of the neonatal intensive care unit: A syntactive model of neonatal behavioral organization. *Physical and Occupational Therapy in Pediatrics, 5,* 3–53.

Als, H., Lester, B. M., Tronick, E., & Brazelton, T. B. (1982). Towards a research for the assessment of preterm infants' behavior (APIB). In H. E. Fitzgerald, B. M. Lester, & M. W. Yogman (Eds.), *Theory and research in behavioral pediatrics* (Vol. 1, pp. 1–35). New York: Plenum Press.

Als, H., Tronick, E., Lester, B. M., & Brazelton, T. B. (1979). Specific neonatal measures: The Brazelton Neonatal Behavioral Assessment Scale. In J. D. Osofsky (Ed.), *Handbook of infant development* (pp. 185–215). New York: Wiley.

American Guidance Service. (1997). *Peabody Individual Achievement Test—Revised.* Circle Pines, MN: Author.

American Psychological Association. (1999). *Standards for educational and psychological testing.* Washington, DC: Author.

Anastasi, A. (1989). Review of the *Stanford–Binet Intelligence Scale—Fourth Edition.* In J. C. Conoley & J. J. Kramer (Eds.), *The tenth Mental Measurements Yearbook* (pp. 771–772). Lincoln: University of Nebraska Press.

Apgar, V. (1975). A proposal for a new method of evaluation of a newborn infant. *Anesthesia and Analgesia, 32,* 260–267.

Ball, R. S. (1977). The Gesell Developmental Schedules: Arnold Gesell (1880–1961). *Journal of Abnormal Child Psychology, 5,* 233–239.

Ballard & Tighe. (1989). *IDEA Proficiency Tests (Pre-IPT).* Brea, CA: Author.

Bayley, N. (2005). *Bayley Scales of Infant Development (BSID—III)* (3rd ed.). San Antonio, TX: Psychological Corp.

Bender, L. (2003). *Bender Visual Motor Gestalt Test for Children (Bender-Gestalt-II)* (2nd ed.). San Antonio, TX: Psychological Corp.

Boehm, A. E. (2000). *Boehm Test of Basic Concepts* (3rd ed.). San Antonio, TX: Psychological Corp.

Bracken, B. A. (1998). *Bracken Basic Concept Scale—Revised (BBCS-R).* San Antonio, TX: Psychological Corp.

Brand, D. A., Altman, R. L., Puttill, K., & Edwards, K. S. (2005, April). Yield of diagnostic testing in infants who have had an apparent life-threatening event. *Pediatrics, 115,* 885–893.

Brazelton, T. B., Berry, T., & Nugent, J. K. (1995). *Neonatal Behavioral Assessment Scale (NBAS)* (3rd ed.). Cambridge, England: Cambridge University Press.

Brazelton, T. B. (1996). A window on the newborn's world: More than two decades of experience with the Neonatal Behavioral Assessment Scale. In S. J. Meisels & E. Fenichel (Eds.), *New visions for the developmental assessment of infants and young children* (pp. 127–146). Washington, DC: Zero to Three: National Center for Infants, Toddlers, and Families.

Brigance, A. H. (2002). *Brigance Head Start Screen II and Early Childhood Screen II.* Woburn, MA: Curriculum Associates.

Brown, E. G. (1983). *Principles of educational and psychological testing* (3rd ed.). New York: CBS College Publishing.

Buros, O. K. (1999). *Tests in print V.* Lincoln: University of Nebraska Press.

Burrill, L. E. (1980). *How a standardized achievement test is built.* Test Service Notebook 125. New York: Psychological Corp.

Burt, M. K., Dulay, H. C., Hernandez-Chavez, C. E, & Taleporos, E. (1980). *Bilingual Syntax Measure II.* New York: Harcourt Brace Jovanovich.

Calhoun, C. L., Gaughan, J. P., Chafitz, R. S., & Mulcahey, M. J. (2009, Spring). A pilot study of observational motor assessment in infants and toddlers with spinal card injury. *Pediatric physical therapy, 21,* 62–67.

Cronbach, L. J. (1989). Review of the *Stanford–Binet Intelligence Scale—Fourth Edition.* In J. C. Conoley & J. J. Kramer (Eds.), *The tenth Mental Measurements Yearbook* (pp. 773–775). Lincoln: University of Nebraska Press.

Cronbach, L. J. (1990). *Essentials of psychological testing* (5th ed.). New York: Harper & Row.

CTB/McGraw-Hill (2000) *Pre-LAS 2000.* Monterrey, CA: Author.

DeGangi, G., Poisson, S., Sickel, R., & Wiener, A. S. (1995). *Infant/Toddler Symptom Checklist: A screening tool for parents (ITSC).* San Antonio, TX: Therapy Skill Builders, Psychological Corp.

Dunn, L. M., & Dunn, L. (1997). *Peabody Picture Vocabulary Test (PPVT-4)* (4th ed.). Circle Pines, MN: American Guidance Service.

Frankenburg, W. K., Dodds, J., Archer, P., Shapiro, H., & Bresnick, B. (1990). *Denver II.* Denver, CO: Denver Developmental Materials.

Geisinger, K. F., Spies, R. A., Carlson, J. F., & Plake, B. S. (Eds.). (2007). *The seventeenth Mental Measurements Yearbook.* Lincoln: University of Nebraska Press.

Gronlund, N. E. (1990). *Measurement and evaluation in teaching* (6th ed.). New York: Macmillan.

Hammill, D. D., Pearson, N. A., & Voress, J. K. (1996). *Test of Visual–Motor Integration.* Austin, TX: PRO-ED.

Harrison, P., Kaufman, A. S., & Kaufman, N. L. (1990). *AGS Early Screening Profiles (ESP).* Circle Pines, MN: American Guidance Service.

Harrison, P., & Oakland, T. *Adaptive Behavior Assessment System (APAS-II)* (2nd ed.). Los Angeles: Western Psychological Services.

High/Scope Educational Research Foundation. (2003). *Preschool Child Observation Record.* Ypsilanti, MI: Author.

Kaplan, R. M., & Saccuzzo, D. P. (1989). *Psychological testing principles: Applications and issues* (2nd ed.). Belmont, CA: Brooks/Cole.

Kaufman, A., & Kaufman, N. (2005). *Kaufman Assessment Battery for Children (K-ABC-II): Sampler manual* (2nd ed.). Circle Pines, MN: American Guidance Service.

Keyser, D. J., & Sweetland, R. C. (1984–1994). *Test critiques* (Vols. I–X). Kansas City, MO: Test Corporation of America.

Krug, S. E. (1993). *Psychware Sourcebook.* Kansas City, MO: Test Corporation of America.

Le Buffe, P. A., & Naglieri, J. A. (1999). *Devereux Early Childhood Assessment (DECA).* Lewisville, NC: Kaplan Early Learning.

Linn, R. L., & Gronlund, N. E. (2000). *Measurement and assessment in teaching* (8th ed.). Upper Saddle River, NJ: Merrill/Prentice Hall.

Mardell-Czundowski, C. D., & Goldenberg, D. S. (1998). *Developmental Indicators for the Assessment of Learning* (3rd ed.). Circle Pines, MN: American Guidance Service.

McCarthy, D. (1983). *McCarthy's Scales of Children's Abilities.* New York: Psychological Corp.

McMillan, J. H. (2007). *Classroom assessment: Principles and practice for effective instruction* (4th ed.). Boston: Allyn & Bacon.

Mehrens, W. A., & Lehmann, I. J. (1991). *Measurement and evaluation in education and psychology* (4th ed.). New York: Harcourt Brace.

Merrell, K. W. (2002). *Preschool and Kindergarten Behavior Scales (PKBS-2)* (2nd ed.). Austin, TX: PRO-ED.

Meisels, S. J., & Atkins-Burnett, S. (2004, January). The Head Start National Reporting System: A critique. *Young Children, 59,* 64–66.

Meisels, S. J., & Atkins-Burnett, S. A. (2005). *Developmental screening in early childhood: A guide* (5th ed.). Washington, DC: National Association for the Education of Young Children.

Meisels, S., Marsden, D. B., Dombro, A. L., Weston, D. R., & Jewkes, A. M. (2008). *The Ounce Scale.* San Antonio, TX: Pearson.

Meisels, S. J., Marsden, D. B., Wiske, M. S., & Henderson, L. W. (2008). *Early Screening*

Inventory—Revised (ESI-R).New York: Pearson Education.

Miller, L. J. (1993). *First Step: Screening Test for Evaluating Preschoolers (First Step)*. San Antonio, TX: Psychological Corp.

Mullen, E. M. (1995). *Mullen Scales of Early Learning, AGS Edition*. Circle Pines, MN: American Guidance Services, Inc.

Murphy, L. L., Spies, R. A., & Plake, B. S. (2006). *Tests in Print, VII*. Lincoln: University of Nebraska Press.

Newborg, J. (2004). *Battelle Developmental Inventory—II (BDI-II)*. Chicago: Riverside Publishing.

Nihira, K., & Lambert, N. (1993). *AAMR Adaptive Behavior Scale—School (ABS-S:2)*. Washington, DC: American Association on Mental Retardation.

Nurss, J. R., & McGauvran, M. E. (1976). *Early School Inventory*. Orlando, FL: Harcourt Brace Jovanovich.

Panitch, H. B. (2004). The role of pulmonary testing in infants. *NeoReviews, 5*. Retrieved September 29, 2009, from http://www.neoreviews. aapublications.org

Payne, D. A. (1997). *Applied educational assessment*. Belmont, CA: Wadsworth.

Spache, G. D. (1981). *Diagnostic reading scales: Examiner's manual*. Monterey, CA: CTB/McGraw-Hill.

Sparrow, S. S., Balla, D. A., & Cicchetti, D. V. (2005). *Vineland Adaptive Behavior Scale* (2nd ed.). Circle Pines, MN: American Guidance Service.

Squires, J., & Bricker, D. (2009). *Ages and Stages Questionnaire (ASQ:3)* (3rd ed.) Baltimore: Brookes.

Stone, M. H., Jastak, S., & Wilkinson, G. (1995). *Wide Range Achievement Test 3*. Wilmington, DE: Jastak Assessment Systems.

Terman, L. M., & Merrill, M. A. (1973). *Stanford–Binet Intelligence Scale: Manual for the Third Revision Form L-M*. Boston: Houghton Mifflin.

Thorndike, R. L., Hagen, E. P., & Sattler, J. M. (1989). *Stanford–Binet Intelligence Scale* (4th ed.). Chicago: Riverside.

U.S. Department of Health and Human Services Head Start Bureau. (2003). *National Reporting System*. Washington, DC: Author.

Walker, H. M., Severson, H. H., & Feil, E. G. (1995). *Early Screening Project (ESP)*. Longmont, CO: Sopris West.

Wechsler, D. (2003). *Wechsler Intelligence Scale for Children (WISC-IV)* (4th ed.). San Antonio, TX: Psychological Corp.

Wechsler, D. (2002). *Wechsler Preschool and Primary Scale of Intelligence (WPPSI-III)* (3rd ed.). San Antonio, TX: Psychological Corp.

Wetherley, A. M., & Prizant, B. M. (1993). *Communication and Symbolic Behavior Scales (CSBS)*. Baltimore: Brookes.

Widerstrom, A. H., Mowder, B. A., & Sandall, S. R. (1991). *At-risk and handicapped newborns and infants*. Upper Saddle River, NJ: Prentice Hall.

Wodrich, D. (1997). *Children's psychological testing: A guide for nonpsychologists*. Baltimore: Brookes.

Woodcock, R. W., & Muñoz-Sandoval. A. F. (2005). *Woodcock-Muñoz Language Survey—Revised (WMLS-R)*. Chicago: Riverside.

Zeitlin, S., Williamson, G. G., & Szczepanski, M. (1988). *Early Coping Inventory (ECI): A Measure of Adaptive Behavior*. Bensenville, IL: Scholastic Testing Service.

Zimmerman, I. L., Steiner, V. G., & Pond, R. E. (2007). *Preschool Language Scale (PLS-4)* (4th ed.). San Antonio, TX: Psychological Corp.

CHAPTER 4

Using and Reporting Standardized Test Results

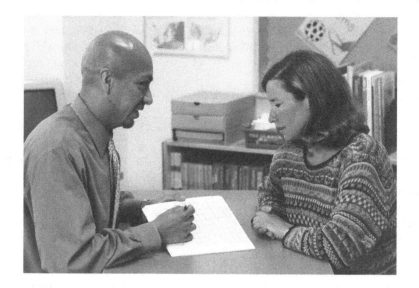

Chapter Objectives

As a result of reading this chapter, you will be able to

1. Explain the difference between norm-referenced and criterion-referenced tests
2. List common characteristics of norm-referenced and criterion-referenced tests
3. Explain the advantages and disadvantages of using tests that have been standardized
4. Understand how test scores are interpreted and reported
5. Describe how individual and group test results are used to report student progress and program effectiveness
6. Discuss the advantages and disadvantages of using norm-referenced and criterion-referenced tests with young children
7. Understand the difficulties in using standardized tests with young children

Tests are administered to young children to acquire beneficial information about them. In chapter 3, we discussed how standardized tests are planned, designed, and standardized.

In this chapter, we discuss in more detail how to use information from children's test scores. In the process of standardizing a test, developers establish the norms that make test score interpretation useful. We not only take a more detailed look at norm-referenced tests, but also study how another type of standardized test, the criterion-referenced test, is used to meet the learning needs of young children. Group test scores can be used to analyze and improve curriculum and instruction at various levels within a school district; individual test scores can be used by the classroom teacher to organize appropriate learning experiences for individual students or the class as a whole.

We also discuss how individual and group test results are used to report student progress and program effectiveness. Test results are important to teachers, school district administrators, parents, and school boards. Results are reported to each in a context that provides meaningful interpretation of the test. Finally, we consider the disadvantages and advantages of using norm- and criterion-referenced tests with young children.

Uses of Norm-Referenced and Criterion-Referenced Tests

Distinctions Between Norm-Referenced and Criterion-Referenced Tests

Norm-referenced and criterion-referenced tests are both standardized instruments. Some standardized tests are designed for norm-referenced results and others for criterion-referenced results. The current trend is to design tests that are both norm and criterion referenced. The two types of tests have different purposes, and test items are used differently when measuring student learning or achievement. **Norm-referenced tests** provide information on how the performance of an individual compares with that of others. The individual's standing is compared with that of a known group. The person's percentile rank is obtained to determine the relative standing in a norm group by recording what percentage of the group obtained the same score or a lower score.

In contrast, **criterion-referenced tests** provide information on how the individual performed on some standard or objective. These test results allow users to interpret what an individual can do without considering the performance of others. Criterion-referenced tests are designed to measure the results of instruction; they determine the individual's performance on specific behavioral or instructional objectives (Wilson, 1980; Zucker, 2003). Linn and Miller (2005) describe the difference between the two types of tests as the ends of a continuum: "The criterion-referenced test emphasizes description of performance and the norm-referenced test emphasizes discrimination among individuals" (p. 44).

Regardless of whether tests are norm or criterion referenced, the process of their design and development is as described in chapter 3. They are constructed and standardized through all the steps that will result in validity and reliability. It is also possible that norm- and criterion-referenced tests have not been standardized; however, criterion-referenced tests are more often nonstandardized (Goodwin & Goodwin, 1993). It is equally important that criterion-referenced tests have validity and reliability if they are to be used to make decisions about young children.

Norm- and criterion-referenced tests have characteristics in common. Linn and Miller (2005) describe these as follows:

1. Both require a relevant and representative sample of test items.
2. Both require specification of the achievement domain to be measured.
3. Both use the same type of test items.
4. Both use the same rules for item writing (except for item difficulty).
5. Both are judged by the same qualities of goodness (validity and reliability).
6. Both are useful in educational measurement. (p. 14)

Both tests measure what students have learned; nevertheless, the objectives for measurement are different. The norm-referenced test is broad in content. Many aspects of the content are measured. Because the test is concerned with overall achievement, only a small sample of behaviors for each objective can be assessed. The criterion-referenced test focuses on mastery of objectives. Each objective has many test questions to determine whether the objective has been mastered (Zucker, 2003).

An achievement test in mathematics provides a good example. The norm-referenced test for the first grade may have items on addition, subtraction, sets, and all other areas included in the mathematics curriculum. Test items are written to sample the student's overall performance in first-grade mathematics. The student's total raw score is then transformed to compare overall achievement with the test norms. On the criterion-referenced test, student performance on individual curriculum objectives is important. Test items are written to measure whether the child has mastered a particular learning objective in subtraction, addition, or other components of the mathematics curriculum (Goodwin & Goodwin, 1982).

Another difference between norm- and criterion-referenced tests also relates to differences in test items. In a norm-referenced instrument, test items must cover a wide range of difficulty. Because the test is intended to discriminate between the performance of students and groups of students, the difficulty of test items ranges above the grade level for which the test is intended. Test items designed primarily for criterion-referenced purposes are written specifically for learning tasks. Easy items are not omitted, and the intent is to evaluate how well the student has learned the objectives for one grade level (Wilson, 1980).

New standardized tests have been developed with dual referencing; that is, they are designed for both norm- and criterion-referenced assessment. Although it is difficult to develop a single test that works equally well for both types of measurements, obtaining both kinds of performance results is helpful to educators. Compromises in test construction are offset by the more effective use of the test (Linn & Miller, 2005). Some criterion-referenced tests have not been standardized. This does not imply that they are not well designed and useful, but readers should be aware of this condition.

Uses of Norm-Referenced Tests With Preschool Children

Norm-referenced test scores are used to measure individual achievement within a designated group. Norms are not standards to be reached; they are numerical descriptions of the test performance of a group of students. Norms can be established at a national or local level. Norm-referenced tests are commonly used to measure school achievement, intelligence, aptitude, and personality traits. Formal tests are administered at the preschool level to identify children who need or can benefit from special instruction, as well as to determine the success of an early childhood program.

Measures of intelligence such as the *Wechsler Preschool and Primary Scale of Intelligence* (Wechsler, 2002) are norm-referenced instruments that allow test examiners to differentiate the knowledge skills of preschool students. As discussed in chapter 2, intelligence tests are described as diagnostic because they include comprehensive examination of children who might be mentally or physically delayed or who are at risk for learning disabilities. Other tests in this category include the *Kaufman Assessment Battery for Children (K-ABC-II)* (Kaufman & Kaufman, 2005) and *McCarthy's Scales of Children's Abilities* (McCarthy, 1983). In addition to identifying children with disabilities, intelligence tests can be used to identify children who are gifted.

The National Reporting System (U.S. Department of Health and Human Services, 2003) discussed in earlier chapters is a controversial norm-referenced test implemented with the purpose of establishing accountability in Head Start programs. Efforts to use test results to determine whether programs would be refunded in 2005 failed. (See chapter 1.) The test is administered orally to individual children. Figure 4-1 shows sample questions on vocabulary and early math.

Norm-referenced tests are used with preschool children to measure their present level of knowledge, skills, or performance. In federally funded programs such as Head Start, a norm-referenced measure may be used to evaluate the learning acquired by the children as a result of the program. The *Peabody Picture Vocabulary Test* (Dunn & Dunn, 1997) provides a measure for language development. The *Boehm Test of Basic Concepts* (Boehm, 2000) and the *Learning Accomplishments Profile—Revised* (Sanford & Zelman, 1995) assess the child's abilities and skills, including the acquisition of concepts.

Uses of Norm-Referenced Tests With School-Age Children

After children enter primary school, achievement tests are the most frequently administered norm-referenced tests. Locally developed achievement tests, as well as state and national tests, can be given in order to measure and analyze individual and group performance resulting from the educational program. Children experiencing difficulties in school are evaluated with screening and diagnostic tests, but all

VOCABULARY
I have said. Let's try one. Put your finger on "ball."
IF THE CHILD RESPONDS CORRECTLY WITHOUT HELP BY POINTING TO THE BALL IN QUADRANT 4 SAY:
Good! Let's try another one. Put your finger on "dog."
(SEE GRAPHIC BELOW.)

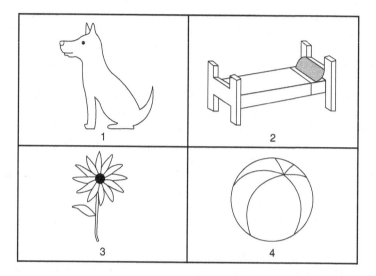

EARLY MATH addresses child outcomes in numbers and operations. The math skills assessed include recognizing one-digit numerals and basic geometric shapes, solving word problems involving counting or simple addition or subtraction, and interpreting simple measurements. The estimated administration time is 3 minutes.

How many trees are on this page?
CORRECT: TWO (NONVERBAL RESPONSES ARE ACCEPTABLE)
(SEE GRAPHIC BELOW)

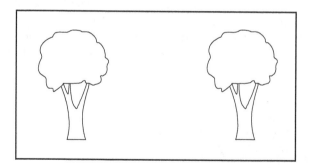

FIGURE 4-1   Sample questions for the Head Start National Reporting System

Source: U.S. Department of Health and Human Resources Head Start Bureau. (2003). *National Reporting System.* Washington, DC: Author.

students take achievement tests as early as kindergarten, more frequently beginning in first grade.

Norm-referenced test results are used for more general comparisons of group test results. One such use is to assess achievement level in subject areas. The achievement of a single class in a school, all classes of a certain grade level in the school, all schools at a grade level in a school district, and all schools within a state with that grade level can be studied to determine general progress in one or more subject areas. The results of batteries of tests can be analyzed for trends in achievement.

In a similar type of analysis, components of an instructional program can be studied by using group test scores. If a new instructional program is to be tried or if an existing method is to be evaluated to help in deciding whether changes are needed, an achievement test can be used to investigate the effectiveness of the program. Particular areas of weakness and strength can be pinpointed, and decisions and plans can be made to improve weak components in the curriculum.

Uses of Criterion-Referenced Tests With Preschool Children

Criterion-referenced test scores are used to describe individual performance on specific objectives. Criterion-referenced measures de-emphasize distinctions among individual performances; rather, they indicate whether the individual has mastered the objectives that were tested. Criterion-referenced tests are used for developmental screening, **diagnostic evaluation,** and instructional planning.

In the preschool years, developmental and diagnostic assessments are the criterion-referenced tests used most frequently. Although **developmental screening** is used primarily to identify children who might profit from early education intervention or from special services before kindergarten or first grade, it is also used as a checkpoint for children who are developing normally. The *Dynamic Indicators of Basic Early Literacy Skills (DIBELS)* (Good & Kaminski, 2002) is an example of a screening for literacy skills. One of the subtests, the *DIBELS Individual Sound Fluency (ISF)* is a measure of phonological awareness. Figure 4-2 shows a page from the scoring manual for the test in which the student is asked to identify/produce the correct beginning sound of a word. This subtest is administered to preschool and kindergarten children.

As introduced in chapter 3, various screening tests have been developed as a result of Public Law 94–142, the Individuals with Disabilities Education Act, which required children with disabilities to be placed in the "least restrictive environment" possible. As described by Meisels (1994), "Early childhood developmental screening is a brief assessment procedure designed to identify children who, because of the risk of a possible learning problem or handicapping condition, should proceed to a more intensive level of diagnostic assessment" (p. 1). Thus, developmental surveys assess affective, cognitive, and psychomotor characteristics to determine whether further testing evaluation is needed to identify disabilities and strategies for remediation.

Various screening tests have been developed for the preschool child. The *Denver II* (Frankenburg, Dodds, Archer, Shapiro, & Bresnick, (1990) is commonly

5. <u>Correct Initial Consonant Sound:</u> If the word starts with an initial consonant sound, the child can respond with the first sound or initial sounds. For example, if the word is "clock" a correct initial sound would be /c/ or /cl/ or /klo/ but not /l/ or "clock."

PROMPT:	*STUDENT SAYS:*	*SCORE:*
What sound does "clock" begin with?	/k/	0 ①
What sound does "clock" begin with?	/kl/	0 ①
What sound does "clock" begin with?	/klo/	0 ①
What sound does "clock" begin with?	/l/	⓪ 1
What sound does "clock" begin with?	"clock"	⓪ 1

6. <u>Correct Initial Vowel Sound:</u> If the word starts with an initial vowel sound, the child can respond with the initial vowel sound or initial sounds. For example, if the word is "elephant" a correct initial sound would be /e/ or /el/ or /ele/, but not the name of the letter /ea/.

PROMPT:	*STUDENT SAYS:*	*SCORE:*
What sound does "elephant" begin with?	/e/	0 ①
What sound does "elephant" begin with?	/el/	0 ①
What sound does "elephant" begin with?	/ea/	⓪ 1
What sound does "elephant" begin with?	/ele/	0 ①

7. Schwa sound (/u/) added to a consonant is not counted as an error. Some phonemes cannot be pronounced correctly in isolation without a vowel, and some early learning of sounds <u>includes</u> the schwa.

PROMPT:	*STUDENT SAYS:*	*SCORE:*
What sound does "clock" begin with?	/ku/	0 ①
What sound does "clock" begin with?	/klu/	0 ①

8. <u>Articulation Difficulty:</u> The student is not penalized for imperfect pronunciation due to dialect, articulation, or second language interference. For example, the student responds /th/ when asked for the first sound in "sink". If the student <u>consistently</u> say /th/ for /s/, as in "thircle" for "circle," he or she should be given credit for a correct initial sound. This is a professional judgment and should be based on the student's responses and any prior knowledge of his/her speech patterns.

PROMPT:	*STUDENT SAYS:*	*SCORE:*
What sound does "sink" begin with?	/th/	0 ①

FIGURE 4-2 Examples of questions from the Initial Sound Fluency (ISF) measure of DIBELS 6th Edition

Source: Good, R. H., & Kaminski, R. A. (Eds.). (2002). *Dynamic Indicators of basic Early Literacy Skills: Administration and scoring guide* (6th ed.). Eugene, OR: Institute for the Development of Educational Achievement. Reprinted by permission of Dynamic Measurement Group.

used by pediatricians and other medical professionals. The *Early Screening Inventory—Revised* (Meisels, Marsden, Wiske, & Henderson, 2008) and *McCarthy's Scales of Children's Abilities* (McCarthy, 1978, 1983) are also used for screening purposes. Figure 4-3 shows some of the criterion-referenced screening items on the *Early Screening Inventory—Revised*.

Uses of Criterion-Referenced Tests With School-Age Children

Diagnostic evaluation measures are used with school-age children as well as preschool children. Intelligence batteries and diagnostic tests in academic content areas are used with students who demonstrate learning difficulties. In addition, criterion-referenced results are used for instructional planning with children at all levels of learning needs and achievement.

Criterion-referenced scores on achievement tests are used to describe individual performance. Reports of individual performance are then used for instructional planning. Individual performance can also be used in teaching groups of children with the same instructional needs.

Mastery testing is a common criterion-referenced measure in which instructional objectives are assessed. After mastery on a test objective has been achieved, instruction proceeds with a new objective. In the case of an achievement test, performance

FIGURE 4-3 Sample of a developmental screening instrument

Source: Early Screening Inventory Revised: © 2001 by Pearson Education, Inc., publishing as Pearson Early Learning. Used by permission. *Early Screening Inventory Revised ESI-R, ESI-P,* and *ESI-K,* and the *ESI-R, ESI-P, ESI-K* logos are trademarks of Pearson Education Inc.

II LANGUAGE AND COGNITION	Circle Points, or F, or R			
A Number Concept	Points	Fail	Refuse	Comments
1 10 Block Counting				
Count these blocks. Point to each one and count out loud so that I can hear you. *Place 10 blocks in random order on a piece of construction paper. Blocks should not touch each other. Child may rearrange blocks when counting.*				
10 Blocks (counting)	2	F	R	
If child passes, proceed <u>promptly</u> to All Together				
or, if child fails 10 Block Counting — 5 Block Counting				
Remove 5 blocks. Count these blocks. Point to each one and count out loud so that I can hear you.				
or 5 Blocks (counting)	or 1	F	R	
If child passes, proceed <u>promptly</u> to All Together				
or, if child fails both counting trials, go directly to Verbal Expression				
2 All Together				
If child passes either counting trial, promptly ask: **How many are there all together?**				
If child begins counting (again): **Tell me without counting.**				
10 Blocks *or* 5 Blocks (all together)	1	F	R	

ESI·K

3

FIGURE 4-3 (*Continued*)

results may be charted to show which objectives the test taker has mastered and which need further attention. This result can be used in planning instruction for a group of students. In a similar manner, individualized instruction can be initiated as a result of criterion-referenced test results. Figure 4-4 gives examples of criterion-referenced objectives in early achievement tests.

In **individualized instruction,** students are taught singly, on the basis of personal needs, rather than in large groups. Instead of planning learning activities for the class as a whole, instructional groups of different sizes are formed, and the teacher diversifies instruction based on the progress of each student. Criterion-referenced tests are one source of information for individualized instruction.

Minimum-competency testing also uses criterion-referenced test results. In minimum-competency testing, a minimum standard is set regarding competence in achieving test objectives. Individual test scores are interpreted to screen for test takers who have reached or exceeded the established level of competency. Many states have instituted minimum-competency tests for students at the elementary school level; the test results help determine promotion or retention.

On a larger scale, criterion-referenced test scores are used for broad surveys of educational accomplishment. Group achievement on a local, state, or national level is assessed to better understand educational progress. The achievement of very large

Criterion-referenced items in beginning reading
1.   Matches uppercase and lowercase letters
2.   Recognizes uppercase and lowercase letters
3.   Matches three-letter words
4.   Matches four-letter words
5.   Recognizes letters, words, and numbers
6.   Recognizes words in context
7.   Demonstrates skill in copying letters, numbers, and words

Criterion-referenced items in mathematics
1.   Counts to 10
2.   Recognizes numbers to 20
3.   Recognizes coins
4.   Matches number to numeral to 10
5.   Adds numbers to 10
6.   Subtracts numbers from 10
7.   Recognizes basic shapes

FIGURE 4-4   Examples of objectives used in criterion-referenced tests

groups of children is analyzed to assess strengths and weaknesses in instruction beyond the level of an individual school district. For example, students tested on a national achievement test in reading were found to be stronger in word identification skills than in comprehension skills. More recently, the National Assessment of Educational Progress report on writing showed that in eleven states only 20% of the students scored at a proficient level or better in the national writing tests, and 31% scored at a proficient level or better in only five states (Heath, 1999). After such information is acquired at a state or national level, curriculum resources and teaching practices can be investigated to correct the problem. In addition to the *California Achievement Test (Terra Nova CAT/6)* (2009), another achievement test that includes criterion-referenced information is the *Comprehensive Tests of Basic Skills (CTBS)* (1989). In the preceding sections, information was given on how tests are used for beneficial purposes with infants and young children, especially for identification of children with developmental delay.

It would be easy to assume that teachers don't need standardized test results because other types of assessment are preferable for classroom use. Information in chapter 2 stressed that assessments should benefit the child, and standardized tests should be used for instructional planning. Although the prevalent use of standardized tests is for accountability of effective instruction and standards-based evaluation of students, teachers, and schools, standardized test results contain valuable information that the teacher can use to understand student needs and accomplishments. In particular, criterion-referenced results provide a guide for general assessment and instructional planning.

Group testing can provide information that teachers can use for both individual and group instructional planning. Individual and class results yield a profile of level of achievement for criterion-referenced test objectives. If the test objectives are a good fit with the learning objectives designed for the classroom, the teacher has a start in determining how to plan instruction at the beginning of the year.

90

....

CHAPTER 4

*Using and
Reporting
Standardized
Test Results*

Chapter 2 recommended that all assessment be integrated with instruction. However, recent studies have shown that teachers perceive standardized tests as separate from instruction. They did not understand that standardized tests could be helpful in planning for student needs (Shepard, 2000). To the contrary, in spite of many concerns about standardized tests, they can be included as one of many tools for instructional planning when used appropriately and effectively by the classroom teacher.

Interpreting Test Scores

A child's performance on a standardized test is meaningless until it can be compared with other scores in a useful way. The raw score must be translated into a score that reports how well the child's performance is compared with that of other children who took the same test. In describing the standardization process, we have discussed how norms are set for comparing individual or group test scores on the basis of the scores made by a norming sample. Although several different scoring systems have been established for translating and interpreting raw scores, the bell-shaped normal curve is the graph on which the distribution of scores is arranged by using some type of standard score.

The Normal Curve

The normal curve (Figure 4-5) represents the ideal **normal distribution** of test scores of groups of people, as well as the distribution of many other human characteristics. Physical and psychological traits are distributed in a bell-shaped frequency polygon, with most scores clustered toward the center of the curve. If, for example, we were to chart the heights of all adult men in the United States, most heights would be grouped around a mean height, with fewer distributed toward very short and very tall heights.

Ideally, group test scores have a similar distribution, and the normal curve can be used as a reference for understanding individual test scores. Any numerical scale can be used with the normal curve to demonstrate the range of scores on a test instrument.

The midpoint of the curve is the **mean**. Because the curve represents the total number of scores in the distribution of scores on a test, the mean divides the curve into two halves. As many scores are distributed above the mean as below it. The normal curve is used to describe or pinpoint an individual's performance on a standardized test. Derived scores are used to specify where the individual score falls on the curve and how far above or below the mean the score falls (Cronbach, 1990).

Standard Deviations

The normal curve is divided further into eight equal sections called **standard deviations** (designated by a sigma, σ). Standard deviations are used to calculate how an individual scored, compared with the scores of the norming group on a standardized test. Standard deviations describe how test scores are dispersed around the mean. For example, an individual score that is one standard deviation above the mean indicates that the individual scored higher than the mean of test scores on the norming sample. Furthermore, the individual scored higher than about 84% of the individuals who normed the test. If we look at the percentage of scores in each standard deviation, we find that about 68% of the scores are found between one standard deviation below the mean and one standard deviation above the mean. The percentage of scores in each successive standard deviation above and below the mean decreases sharply beyond one standard deviation. When raw scores are transformed into percentiles, or standard scores, standard deviations further explain individual scores compared to the normal distribution of scores (Brown, 1983).

All scoring scales are drawn parallel to the baseline of the normal curve. Each uses the deviation from the mean as the reference to compare an individual score with the mean score of a group. In the next section, the transformation of raw scores into standard scores is explained in terms of percentile ranks, stanines, and Z scores and T scores, as illustrated in Figure 4-5.

Percentile Ranks and Stanines

After a test is standardized, percentile ranks and stanines may be used as the measures of comparison between the norming sample and individual test scores. Figure 4-5 shows how **percentile ranks** are arrived at by looking at cumulative

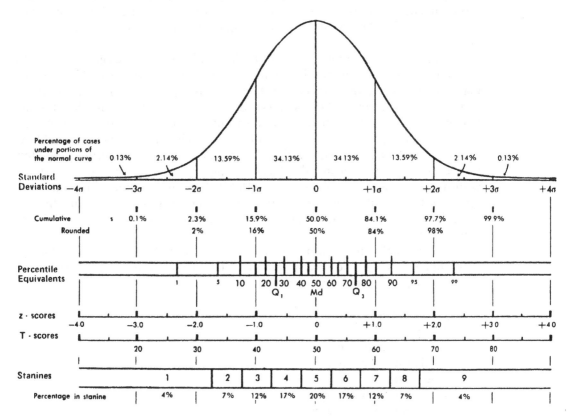

FIGURE 4-5 Normal curve

percentages and percentile equivalents under the normal curve. We already understand that a percentage of the total distribution of scores is arranged within each standard deviation on the normal curve, with a smaller percentage located in each deviation as we move away from the mean. These percentages can also be understood in a cumulative fashion.

Beginning at the negative end of the curve, percentages in each standard deviation can be added together. At the mean, the cumulative percentage is 50%, while 99.9% is reached at three standard deviations above the mean.

Percentile equivalents are derived from the accumulated percentages. If the cumulative percentages represent the percentage of test scores falling into standard deviations along the normal curve, **percentiles** represent a point on the normal curve below which a percentage of test scores is distributed. A score at the 40th percentile equals or surpasses 40% of the scores on the test being used. A student's percentile rank on a test thus indicates the percentage of students who scored lower in the comparison group. If a student's percentile rank is 60%, the student scored better than 60% of the comparison group who took the test. Most important, the percentile rank is compared to scores of a particular group when the test was standardized and norms were established.

After a percentile rank norm is established for a standardized test, the developers determine how the distribution of scores acquired from the norming sample is arranged on the normal curve. Standard deviations and percentiles calculate the distribution. Future test users can then use these norms as measures of comparison to interpret individual or group scores in comparison with the scores of the original norming group.

Stanines provide another way to understand the distribution of scores. As shown in Figure 4-5, stanines divide the norm population represented by the normal scale into nine groups. Except for stanine 9, the top, and stanine 1, the bottom, each stanine represents half of a standard deviation. Stanines provide a helpful way to compare cumulative percentages and percentile ranks on the normal curve. One can look at the percentage of scores distributed in each stanine and understand how the percentile rank is correlated with the overall distribution. In reporting group test scores, the stanine rank of an individual score measures how the individual is ranked within a group of test takers (Seashore, 1980). Thus, the stanines clustered at the center of the normal curve represent the highest percentage of scores, while the stanines one or more standard deviations above or below the mean reflect much lower percentages of scores.

Parents usually find stanine results the easiest to understand when looking at their child's performance on a standardized test. They can understand where the child's score falls when described as follows:

9. Very superior
8. Superior
7. Considerably above average
6. Slightly above average
5. Average
4. Slightly below average
3. Considerably below average
2. Poor
1. Very poor (Psychological Corporation, 1980, p. 4)

Z Scores and T Scores

Some standardized test results are reported in terms of Z scores or T scores because they provide a simple way to locate an individual score along the normal curve. **Z scores** and **T scores** are called **standard scores** because they report how many standard deviations a person's transformed raw score is located above or below the mean on the normal curve.

Using Achievement Test Results to Improve Teaching and Learning

The school board in Lucky analyzed the yearly report on school achievement in their community. Results indicated that students achieved at the national norm through the third grade, but thereafter scores tended to drop off steadily among some groups of students. Minority student scores dropped more significantly than the scores of Anglo students. Students from low-income homes did less well than those from middle-income homes.

The teachers in the elementary schools studied the criterion-referenced test results to discover whether certain objectives on the results were weak. Consistent indicators of weakness were found in reading comprehension and in problem solving in mathematics. As a group, students in the school district were stronger in word attack skills in reading and computation in mathematics than they were in higher-order skills that involved analysis and synthesis.

A committee of teachers at each grade level was assigned to search instructional resources to find supplementary materials that would strengthen teaching in those areas. The committees were particularly interested in finding materials that would involve the students in applying what they were learning in mathematics and allow students to engage in meaningful reading experiences.

The grade-level committees first searched through reading and math materials available in their own classrooms. They then surveyed materials available through the school district's central resource center. Finally, they traveled to a regional educational service center, where an educational consultant helped them find additional resources that addressed their students' needs in mathematics and reading. The consultant also worked with the committees in designing workshops to share materials and teaching strategies with the other teachers at each grade level.

The second year after the supplementary materials were included, a small improvement was noted in the test scores. Another gain occurred in the third year.

Now, each year, a committee of teachers studies test results to see where the students are encountering difficulty in order to determine whether the instructional program should be modified. The committee is especially attentive to students who are likely to have lower scores. The school board is pleased with the steady improvement in elementary achievement scores.

Z scores are considered the most basic of all standard scores and the building blocks for other standard scores. They are used to determine how far above or below the mean a score is located in standard deviation units. Percentile ranks are understood by looking at where cumulative percentages fall on the normal curve. Z scores make a similar comparison; however, with Z scores the standard deviations are used as the criteria for determining where an individual score falls. Z scores are parallel to standard deviations in that the mean is at the center of the normal distribution; if a score falls within one standard deviation above the mean, the Z score is +1. If the score falls two standard deviations below the mean, the Z score is −2.

T scores also report scores that are parallel to standard deviations on the normal curve. Like percentiles, T scores are cumulative along the curve. T scores range from 0 to 100, with a range of ten points from one standard deviation to the next. T scores are almost the same as Z scores; Z scores have a mean of 0 and a standard deviation of 1.0, while T scores have a mean of 50 and a standard deviation of 10 (Hopkins, 1997; Kubiszyn & Borich, 1996). Various standardized tests use T scores. *McCarthy's Scales of Children's Abilities* (McCarthy, 1983) report T scores, as do IQ tests such as the *Stanford–Binet Intelligence Scale* (Terman & Merrill, 1973).

Reporting Standardized Test Results

After a standardized test has been administered and scored and individual and group scores have been interpreted, test users can use the information to report not only to professionals within the school district but also to parents of the students. Reporting originates with individual test results, which are then combined and recombined with the scores of other individuals to form class, school, and district reports.

Individual Test Record

The individual test record in Figure 4-6 is from the *Stanford Achievement Test Series*, 9th ed. (1996). The hypothetical student is student number 8, who is in the fourth grade. The test was administered in April, the eighth month of the school year. In this form of the test report, both norm-referenced and criterion-referenced scores are reported. In Figure 4-6, the norm-referenced scores are listed in the section at the top of the page. The criterion-referenced scores are located at the bottom of the page.

Norm-Referenced Scores

The individual record includes the subtests or content areas of the test battery. In this particular test, Reading, Mathematics, Language, Spelling, Science, Social Science, Listening, and Thinking Skills are included. Reading, mathematics, and language also have subtests. Within each test and subtest, the scaled score, national percentile rank and stanine, and grade equivalent are reported. The scaled score is a

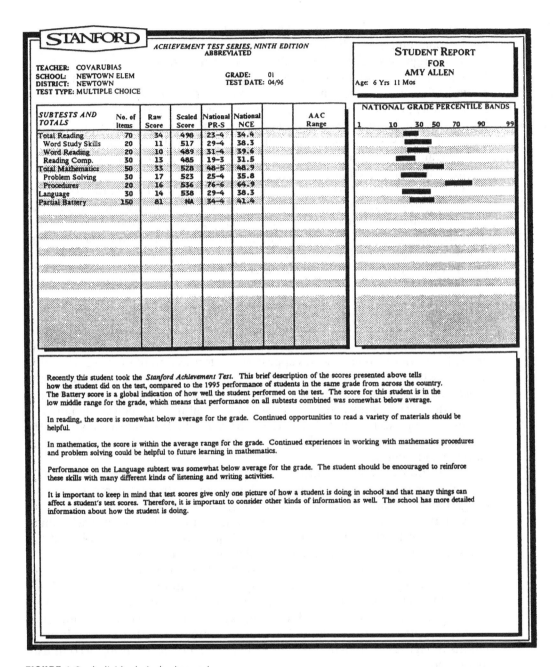

FIGURE 4-6 Individual student report

Source: Stanford Achievement Test Series (9th ed.). Copyright © 1996 by Harcourt Assessment, Inc.
Reproduced by permission. All rights reserved.

continuous score measured over all grade levels. It indicates the student's progress on the continuum for each category.

To the right of student number 8's norm-referenced scores is the National Grade Percentile Bands report. In these bands the percentile score is reported as a possible range for the score that accounts for the standard error of measurement on the test. For example, this student's total reading score was in the 59th percentile; however, the percentile band ranged between about the 50th and 68th percentiles. Examination all scores demonstrate that generally fall within the range that is close to the mean or above the mean; however, language expression and listening range as low at the 30th percentile.

Criterion-referenced scores are all broken down into subcategories. For example, in the norm-referenced results Social Science only showed the overall score, while the criterion-referenced scores included eight subcategories. In addition to individual national percentile scores, the student was ranked below average, average, or above average on each subtest. This student's scores were predominantly in the average category with few scores above average or below average.

Class Reports

Figure 4-7 is a class report on the *Stanford Achievement Test*, 9th ed., also for fourth grade. The norm-referenced scores appear on the top section of the page. The information includes how many were tested (22), the number correct on each test and subtest, and the mean scaled score, national individual percentile range and stanine, and median grade equivalent. This class report combines the percentile rank and stanine into one section and also includes the normal curve equivalent scores. The NCE mean score on this test reflects the class average score on the normal curve for each test and subtest.

The National Grade Percentile Ranks appear on the top right of the page. As a class, the percentile ranks were average. There were no strong differences between categories in the National Grade Percentile Ranks.

Criterion-referenced scores are shown at the bottom of the page. Each subtest is represented by the categories or types of questions and the number of test items for each category. The teacher can determine strengths and weaknesses in the class by examining what percentage of the class was below average, average, or above average. The results can be compared with individual reports to determine students who would benefit from additional instruction and those who are ready to move to more advanced learning experiences. Note that the individual student report shown in Figure 4-6 can be compared with the overall grade reports in Figure 4-7 to determine the individual student's learning accomplishments and needs.

School and District Reports

Summaries of class reports can be grouped to form school and district reports. Both norm- and criterion-referenced information can be organized in a useful form for building principals, school district evaluators, superintendents, and governing

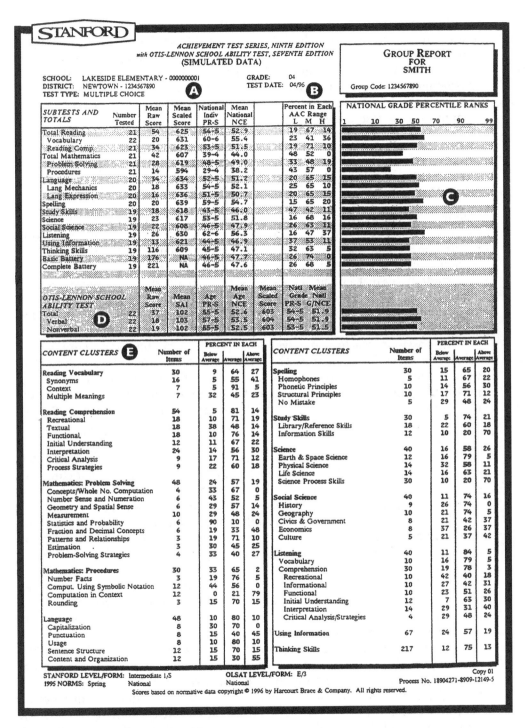

FIGURE 4-7 Group test report

Source: Stanford Achievement Test (9th ed.). Copyright © 1996 by Harcourt Assessment, Inc. Reproduced by permission. All rights reserved.

boards. Achievement reports can be studied by grade level, across a school, or among all the schools in the district serving a grade level. Instructional strengths and weaknesses can be analyzed by content areas, as well as by school and grade level. Achievement can be compared over several years to determine long-term improvement or decline in achievement. Each type of analysis must take into account the error of measurement on the test so that realistic conclusions are drawn from the study of test results.

Reporting Test Results to Parents

Parents have the right to know about their child's performance in school, and schools have the responsibility to keep parents informed. One method used to report student learning is the standardized achievement test. The school should report the test results in a manner that is helpful to the parents.

Statistical data that are part of standardized test reports can be confusing to parents. Because of the seeming complexity of test reports, it is important to give parents an opportunity to meet with the teacher for an explanation of their child's test results. Test results can be discussed in a parent–teacher conference.

The classroom teacher can have the major responsibility for explaining standardized test results to parents. The teacher not only knows the children from working with them every day, but is also aware of the kinds of information that individual parents will understand and want to acquire. It is helpful for the teachers to explain both the value and the limitations of the test scores. Parents may also benefit from knowing why the test was chosen and how the results will be used.

It may be helpful for parents to understand how the criterion-referenced test results may be used to plan appropriate learning experiences for their child. For example, the teacher may use test results to suggest activities that the parent can use at home to help the child, such as those suggested in Figure 4-6.

The teacher may also advise against the comparison of test scores among children, particularly siblings. Parents can be reassured that individual differences in test scores result from many variables. Comparing test scores of different children is neither accurate nor useful.

Once children enter the primary grades, parents are eager to know how well their child is progressing and whether the child is achieving as well as he or she should be at that grade level. Analysis of the results of a standardized test can provide the information that parents need.

The *Stanford Diagnostic Reading Test* (1995) shown in Figure 4-8 demonstrates how performance on specific objectives can be reported to parents. The test was administered in November to a child in the second grade. Phonetic Analysis, Vocabulary, and Comprehension were the subtests in reading that were included on the test. The norm-referenced scores are listed across the top of the page, with the National Percentile Bands at the right of the page. Note that all the percentile bands are above the 50th percentile, indicating that the child's overall performance was well above average.

FIGURE 4-8 *Stanford Diagnostic Reading Test*: Primary-grade individual record

Source: Stanford Diagnostic Reading Test (4th ed.). Copyright © 1995 by Harcourt Assessment, Inc. Reproduced by permission. All rights reserved.

100

....

CHAPTER 4

*Using and
Reporting
Standardized
Test Results*

This test reports a score not seen in the other test examples, the comprehension **grade equivalent**. The grade equivalent is a method of comparing student achievement at particular grade levels. The score is expressed in terms of grade levels and the number of months that school has been in session.

After a test has been given at a grade level, the results are compared with test results from grades above and below that grade level. In Figure 4-8 the child's test scores for Phonetic Analysis is 2.5—second grade, fifth month. However, the grade equivalent is 4.4, or fourth grade, fourth month. These test results show that in this category, the child made the same number of correct responses as children in the norming group in fourth grade.

The grade-equivalent score indicates whether the child performed above or below average, but it does not indicate grade-level placement in school. If the child's comprehension grade equivalent is compared with the local or national percentile ranks, both show that the child performed well above average in the number of correct responses.

Some test publishers recommend that grade equivalents not be used to report to parents because they can be misunderstood. Parents can understand that the grade-equivalent score is reported in years and months in school, but they may not understand that the score does not mean the child should be placed in a higher or lower grade. The child reflected in the *Stanford Diagnostic Reading Test* was tested in November, the third month of school. All the grade-equivalent scores are higher than 2.3 but do not indicate that the child should be placed at a higher grade level.

The criterion-referenced scores at the bottom of the page are reported in a different format. Each skill is reported in the ovals as the number of correct responses compared to the total number. A shaded oval indicates that the score is at or above a progress indicator cutoff score indicating mastery. A note below the scores indicates that none of the ovals is shaded because the student's scores were higher than the level of the test. In other words, the student mastered all the skills at a high level for second grade.

Advantages and Disadvantages of Standardized Tests

Norm-referenced and criterion-referenced achievement tests can provide valuable information regarding the effectiveness of curriculum and instruction. At the beginning of the school year, such tests can show what children know in relation to an instructional program. Likewise, achievement tests administered at the end of the school year can demonstrate how well children learned the content of a program. Teachers can use the test results to determine how to reteach or change program content or instructional methods. In other words, teachers can use test results to evaluate their program and to make changes to more effectively meet the instructional needs of their students. In the sections that follow, we continue the discussion of the advantages of using standardized tests. Then we discuss the disadvantages of using standardized tests, including concerns regarding their inappropriate use with young children.

Advantages of Standardized Tests

Standardized tests can be described as measuring instruments. Each test is constructed, administered, and scored to measure some human characteristic. An individual's responses to the test items provide samples of his or her behavior, which can be scored and evaluated according to an established standard. In contrast to informal strategies, standardized tests have unique qualities that are advantageous for measuring human behavior. Among these characteristics are uniformity in test administration, quantifiable scores, norm referencing, and validity and reliability.

Uniformity in Test Administration

Standardized tests have precise administration procedures. Because the results should be dependable, test designers must be sure that all examiners who give the test to children will follow the instructions exactly. Whether the test is being given in Wisconsin or in Florida, the procedures are the same. Informal methods are less specific; the examiner uses personal strategies for assessment.

Quantifiable Scores

Standardized tests are quantifiable because they have numerical scores. The correct answers are totaled to determine the raw score. The raw score is then translated into a derived score so that the child's performance on the test can be compared with the performance of other test takers. The derived score can be interpreted to evaluate the child's performance when compared to the established standard.

Norm Referencing

Norm referencing refers to the process of developing a standard for interpreting test scores on a standardized test. To compare a child's performance on a test with the performance of other children, a norm group is selected. The test is administered to that group to determine what normal performance is. The norm group's test responses result in a range of scores with which a child's performance can be compared.

Validity and Reliability

Unlike informal evaluation and measurement strategies, standardized tests have established dependability through determination of validity and reliability. Reliability is the test's ability to measure the child's characteristics accurately under different conditions. If the child were given the test more than once, would the results be similar?

Validity establishes whether a test measures the characteristics it was designed to measure. If the test is designed to measure intelligence, does it actually yield results that show the child's level of intelligence?

Tests that have proven reliability and validity are dependable. They can be administered to many children, either individually or as a group, and children's scores can be interpreted with confidence that the results accurately reflect each child's behaviors or characteristics.

Validity, reliability, norm referencing, and other test characteristics that contribute to the effectiveness of the standardized test result from careful and thorough

102

CHAPTER 4

*Using and
Reporting
Standardized
Test Results*

Improving Shirley's Comprehension Skills

Shirley is in the second grade. Although she is able to use phonics to decode words and has a good vocabulary, she has difficulty demonstrating her understanding of the reading materials she has read. The reading specialist at her school discussed Shirley's lack of progress in reading and administered a diagnostic reading test.

The results of the test showed that Shirley has the most difficulty in answering questions about reading content. The reading specialist and the classroom teacher discussed comprehension strategies that might be used to help Shirley focus on the meaning of what she is reading. Shirley's mother was given activities and tips on how to discuss books that are read to and with Shirley at home.

test design. Each step in test construction has the goal of producing a dependable test to measure a human characteristic accurately.

Disadvantages of Standardized Tests

Although standardized tests are carefully designed and normed before they are used with children, they are not necessarily the best method of evaluation of young children. In chapters 1 and 2, this concern was discussed in terms of the fact that a variety of strategies should be used in assessing children. No matter how good a standardized test is, other methods of assessment should also be used. Other issues introduced in chapters 1 and 2 were concerns about the increased use of standardized tests, the use of tests with children from a different culture or whose first language is not English, and the use of standardized tests to deny childrens' promotion in grade.

Concerns about the use of standardized tests were first introduced in the 1970s. Educators were particularly concerned about the poor performance of children from low-socioeconomic and minority populations (Wesson, 2001). Another early concern was the control that testing imposed on instruction, labeled by some as *measurement-driven instruction*. In the late 1990s, many of the concerns published in the 1970s persisted in spite of improvements in test design. New exams were matched to the curriculum, particularly in state achievement tests. In addition, essay questions and short-answer questions were added to the traditional multiple-choice questions (McGinn, 1999). More recently, the *California Achievement Test (Terra Nova CAT/6)* (2009) has added writing tasks and performance assessments in keeping with advances in assessment. However, on some tests, the results could be based on the answers to a few questions, and time limitations for achievement tests precluded adequate assessment of student achievement (Popham, 1999). Although standardized tests can give accurate information about students' relative strengths and weaknesses across content areas, most tests contain too few items to provide meaningful within-subject comparisons of strengths and weaknesses.

Despite these concerns about standardized tests, the long-term campaign to reduce their use has failed. Educational reforms responding to calls for excellence in education increased the reliance on standardized testing (Fair Test, 2007; McGinn, 1999; Popham, 2001). In the late 1990s, states had already raised new standards for what children should learn in each grade. Failure to pass the test could result in retention, mandatory attendance in summer school, or denial of a high school diploma. In some states, poorly performing schools faced state takeover, and educators were fired or given a reduction in pay (McGinn, 1999).

The advent of NCLB and the requirements of the Head Start *National Reporting System* (NRS) have expanded the dependence on standardized tests as the primary measure of a child's progress and achievement. The practice is now called *high-stakes testing*, with negative impact on younger preschool children and students at all levels of K–12 education.

High-Stakes Testing

The concerns about high-stakes testing are related to the use of standardized tests to admit children into schools; place them in programs such as special education, ELL, and bilingual programs; promote or retain students; or determine whether they can graduate from high school (Heubert, 2002). Dependence on standardized tests limits teachers, parents, and administrators from including other resources when making program and evaluation decisions with the intent of benefiting the child.

When major decisions are based on the outcomes of a single test, it is known as a high-stakes test. When children are denied promotion to the next grade, entry into school, or exit from high school based on a standardized test, they have had decisions made about their future based on high-stakes testing (American Psychological Association, 2002; Fair Test, 2007; Heubert, 2002).

Measurement Limitations

Standardized tests are limited in what they measure. They are limited in how long they can be and how many learning objectives can be properly evaluated. The organization Fair Test (2007) proposes that they cannot be a fair and helpful evaluation tool as follows:

> Standardized tests are tests on which all students answer the same questions, usually in multiple-choice format, and each question has only one correct answer. They reward the ability to quickly answer superficial questions that do not require real thought,. They do not measure the ability to think or create in any field. Their use encourages a narrowed curriculum, outdated methods of instruction, and harmful practices such as retention in grade and tracking. They also assume all test-takers have been exposed to a white, middle-class background. (p. 1)

There are also limitations in the test design for the standardized tests developed by individual states to comply with NCLB. Although NCLB required all states to design and implement tests for accountability in learning, the tests are more rigorous in some states than in others. In addition, varying poverty levels from state to state impacted how much improvement could be demonstrated within and among school districts. As implementation and accountability deadlines approached, some

104

CHAPTER 4

*Using and
Reporting
Standardized
Test Results*

states applied for and received waivers for reaching accountability targets while others did not. More recently, the Department of Education relaxed the rules about testing, and efforts were begun to have a national standard for learning objectives with the eventual development of a national test.

Assessment of Students With Disabilities and/or Limited English Proficiency (LEP)

NCLB required that all students be assessed regardless of their special needs. For decades, these students had not been required to be included in standardized testing because of their limitations. A negative impact of this practice was that these students were also neglected in their opportunities for an education.

The limitations of the tests designed for NCLB when used with these populations immediately became an issue. Accommodations had to be made for students with disabilities and for those who spoke a language other than English or had limited English. In 2006, the development of appropriate tests was still in progress, with some states threatened with loss of funds because of noncompliance in developing appropriate tests. Validity and reliability of the new instruments that had been developed was another issue to be addressed. By 2010, states were working together to design national tests to be used in all states.

Lack of validity and reliability was a limitation of the NRS. As discussed in earlier chapters, efforts to hold Head Start programs accountable for children's achievement though the NRS failed in 2005 because it lacked validity and reliability. Work to improve and refine the NRS continued.

Effects on Curriculum and Instruction

Pressures for higher test scores result in limitations on the curriculum that is taught in the classroom. Instruction becomes focused on what will be tested and limits the balance of curriculum that is desired for young children. This effect is now reflected in Head Start programs as teachers focus only on language, literacy, and math skills that are tested in the NRS.

Concerns About High-Stakes Testing

*T*he potential problem with the current increased emphasis on testing is not necessarily the test, per se, but the instances when tests have unintended and potentially negative consequences for individual students, groups of students, or the educational system more broadly. But it also critical to remember that, in many instances, without tests, low-performing students and schools could remain invisible and therefore not get the extra resources or remedial help that they need.

Source: American Psychological Association. (2001). Appropriate use of high-stakes testing in our nation's schools. Retrieved January 29, 2007, from http://www.apa.org/pubs/info/brochures/testing.aspx

105

CHAPTER 4

*Using and
Reporting
Standardized
Test Results*

A Misinterpretation of Julio's Achievement Test Scores

*J*ulio's family recently immigrated to the United States from Puerto Rico. Julio has been attending a school in Florida for about 2 years. He has now entered fourth grade and is required to take standardized achievement tests as a part of the requirements of NCLB. Julio's scores in reading and math were both very low, although he scored higher in mathematics than in reading. Julio's teacher is considering referring Julio for the special education program. The school counselor, however, realizes that Julio's low scores are due to his limitations in using English rather than a delay or disability. She shows the teacher how Julio's computation skills in mathematics are higher than problem-solving questions. The decision is made to provide additional ESL training and tutoring to address Julio's language limitations.

Misapplication of Test Results With Young Children

In chapter 1, the inappropriate use of standardized tests to prevent school entry or the placement of children in transitional classrooms in early childhood programs was discussed. Although there have been challenges to this practice and many states have dropped such policies, there is still evidence that it continues to be a problem (National Association of Early Childhood Specialists in State Departments of Education, 2000). It is appropriate at this point to further explain the concerns about the use of standardized tests for this purpose.

Early childhood specialists in the 1980s expressed concern about the use of individual intelligence tests, developmental screening measures, and school readiness tests for making decisions about school entry. They pointed out that developmental tests and IQ tests do not differentiate between limited intelligence and limited opportunities to learn. Like readiness tests, IQ tests and developmental tests should not be used to determine school entry (Shepard & Graue, 1993).

The use of developmental screening tests was recommended to predict quickly whether a child could profit from special education placement if such tests have predictive validity, developmental content, and normative standardization (Meisels, 1987; Meisels, Steele, & Quinn-Leering, 1993). Nevertheless, Meisels stated that developmental screening tests should be used to identify children who need further evaluation. Decisions on such issues as enrollment, retention, and placement in special classes should never be based on a single test score. Other sources of information, including systematic observation and samples of children's work, should be part of the evaluation process (Bredekamp & Copple, 1997; National Association for the Education of Young Children, 1988).

Another concern about misapplication of standardized test results surfaced in 2003. President Bush announced that in the fall of 2003, all Head Start students would be given a national standardized skills assessment test (McMaken, 2003). An immediate issue was whether preschool children should be given a standardized

106
....

CHAPTER 4

*Using and
Reporting
Standardized
Test Results*

test and whether the test, the National Reporting System, had the desired reliability and validity (Raver & Zigler, 2004). Other issues related to the limitations of the test to measure only cognitive skills and omit measurement of children's competence, emotional development, and cultural diversity (Schumacher, Greenberg, & Mezey, 2003). It was proposed that a narrow test of skills and literacy and math should not be used to measure the overall quality of the Head Start program (Meisels & Atkins-Burnett, 2004).

A new direction is being taken to overcome the limitations of standardized tests for identifying and diagnosing children with disabilities. **Play-based assessment,** which uses observation of children's play as the major assessment strategy, is becoming more common as educators of children with disabilities seek more natural approaches to assessment (Segal & Webber, 1996).

Play-based assessment is a structured observation of an individual child's play. An adult follows the child engaged in play and talks and plays with the child, using the toys and activities the child chooses. In four phases of the observation, the child engages in more structured play, child–child play, parent–child interaction, and motor play (Brookes Publishing, 2002; Linder, 2008).

Play-based assessment is used in addition to the administration of standardized tests and other developmental assessments. Play-based assessment will be discussed further in chapter 5.

Summary

Standardized tests have a role in measuring young children. Many early childhood educators are not opposed to the use of standardized tests per se, but rather to specific tests. While teacher intuition for evaluation can be biased, systematic measurement and evaluation can have advantages. Although there are shortcomings in standardized tests used with young children, more is needed than informal measures and teacher observations, especially for young children with disabilities. The need for appropriate instruments to identify at-risk children and to plan programs for remediation will continue pressures for valid and reliable instruments.

On the one hand, information from norm- and criterion-referenced tests can be very useful in evaluating achievement and in considering instructional improvement. On the other hand, misuse of test results or lack of consideration of test errors and limitations can have a negative impact on instructional decisions affecting preschool and school-age children.

Despite ongoing concerns about their weaknesses, the use of standardized tests is increasing, and new instruments are being developed in response to pressures for accountability for the quality of education and minimum-competency standards for students and teachers.

Increasingly, early childhood educators and specialists are urging the use of a variety of methods to evaluate or test children, particularly preschool children. Standardized tests have a role, but they are only one method that should be used to evaluate young children. Informal methods, such as teacher observation and teacher-designed tasks, can also be used to obtain a more accurate picture of what preschool and primary-grade children have learned and achieved.

REVIEW QUESTIONS

1. How do norm- and criterion-referenced tests report achievement differently?
2. Why are tests with dual referencing difficult to design?
3. Why is a normal curve used to chart the distribution of test scores?
4. What is the function of the mean on the normal curve?
5. How do standard deviations serve as reference points when interpreting test scores?
6. How are percentile ranks and stanines used with standardized test scores?
7. Why are Z scores and T scores useful?

SUGGESTED ACTIVITIES

1. Visit with an elementary school counselor to find out how standardized test results are used and reported, especially in the area of parental reporting. Write a report on the processes used.
2. Discuss with a teacher of children with special needs how standardized tests are used to identify such children and create individual plans for them. Write a report of the process used with one child without including any names.
3. With a classmate, role-play a conference between a teacher and a parent to explain a child's results on a standardized test. The responsibility of the teacher is to explain the results of the standardized test; the role of the parent is to ask questions and contribute information about a hypothetical child.

KEY TERMS

criterion-referenced test
developmental screening
diagnostic evaluation
grade equivalent
individualized instruction
mastery testing
mean
minimum-competency testing
normal distribution
norm-referenced test
percentile
percentile rank
play-based assessment
standard deviation
standard score
stanine
T score
Z score

SELECTED WEB SITES

Pearson Education Assessments
http://www.pearsonassessments.com

American Psychological Association
http://www.apa.org/pubs/info/brochures/testing.aspx

Fair Test
http://www.fairtest.org

References

American Psychological Association. (2001, May). *Appropriate use of high-stakes testing in our nation's schools.* Retrieved October 7, 2009 from http://www.apa.org/pubs/info/brochures/testing.aspx

Boehm, A. E. (2000). *Boehm Test of Basic Concepts* (3rd ed.). San Antonio, TX: Psychological Corp.

Bredekamp, S., & Copple, C. (1997). *Developmentally appropriate practices in early childhood programs* (Rev. ed.). Washington, DC: National Association for the Education of Young Children.

Brookes Publishing. (2002). *Using Transdisciplinary play-based assessment: Structuring a play session.* Retrieved October 20, 2009, from http://www.brookespublishing.com/email/archive...july02EC4.hrm/

Brown, E. G. (1983). *Principles of educational and psychological testing* (3rd ed.). New York: CBS College Publishing.

California Achievement Test (Terra Nova CAT/6) (6th ed.). (2009). Monterey, CA: CTB/McGraw-Hill.

Comprehensive Tests of Basic Skills (Level K) (4th ed.). (1989). Monterey, CA: CTB/Macmillan/McGraw-Hill.

Cronbach, L. J. (1990). *Essentials of psychological testing* (5th ed.). New York: Harper & Row.

Dunn, L. M., & Dunn, L. (1997). *Peabody Picture Vocabulary Test* (3rd ed.). Circle Pines, MN: American Guidance Service.

Fair Test (2007, December). *What's wrong with standardized tests?* Retrieved October 20, 2009, from http://www.Fairtest.org/whats-wrong-standardized-tests

Frankenburg, W. K., Dodds, J., Archer, P., Shapiro, H., & Bresnick, B. (1990). *Denver II.* Denver, CO: Denver Developmental Materials.

Good, R. H., & Kaminski, R. A. (Eds.). (2002). *Dynamic Indicators of Basic Early Literacy Skills (DIBELS)* (ed.). *Administration and Scoring guide* (6th ed.). Eugene, OR: Institute for the Development of Educational Achievement.

Goodwin, W. L., & Goodwin, L. D. (1982). Measuring young children. In B. Spodek (Ed.), *Handbook of research in early childhood education* (pp. 523–563). New York: Free Press.

Goodwin, W. L., & Goodwin, L. D. (1993). Young children and measurement: Standardized and nonstandardized instruments in early childhood education. In B. Spodek (Ed.), *Handbook of research on the education of young children* (pp. 441–463). New York: Macmillan.

Heath, J. (1999, September, 29). Texas No. 4 on U.S. test. *Austin American–Statesman,* pp. A1, A6.

Heubert, J. P. (2002). *High-stakes testing: Opportunities and risks for students of color, English-Language Learners, and students with disabilities.* Wakefield, MA: National Center on Accessing the General Curriculum. Retrieved October 20, 2009, from http://www.cast.org/publications/ncac/ncac_highstakes.html

Hopkins, K. D. (1997). *Educational and psychological measurement and evaluation* (8th ed.). Upper Saddle River, NJ: Prentice Hall.

Kaufman, A., & Kaufman, N. (2005). *Kaufman Assessment Battery for Children (K-ABC-II).* Circle Pines, MN: American Guidance Service.

Kubiszyn, T., & Borich, G. (1996). *Educational testing and measurement: Classroom application and practice* (5th ed.). Hoboken, NJ: John Wiley & Sons.

Linder, T. (2008). *Transdisciplinary play-based assessment* (2nd ed.). Retrieved October 20, 2009, from http://www.brookespublishing.com/stor/books/linder-tbai2/

Linn, R. L., & Miller, M.D. (2005). *Measurement and assessment in teaching* (9th ed.). Upper Saddle River, NJ: Merrill/Prentice Hall.

McCarthy, D. (1978). *McCarthy Screening Test.* New York: Psychological Corp.

McCarthy, D. (1983). *McCarthy Scales of Children's Abilities.* New York: Psychological Corp.

McGinn, D. (1999, September 6). The big score. *Newsweek,* pp. 46–49.

McMaken, J. (2003, March). *Early childhood assessment.* Denver, CO: Education Commission of the United States. Retrieved January 29, 2007, from http://www.ecs.org/html.IssueSection.asp?issued=77...0...

Meisels, S. J. (1987). Uses and abuses of developmental screening and school readiness testing. *Young Children, 42,* 68–73.

Meisels, S. J. (1994). *Developmental screening in early childhood: A guide* (5th ed.). Washington, DC: National Association for the Education of Young Children.

Meisels, S. J., & Atkins-Burnett, S. (2004, January). The Head Start National Reporting System: A critique. *Young Children, 59,* 64–66.

Meisels, S. J., Marsden, D. B., Wiske, M. S., & Henderson, L. W. (1997). *Early Screening Inventory—Revised.* Ann Arbor, MI: Pearson Early Learning.

Meisels, S. J., Steele, D. M., & Quinn-Leering, K. (1993). Testing, tracking, and retaining young children: An analysis of research and social policy. In B. Spodek (Ed.), *Handbook of research on the education of young children* (pp. 279–292). New York: Macmillan.

National Association for the Education of Young Children. (1988). Position statement on standardized testing of young children age 3 through age 8. *Young Children, 43,* 42–47.

National Association of Early Childhood Specialists in State Departments of Education. (2000). *Still! Unacceptable trends in kindergarten entry and placement.* Washington, DC: Author.

Popham, W. J. (1999). Why standardized tests don't measure educational quality. *Educational Leadership, 56,* 8–16.

Popham, W. J. (2001). *The truth about testing: An educator's call to action.* Alexandria, VA: Association for Supervision and Curriculum Development.

Psychological Corporation. (1980). *On telling parents about test results.* Test Service Notebook 154. New York: Author.

Raver, C. C., & Zigler, E. F. (2004, January). Another step back? Assessing readiness in Head Start. *Young Children, 59,* 58–63.

Sanford, A. R., & Zelman, J. G. (1995). *Learning Accomplishment Profile—Revised.* Chapel Hill, NC: Chapel Hill Training Outreach.

Schumacher, R., Greenberg, M., & Mezey, J. (2003). *Head Start reauthorization: A preliminary analysis of HR 2210, the "School Readiness Act of 2003."* Washington, DC: Center for Law and Social Policy.

Seashore, H. C. (1980). *Methods of expressing test scores.* Test Service Notebook 148. New York: Psychological Corp.

Segal, M., & Webber, N. T. (1996). Nonstructured play observations: Guidelines, benefits, and caveats. In S. J. Meisels & E. Fenichel (Eds.), *New visions for the developmental assessment of infants and young children* (pp. 207–230). Washington, DC: Zero to Three: National Center for Infants, Toddlers, and Families.

Shepard, L. A. (2000). The role of assessment in a learning culture. *Educational Researcher, 29,* 4–14.

Shepard, L. A., & Graue, M. E. (1993). The morass of school readiness screening: Research on test use and test validity. In B. Spodek (Ed.), *Handbook of research on the education of young children* (pp. 293–305). New York: Macmillan.

Stanford Achievement Test Series (9th ed.). (1996). San Antonio, TX: Harcourt Brace.

Stanford Diagnostic Reading Test (4th ed.). (1995). San Antonio, TX: Harcourt Brace.

Terman, L. M., & Merrill, M. A. (1973). *Stanford–Binet Intelligence Scale: Manual for third revision forms L–M.* Boston: Houghton Mifflin.

U.S. Department of Health and Human Services Head Start Bureau. (2003). *National Reporting System.* Washington, DC: Author.

Wechsler, D. (2002). *Wechsler Preschool and Primary Scale of Intelligence (WPPSI-III)* (3rd ed.). San Antonio, TX: Psychological Corp.

Wesson, K. A. (2001). The "Volvo effect"—Questioning standardized tests. *Young Children, 56*(2), 16–18.

Wilson, R. (1980). *Criterion-referenced testing.* Test Service Notebook 37. New York: Psychological Corp.

Zucker, S. (2003, December). *Fundamentals of standardized testing.* San Antonio, TX: Pearson, Inc. Retrieved October 19, 2009, from http://www.hemweb.com/libraryresearchreports/index.htm

CHAPTER 5

Observation

Chapter Objectives

As a result of reading this chapter, you will be able to

1. Understand the purposes of teacher assessments
2. Understand the purposes of observation
3. Use different types of observation
4. Conduct observations of physical, social, cognitive, and language development by using appropriate observation strategies

In the three previous chapters, we discussed standardized tests—tests that have been tried and tested with a population of test takers to establish standards for analyzing and reporting the results. We covered how standardized tests are developed and used, their advantages and limitations, and some of the concerns of early childhood specialists concerning their use with young children.

In chapter 2, we discussed informal ways of assessing and evaluating young children. These included instruments and other strategies designed by teachers, other school staff members, early childhood specialists, curriculum textbook writers, and others to assess what children already know, what they have learned, and what they are prepared to learn. Types of informal assessments introduced in chapter 2 included observation, checklists and rating scales, rubrics, teacher-designed tests, and performance assessments. In contrast with standardized tests, informal assessments designed by teachers are not standardized (Linn & Gronlund, 2000). However, some of the assessment instruments used by teachers have been standardized. They are not standardized tests, but have established reliability and validity. Checklists and rating scales fall into this category. Although many checklists and rating scales are designed for classroom use by teachers and other educators and are considered informal measures, others, such as the *Preschool Child Observation Record (COR)* (High/Scope Educational Research Foundation, 2003) and the *Early Childhood Environment Rating Scale—Revised (ECERS)* (Harms, Clifford, & Cryer, 1998), have been developed through a formal process and have established validity and reliability.

In this chapter, we will discuss how informal assessments or teacher assessment strategies are used and their advantages and disadvantages. In the remainder of the chapter, we will focus on observation strategies.

Uses of Teacher Assessment Strategies

As discussed in chapters 3 and 4, standardized tests are used for two purposes: (1) to evaluate achievement in comparison with a sample group of children and (2) to measure a child's achievement on specific test objectives. The norm-referenced test measures achievement; the criterion-referenced test evaluates mastery of test objectives. Teachers can use criterion-referenced test results to determine an individual child's strengths and weaknesses in the content areas measured by the test. Test results provide a rough idea of the child's learning needs. However, because many objectives are measured on the standardized test, there are few test questions for each objective. Consequently, criterion-referenced test results cannot be considered a completely reliable picture of the individual child's progress and instructional needs. Teacher-conducted assessments allow the teacher to obtain more specific information about each student's knowledge and skills relative to the instructional objectives of the class. These informal assessments can be used for placement, diagnostic evaluation and instructional planning, and formative and summative evaluation.

Placement Evaluation

At the beginning of the school year and periodically during the year, preschool and primary-grade teachers must decide how to place or group children. With preschool children, the teacher needs to know the skills and knowledge of each child. Because the backgrounds of the children can vary widely, the teacher evaluates all students to determine how to plan for them in the instructional program. In preschool programs, designed to prevent or deal with learning problems, the evaluation may determine whether the child is eligible for the program. Of particular concern currently are children who are limited in English-speaking ability and children who have delays and disabilities. Formal testing is done with these children to determine their eligibility for special services. When considering LEP students and bilingual programs teachers need to conduct additional assessments to track progress and determine whether the students need to continue in a LEP program or be dismissed from the program. School districts are responsible for understanding and following federal requirements for providing instruction that will lead to adequate yearly progress under Title I regulations (U.S. Department of Education, 2006).

Students with delays or disabilities also need individual attention for instructional placement. These children have a yearly plan, which must be reviewed to determine whether the child has made sufficient progress. Each new school year, the child's needs are reassessed and new plans are made for maximum progress. Teachers are responsible for providing placement assessment beyond standardized testing to support adequate improvement each year.

The same process just described for preschool children is continued for children in elementary grades who are ELLs or have special needs. In addition, teacher-conducted testing may result in placement in a group for reading and mathematics. The teacher or team of teachers gives tests at the beginning of the school year to determine the child's mastery of content objectives; the purpose is to group children with similar learning needs for instruction. This type of evaluation may be repeated whenever teachers believe that regrouping is needed to improve instructional services for the children.

Diagnostic Evaluation and Instructional Planning

Diagnostic evaluation is more specific than placement evaluation. When assessing for diagnostic purposes, the teacher investigates the child's ability in specific objectives. With preschool children, the teacher may assign tasks involving knowledge of colors to determine which children know the colors and which children need activities to learn them. With school-age children, the teacher may administer a paper-and-pencil test to determine which children have learned to add and which children need to be taught this skill. Diagnostic evaluation continues throughout the year with children who have disabilities. Indicators of progress in specific skills are monitored and instruction adapted if necessary.

Formative and Summative Evaluation

Formative evaluation and summative evaluation occur after instruction on a particular objective or a series of objectives. **Formative evaluation** is done throughout the year to determine how students are progressing toward mastery of objectives. In some schools formative evaluation is conducted every 6 weeks or every 9 weeks. In individual classrooms formative evaluation may take place more frequently as students move through specific objectives in the curriculum. After students practice a skill or learn information, the teacher evaluates them to determine which ones have achieved mastery and which need additional work through different instructional methods or learning experiences.

Summative evaluation is a final assessment of what children have learned. It is conducted after diagnostic and formative evaluation. For some grade levels, summative evaluation is done for grading purposes: The child receives a grade for performance on the objectives tested. Whether or not grades are used, it is hoped that children who have not mastered the information or skills tested will have more opportunities to learn.

Advantages of Using Classroom Assessments

Classroom assessments have certain advantages over standardized tests. Although they have not been validated with large numbers of students before being used in the classroom, teacher assessments include measurement opportunities that standardized tests cannot provide.

The focus of classroom assessments is to encourage students to produce knowledge, rather than to reproduce knowledge. In keeping with Piaget's position that children construct knowledge, assessments can stress the child's active involvement in learning, which is exhibited through performance of tasks or samples of work, rather than through assessments that are limited to mastery of discrete skills (Goodwin & Goodwin, 1993; Wiggins, 1989, 1993). The goal of classroom evaluation is to measure long-term development that occurs slowly over a period of time, rather than short-term learning that is assessed without acknowledging interrelationships in development.

One advantage of classroom assessments is that they can be derived directly from the teacher's educational objectives and curriculum or from a commercial textbook curriculum. Standardized tests, by contrast, are developed to measure general objectives applicable to many children in different school districts and areas of the country. With assessments, individual teachers or groups of teachers design both the curriculum and the measures to assess children's knowledge of the curriculum. Consequently, evaluation items can focus specifically on the teacher's instruction and assessment plans. Commercial publishers also can design informal means of assessment specifically for their instructional materials.

In chapter 4, we established that standardized tests may not measure how children are being taught in the classroom. Because these tests are developed over a long period of time, the test items may reflect outdated learning objectives. As a result, teacher-designed evaluation strategies may measure learning more accurately than standardized tests.

The reality is that standardized tests are not likely to be replaced. However, teacher-designed assessments have an important role as part of an assessment program. One response is to design instruction and informal testing to maintain the integrity of a constructivist approach to learning, while also helping students perform on standardized tests (Taylor & Walton, 1997). In the same approach, assessment specialists propose the use of sound assessments that are consistent with local educational goals in addition to the use of externally imposed standardized tests (Bernauer & Cress, 1997).

Research in reading instruction suggests that young readers use available resources such as text, prior knowledge, and environmental clues to make sense of reading material, whereas standardized tests evaluate reading as a set of discrete skills. As a result, teachers teach reading as discrete skills or teach so that students will do well on the standardized tests (Valencia & Pearson, 1987). Valencia and Pearson recommend not only that formal testing strategies be modified to better match reading research findings about effective instruction, but also that teachers use a combination of strategies that more accurately assess the reading process.

The developmental nature of emergent literacy is also cited as a rationale for using classroom evaluation measures. Literacy includes the development of language, listening, writing, and reading, which are interrelated and concurrent. The process of literacy begins at birth and continues throughout the early childhood years. The developmental progress of literacy is followed and evaluated by using the child's performance and examples of work collected over a period of time that reflect advances toward the ability to communicate through reading and writing. More specifically, assessment of literacy occurs through emergent writing samples, emergent reading of books, and oral discussions founded on the philosophy that the child's emerging skills reflect the child's ability to construct literacy through experiences with literacy over time (Goodwin & Goodwin, 1993; Sulzby, 1990; Teale, 1988). Likewise, stages of emergent literacy that are skills related, such as knowledge of letter–sound correspondence and encoding and decoding words, are assessed through learning activities and instructional events (Schickedanz, 1989). Although federal guidelines for successful reading in the primary grades stress the importance of phonics, emergent literacy is still a very appropriate choice for developing literacy in young children (Fields & Spangler, 2000; Newman, Copple, & Bredekamp, 2000; Owocki, 2001). Moreover, emergent literacy incorporated with other strategies that use a constructivist approach can be incorporated into assessment activities. Open-ended tasks and performance activities reflect the developmental nature of emergent literacy (Shepard, 2000).

Using limited, teacher-directed instructional methods so that children will perform well on standardized tests can affect mathematics as well as reading. Although current theory of mathematics instruction stresses that children construct concepts by becoming actively involved with concrete materials, tests still measure knowledge of numerals (Kamii, 1985a, 1985b). School systems teach to the test rather than follow methods that are best for children, especially in "at-risk" schools where the stakes are high for both achievement and failure (Shepard, 2000). Moreover, the tests stress lower-order thinking rather than higher-order thinking, and improvement in test scores reflects improvement in computation rather than in problem solving (Dossey, Mullis, Lindquist, & Chambers, 1988; Kamii & Kamii, 1990). Although newer standardized tests, particularly achievement tests, developed at the state level, have included more performance questions, particularly in writing, in general they are still multiple-choice tests with the same limitations (Popham, 1999). Alternative assessments such as interviews, projects, games, and observations are recommended to evaluate the constructivist nature of learning in mathematics (Kamii & Kamii, 1990).

In contrast to standardized tests, locally designed assessments are current. Because standardized tests are developed over a period of time, there may be a lag of two years or more between test design and implementation. A test cannot be easily updated or modified. Teacher-designed evaluation measures, however, can be altered when necessary. If instructional materials are changed or learning objectives modified, the teacher can keep classroom measures current by redesigning assessment strategies to reflect the changes.

Another advantage of classroom assessments is that they can be correlated with diagnostic needs. If the teacher wants certain types of information for placement, grouping, and individual instructional needs, the assessment measures can be easily adapted for these purposes. Although criterion-referenced standardized tests also serve diagnostic purposes, they are generally a starting point for effective teachers. The teacher must follow criterion-referenced results with classroom strategies that provide additional diagnostic information. For preschool children who have not been given standardized tests, teacher-designed strategies are a first step in evaluation. Criterion-referenced standardized tests can be administered later, when the child has the developmental skills to take them.

The flexibility of teacher-designed assessment strategies is an important advantage. The objectives to be evaluated on a standardized test are established early in the test development process. Thereafter, objectives are not changed, and test items to measure them are evenly distributed and measure all general objectives equally. Individual teachers design both the curriculum and the measures to assess children's mastery of it; consequently, evaluation items can be tailored to the teacher's instruction and assessment plans.

Disadvantages of Using Classroom Assessments

Although classroom assessments have certain advantages, they also have limitations and weaknesses. Classroom teachers are more likely to use local assessments than the results of standardized tests. Therefore, they must learn how to design and use informal measures appropriately if these measures are to be effective for evaluation and instructional planning. Improper development and implementation are the main disadvantages of teacher-designed assessments—specifically, problems centered on their validity and reliability, misapplication, and inappropriate use.

Locally designed assessment instruments are widely used in preschools and elementary schools. Since the 1970s, when measures such as instructional checklists first became popular, many school districts have developed their own checklists and other assessment measures. At the preschool level, teachers and administrators have devised screening tests to determine eligibility for preschool intervention programs. For example, in some states, only children who are at risk for academic failure are eligible for state-supported kindergarten programs. Local schools are expected to determine the eligibility of the 5-year-old children in their district. The screening instruments vary greatly from one community to another.

Teachers and other educators in public schools can take steps to develop quality assessments. One method is to establish interrater reliability. Several teachers use the same instrument, such as a checklist or observation, to determine whether they get similar results from using the strategy. Likewise, teachers can collaborate on developing multiple-choice or true–false test items to ensure that they locate weaknesses in test items before tests are administered. These testing strategies can be piloted with students to conduct an item analysis to retain or replace test questions as needed. More about establishing quality in assessment strategies will be discussed in the chapters that follow.

Another disadvantage of classroom measures is that teachers may misuse them. Locally designed checklists are frequently used as a framework for organizing or designing the curriculum, as well as a record of evaluation of student learning. Children are tested on the checklist's objectives, and the record of their progress follows them from grade to grade. Because teachers develop their own tasks or tests to assess checklist objectives, confusion over what constitutes mastery and what kind of assessment is appropriate can cause major problems within a school or throughout a school district. In an effort to arrive at consensus on how to assess the objectives, the strategies used by individual teachers may be severely limited. In the primary grades, teachers must frequently place a workbook page or other pencil-and-paper documentation in the child's record as proof of successful performance. This requirement eliminates the use of other classroom strategies, such as teacher observation or developmental tasks, for evaluation.

The current movement to incorporate authentic or performance-based assessments in early childhood programs offers additional options for evaluating young children. Interviews, directed assignments, narrative reports, and portfolios offer new techniques that permit teachers to develop assessments congruent with their teaching style and the constructivist approach to learning (Wiggins, 1993, 1998). However, there are serious concerns about the possible disadvantages to these new approaches to informal assessment, especially in the light of federal requirements for accountability. One is that these measures may not present evidence of validity, reliability, and freedom from bias. Another disadvantage is the extensive training needed by teachers to feel comfortable with the new techniques (Winograd & Webb, 1994). Furthermore, teachers have concerns about the issue of accountability with authentic assessments. The amount of time needed to conduct the newer measures and to keep records is a concern. Finally, there are concerns about acceptance by parents, the public in general, and policy makers (Goodwin & Goodwin, 1993, 1997; Smith, 1990; Teale, 1990).

The major disadvantage of classroom assessments seems to be that teachers are not prepared to develop and use them. They misuse or are unaware of the proper application of either standardized or informal measures. Some writers advocate the use of a variety of formal and informal strategies to assess young children. Observation, like other teacher strategies, requires an informed, well-prepared teacher who will use it effectively. In the rest of this chapter, we discuss the purposes of observation and describe how observations are conducted and interpreted.

Purposes of Observation

Observation is the most direct method of becoming familiar with the learning and development of the young child. Because it requires a focus on the child's behaviors, observation allows the teacher to get to know the child as a unique individual, rather than as a member of a group. It is very important for teachers of young children to have training in early childhood development in order to understand appropriate behaviors when observing children. Further, such training is a prerequisite to understand what they are seeing in the context of all types of development.

Learning the importance of observation is important, as is developing the skills of how to observe. Many students studying to become teachers, as well as practicing teachers, do not understand how skilled observations are central to the teacher's work or what can be learned from well-conducted observations. Once the importance of observation is understood, teachers and future teachers need to develop observational skills appropriate to the objectives of the observation and the information they desire from the observation (Billman & Sherman, 1997; Harrington, Meisels, McMahon, Dichtelmiller, & Jablon, 1997; Pelo, 2006). Observation can be used for three major purposes: (1) to understand children's behavior, (2) to evaluate children's development, and (3) to evaluate learning progress.

Understanding Children's Behavior

Because young children have not yet mastered language and the ability to read and write, they are unable to express themselves as clearly as older children and adults. They cannot demonstrate how much they know or understand through formal or informal assessments involving tasks and standardized tests. According to child development specialists, one of the most accurate ways to learn about children is to observe them in daily activities. Because children cannot explain themselves sufficiently through language, evidence of why they behave as they do is obtained through on-the-spot recording of their actions (Irwin & Bushnell, 1980). Children who are English language learners especially need this type of perception about what they understand, even if they cannot express themselves adequately in English. Observation of this population of children reveals information about them that may not be obvious within the larger group of students.

Skilled observation is important to correctly determine what is behind a child's classroom behavior. Misinterpretation leads to difficulties for both teacher and child stemming from the teacher thinking that one cause has led to the child's behavior, while the truth may be quite different (MacDonald, 2006).

Children communicate through their bodies. Their physical actions reveal as much about them as the things they say. Cohen, Stern, and Balaban (1997) describe how observing children's behavior provides information or clues to their thoughts and feelings:

> Children communicate with us through their eyes, the quality of their voices, their body postures, their gestures, their mannerisms, their smiles, their jumping up and down, and their listlessness. They show us, by the way they do things as well as by what they do, what is going on inside them. When we come to see children's behavior through the eyes of its meaning to them, from the inside out, we shall be well on our way to understanding them. Recording their ways of communicating helps us to see them as they are. (p. 5)

Observation of Social Behavior

A major accomplishment during the early childhood years is the development of social skills. Beginning as toddlers and preschoolers, young children evolve into

Muniru

*M*uniru has had a "no good, very bad day" in the toddler room at the Delgado Child Enrichment Center. His regular teacher was delayed for part of the day and the substitute teacher was very impatient with him. First, Muniru's father was late for work and he did not get to finish his breakfast. Later, he bit a child, which is unusual behavior for him. He fussed and cried all morning and did not enjoy any of the play activities. By the time the regular teacher returned in the afternoon, the substitute was exasperated with Muniru. The regular teacher observed Muniru for a few minutes and noticed that he was drooling. When she checked his mouth, she discovered that a new tooth was erupting. She put some ice in a clean cloth and let Muniru suck on it. Before Muniru's father returned to pick him up, Muniru had been able to participate in classroom play and story time.

social beings who learn to interact with each other. First efforts to become part of a social group are often ineffective, but with continued opportunity to engage in group activities, most young children develop the ability to work and play with each other. Observation of children at play or interacting in classroom centers reveals how social development and behavior are progressing. Social behavior is part of social development, discussed in the next section.

Evaluating Children's Development

A second major purpose of observing children is to evaluate their development. When teachers study development, observation is specific. Rather than considering behavior in general, the observer's purpose is to determine the child's progress in physical, cognitive, social, or emotional development. Observing development not only makes it easy to understand sequences of development but also helps teachers of young children to be aware of individual growth and aid children who have delays in specific areas of development. Skilled observation of developmental domains requires a sound foundation in child development. The ability to conduct developmental observations increases with practice when the practicing teacher is able to match the developmental characteristics and norms with the activities of the children he or she observes.

Beaty (1997) describes observation of development as systematic. There are specific purposes for observing and particular methods for collecting and recording observation data. Beaty proposes eight reasons for systematically observing and recording the development of young children:

1. To make an initial assessment of the child's abilities
2. To determine a child's areas of strength and areas needing strengthening
3. To make individual plans based on observed needs

4. To conduct an ongoing check on the child's progress
5. To learn more about child development in particular areas
6. To resolve a particular problem involving the child
7. To report to parents or to specialists in health, speech, and mental health
8. To gather information for the child's folder, for use in guidance and placement. (p. 5)

Observing Infant and Toddler Development

The years between birth and age 2 are the most rapid period of development. They are also the years when the infant and toddler are least able to communicate with others. Observation is the primary means to interpret the meaning of a very young child's behaviors. Mothers learn the differences in their baby's cries to be able to respond to their needs. Infant caregivers observe the infants in their care throughout the day to understand when the infants are tired, hungry, wet, or not feeling well. Observation of changes in an infant's daily sleeping and eating patterns might signal advances in development or an impending illness. Opportunities for adult–child interactions are also determined by observing the infant's readiness to be attentive.

Observing English Language Learners

Children who enter a preschool program or elementary school with limited English have a special need to acquire or expand their language. Observation by the classroom teacher and other staff members provides input on what the child understands and is learning to express. Many times a language limitation is hidden because a child seems extremely shy, when in reality he or she does not understand the language being spoken. Although tests are commonly administered to admit a child into an English language development program or a bilingual program, daily observation is the key to knowing what the child needs to learn to become proficient in English. The teacher can provide instant feedback and amplification of the child's speaking attempts to further expand vocabulary and functional use of language.

Assessment of Young Children With Disabilities

In recent years, educators who work with children who have developmental delays or disabilities have begun to use observation as a tool for assessment. Traditionally, tests for infants and preschool children were used almost exclusively to identify and diagnose the development of children with disabilities or at risk to develop disabilities. Observation of play has been found more effective than testing for some types of assessment. Sometimes referred to as *play-based assessment*, both structured and nonstructured observations can be used to assess the young child's developmental strengths and weaknesses (Segal & Webber, 1996).

Play-Based Assessment

Assessment during child play, or **play-based assessment**, is particularly useful for learning about development in children with disabilities. The procedures described in this chapter can be used with children without disabilities; however, play observation provides unique ways to assess children who may be delayed in development.

For example, children with disabilities and children who are developing normally can be presented with the same toys. The observer can then compare how the two groups play with the toys to determine possible deficits in children with disabilities. Toys can also be given to a child with disabilities to observe it and rate the developmental sequences of play (Fewell & Glick, 1998).

All children are assessed through observation of play. Naturally occurring play is observed for developmental indicators as described earlier in the chapter. Play-based assessment is uniquely designed to assess children who may be delayed in development.

A team of adults usually serves children with disabilities. Assessment and intervention teams have different specializations and purposes of assessment. Parents are included on each child's team to conduct the assessment. The play session is flexible enough to be adapted to individual needs and interests (Bergen, 1994; Fewell & Glick, 1998; Linder, 1993). The play activities are conducted with a facilitator, the child's parents, and a peer. Both structured and unstructured play activities are included within five phases taking place for about 60–70 minutes. The phases are as follows:

Phase 1: Unstructured Facilitation (20–25 minutes)

The child initiates the activities. The facilitator follows along in playing and conversations using the toys the child selects. The facilitator can model slightly higher play skills but should avoid trying to teach the child.

Phase 2: Structured Facilitation (10–15 minutes)

The facilitator leads the activities and asks the child to perform spatial tasks (games) that provide an additional opportunity to observe language and cognitive development. The child should be allowed to initiate activities as well.

Phase 3: Child–Child interaction (5–10 minutes)

The child plays with another child who is slightly older, familiar to the child being assessed and who is developing typically. The children play wherever they choose, with the facilitator encouraging interaction. The team observes the child's play interactions and social patterns.

Phase 4: Parent–Child Interaction (5 minutes)

The parent and child engage in the play activities that they do at home. The team observes how the child interacts with the parent and if behaviors are different than in other phases in the assessment. At the end the parents are asked to leave the room and then return in a few minutes. The child's behavior during separation and return is observed. The parents again play with the child in a more structured activity or teach the child a new task.

Phase 5: Motor Play (10–20 minutes)

Again, the child engages in unstructured play for a few minutes followed by specific motor activities guided by the facilitator. This phase may include an occupational or physical therapist.

Phase 6: Snack (5–10 minutes)

The child is given a snack. The team observes self-help skills, adaptive behavior, and oral motor skills. The snack can include the peer play partner from Phase 3.

The entire session is recorded using a video camera so that team members can observe it again later (Brookes Publishing, 2002).

Functional Behavioral Assessment

The Functional Behavioral Assessment looks at the child's behaviors to address problem behaviors and is most frequently used with children with disabilities. The assessment uses a problem solving process that is integrated with the process of using IEPs. A variety of techniques is used to identify the causes of the behavior. Why does the child use the behavior?

The inappropriate behaviors are examined to identify the purpose or function of the behavior. The child might be using the behavior to get something, avoid something, or to make something happen. Once the behavior and function are identified, the child is helped to succeed in a more positive, appropriate way (Center for Effective Collaboration and Practice, 2001; Miller, n.d.).

The process of conducting a Functional Behavioral Assessment includes the following steps (Sugai et al., 1999):

1. Collect information on the problem behavior and the conditions when it is observed.
2. Develop testable hypotheses about changing the problem behavior to an acceptable behavior.
3. Collect information through direct observation.
4. Design behavior support plans.
5. Develop implementation strategies.
6. Collect information on the effectiveness of the support plan and redesign, if needed.

Evaluating Learning Progress

Once children have entered any type of early learning program or school setting, teachers need to acquire information on what children have learned from classroom instruction and learning activities. Although other strategies such as teacher-designed tasks and tests are commonly used, observation is also a useful tool, especially to understand the individual learning styles used by children. The teacher might use a planned observation such as the strategies described later in the chapter or an incidental observation that is employed when the teacher notices a child's activity or behavior that can provide insight into the child's learning. Both planned and incidental observations are effectively conducted during children's play. Almost every area of development can be assessed through the observation of play. Teachers can observe social skills, language skills, cognitive skills, and motor skills using incidental or structured observations (Fewell & Glick, 1998). One effective type of activity is a performance activity whereby the child demonstrates learning through some type of performance, such as motor skills on the playground or the ability to put together a complex puzzle. This type of performance assessment will be discussed in more detail in chapter 8.

A teacher can use Vygotsky's zone of proximal development (ZPD) in observations to determine the child's progress toward mastery of skills (Bodrova & Leong, 1996).

Vygotsky (1978) proposed that there is a range or zone between what the child cannot do, can do with assistance, and can do independently. The teacher observes the child's activities and works to determine where the child's progress lies in the ZPD. An example in kindergarten or first grade might be the student's ability to use fine-motor skills to construct a model or make a collage. The teacher observes the child at work to determine the level of competency in drawing, cutting, and putting materials together to determine his or her ZPD in fine-motor skills needed for the task.

Because what is observed must be interpreted, the observer must know how to use observation to gather specific data. Background information on how children develop and learn is important if the observer is to convert the child's behaviors into information that can be used to understand the child's level of development and the need for experiences that will further this development.

Obviously, the quality of the information gained from an observation depends on the skills of the observer. The sophisticated observer uses knowledge of developmental theories and stages of development to identify the significant events of an observation and to interpret these events in a way that is useful in understanding the child. For example, a teacher may notice that a child is exploring or playing with a collection of buttons by making a pile of all the buttons with four holes. Knowledge of Piaget's cognitive developmental theory enables the teacher to interpret this activity as the ability to classify objects.

Bentzen (1997) states that observation is not simply looking at something; it is a disciplined, scientific process of searching for a behavior in a particular way. The observer must know what to look for, how to record the desired information, and how to explain the behavior.

Young children develop rapidly, and their level of development changes continually. By observing frequently, teachers can track the child's development and respond to changes and advances in development with new opportunities and challenges.

Observation to Improve the Classroom Environment and Instruction

Teachers of toddler groups closely observe to see what their children enjoy and take clues for adding to or changing the environment to reflect the children's interest in play. What teachers think children will do and how they interact with the environment can be very different. A teacher of toddlers was interested in generating an outdoor area especially for toddlers. A track was set up for wheeled toys, a variety of clothing articles for role-play were placed in a plastic container, and small vehicles were located nearby. To the teacher's surprise, the children did not ride or play with wheel toys on the track. Instead, they took some headbands out of the clothes items, put them on, and jogged around the track as they had experienced with their parents. The teacher learned from her observation to respond to the children's interests and introduced additional items that might enhance role-play as well as physical play.

Observation and Documentation

Observation of children's learning can include reflecting upon their accomplishments. Much of a teacher's understanding of what children have learned can be gleaned through observation of the children working and study of the product of that learning. *Documentation* is a strategy used to evaluate children's learning in Reggio

Seeing From the Child's Point of View

*O*ne morning, the toddler teacher brought a bucket full of sparkly plastic bracelets into the classroom. As she observed the children, they used the bracelets for several purposes. Some children waved the bracelets about and noticed how they glittered in the light. One child put as many bracelets on his arm as possible. Another child threw the bracelets on the floor so that they twirled in circles. After many practice throws, the child learned that they would spin like a top if he threw them in a certain way. Finally, some children just enjoyed taking the bracelets out of the bucket and then putting them back in over and over. As the teacher observed the children, and they observed each other, they learned new ideas about how they could play with the bracelets. The teacher learned more about individual children as they experimented with the bracelets. She used some of their ideas when the bracelets were introduced to the play environment again.

Source: Curtis, D. (2006, November/December). No ordinary moments: Using observations with toddlers to invite further engagement. *Exchange, 172,* 36–40.

Emilia schools. The teacher documents the progress of a period of time or work by taking notes, photographs, or using a video camera to record steps in the process. The work that the children produce also serves as documentation of what has transpired. The important factor in the observation and documentation is that the teacher is observing the children in depth from the children's perspective. The documentation reflects how the children engaged in the learning, not how the teacher planned for learning. A teacher who has been learning the Reggio Emilia approach to documentation commented, "The most persistent and persuasive challenge has been to shift our vision to see what the children are really doing in the classrooms every day, to see the interactions, to hear their real conversations, to record these explorations and to share them with the parents, children, and teachers" (MacDonald, 2006, p. 46).

Documentation has commonly been described as pictures, photographs, and written explanations mounted on a wall. However, documentation can be expanded to a variety of formats. Documentation assessment strategies can include portfolios, products of investigations, videotapes, class books, and slide shows (Helm, Beneke, & Steinheimer, 2007; Seitz, 2008). While the original descriptions of documentation referred to wall displays related to a project, the process has been enriched to include more possibilities on how and where documentation is used to demonstrate what children have learned through their own work. Figure 5-1 shows possibilities for documentation of student achievement.

The type of documentation used can depend on the intended audience. If families and administrators are the target audiences, the teacher might use photos of children engaging in classroom activities that meet specific learning standards. The focus would be on how children learn. If, however, the children in the classroom are the

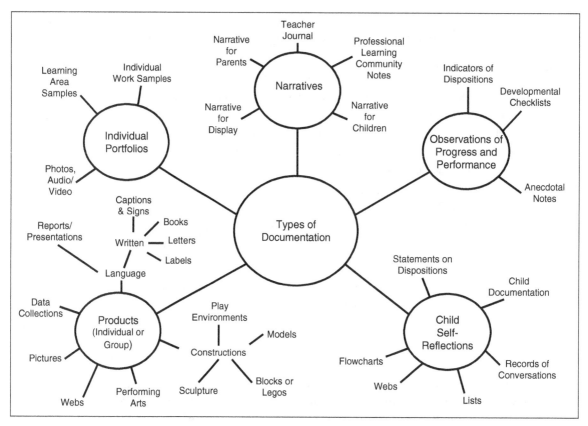

FIGURE 5-1 Examples for types of documentation of student achievement

Source: Judy Helm and Sally Beneke, windows on Learning: Documenting Young Children's Work. 2nd Edition published in 2007 by Teachers College Press.

intended audience, the teacher might feature webs of children's ideas and children's work examples to demonstrate how the ideas were implemented and what was learned using the web (Seitz, 2008).

Types of Observation

What happens during an observation? What does the observer actually do? When conducting an observation, the student, teacher, or researcher visits a classroom or other place where a group of children may be observed as they engage in routine activities. The observer, having already determined the objectives or purpose of the observation, the time to be spent studying the child or children, and the form in which the observation will be conducted and recorded, sits at the side or in an observation booth and watches the children. The types of observations used include anecdotal records, running records, specimen records, time sampling, event sampling, and checklists and rating scales.

Child Name(s): <u>Robbie, Mary, Janie</u>	
Age: <u>4</u>	
Location: <u>Sunnyside Preschool</u>	
Observer: <u>Sue</u>	
Type of Development Observed: <u>Social/Emotional</u>	
Date: October 5, 2008	

Incident	Social/Emotional Notes or Comments
Mary and Janie were in the Housekeeping Area pretending to fix a meal. Robbie came to the center and said he wanted to eat. The girls looked at him. Janie said, "You can't play here, we're busy." Robbie stood watching the girls as they moved plastic fruit on the table. Robbie said, "I could be the Daddy and do the dishes." Mary thought for a minute, looked at Janie, and replied, "Oh, all right, you can play."	The girls play together frequently and tend to discourage others from entering their play. Robbie has learned how to enter a play group. He was careful not to upset the girls. They relented when he offered to be helpful. Robbie is usually successful in being accepted into play activities.

FIGURE 5-2 Example of an anecdotal record

Anecdotal Record

An **anecdotal record** is a written description of a child's behavior. It is an objective account of an incident that tells what happened, when, and where. The record may be used to understand some aspect of behavior. A physician, parents, or teacher may use anecdotal records to track the development of an infant or a young child in order to explain unusual behavior. Although the narrative itself is objective, comments may be added as an explanation of or a reaction to the recorded incident.

The anecdotal record has five characteristics (Goodwin & Driscoll, 1980):

1. The anecdotal record is the result of direct observation.
2. The anecdotal record is a prompt, accurate, and specific account of an event.
3. The anecdotal record includes the context of the behavior.
4. Interpretations of the incident are recorded separately from the incident.
5. The anecdotal record focuses on behavior that is either typical or unusual for the child being observed.

Figure 5-2 is an example of the form and content of an anecdotal record. Teachers can use anecdotal records in the classroom to record observed behaviors. The caregiver in an infant or toddler classroom might keep a daily logbook or index cards on a child's eating or health patterns or acquisition of a new skill to share with parents. A preschool teacher might use blank address labels to record a significant or changing behavior to note and place in a child's folder. Likewise, a primary-grade teacher might note a child's daily work habits in the classroom on sticky notes to record and document the ability or inability to focus on tasks, dependency on others, or improvements in a child's social behavior (Fields & Spangler, 2000; Martin, 1994).

Advantages and Disadvantages of Using Anecdotal Records

Anecdotal records are quick and easy to use. It just takes a moment or two for the teacher to record the information that has been observed. The teacher can later reflect on the observation and its importance. A disadvantage of using anecdotal records is that they might not contain enough information for the teacher to analyze the content of the observation. The teacher will also have to be creative on how to develop a system to keep the observations organized.

Running Record

Using a **running record** is another method of recording behavior. It is a more detailed narrative of a child's behavior that includes the sequence of events. The running record includes everything that occurred over a period of time—that is, all behavior observed—rather than the particular incidents that are used for the anecdotal record. The description is objective. An effort is made to record everything that happened or was said during the observation period. Running records may be recorded over a period ranging from a few minutes to a few weeks or even months.

The observer comments on or analyzes the behaviors separately after studying the record. His or her task is to record the situation so that future readers can visualize what occurred (Cohen et al., 1997). Figure 5-3 is an example of a running record.

Running records are also used to assess emergent literacy. When the teacher desires to acquire information about the child's current abilities and weaknesses in reading, the teacher may listen to the child read, and record errors and corrections that are made as the child reads the passage. The teacher might mark on a copy of the material that the child is reading, using a systematic method of identifying errors such as reversals, substitutions, self-corrections, or omissions. As an alternative, the teacher might use a running record form separate from the passage being read. The intent is to conduct an informal assessment when the child is actually reading (Sulzby, 1993).

Running records may be used for reading instruction. A teacher might observe a child's oral reading and write down unknown words, fluency changes, or difficulty in pronouncing some words. At the end of the reading activity, the teacher has needed information to help the child immediately and in succeeding instructional periods.

Marie Clay (1993) developed a standardized running record to document oral reading behaviors in the Reading Recovery Program. In this program designed to detect and correct problems at early reading stages, checks are used to mark words read correctly, while a dash is used for words missed. Figure 5-4 shows an adaptation of a running record and analysis of errors and self-corrections. The left-hand side of the page shows how each word was recorded on the twenty pages of the story. Errors, self-corrections, and strategies used for identifying words are recorded in the columns at the right-hand side of the page. The check marks on each line record words the child read correctly. Where one word is written above the other, the child either self-corrected the word or made an error. The columns on the right indicate that three words were errors and four were self-corrected (Fields & Spangler, 2000).

Child Name(s): <u>Christopher</u>
Age: <u>4</u>
Location: <u>KinderKare</u>
Date and Time: <u>June 21, 20XX</u>   <u>8:40–9:10</u>
Observer: <u>Perlita</u>
Type of Development Observed: <u>Social and Cognitive</u>

Observation	Notes or Comments
Chris is playing with a toy. He says, "Kelly, can I keep it?" several times until he gets an answer. He moves on to a toy guitar and plays it while he supervises the other children by walking around the room. He tells everyone to sit down at the tables after the teacher says to.	Chris is polite to others. Chris is helping his classmates follow the rules.
Chris sits by a friend and talks about eating granola bars. He watches and listens to the conversation on either side of him. He's still unaffected by the loud temper tantrum of another child. Then he notices her and watches. He tries to explain this behavior to the others by saying a plant was spilled.	Chris is interested in what others have to say. Chris tries to make sense of a child's behavior.
He follows the teacher's directions. Then he decides he wants to be in on a secret. A boy shoves him away. Chris informs him that he *can* hear if he wants to. This has caused him to disobey the teacher. He has to sit out of the circle. He walks over to the chair, sits down, gets up immediately, and comes back to the circle undetected by the teacher. He joins the circle.	Chris chooses appropriate ways to assert himself.

FIGURE 5-3   Example of a running record

Advantages and Disadvantages of Using Running Records

Running records are adaptable to different purposes as demonstrated in Figure 5-3 and Figure 5-4. It includes more information than an anecdotal record and provides a snapshot of what occurred over a period of time. Other interested staff members can use the information to better understand the child. A disadvantage is that this type of observation must be scheduled and time designated for this purpose. In the case of beginning reading, the observation can be built into instructional time. Other types of running record observations might be more difficult to manage.

Observation	Notes or Comments
Chris tattles on a child hiding money. He is told to switch places and wants to know why. He gets up to push the chairs under the table without being asked directly. He wants to explain the temper tantrum to another child (it is still going on) who is curious.	Chris needs to know why he does some things.
Chris attends to the teacher's questions and the story that she is now reading. He begins to look around the circle and then back to the book. He plays with his socks and participates in the group answers to questions about the story (*Now One Foot, Now the Other Foot* by Tomie dePaola [he is in continuous motion with some part of his body during the story]). Now he becomes very still and attends to the story. He puts both hands over his ears when students remark about events in the story. He immediately makes his own remarks. He becomes very still again. The whole circle is quiet for the ending of the book.	Chris shows he has self-control. Chris responds to and sympathizes with the characters in the story.
As soon as the story is finished, Chris says, "I got a cut from a thorn bush." He sits very quietly but moves around. "How do we kill our plants over there?" he asks the teacher. (A plant was knocked off earlier.) "Not mine, not me!" he says.	

FIGURE 5-3 *(Continued)*

Time Sampling

The purpose of **time sampling** is to record the frequency of a behavior for a designated period of time. The observer decides ahead of time what behaviors will be observed, what the time interval will be, and how the behaviors will be recorded. The observer observes these behaviors and records how many times they occur during preset, uniform time periods. Other behaviors that occur during the observation are ignored. After a number of samplings have been completed, the data are studied to determine when and perhaps why a behavior is occurring. The observer can use the information to help the child if a change in behavior is desired.

Child's name *Felicia*   Date *Dec 15*

Book *Catch that Frog*

PAGE:		E	Sc	M	S	V
				Strategy		
1						
2	✓ ✓ ✓ ✓ ✓ ✓ ✓ ✓ ✓ ✓ ✓ ✓ ✓					
3						
4	✓ ✓ ✓ ✓ ✓ ✓ ✓ ✓ ✓ ✓ ✓ ✓ ✓					
5						
6	✓ ✓ ✓ ✓ ✓ her/Carol's /sc ✓ ✓ ✓ ✓ ✓ R ✓			1		sc
7	✓✓✓ around/across ✓ ✓ ✓ ✓ ✓	1		t		
8	✓ ✓ ✓ ✓ ✓ ✓ ✓ ✓ ✓ ✓					
9						
10	✓ got/caught /sc ✓ ✓ ✓ ✓ ✓ along/again	1	1			✓
11						
12	✓ ✓ ✓ ✓ ✓ ✓ ✓ ✓ ✓ ✓ ✓✓✓					
13						
14	✓ ✓ ✓ ✓ ✓ ✓ ✓ ✓ ✓ ✓					
15						
16	✓ ✓ ✓ ✓ ✓ ✓					
17						
18	✓ ✓ after/around /sc ✓ ✓ R ✓ that/the ✓		1	sc		
19						
20	✓ ✓ ✓ after/around /sc ✓ ✓ get/after ✓ ✓	1	1	t		sc

Analysis of **E**rrors and **S**elf **C**orrections (**SC**): Strategies (**M**eaning, **S**tructure, **V**isual)

Comments:

x checks with visual and meaning clues
this was an easy book for Felicia

FIGURE 5-4 Adaptation of a running record for reading

Source: M. V. Fields, L. Groth, and K. L. Spangler, *Let's begin reading right: A developmental approach to emergent literacy* (5th ed.), p. 322. Adapted by permission of Pearson Education, Inc., Upper Saddle River, NJ.

Time sampling may be used with young children because many of their behaviors are brief. By using time sampling, the observer can gain comprehensive information about the behavior. The length of the observation can be affected by the target behavior, the children's familiarity with the observer, the nature of the situation, and the number of children to be observed (Webb, Campbell, Schwartz, & Sechrest, 1966).

Teachers or other school staff members frequently use time sampling when a child is behaving inappropriately at school—for example, one who behaves aggressively with other children and does not cooperate in classroom routines at certain times. It is used over a period of time during the hours of the daily schedule when the unwanted behavior occurs. After the time samples are studied, the teacher can determine what to do to modify the behavior. Figure 5-5 is an example of time sampling as an observation method.

Advantages and Disadvantages of Using Time Sampling

The primary advantage of using time sampling is that the purpose is very clear. The teacher is concerned about a behavior and wants to observe the child to determine how often it occurs. The framework for the observation is planned ahead of time and only the target behavior is recorded. It also gives the teacher the opportunity to focus on what is happening without being distracted by other events occurring in the classroom. A disadvantage is that time for the observation may be difficult to manage on a regular timed schedule. It is a skill that has to be practiced and learned. Observing a behavior on the playground might be much easier than observing during classroom instruction.

Child Name(s): <u>Joanie</u>
Age: <u>5</u>
Location: <u>Rosewood School Kindergarten</u>
Date and Time: <u>May 17, 10:45–11:00</u>
Observer: <u>Susanna</u>
Type of Development Observed: <u>Joanie Has Difficulty Completing Tasks</u>

Event	Time	Notes or Comments
Art Center—leaves coloring activity on table unfinished	10:45	Some of Joanie's behaviors seem to be resulting from failure to follow procedures for use of materials.
Library—looks at book, returns it to shelf.	10:50	
Manipulative Center—gets frustrated with puzzle, piles pieces in center—leaves on table. Pulls out Lego blocks, starts to play. When teacher signals to put toys away, Joanie leaves Lego blocks on table and joins other children.	10:55	Behavior with the puzzles may come from frustration.
	11:00	Joanie may need help in putting away with verbal rewards for finishing a task and putting materials away.
		Encourage Joanie to get help with materials that are too hard.

FIGURE 5-5   Example of time sampling

Observing Bullying Behavior

*O*scar enjoys teasing his fellow first-graders and challenging them to a fight. Although he usually picks on other boys in his own classroom, his teacher, Mary Oltorf, has been getting complaints from other teachers. Mary decides to observe how often Oscar exhibits this kind of behavior. While supervising her class during recess, she records how often Oscar bullies other children. Each time Oscar uses an aggressive or teasing behavior, she marks down the time that it occurred and the behavior used. At the end of the recess period, she evaluates the frequency of Oscar's behavior and finds that he disturbed children five times during the play period. After making these observed time recordings every day for a week, she and the other teachers determine that Oscar bullies other children regularly and plans how to intervene and guide Oscar to more acceptable play behaviors. Mary found that she was vaguely aware that Oscar upset other children, but until she made a timed observation, she was not aware of how serious the problem was for Oscar and the other children on the playground.

In the example described, the teacher did not observe Oscar at regular time intervals as shown in Figure 5-6. Instead, she marked the times that the targeted behavior occurred during the recess period each day. Nevertheless, she was able to record the frequency of Oscar's bullying behavior for a designated period of time.

Child Name(s): <u>Tamika</u>
Age: <u>4</u>
Location: <u>May's Child Enrichment Center</u>
Date and Time: <u>2/4   2:30–3:30</u>
Observer: <u>Marcy</u>
Type of Development Observed: <u>Social/Emotional</u>
   Tamika uses frequent hitting behavior

Time	Antecedent Event	Behavior	Consequent Event
2:41	Tamika and Rosie are eating a snack. Rosie takes part of Tamika's cracker.	Tamika hits Rosie.	Rosie calls to the teacher.
3:20	John is looking at a book in the Library Center. Tamika asks for the book. John refuses.	Tamika grabs the book and hits John.	John hits back and takes back the book. Tamika gets another book and sits down.

FIGURE 5-6   Example of event sampling

Event Sampling

Event sampling is used instead of time sampling when a behavior tends to occur in a particular setting, rather than during a predictable time period. The behavior may occur at odd times or infrequently; event sampling is commonly used to discover its causes or results. The observer determines when the behavior is likely to occur and waits for it to take place. The drawback of this method is that if the event does not occur readily, the observer's time will be wasted.

Because event sampling is a cause-and-effect type of observation, the observer is looking for clues that will help solve the child's problem. Bell and Low (1977) use *ABC analysis* with the observed incident to understand the cause of the behavior. *A* is the antecedent event, *B* is the target behavior, and *C* is the consequent event. Using ABC analysis with event sampling permits the observer to learn how to address the problem with the child. Figure 5-6 is an example of event sampling with ABC analysis to interpret the incident. Because event sampling is used typically for inappropriate behaviors, its primary usefulness is to determine the cause of the behavior and to address the problem. For example, Sheila, age 4, frequently approached the teacher on the playground because she had "nothing to do." The teacher assumed Sheila just wanted attention until she observed Sheila's play using the ABC process and realized that she approached the teacher after being rejected by her playmates. Moreover, the other girls had noticed that Sheila "tattled" to the teacher and enjoyed the success of their actions. By probing the cause of Sheila's difficulty in group play, the teacher realized that both Sheila and the other playmates needed to change their behaviors. She helped Sheila learn acceptable ways to be a part of the play group. At the same time, the other girls were redirected to more positive interactions with Sheila.

Figure 5-7 is an observation form that is adaptable to various types of observations. The summary of important behaviors at the bottom of the page can be expanded into a narrative report if desired. Narrative reports will be discussed in chapter 10.

Advantages and Disadvantages of Using Event Sampling

Like the time sampling observation, event sampling focuses on a particular purpose: to find out why a child uses a particular behavior. The teacher focuses on what triggers the behavior rather than on all behaviors. The teacher is able to anticipate when a behavior occurs and observe why it occurs. A disadvantage is that the targeted behavior may be difficult to anticipate and the time spent observing could be used for another purpose.

Checklists and Rating Scales

Although chapter 6 is devoted to checklists and rating scales, it is useful to include them in this discussion of observation techniques. A **checklist** is a list of sequential behaviors arranged in a system of categories. The observer can use the checklist to determine whether the child exhibits the behaviors or skills listed. The checklist is useful when many behaviors are to be observed. It can also be used fairly quickly and easily.

Name _____

Date _____

Time _____

Location _____

Child(ren) Observed _____

_____

Age _____

Type of Development Observed: _____

Type of Observation Used: _____

Purposes of Observation:

1.

2.

3.

Questions Answered:

1.

2.

3.

Description of Observation (Anecdotal, Time Sampling, Running Record,
        Event Sampling):

Summary of Important Behaviors Recorded and Comments:

FIGURE 5-7   Sample observation form

The **rating scale** provides a means to determine the degree to which the child exhibits a behavior or the quality of that behavior. Each trait is rated on a continuum, allowing the observer to decide where the child fits on the scale. Rating scales are helpful when the teacher needs to evaluate a wide range of behaviors at one time. For example, a rating scale of social skills might be used to record social behaviors not yet exhibited by a child in conjunction with an observation of social play. A checklist of independent work behaviors might be used during an observation of children in the classroom to identify problematic behaviors, such as attention seeking or actions used to delay completing assigned work.

Observations and Technology

In each of the types of observations discussed in this chapter, suggestions have been offered for how observations can be recorded and analyzed. With the constant evolution of new technologies, much of the observation results can be stored in an electronic form. Notebook computers are becoming smaller in size and lighter in weight. It is easier to keep such a device close at hand to record information. Observation forms can be transferred to a small computer with entries quickly typed in.

Taping observations can be a useful tool to record activities observed during an observation. Audiotapes are helpful when children's language is important to the observation. Instead of trying to record what children say, the observer can use the tape recorder to document the language used. Later, the tape can be reviewed to analyze children's conversations.

Videotapes can also be helpful to augment an observation. Although the observer can record significant events during the observation, the videotape can provide opportunities for further study and analysis after the observation has been completed. It can also help in interpretation and analysis when several observers are working together. Digital cameras are especially useful in displaying results of an observation for teachers and children to share together. This is an immediate response to observations that can then be printed out in a more permanent form for future use.

A newer electronic device is the digital whiteboard. The whiteboard is a large interactive display screen that can be connected to a computer or projector. The teacher can project observation information to share with parents and other teachers. Photo documentation can be displayed as well. The teacher can use a finger or digital pen to write or draw on the screen. Information displayed on the screen can be saved in the computer (Lisenbee, 2009).

Observing Development

Young children develop rapidly. At this time, we need to consider the meaning of development in more detail. Development is continuous and sequential and involves change over time.

Development can be defined, in part, as the process of change in an individual over time. As the individual ages, certain changes take place. Development is thus affected by the child's chronological age, rate of maturation, and individual experiences.

Children of the same chronological age are not necessarily at the same stage or level of development, possibly because they mature at different rates and have different experiences and opportunities. The child who has many opportunities to climb, run, and jump in outdoor play may demonstrate advanced motor development skills, compared to the child who spends most play periods indoors.

Developmental change can be both quantitative and qualitative. Physical growth is quantitative and cumulative. New physical skills are added to those already present. Developmental change can also be qualitative. When changes in psychological characteristics such as speech, emotions, or intelligence occur, development is reorganized at a higher level.

Development is characterized as continuous. The individual is constantly changing. In quantitative change, the individual is continually adding new skills or abilities. In qualitative change, the individual is incorporating new development with existing characteristics to create more sophisticated psychological traits.

Finally, development is sequential. Each individual develops at a different rate; however, the sequence or pattern of development is the same. All children move through stages of development in the same sequence, the characteristics of which are described by Bentzen (1997) as follows:

1. Stages or steps in development do not vary. Children do not skip a stage of development.
2. Children progress through the stages in the same order.
3. All children, regardless of cultural or social differences, progress through the stages in the same order. The stages are universal. (p. 21)

Physical Development

Preschool children are in the most important period of physical and motor development. Beginning with babies, who are in the initial stages of learning to control their bodies, physical development is rapid and continues into the primary school years.

Observations of physical development focus on both types of motor development: gross- and fine-motor skills. *Gross-motor skills* involve the movements and abilities of the large muscles of the body in physical activities. Gross-motor development includes locomotor dexterity movements that permit the child to move about in some manner, such as jumping, hopping, running, and climbing. This basic list was extended (Jambor, 1990) to include rolling, creeping, crawling, stepping up and down, bouncing, hurdling, pumping a swing, galloping, and skipping. In the preschool years, gross-motor skills advance from riding a tricycle to a bicycle. Some older preschoolers are able to roller-skate and kick a soccer ball (Johnson, 1998).

Fine-motor skills involve the body's small muscles, specifically the hands and fingers. Preschool children gain more control of finger movement, which allows them to become more proficient in using materials that require grasping and manipulating. These skills are used for eating, dressing, writing, using small construction toys, and performing other tasks. Preschool children learn to work with puzzles; cut with scissors; use brushes, pens, pencils, and markers; and manipulate small blocks, counters, and modeling clay. Fine-motor skills emerge after gross-motor skills have been mastered.

Assessing physical development through observation.

Purposes for Observing Physical Development

Physical development is observed for the following reasons:

1. To learn how children develop gross- and fine-motor skills
2. To become familiar with the kinds of physical activities young children engage in as they practice the use of gross- and fine-motor skills
3. To become familiar with individual differences in physical development

Questions Answered by Observation of Physical Development

Physical development is observed to answer the following questions:

1. Observe a child on the playground. What gross-motor movements can you record?
2. What types of large-motor activities does the child enjoy using play equipment?
3. Observe a child working or playing in activity centers in the classroom. What kinds of fine-motor movements can you record?
4. Observe two children engaged in art activities. Can you see differences in fine-motor development and dexterity? Describe them.

Social and Emotional Development

Social development and emotional development are significant areas of development during the preschool years. In this period, the child moves from egocentricity to social interaction with others. When a child is able to use social behaviors, he or she influences others and is influenced by them. As children interact in various contexts, they develop and expand their repertoire of social skills.

Emotional development parallels and affects social development. The preschool child refines behaviors as he or she experiences such emotions as happiness, anger, joy, jealousy, and fear. The most common emotions in preschool children are aggression, dependency, and fear (Bentzen, 1997). *Aggression* is a behavior intended to hurt another person or property. *Dependency* causes such behaviors as clinging; seeking approval, assistance, and reassurance; and demands for attention. *Fear* includes behaviors such as crying and avoiding the feared situation.

Important characteristics of social and emotional development are self-concept, self-esteem, and self-regulation of emotions. In self-concept, young children develop awareness that they are different from other children and have individual characteristics that are defined by mastery of skills and competencies (Berger, 2000; Berk, 2001).

Self-regulation of emotions results when children develop an awareness of their feelings and can initiate behaviors that permit them to cope. Self-esteem emerges when children begin to make judgments about their own worth and competencies. They feel they are liked or disliked depending on how well they can do things and are influenced by parental and peer approval or disapproval. They translate accomplishments and new skills into positive or negative feelings about themselves.

Purposes for Observing Social and Emotional Development

Social and emotional development is observed for the following reasons:

1. To learn how children develop social skills
2. To become familiar with how children learn about social interactions
3. To understand how children differ in social skill development
4. To become familiar with the ways preschool children handle their emotions
5. To be aware of differences in children's emotional behaviors and responses

Questions Answered by Observations of Social and Emotional Development

Social and emotional development are observed to answer the following questions:

1. How has a child demonstrated social awareness and prosocial skills?
2. How do children develop leadership skills? Observe a child who is able to lead peers in play and describe how that role was initiated.
3. How does the child resolve conflict? Observe children dealing with a problem and describe how the conflict was handled.
4. How do children use and handle aggressive behavior? Observe a child who is behaving aggressively. How does this child use aggression and what is the response of the victim?
5. What kinds of events trigger dependence or fear? Observe a child who has encountered either situation and describe how the child reacts.

Cognitive Development

Cognitive development, which stems from mental functioning, is concerned with how the child learns about and understands the world. Cognitive abilities develop as the child interacts with the environment. Our descriptions of cognitive development are derived largely from Piaget's theory of development.

Piaget described cognitive development in terms of stages. The quality of the child's thinking progresses as the child moves through the stages. The infant is in the sensorimotor stage, which lasts until about age 18 months. During this stage, intellectual growth occurs through the senses and innate reflexive actions. In the latter part of the sensorimotor stage, symbolic thought develops, which is characterized by improved memory.

Between ages 2 and 6, the child moves through the preoperational stage. In this stage, the ability to use language is developed. The child is egocentric, unable to view another person's perspective. Thinking is bounded by perception. Later, when the child reaches the stage of concrete operations, he or she is able to move beyond perceptual thinking. Cognitive abilities become qualitatively different. The child is now able to grasp concepts such as classification, seriation, one-to-one correspondence, and causality because he or she has attained conservation.

The child's use of mental processes to understand knowledge develops gradually, and cognitive abilities evolve over a long period of time. Piaget attributed cognitive development to maturity, experiences, and social transmission. Therefore, the child's family, environment, and opportunities for experiences affect the development of cognitive abilities. Knowledge is reconstructed as the child organizes and restructures experiences to refine and expand his or her own understanding.

Purposes for Observing Cognitive Development

Cognitive development is observed for the following reasons:

1. To understand how children use their cognitive abilities to learn
2. To understand the differences in children's cognitive styles
3. To become familiar with how children develop the ability to use classification, seriation, and one-to-one correspondence
4. To understand how the child uses play and interaction with materials to extend his or her cognitive abilities
5. To become familiar with how children think and what they are capable of learning
6. To evaluate what children have learned

Questions Answered by Observation of Cognitive Development

Cognitive development is observed to answer the following questions:

1. How is the child's learning affected by cognitive abilities? Observe two children and compare how they address an activity that requires solving a problem.
2. How does the child use emerging cognitive abilities? Find examples of children using conservation, one-to-one correspondence, or seriation and describe their activities.

3. How do children differ in cognitive development and cognitive characteristics? Observe two children who seem to have different levels of cognition and compare how they work with drawings, work a puzzle, or make a construction.

4. How do classroom experiences affect opportunities for cognitive development? Study learning centers in a preschool classroom and describe opportunities for learning.

5. How is a child's cognitive knowledge demonstrated nonverbally? Observe a child and describe how the child's actions reveal that learning is occurring or being applied to an activity.

Language Development

Acquisition of language is a major accomplishment of children during the preschool and primary-grade years. During the first 8 years of life, the child rapidly acquires vocabulary, grammar, and syntax. As in other types of development, the child's use of language changes, increases, and is refined over a period of time.

Whereas babies begin using speech as single utterances, toddlers and preschoolers expand their repertoire into two words, three words, and increasingly complex statements. As the child's ability to use language expands to include questions and other grammatical elements, the child uses trial and error to more closely approximate the syntax and grammar of adult speech.

Language development is also related to cognitive development. When the child's thinking is egocentric, his or her language reflects this pattern. The egocentric child talks to herself and does not use language to communicate with other children. The child who is shedding egocentric thinking uses socialized speech to communicate with others. He or she not only shares conversations with peers and adults, but also listens and responds to what others are saying.

During the preschool years, young children learn about 10,000 words. Concurrent with acquisition of a remarkable number of words, they learn the rules of their language: morphology rules, syntax rules, and semantic rules. Morphology and syntax rules relate to understanding the sounds and grammar of language; semantic rules explain vocabulary and meaning development.

Preschool children also learn the rules of conversation, or the pragmatics of language. The ability to participate in a conversation develops at an early age and is extended and refined with expanded language abilities and experiences with conversations. By age 4, preschool children understand how to carry on a conversation in their language community and culture.

Purposes for Observing Language Development

Language development is observed for the following reasons:

1. To become aware of the child's ability to use language to communicate
2. To understand the difference between egocentric and socialized speech
3. To learn how the child uses syntax, grammar, and vocabulary in the process of expanding and refining his or her language

4. To become aware of differences in language development among individual children, particularly children from homes where another language or dialect is spoken

5. To determine how children are progressing in learning English as their second language and to determine their individual needs for language experiences

6. To determine a child's dominant language when placed in a bilingual program (Which language does the child use in the classroom, with friends at school, and at home?)

Questions Answered by Observation of Language Development

Language development is observed to answer the following questions:

1. How does the child use language to communicate? Describe how two different children use language to communicate with a friend.

2. When do children tend to use egocentric speech? Socialized speech? Describe events when children use each type.

3. What can be observed about the child's use of sentence structure? Record several of a child's utterances and describe the sentence structure used.

4. How can errors in the use of language reveal the child's progress in refining language? Record some child conversations. Describe utterances that reveal an error that will later be expressed correctly.

Advantages and Disadvantages of Using Observation for Assessment

Observation is a valuable evaluation tool. Teachers may use it to gather the kind of information that may not be available from structured methods of measurement.

When observed, children are engaged in daily activities that are a natural part of the classroom routine. The observer sees the typical ways children respond to learning tasks, play activities, and individual and group lessons. The observer can notice the child's behaviors and the background factors that influence the behaviors.

Learning can also be evaluated by observation. The teacher can observe the child's responses in a group during a lesson or while the child engages in exploration with construction materials. Areas of development such as gross-motor skills can be observed on the playground; language skills can be noted by listening to the language of two children in the art center.

An advantage of observation is that the observer can focus on the behavior or information that is needed. If a child is exhibiting aggression, the observer can focus on aggressive incidents to help the child to use more appropriate behaviors in interactions with other children. If a child is beginning to use prosocial skills more effectively, the teacher can observe group interactions and encourage the child to continue to improve.

Although observation allows one to concentrate on specific behaviors, it can also cause difficulties. The observer can miss details that make a significant difference in the quality of the data gathered. Because many incidents and behaviors may occur during the observation, the danger is that the observer may focus on the wrong behaviors. Or the observer may become less attentive during the observation period, resulting in variations in the information obtained (Webb et al., 1966).

Observer bias is another disadvantage. If the observer has preconceived notions about how the child behaves or performs, these ideas can affect the observer's interpretation of the information obtained from watching the child.

Observations can be misleading when the incident observed is taken out of context. Although an observed behavior is often brief, it must be understood in context. A frequent mistake of inexperienced observers is to interpret a single incident as a common occurrence. For example, the observer who witnesses a teacher losing patience with a child may interpret the incident as that teacher's normal behavior. In reality, however, this behavior may be rare. The presence of the observer can also affect children's behavior. Because children are aware that they are being watched, their behaviors may not be typical. As a result, the validity of the observation may be doubtful (Webb et al., 1966).

Observation Guidelines

For college students and teachers who have limited experience in conducting observations or wish to improve their observation skills, certain guidelines are now presented. The student seeking a site for observation needs to know how to go about finding a school or early childhood center and how to observe effectively once it has been selected. Classroom teachers have a ready site in their own classroom or in the classroom of a colleague. However, teachers may want to observe a different type of program and will need to visit a different setting. Although observation is valuable for many reasons, it is usually the least used by teachers because of time constraints. Therefore, new teachers may need specific training on how to accomplish successful observation times.

Determining the Observation Site

The observation site depends on the type of observation to be done. First, the observer must determine the purpose of the observation. He or she will want to know that children at the school or early childhood center engage in the activities of interest to the observer. For example, if the observer wishes to see activities typical of a Montessori classroom, it would be wise to find out whether these activities will be taking place during the observation period. Once the purpose of the observation has been determined, the observer must decide on an optimum location. If the objective is to learn about creativity in the young child, it is frustrating to spend time in a program in which art experiences are limited or infrequent. Likewise, if the purpose is to observe behaviors in a child-centered environment, it would be inappropriate to visit a structured program directed by the teacher.

Once the center or school has been selected, the observer should contact it ahead of time. Although many settings welcome observers on a walk-in basis, most early childhood programs request or require advance notification. Some settings do not allow observers or schedule them in ways designed to protect children from interruptions. Some schools allow observations on certain days. Others wish to be contacted well in advance because many people wish to observe their program. Many child-care centers schedule field trips frequently and wish to avoid inconveniencing their observers. Whatever the reason, it is best to contact the observation site before scheduling the observation.

Observer Behaviors During the Observation Visit

The observer is a guest of the center or school. Although the opportunity to study the children is important, it is also important to avoid disrupting activities in progress. The observer may want to share the purpose of the observation with staff members or the teacher in the classroom being visited. In addition, the observer should conduct the observation in a manner that is compatible with the teacher's style of leadership in the type of program being observed. For example, Montessori schools frequently restrict visitors to certain areas of the classroom and may discourage any interaction with the children. Another school or program may encourage the observer to talk to the children or to take part in their activities.

Most schools and preschool centers require that all who will be working in the building undergo a background check. In addition, observers are required to check in at the office when arriving at the location to be observed. Identification badges are usually required so that the observer's approved presence is readily apparent to teachers and other staff members.

In most cases, the observer should be unobtrusive. Because children are sensitive to the presence of visitors and may alter their behaviors when a stranger is in the room, observers can minimize such changes by drawing as little attention to their presence as possible. Observers may seat themselves in a position that does not draw the children's attention. Sometimes it is helpful to avoid looking at the children for a few minutes, until they become acclimated. Postponing the writing of observation notes for a few minutes may also help prevent disruption.

Dress can make a difference. Observers dressed in simple clothing of one color rather than bright garments with bold patterns are less likely to draw undue attention to their presence. Dress should also be appropriate. Clothing that is too casual may be offensive to the adults in the early childhood center. Observers should err on the side of being dressed too formally, rather than in an unprofessional manner (Irwin & Bushnell, 1980).

Ethics During the Observation Visit

Observers must be alert to the proper way to use the information gathered during an observation. The privacy of the children, the children's families, and school staff members must be considered. When individual children are observed, only the child's first name should be used. Information from any observation should be considered confidential and safeguarded from casual perusal by others. The child

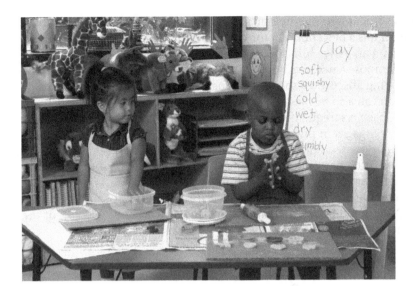

Observations can reveal information about different domains of development.

should not be discussed in an unprofessional manner with other observers, school staff members, or outsiders. It may be necessary to obtain permission from the child's family prior to making an observation. If this is necessary, the observer should acquire the necessary forms and have them sent to the parents for their approval prior to conducting any observations.

Teachers in training and professional teachers should be very aware of the professional ethics of the profession. The NAEYC position statement or *NAEYC Code of Ethical Conduct and Statement of Commitment* (2005) is a comprehensive document that serves as a professional guide for ethical behavior. It has sections on ethical responsibilities to children, to families, to colleagues, and to community and society. Each section has description of principles that give examples of indicators for that section. Individuals engaged in conducting observations can find many items that refer to ethical behaviors.

Avoiding Personal Bias

Personal bias can affect the observer's reaction to and report of an observation. If observers are aware of how their background and previous experiences can influence their report, they can avoid using personal opinion when analyzing the data collected during an observation.

One cause of observer bias is differences in value systems. It is easy to apply one's own value system when observing in a school. For example, a middle-class observer may misunderstand the nature of aggression exhibited by young children in an inner-city school. It is also possible to impose personal values on the language of a child from a home where cursing is a common form of communication. The observer needs to be aware of such possible biases and avoid them when interpreting observational information.

The observer's reaction to the site can also distort his or her use of observational data. Each observer has a perception of the characteristics of a "good" school or center. When observing an early childhood program that does not fit this definition, the observer may impose a negative interpretation on the information gathered. The reaction to the setting affects how the observer perceives the behaviors observed.

An observation can also be biased by the time of the observation or by the briefness of the visit. Observers frequently react to a teacher's behavior and conclude that the teacher always engages in practices that the observer considers inappropriate. Observers need to understand that what they see during a short visit may give them an incomplete, distorted perception of the teacher or setting. The observer would have to make many visits during different times of the day over a long period of time before being able to draw conclusions about the quality of teaching or the environment. One or two brief observations provide only a small glimpse of the nature of the teacher and the classroom visited.

Summary

Although standardized tests are used to evaluate children's learning, informal strategies are also essential, particularly for use by classroom teachers. They provide a variety of evaluation methods by which teachers can acquire comprehensive information about their students' development and learning.

Observation is used to assess learning and to gather information regarding children's development. Because young children cannot demonstrate knowledge in a written test, teachers of preschool children use observation to learn about children's development, as well as about the knowledge the children have acquired.

Observations are of several types, each with a specific purpose. Observers can use anecdotal records, running records, time sampling, event sampling, and checklists and rating scales to gather information about young children. Another type of observation is documentation. In this approach the teacher follows the children's lead in what they are doing, how they are interacting, and what they are gaining from the experience. In this case the teacher does not predetermine what is to be observed but observes what is occurring with the children.

REVIEW QUESTIONS

1. Why is it important to use informal assessment methods, particularly with preschool and primary-grade children?

2. How do the purposes of informal assessment differ from the purposes of standardized testing?

3. Do the advantages of informal assessment strategies outweigh the disadvantages? Why or why not?

4. Describe some ways that teachers can use informal assessment strategies for instructional planning.

5. What is diagnostic evaluation?

6. What are the differences between formative and summative assessment?

7. Why do informal assessments produce immediate results, compared with standardized test results?

8. How may informal assessments be misused in elementary schools?

9. How may teachers be unaware of the proper use of formal and informal assessments?

10. Describe some purposes of using observation techniques with preschool and school-age children.
11. Why is observation of development systematic and specific?
12. Explain the purposes of the different types of observations: (a) anecdotal records, (b) running records, (c) specimen records, (d) time sampling, (e) event sampling, and (f) checklists and rating scales. What is unique about specimen records?
13. How are other types of development related to the child's cognitive development?
14. How does egocentrism affect cognitive, social, and language development?
15. How can an observer's experience and skills affect the quality of the information gained from observing young children?

$\mathcal{S}$UGGESTED ACTIVITY

1. Conduct three observations of development. Use a different category of development for each observation. Use a different type of observation for each, selected from anecdotal records, running records, time sampling, and event sampling. Use an adaptation of the sample observation form in Figure 5-7 for each of the three observations.

$\mathcal{K}$EY TERMS

anecdotal record
checklist
event sampling
formative evaluation
play-based assessment

rating scale
running record
summative evaluation
time sampling

$\mathcal{S}$ELECTED WEB SITES

Center for Effective Collaboration and Practice
Functional Behavioral Assessment
http://Cecp.air.org/fba

Pearson Achievement Solutions
http://www.pearsonachievementsolutions.com/

National Association for the Education of Young Children
http://www.naeyc.org

$\mathcal{R}$EFERENCES

Beaty, J. J. (2006). *Observing development of the young child* (6th ed.). Upper Saddle River, NJ: Merrill/Prentice Hall.

Bell, D., & Low, R. M. (1977). *Observing and recording children's behavior.* Richland, WA: Performance Associates.

Bentzen, W. R. (1997). *Seeing young children: A guide to observing and recording behavior.* Albany, NY: Delmar.

Bergen, D. (1994). *Assessment methods for infants and toddlers.* New York: Teachers College Press.

Berger, K. S. (2000). *The developing person through childhood* (2nd ed.). New York: Worth.

Berk, L. E. (2001). *Infants, children, and adolescents* (3rd ed.). Boston: Allyn & Bacon.

Bernauer, J. A., & Cress, K. (1997). How school communities can help redefine accountability assessment. *Phi Delta Kappan, 79,* 71–75.

Billman, J., & Sherman, J. A. (1997). *Observation and participation in early childhood settings.* Boston: Allyn & Bacon.

Bodrova, E., & Leong, D. J. (2007). *Tools of the mind: The Vygotskian approach to early childhood education* (2nd ed.). Upper Saddle River, NJ: Merrill/Prentice Hall.

Brookes Publishing. (2002, July). *Using transdisciplinary play-based assessment: Structuring a play sessions.* Retrieved October 20, 2009, from http://www.brookespublishing.com/email/archive . . . july02EC4.htm

Center for Effective Collaboration and Practice (2001). *Functional Behavioral Assessment.* Retrieved October 7, 2009, from http://Cecp.air.org/fba

Clark-Stewart, A. (1987). Predicting child development from child care forms and features: The Chicago study. In D. A. Phillips (Ed.), *Quality in child care: What does research tell us?* (pp. 21–41). Washington, DC: National Association for the Education of Young Children.

Clay, M. (1993). *An observation survey of early literacy achievement.* Portsmouth, NH: Heinemann.

Cohen, D. H., Stern, V., & Balaban, N. (1997). *Observing and recording the behavior of young children* (4th ed.). New York: Teachers College Press.

Curtis, D. (2006, November/December). No ordinary moments: Using observations with toddlers to invite further engagement. *Exchange, 172,* 36–40.

Dossey, J. A., Mullis, I. V. S., Lindquist, M. M., & Chambers, D. L. (1988). *The mathematics report card: Are we measuring up?* Princeton, NJ: Educational Testing Service.

Fewell, R., & Glick, M. (1998). The role of play in assessment. In D. Fromberg & D. Bergen (Eds.), *Play from birth to twelve and beyond* (pp. 202–207). New York: Garland.

Fields, M. V., & Spangler, K. L. (2000). *Let's begin reading right: A developmental approach to emergent literacy* (4th ed.). Upper Saddle River, NJ: Merrill/Prentice Hall.

Foley, G. M. (1992). Portrait of the arena evaluation: Assessment in the transdisciplinary approach. In E. D. Gibbs & D. M. Teti (Eds.), *Interdisciplinary assessment of infants: A guide for early intervention professionals* (pp. 271–286). Baltimore: Brookes.

Goodwin, W. L., & Driscoll, L. A. (1980). *Handbook for measurement and evaluation in early childhood education.* San Francisco: Jossey-Bass.

Goodwin, W. L., & Goodwin, L. D. (1993). Young children and measurement: Standardized and nonstandardized instruments in early childhood education. In B. Spodek (Ed.), *Handbook of research on the education of young children* (pp. 441–463). New York: Macmillan.

Goodwin, W. L., & Goodwin, L. D. (1997). Using standardized measures for evaluating young children's learning. In B. Spodek & O. N. Saracho (Eds.), *Issues in early childhood educational assessment and evaluation* (pp. 92–107). New York: Teachers College Press.

Harms, T., Clifford, R. M., & Cryer, D. (1998). *Early Childhood Environment Rating Scale—Revised.* New York: Teachers College Press.

Harrington, H. L., Meisels, S. J., McMahon, P., Dichtelmiller, M. L., & Jablon, J. R. (1997). *Observing, documenting, and assessing learning: The work sampling system handbook for teacher educators.* Ann Arbor, MI: Rebus.

Helm, J. H., Beneke, S., & Steinheimer, K. (2007). *Windows on learning: Documenting young children's work* (2nd ed.). New York: Teachers College Press.

High/Scope Educational Research Foundation. (2003). *Preschool Child Observation Record.* Ypsilanti, MI: Author.

Irwin, D. M., & Bushnell, M. M. (1980). *Observational strategies for child study.* New York: Holt, Rinehart & Winston.

Jambor, T. (1990). Promoting perceptual–motor development in young children's play. In S. C. Wortham & J. L. Frost (Eds.), *Playgrounds for young children: National survey and perspectives* (pp. 147–166). Reston, VA: American Alliance for Health, Physical Education, Recreation, and Dance.

Johnson, J. E. (1998). Play development from ages four to eight. In D. Fromberg & D. Bergen (Eds.), *Play from birth to twelve and beyond* (pp. 146–153). New York: Garland.

Kamii, C. (1985a). Leading primary education toward excellence: Beyond worksheets and drill. *Young Children, 40,* 3–9.

Kamii, C. (1985b). *Young children reinvent arithmetic.* New York: Teachers College Press.

Kamii, C., & Kamii, M. (1990). Negative effects of achievement testing in mathematics. In C. Kamii (Ed.), *Achievement testing in the early grades: The games grown-ups play* (pp. 135–145). Washington, DC: National Association for the Education of Young Children.

Linder, T. W. (1993). *Transdisciplinary play-based assessment (TPBA): A functional approach to working with young children* (Rev. ed.). Baltimore: Brookes.

Linder, T. W. (1998). *Transdisciplinary play based assessment* (Rev. ed.). Baltimore: Brookes.

Linn, R. L., & Gronlund, N. E. (2000). *Measurement and assessment in teaching* (8th ed.). Upper Saddle River, NJ: Merrill/Prentice Hall.

Lisenbee, P. (2009, November). Whiteboards and Websites. *Young Children, 64,* 92–95.

MacDonald, B. (2006, November/December). Observation—The path to documentation. *Exchange, 172,* 45–49.

Martin, S. (1994). *Take a look: Observation and portfolio assessment in early childhood.* Don Mills, Ontario: Addison-Wesley.

Miller, J. (n.d.). *Conducting a functional behavioral assessment. Teachnology tutorials* Retrieved October 7, 2009, from http://www.teach-nology.com/tutorials/teaching/fba/

National Association for the Education of Young Children. (2005). *NAEYC code of ethical conduct and statement of commitment. A position statement of the National Association for the Education of Young Children.* Washington, DC: Author.

Newman, S. B., Copple, C., & Bredekamp, S. (2000). *Learning to read and write.* Washington, DC: National Association for the Education of Young Children.

Owocki, G. (2001). *Make way for literacy.* Portsmouth, NH: Heinemann.

Pelo, A. (2006, November/December). Growing a culture of inquiry: Observation as professional development. *Exchange, 172,* 50–53.

Popham, W. J. (1999). Why standardized tests don't measure educational quality. *Educational Leadership, 56,* 8–16.

Schickedanz, J. A. (1989). The place of specific skills in preschool and kindergarten. In D. S. Strickland & L. M. Morrow (Eds.), *Emerging literacy: Young children learn to read and write* (pp. 96–106). Newark, DE: International Reading Association.

Segal, M., & Webber, N. T. (1996). Nonstructured play observations: Guidelines, benefits, and caveats. In S. J. Meisels & E. Fenichel (Eds.), *New visions for the developmental assessment of infants and young children* (pp. 207–230). Washington, DC: Zero to Three: National Center for Infants, Toddlers, and Families.

Shepard, L. A. (2000). The role of assessment in a learning culture. *Educational Researcher, 29,* 4–14.

Seitz, H. (2008, March). The power of documentation in the early childhood classroom. *Young Children, 63,* 88–93.

Smith, J. K. (1990). Measurement issues in early literacy assessment. In L. M. Morrow & J. K. Smith (Eds.), *Assessment for instruction in early literacy* (pp. 62–74). Upper Saddle River, NJ: Prentice Hall.

Sugai, G., Horner, R. H., Dunlap, G., Hieneman, M., Lewis, T. J., Nelson, C. M., Scott, T., Liaupsin, C., Sailor, W., Turnbull, H. R., Wickhom, D., Ruef, M., & Wilcox, B. (1999). *Applying positive behavioral support and functional behavioral assessment in schools.* Technical Assistance Guide I, Version 1.4.4. Washington, DC: U. S. Department of Special Education.

Sulzby, E. (1990). Assessment of writing and children's language when writing. In L. M. Morrow & J. K. Smith (Eds.), *Assessment for instruction in early literacy* (pp. 83–109). Upper Saddle River, NJ: Prentice Hall.

Sulzby, E. (1993). *Teacher's guide to evaluation: Assessment handbook.* Glenview, IL: Scott, Foresman.

Taylor, K., & Walton, S. (1997). Co-opting standardized tests in the service of learning. *Phi Delta Kappan, 79,* 66–70.

Teale, W. H. (1988). Developmentally appropriate assessment of reading and writing in the early childhood classroom. *Elementary School Journal, 89,* 173–183.

Teale, W. H. (1990). The promise and challenge of informal assessment in early literacy. In L. M. Morrow & J. K. Smith (Eds.), *Assessment for instruction in early literacy* (pp. 45–61). Upper Saddle River, NJ: Prentice Hall.

U.S. Department of Education. (2006, September 11). *New No Child Left Behind regulations: Flexibility and accountability for limited English proficient students.* Washington, DC: Author. Retrieved January 29, 2007, from http://www.ed.gov/admins/lead/account/lepfactsheet. html

Valencia, S., & Pearson, P. D. (1987). Reading assessment: Time for a change. *Reading Teacher, 40,* 726–732.

Vygotsky, L. S. (1978). *Mind and society: The development of higher mental processes.* Cambridge, MA: Harvard University Press.

Webb, E. J., Campbell, D. T., Schwartz, R. D., & Sechrest, L. (1966). *Unobtrusive measures.* Chicago: Rand McNally.

Wiggins, G. (1989). Teaching to the (authentic) test. *Educational Leadership, 46,* 41–47.

Wiggins, G. P. (1993). *Assessing student performance.* San Francisco: Jossey-Bass.

Wiggins, G. P. (1998). *Educative assessment.* San Francisco: Jossey-Bass.

Winograd, P., & Webb, K. S. (1994). Impact on curriculum and instruction reform. In T. Guskey (Ed.), *High stakes performance assessment: Perspectives on Kentucky's educational reform* (pp. 19–36). Thousand Oaks, CA: Corwin Press.

Checklists, Rating Scales, and Rubrics

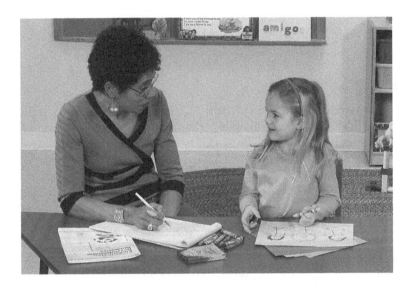

Chapter Objectives

As a result of reading this chapter, you will be able to

1. Describe the purposes of using checklists for informal assessment
2. Explain how developmental checklists are used with preschool children
3. Explain the differences between the uses of checklists with preschool and primary-grade children
4. Identify the four basic steps in checklist design
5. Discuss the advantages and disadvantages of using checklists for informal assessment
6. Describe the purposes of using rating scales for informal evaluation
7. Discuss the advantages and disadvantages of using rating scales
8. Describe the purposes of using rubrics for informal evaluation
9. Discuss how rubrics are used with preschool and primary-grade children
10. Discuss how rubrics are designed
11. Discuss the advantages and disadvantages of using rubrics

In chapter 5, we considered the topic of classroom assessment strategies. The purposes of classroom assessments were discussed, as well as their strengths and weaknesses. One assessment strategy—observation—was described in detail. In this chapter, we discuss another type of evaluation strategy that involves the use of teacher-designed instruments: checklists, rating scales, and rubrics. Because checklists are used more extensively than rating scales by infant–toddler, early childhood, and primary school teachers, we discuss them first. A description of rating scales follows so that the reader can understand how they are designed and used and how they differ from checklists. Rubrics are used most commonly with performance assessments. They will be discussed in that context.

Checklists

Purposes of Checklists

Checklists are made from a collection of learning objectives or indicators of development. The lists of items are arranged to give the user an overview of their sequence and of how they relate to each other. The lists of items are then organized into a checklist format so that the teacher can use them for various purposes in the instructional program. Because the checklists are representative of the curriculum for the grade level, they become a framework for assessment and evaluation, instructional planning, record keeping, and communicating with parents about what is being taught and how their child is progressing.

Using Checklists With Infants, Toddlers, and Preschool Children

Children in the years from birth to age 8 move rapidly through different stages of development. Doctors, psychologists, parents, and developmental specialists want to understand and monitor the development of individual children and groups of children. The developmental indicators for children at different stages and ages have been established; lists and checklists of these indicators can be used to monitor development. Many types of professionals use a **developmental checklist** format to evaluate a child's development and record the results.

Developmental checklists are usually organized into categories of development: physical, cognitive, and social. Physical development is frequently organized into fine- and gross-motor skills. Cognitive, or intellectual development might include language development. Some checklists have language development as a separate category. Social development checklists can also be organized to include emotional development and development of social skills.

Preschool teachers use checklists to evaluate and record preschoolers' developmental progress. The individual child's developmental progress provides important clues to the kinds of experiences he or she needs and can enjoy. For instance, the teacher tracks the child's use of fine-motor skills. After the child is able to use the fingers to grasp small objects, cutting activities may be introduced. In language development, the teacher can evaluate the child's speaking vocabulary and use of syntax and thus choose the best stories to read to the child.

Teachers often use checklists to screen children who enter preschool programs or to select children for programs. Developmental or cognitive tasks are used to identify children with special needs. Because these checklists include behaviors that are characteristic of a stage of development, children who do not exhibit these behaviors can be referred for additional screening and testing (Spodek & Saracho, 1994).

Checklists are also used to design learning experiences at the preschool level. The teacher surveys the list of learning objectives appropriate for that age group of children and uses the list to plan learning activities in the classroom. These checklists can be used to assess the child's progress in learning the objectives and to keep records of progress and further instructional needs. When talking to parents about the instructional program, the teacher can discuss what is being taught and how their child is benefiting from the learning experiences.

Using Checklists With School-Age Children

The use of checklists for primary-grade children is very similar to their use with preschool children. In fact, curriculum checklists can be a continuation of those used in the preschool grades. However, there are two differences. First, fewer developmental characteristics are recorded, and cognitive or academic objectives become more important. Second, school-age checklists become more differentiated in areas of learning. Whereas teachers are concerned with motor development, language development, social and emotional development, and cognitive development at the preschool level, at the primary level, curriculum content areas become more important. Thus, with primary-grade checklists, objectives are more likely to be organized in terms of mathematics, language arts, science, social studies, and physical education (Ratcliff, 2001/2002). Checklists that can be used quickly are a particular advantage to classroom teachers because of time restraints in the daily schedule.

Diagnosis of learning strengths and weaknesses in curriculum objectives becomes more important in the primary grades, and assessment of progress in learning may become more precise and segmented. Checklist objectives may appear on report cards as the format for reporting the child's achievement to parents. Likewise, the checklist items may be representative of achievement test objectives, state-mandated objectives, textbook objectives, and locally selected objectives.

Using Checklists to Assess Children With Delays in Development

Checklists can be used with children who have exhibited developmental delay and are served in intervention programs. Children who are English language learners (ELLs) are included in this category. Language assessment is the focus for ELLs children. Checklists can be part of an integrated assessment system that has multiple purposes, including continuous assessment of developmental progress. The components of such a system include tracking the child's growth and development through ongoing assessment, documenting and monitoring child growth for caregivers and other professional staff, and providing a structure for families to develop and monitor goals for their children. Checklists in this context are used with a family portfolio, developmental guidelines and checklists, and summary reports of the child's progress (Meisels, 1996).

How Checklists Are Designed and Used

Checklists of developmental and instructional objectives have been used in education for several decades. When educators and early childhood specialists worked with Head Start and other programs aimed at improving education for special populations of students, they developed outlines of educational objectives to describe the framework of learning that children should experience. Since that time, checklists have been further developed and used at all levels of education. Reading series designed for elementary grades include a scope and sequence of skills, and many school districts have a list of objectives for every course or grade level. The scope of a curriculum is the different categories that are included, while the sequence is the individual objectives that appear under each category. Figure 6-1 is a typical checklist developed by a school district for mathematics at the elementary level.

Curriculum objectives and skills can be developed at a state or national level. The U.S. Department of Education held a reading summit in September 1998 to discuss prevention of reading difficulties in young children. The National Research Council (NRC) undertook a study of research on early reading development to provide suggestions about how to prevent reading problems in young children. Part of its report included accomplishments in reading that might be expected from birth through grade 3. Following is a partial list of second-grade accomplishments suggested by the NRC (Bickart, 1998):

- Reads and comprehends both fiction and nonfiction that is appropriately designed for grade level.
- Accurately decodes orthographically regular multisyllable words and nonsense words (e.g., *capital, Kalamazoo*).
- Uses knowledge of print–sound mappings to sound out unknown words.
- Accurately reads many irregularly spelled words and such spelling patterns as diphthongs, special vowel spellings, and common word endings.
- Shows evidence of expanding language repertory, including increasing use of more formal language registers.
- Reads voluntarily for interest and own purposes.
- Rereads sentences when meaning is not clear.
- Interprets information from diagrams, charts, and graphs.
- Recalls facts and details of texts.
- Reads nonfiction materials for answers to specific questions or for specific purposes.
- Takes part in creative responses to texts such as dramatizations, oral presentations, fantasy play, and so on. (p. 29)

CHECKLIST
LEVEL 1

Name _____   Date _____

Age _____   Math Teacher _____   Unit _____

Advisor _____

Dates	
I	M

NUMERATION

0. Knows vocabulary:
   ___ same   ___ different   ___ more   ___ less   ___ before   ___ after

1. Rote counts:
   __ 1 __ 2 __ 3 __ 4 __ 5 __ 6 __ 7 __ 8 __ 9 __ 10

2. Counts objects:
   __ 1 __ 2 __ 3 __ 4 __ 5 __ 6 __ 7 __ 8 __ 9 __ 10

3. Matches equivalent sets with concrete objects.
4. Reproduces equivalent sets with concrete objects.
5. Matches like pairs
6. Matches unlike pairs
7. Compares nonequivalent sets with concrete objects
8. Reproduces nonequivalent sets with concrete objects
9. Sorts objects using more than one classifying characteristic
10. Matches numerals:
    __ 1 __ 2 __ 3 __ 4 __ 5 __ 6 __ 7 __ 8 __ 9 __ 10

11. Identifies numerals:
    __ 1 __ 2 __ 3 __ 4 __ 5 __ 6 __ 7 __ 8 __ 9 __ 10

12. Constructs sets for numerals:
    __ 1 __ 2 __ 3 __ 4 __ 5

13. Names numerals:
    __ 1 __ 2 __ 3 __ 4 __ 5

MEASUREMENT

A. Linear
   1. Matches objects
      ___ size ___ length ___ width ___ height
   2. Compares objects
      ___ size ___ length ___ width ___ height
   3. Seriates objects
      ___ size ___ length ___ width ___ height

B. Weight
   1. Classifies objects according to weight
      ___ heavy ___ light
   2. Compares objects according to weight
      ___ heavy ___ light
   3. Demonstrates use of balance
   4. Identifies instruments for measuring weight

FIGURE 6-1   Mathematics checklist: Level 1

Preschool developmental checklists and curriculum checklists in the elementary grades are used in the same manner for the same purposes; however, developmental checklists add the developmental dimension to curriculum objectives. Because the young child's developmental level is an important factor in determining the kinds of experiences the teacher will use, our discussion of the purposes of checklists includes the implications of child development during the early childhood years. Those purposes are as follows:

1. To understand development
2. To serve as a framework for curriculum development
3. To assess learning and development

Checklists as a Guide to Understand Development

All developmental checklists are organized to describe different areas of growth, including social, motor, and cognitive development. The checklist items in each area for each age or developmental level indicate how the child is progressing through maturation and experiences. When teachers, caregivers, and parents look at the checklists, they can trace the sequence of development and also be realistic in their expectations for children. Checklists for infant and toddler development are significant because of the rapid pace of development in the first 2 years after birth. Figure 6-2 shows an example of a simple developmental checklist for infants ages 6 to 12 months, while Figure 6-3, the *Infant/Toddler Checklist for Communication and Language Development,* is used to identify infants and toddlers who might have a delay in language development and to monitor changes. *The Work Sampling System: Preschool–4 Developmental Guidelines* (Marsden, Meisels, Jablon, & Dichtelmiller, 2001) provides a checklist for physical development as shown in Figure 6-4. Figure 6-4 also includes some of the expanded explanations of checklist items.

Checklists as a Guide to Develop Curriculum

Because developmental checklists describe all facets of development, they can serve as a guide in planning learning experiences for young children. Curriculum is not necessarily described as content areas such as science, art, or social studies, as these are commonly organized in elementary school; rather, it follows the experiences and opportunities that young children should have in the early childhood years. Thus, teachers and caregivers who study the objectives on the checklists have guides for learning activities that will be appropriate for their children.

Because checklists are organized by developmental level or age, they also serve as a guide for sequencing learning. Teachers can match the experiences they wish to use with the checklist to determine whether they are using the correct level of complexity or difficulty. They can determine what came before in learning or development and what should come next. The story retelling assessment sheet for early childhood classrooms shown in Figure 6-5 includes objectives and skills for retelling stories (Polakowski, 1993). By studying the items on the checklist and the student's level of performance in previous experiences, the teacher can plan for

AGE: 6 TO 12 MONTHS			
PHYSICAL-COGNITIVE DEVELOPMENT	Date	Date	Date
1. Sits alone			
2. Transfers object from one hand to another			
3. Drinks from a cup			
4. Picks up small things with thumb and forefinger			
5. Uncovers hidden toy			
6. Looks at picture book			
7. Holds two toys			
8. Imitates speech sounds			
9. Creeps or gets from one place to another			
10. Attains sitting position independently			
11. Stands holding on			
12. Walks holding on			
13. Drops or places objects into a container			
14. Manipulates objects			
15. Says single words such as "mama" and "dada"			
16. Imitates actions			
17. Attempts self-feeding with a cup and spoon or fingers			
SOCIAL-EMOTIONAL DEVELOPMENT			
1. Shows likes or dislikes of people, objects, places			
2. Plays with image in mirror			
3. Understands "No"			
4. Responds to presence of a new person			
5. Squeals with joy or pleasure			
6. Demostrates anxiety over departure of parents			
7. Enjoys and plays games with others (e.g., "pat-a-cake")			
8. Uses motions or gestures to communicate (holds out arms to be picked up)			

FIGURE 6-2 Wortham developmental checklist: Infants and toddlers, 6 to 12 months

Source: Wortham, Sue C. (2010). *Early childhood curriculum: Developmental bases for learning and teaching* (5th ed.) © 2010, p. 91. Reprinted by permission of Pearson Education, Inc., Upper Saddle River, NJ.

instruction and future activities. Moreover, because the checklist includes kindergarten through second grade, a range of levels of reading and writing ability is accommodated. Teachers can attach samples of the student's work to the checklist for use in a portfolio.

Developmental checklists help teachers and caregivers plan for a balance of activities. With the current emphasis on academic subjects even in preschool programs, teachers feel compelled to develop an instructional program that is limited to readiness for reading, writing, and mathematics. Preschool teachers are caught between the emphasis on "basics" and developmentally appropriate instruction that

CSBS DP Infant-Toddler Checklist

(CSBS DP)

Child's name: **Sharla Thompson**   Date of birth: **(18 months)** Date filled out: _____

Was birth premature? **No**   If yes, how many weeks premature? _____

Filled out by: **Dorothy Cook**   Relationship to child: **Caregiver**

Instructions for caregivers: This Checklist is designed to identify different aspects of development in infants and toddlers. Many behaviors that develop before children talk may indicate whether or not a child will have difficulty learning to talk. This Checklist should be completed by a caregiver when the child is between **6 and 24 months of age** to determine whether a referral for an evaluation is needed. The caregiver may be either a parent or another person who nurtures the child daily. Please check all the choices that best describe your child's behavior. If you are not sure, please choose the closest response based on your experience. **Children at your child's age are not necessarily expected to use all the behaviors listed.**

Emotion and Eye Gaze

1. Do you know when your child is happy and when your child is upset?	☐ Not Yet	☐ Sometimes	☒ Often
2. When your child plays with toys, does he/she look at you to see if you are watching?	☐ Not Yet	☒ Sometimes	☐ Often
3. Does your child smile or laugh while looking at you?	☐ Not Yet	☐ Sometimes	☒ Often
4. When you look at and point to a toy across the room, does your child look at it?	☐ Not Yet	☒ Sometimes	☐ Often

Communication

5. Does your child let you know that he/she needs help or wants an object out of reach?	☐ Not Yet	☒ Sometimes	☐ Often
6. When you are not paying attention to your child, does he/she try to get your attention?	☐ Not Yet	☐ Sometimes	☒ Often
7. Does your child do things just to get you to laugh?	☒ Not Yet	☐ Sometimes	☐ Often
8. Does your child try to get you to notice interesting objects—just to get you to look at the objects, not to get you to do anything with them?	☒ Not Yet	☐ Sometimes	☐ Often

Gestures

9. Does your child pick up objects and give them to you?	☐ Not Yet	☒ Sometimes	☐ Often
10. Does your child show objects to you without giving you the object?	☐ Not Yet	☒ Sometimes	☐ Often
11. Does your child wave to greet people?	☐ Not Yet	☐ Sometimes	☒ Often
12. Does your child point to objects?	☐ Not Yet	☒ Sometimes	☐ Often
13. Does your child nod his/her head to indicate *yes*?	☐ Not Yet	☐ Sometimes	☒ Often

Sounds

14. Does your child use sounds or words to get attention or help?	☐ Not Yet	☒ Sometimes	☐ Often
15. Does your child string sounds together, such as *uh oh, mama, gaga, bye bye, bada*?	☐ Not Yet	☐ Sometimes	☒ Often
16. About how many of the following consonant sounds does your child use: *ma, na, ba, da, ga, wa, la, ya, sa, sha*?	☐ None ☐ 1–2 ☐ 3–4 ☒ 5–8 ☐ over 8		

Words

17. About how many different words does your child use meaningfully that you recognize (such as *baba* for bottle; *gaggie* for doggie)?	☐ None ☐ 1–3 ☒ 4–10 ☐ 11–30 ☐ over 30		
18. Does your child put two words together (for example, *more cookie, bye bye Daddy*)?	☐ Not Yet	☐ Sometimes	☐ Often

Understanding

19. When you call your child's name, does he/she respond by looking or turning toward you?	☐ Not Yet	☒ Sometimes	☐ Often
20. About how many different words or phrases does your child understand without gestures? For example, if you say "where's your tummy," "where's Daddy," "give me the ball," or "come here," without showing or pointing, your child will respond appropriately.	☐ None ☐ 1–3 ☒ 4–10 ☐ 11–30 ☐ over 30		

Object Use

21. Does your child show interest in playing with a variety of objects?	☐ Not Yet	☐ Sometimes	☒ Often
22. About how many of the following objects does your child use appropriately: cup, bottle, bowl, spoon, comb or brush, toothbrush, washcloth, ball, toy vehicle, toy telephone?	☐ None ☐ 1–2 ☐ 3–4 ☒ 5–8 ☐ over 8		
23. About how many blocks (or rings) does your child stack? **Stacks**	☐ None ☒ 2 blocks ☐ 3–4 blocks ☐ 5 or more		
24. Does your child pretend to play with toys (for example, feed a stuffed animal, put a doll to sleep, put an animal figure in a vehicle)?	☐ Not Yet	☒ Sometimes	☐ Often

Do you have any concerns about your child's development?   ☐ yes   ☒ no   **If yes, please describe on back.**

Communication and Symbolic Behavior Scales Developmental Profile by Amy M. Wetherby & Barry M. Prizant
© 2002 by Paul H. Brookes Publishing Co., Inc. All rights reserved.

FIGURE 6-3   Infant/toddler developmental checklist

Source: Wetherby, A. M., & Prizant, B. M. (2002). *Communication and Symbolic Behavior Scales Developmental Profile (CSBS DP™), First Normed Edition.* Baltimore: Brookes Publishing Co.; reprinted by permission. For blank copies and scoring instructions, please visit http://www.brookespublishing.com

D Geometry and spatial relations   F W S

1 Begins to recognize and describe the attributes of shapes. (p. 12)
Not Yet ☐☐☐
In Process ☐☐☐
Proficient ☐☐☐

2 Shows understanding of and uses several positional words. (p. 12)
Not Yet ☐☐☐
In Process ☐☐☐
Proficient ☐☐☐

E Measurement   F W S

1 Orders, compares, and describes objects according to a single attribute. (p. 13)
Not Yet ☐☐☐
In Process ☐☐☐
Proficient ☐☐☐

2 Participates in measuring activities. (p. 13)
Not Yet ☐☐☐
In Process ☐☐☐
Proficient ☐☐☐

IV Scientific Thinking

A Inquiry   F W S

1 Asks questions and uses senses to observe and explore materials and natural phenomena. (p. 15)
Not Yet ☐☐☐
In Process ☐☐☐
Proficient ☐☐☐

2 Uses simple tools and equipment for investigation. (p. 15)
Not Yet ☐☐☐
In Process ☐☐☐
Proficient ☐☐☐

3 Makes comparisons among objects. (p. 16)
Not Yet ☐☐☐
In Process ☐☐☐
Proficient ☐☐☐

V Social Studies

A People, past and present   F W S

1 Identifies similarities and differences in personal and family characteristics. (p. 17)
Not Yet ☐☐☐
In Process ☐☐☐
Proficient ☐☐☐

B Human interdependence   F W S

1 Begins to understand family needs, roles, and relationships. (p. 17)
Not Yet ☐☐☐
In Process ☐☐☐
Proficient ☐☐☐

2 Describes some people's jobs and what is required to perform them. (p. 17)
Not Yet ☐☐☐
In Process ☐☐☐
Proficient ☐☐☐

3 Begins to be aware of technology and how it affects life. (p. 18)
Not Yet ☐☐☐
In Process ☐☐☐
Proficient ☐☐☐

C Citizenship and government   F W S

1 Demonstrates awareness of rules. (p. 18)
Not Yet ☐☐☐
In Process ☐☐☐
Proficient ☐☐☐

2 Shows awareness of what it means to be a leader. (p. 18)
Not Yet ☐☐☐
In Process ☐☐☐
Proficient ☐☐☐

D People and where they live   F W S

1 Describes the location of things in the environment. (p. 19)
Not Yet ☐☐☐
In Process ☐☐☐
Proficient ☐☐☐

2 Shows awareness of the environment. (p. 19)
Not Yet ☐☐☐
In Process ☐☐☐
Proficient ☐☐☐

VI The Arts

A Expression and representation   F W S

1 Participates in group music experiences. (p. 21)
Not Yet ☐☐☐
In Process ☐☐☐
Proficient ☐☐☐

2 Participates in creative movement, dance, and drama. (p. 21)
Not Yet ☐☐☐
In Process ☐☐☐
Proficient ☐☐☐

3 Uses a variety of art materials for tactile experience and exploration. (p. 21)
Not Yet ☐☐☐
In Process ☐☐☐
Proficient ☐☐☐

B Understanding and appreciation   F W S

1 Responds to artistic creations or events. (p. 22)
Not Yet ☐☐☐
In Process ☐☐☐
Proficient ☐☐☐

VII Physical Development and Health

A Gross motor development   F W S

1 Moves with balance and control. (p. 23)
Not Yet ☐☐☐
In Process ☐☐☐
Proficient ☐☐☐

2 Coordinates movements to perform simple tasks. (p. 23)
Not Yet ☐☐☐
In Process ☐☐☐
Proficient ☐☐☐

B Fine motor development   F W S

1 Uses strength and control to perform simple tasks. (p. 23)
Not Yet ☐☐☐
In Process ☐☐☐
Proficient ☐☐☐

2 Uses eye-hand coordination to perform tasks. (p. 24)
Not Yet ☐☐☐
In Process ☐☐☐
Proficient ☐☐☐

3 Shows beginning control of writing, drawing, and art tools. (p. 24)
Not Yet ☐☐☐
In Process ☐☐☐
Proficient ☐☐☐

C Personal health and safety   F W S

1 Performs some self-care tasks independently. (p. 24)
Not Yet ☐☐☐
In Process ☐☐☐
Proficient ☐☐☐

2 Follows basic health and safety rules. (p. 24)
Not Yet ☐☐☐
In Process ☐☐☐
Proficient ☐☐☐

FIGURE 6-4   Preschool checklist and developmental guidelines for physical development

Source: The Work Sampling System® The Developmental Checklist Preschool 4: © 2001 by Pearson Education, Inc., publishing as Pearson Early Learning, an imprint of Pearson Learning Group. Used by permission. *The Work Sampling System* is a registered trademark of Pearson Education, Inc., publishing as Pearson Early Learning, an imprint of Pearson Learning Group.

recognizes that young children learn through active learning based on interaction with concrete materials. Developmental checklists help the preschool teacher maintain a perspective between developmentally appropriate instruction and pressures to prepare children for first grade. Inclusion of developmental experiences helps the teacher ensure a balanced curriculum that is best for the children's level of development.

Story Retelling Assessment Checklist

Child's Name _____ Date _____

Teacher _____ Grade _____

Book Title _____ Author_____

Story was read independently ☐
Story was read to the child   ☐
Type of response: oral ☐   picture ☐   written ☐

Setting/Character	**Independently**	**With Prompting**
Retells from beginning of story		
Names main character		
Plot/Events		
Includes all major events		
Tells events in order		
Identifies the plot or problem		
Resolution		
Tells how the story ended or how the problem was solved		

Assessment Comments

FIGURE 6-5 Story retelling assessment sheet

In planning the curriculum and instruction in early childhood or preschool programs, teachers must incorporate the use of learning centers in classroom experiences. Developmental checklists with a sequence of objectives provide guidelines for selecting the materials to place in centers to support curriculum and instruction. For example, for 5-year-olds, the sequence on a checklist for fine-motor development might be similar to the following:

Cuts and pastes creative designs
Creates recognizable objects with clay
Ties shoes

Puts together a 20-piece puzzle

Creates or copies a pegboard design

Copies letters

Can copy numerals (Wortham, 1984, p. 33)

By studying the sequence, the teacher can determine that activities for cutting and pasting should be part of center activities earlier in the year. Later, when fine-motor skills are better developed, opportunities to copy letters and numerals should be included in centers to complement instructional activities in writing. Thus, developmental checklists help teachers decide what to select for learning centers as the year progresses. Early in the year, the teacher may introduce simple toys, puzzles, and construction materials in centers. Later, more complex, challenging activities and materials are more appropriate. As the year progresses, the materials available in the centers should be compatible with developmental growth.

Because the rate of development varies from child to child, the sequence of development reflected in the checklists allows the teacher to vary materials for individual children. Certain games, activities, and materials can be placed in the centers and designated for a particular child's needs or interests. Materials for experiences placed in centers provide a means of individualizing learning, with checklists serving as the guide for a sequence from simple to complex. The more complex concepts or objectives lead to the selection of materials for the child whose development is more advanced.

Checklists as a Guide to Assess Learning and Development

Having information on how children are growing and learning is one of the important requirements of an early childhood program. Teachers must know how children's development and learning are progressing, and must be able to discuss it with parents, other teachers, and staff members of other schools that later may teach the child. Figure 6-4, the checklist for physical development (Marsden et al., 2001), is a part of a set of developmental checklists that can be used for these purposes.

Because the checklists cover all kinds of development, they allow teachers to track individual children and groups of children. When teachers keep consistent records on individual children, they can give parents information about the child's progress. Parents then have a clear idea of what is happening in school and what their child is accomplishing.

Teachers who use developmental checklists to assess, evaluate, and record children's progress may eventually realize that they have a better understanding of each child in the class than they had before. If a teacher uses a checklist for gross-motor skills to keep track of large-muscle development in his or her students, systematic observation of students engaged in physical activities will make the teacher more aware of how each child is progressing and will reveal individual differences in development. When reporting to one child's parent, for example, the teacher may discuss the improvement in throwing and catching a ball. In another case, the teacher may focus on the child's ability to ride a bicycle or to jump rope.

Evaluating and Assessing With Checklists

If a checklist is used as a framework for curriculum development and instruction, it can also be used for evaluation and assessment. The curriculum objectives used to plan instructional experiences can also be used to evaluate the children's performance on the same objectives. After a series of activities is used to provide opportunities to work with new concepts or skills, the children are assessed to determine how successful they were in learning the new skill or information. Evaluation can be accomplished through observation, during ongoing learning activities, and through specific assessment tasks.

Evaluating Checklist Objectives by Observation

Observing young children is the most valuable method of understanding them. Because children in early childhood programs are active learners, their progress is best assessed by watching their behaviors, rather than by using a test. If you look at the items on developmental checklists, you will see that some objectives or indicators of development can be evaluated only by observing the child. For example, in the area of language development, if a teacher wants to know whether a child is using complete sentences, he or she observes the child in a play activity and listens for examples of language. Likewise, if the teacher is interested in evaluating social development, he or she observes the children playing outdoors to determine whether they engage mostly in solitary or parallel play or whether individual children play cooperatively as part of a group. Because very young children learn through play, the teacher can notice how a child is learning during play activities. Likewise, the infant–toddler caregiver will become aware of each child's physical and language advances at the very beginning stages of development while children explore the environment through play.

Chapter 5 included information on how observation can be incidental or planned. The teacher may decide to evaluate during center time and may determine in advance which items on a checklist can be evaluated by observing children in the art center or the manipulative center. The teacher then places materials in those centers that are needed to observe specific behaviors, and records which children are able to use the materials in the desired manner. For example, the ability to cut with scissors can be assessed by having a cutting activity in the art center. As an alternative, the teacher might use a cutting activity with an entire group and observe how each child is performing during the activity.

Evaluating Checklist Objectives With Learning Activities

Some objectives cannot be assessed through observation alone. Objectives in a cognitive area such as mathematics may require a specific learning activity for evaluation. However, instead of having a separate assessment task, the teacher can have children demonstrate their performance on a particular skill as a part of the lesson being conducted. The teacher notes which children demonstrate understanding of the concept or mastery of the skill during the lesson. If a mathematics objective to be assessed involves understanding numbers through five, the teacher might instruct a small group of children to make groups of objects ranging in number from one to five and note which children are successful.

Evaluating Checklist Objectives With Specific Tasks

Sometimes, at the beginning or end of a school year or grading period, the teacher wants to conduct a systematic assessment. He or she assesses a series of objectives at one time. In this situation, the teacher determines a number of objectives that can be evaluated at one time and devises tasks or activities to conduct with a child or a small group of children. The activities are presented in the same fashion as in a lesson, but the teacher has the additional purpose of updating and recording progress. Assessment tasks are organized on the basis of children's previous progress and vary among groups of children. Some children perform one group of activities; others have a completely different set of activities related to a different set of objectives.

There is a time and place for each type of evaluation. The more experience a teacher has in including assessment in the instructional program, the easier it becomes. It is important to use the easiest and least time-consuming strategy whenever possible.

Steps in Checklist Design

A checklist is an outline or framework of development and curriculum. When designing a checklist, the developer first determines the major categories that will be included. Thereafter, development follows four basic steps:

1. Identification of the skills to be included
2. Separate listing of target behaviors
3. Sequential organization of the checklist
4. Record keeping

Identification of the Skills to Be Included

The teacher studies each checklist category and determines the specific objectives or skills to be included. Using established developmental norms or learning objectives, the teacher decides how to adapt them for his or her needs. For example, on a checklist

Conflicts About Informal Assessment Results

ary Howell and Francesca Carrillo are having a heated argument in the teachers' lounge. Mary teaches first grade, and Francesca teaches second grade. At issue is the checklist from the first grade that is placed in students' folders at the end of the year, before they are promoted to second grade. Francesca's complaint is that the first-grade teachers' assessments are inaccurate. They have indicated that students accomplished first-grade objectives, but these objectives have to be retaught in the second grade because the students either never know them or forget them over the summer.

Mary clearly is offended that her professionalism has been questioned. She defends the process by which first-grade teachers determine whether the children have learned the objectives. Josie, another teacher sitting nearby, says nothing. Under her breath, she mutters, "It's all a waste of time. I wait until the end of the year and then mark them all off, anyway."

After Mary and Francesca have left, the conversation about the merits of using checklists for assessment and record keeping continues. Gunther Sachs, a third-grade teacher, supports the use of checklists for evaluating the students. He observes that he uses the checklist record when having conferences with parents. He believes that the parents gain a better understanding of what their child is learning in school when he can tell them how the child is progressing on curriculum objectives listed on the checklist. Lily Wong, another third-grade teacher, strongly disagrees. Her experience with the checklists leads her to believe that record keeping takes a great deal of time that she would rather use to plan lessons and design more interesting and challenging learning activities for her students.

for language development and reading under the category of language and vocabulary, the following objectives might be included:

Listens to and follows verbal directions
Identifies the concept of *word*
Identifies the concept of *letter*
Invents a story for a picture book

Separate Listing of Target Behaviors

If a series of behaviors or items is included in an objective, the target behaviors should be listed separately so that they can be recorded separately (Irwin & Bushnell, 1980). For the objective of identifying coins, the best way to write the item would be as follows:

Identifies:
Penny

Nickel

Dime

Quarter

When the teacher is assessing the child's knowledge of coins, he or she may find that the child knows some of the coins but not others. Information can be recorded on the mastery status of each coin such as *developing* or *mastered*.

Sequential Organization of the Checklist

The checklist should be organized in a sequential manner. Checklist items should be arranged in order of difficulty or complexity. If the checklist is sequenced correctly, the order of difficulty should be obvious. For example, the ability to count on a mathematics checklist might be listed as "Counts by rote from 1 to 10." At the next higher level, the checklist item would be "Counts by rote from 1 to 50."

Record Keeping

A system of record keeping must be devised. Because a checklist indicates the objectives for curriculum development or developmental characteristics, it must have a method of recording the status of the items. Although many record-keeping strategies have been used, commonly two columns indicate that the child either has or has not mastered the skill or behavior. Two types of indicators frequently used are a simple *Yes/No* or *Mastery/Nonmastery*. Another approach is to record the date when the concept was introduced and the date when it was mastered. In this instance, the columns would be headed *Introduced/Mastery* or could indicate an intermediate step in evaluation with three columns headed *Introduced/Progress/Mastery*. Figure 6-6 is a checklist with three columns for record keeping in physical development. In this example, the columns indicate when the assessment was conducted in the fall, winter, and spring. The codes *Not Yet, In Process,* and *Proficient* are used to indicate the child's progress (Marsden et al., 2001).

The teacher can use a checklist to record individual or group progress. Whether the teacher uses observation, lesson activities, or tasks for assessment, the checklist is used to keep a record of the child's progress. Checklist information can be shared periodically with parents to keep them informed about what their child is learning or is able to do.

Checklists can also be used to keep a record of all the children in the class or group. The group record lists all the children's names, as well as the checklist objectives. By transferring information about individual children to a master or group record, the teacher can plan instruction for groups of children as the group record indicates their common needs. Figure 6-6 is a checklist record for a group of students in language development.

NAME	LANGUAGE ABILITY													FOLLOWING DIRECTIONS			
	1. Shares personal experiences	2. Voluntarily participates	3. Voluntarily answers	4. Tells observed activity	5. Answers factual questions	6. Answers probing questions	7. Answers higher-order questions	8. Answers divergent questions	9. Problem solving	10. Asks factual questions	11. Interprets story picture	12. Comprehension	13. Attention span	14. Follows simple directions	15. Carries messages	16. Two or more directions	17. Makes simple object with specified materials

FIGURE 6-6 Language arts: Class record sheet

Using checklists for assessment and evaluation has definite advantages and disadvantages or problems. Teachers must weigh both sides before deciding how extensively they will use checklists for measurement and record-keeping purposes.

Advantages of Using Checklists

Checklists are easy to use. Because they require little instruction or training, teachers can quickly learn to use them. Unlike standardized tests, they are available whenever evaluation is needed.

Checklists are flexible and can be used with a variety of assessment strategies. The teacher can evaluate in the most convenient manner and obtain the needed information. Because of this flexibility, the teacher can combine assessment strategies when more than one assessment is indicated.

Behaviors can be recorded frequently; checklists are always at hand. Whenever the teacher has new information, he or she can update records. Unlike paper-and-pencil tests or formal tests, the teacher does not have to wait for a testing opportunity to determine whether the child has mastered an objective.

Disadvantages of Using Checklists

Using checklists can be time-consuming. Particularly when teachers are just beginning to use checklists, they report that keeping records current on checklists reduces the time spent with children. Teachers have to become proficient in using checklists without impinging on teaching time.

Teachers may find it difficult to get started. When they are accustomed to teaching without the use of checklists, teachers often find it difficult to adapt their teaching and evaluation behaviors to include checklists. In addition, teachers can have too many checklists. They become frustrated by multiple checklists that overwhelm them with assessment and record keeping.

Some teachers may not consider assessment strategies used with checklists as valid measures of development and learning. For some teachers, particularly those in the primary grades who are accustomed to conducting a test for evaluation, the observation and activity strategies used to measure progress may seem inconclusive. They may feel the need for more concrete evidence of mastery of learning objectives for accountability.

Checklists do not indicate how well a child performs. Unlike a paper-and-pencil test that can be used to record levels of mastery, checklists indicate only whether the child can perform adequately. For teachers who are required to give grades at the elementary level, checklists can be an incomplete strategy for assessment (Irwin & Bushnell, 1980).

A checklist is not itself an assessment instrument. It is a format for organizing learning objectives or developmental indicators. The teacher's implementation of evaluation strategies by using a checklist makes it a tool for evaluation. In addition,

A teacher and students evaluate written work together.

recording the presence or absence of a behavior is not the main purpose of the checklist. The significant factor is what the teacher does with the assessment information recorded. If the information gained from evaluating the objectives is not used for instructional planning and implementation followed by further ongoing evaluation, the checklist does not improve learning and development.

Rating Scales

Rating scales are similar to checklists; however, there are important differences. Whereas checklists are used to indicate whether a behavior is present or absent, rating scales require the rater to make a qualitative judgment about the extent to which a behavior is present. A rating scale consists of a set of characteristics or qualities to be judged by using a systematic procedure. Rating scales take many forms; **numerical rating scales** and **graphic rating scales** seem to be used most frequently.

Types of Rating Scales

Numerical Rating Scales

Numerical rating scales are among the easiest rating scales to use. The rater marks a number to indicate the degree to which a characteristic is present. A sequence of numbers is assigned to descriptive categories. The rater's judgment is required to rate the characteristic. One common numerical system is as follows:

1—Unsatisfactory

2—Below average

3—Average
4—Above average
5—Outstanding

The numerical rating system might be used to evaluate classroom behaviors in elementary students as follows:

1. To what extent does the student complete assigned work?

   1 2 3 4 5

2. To what extent does the student cooperate with group activities?

   1 2 3 4 5

Numerical scales become difficult to use when there is little agreement on what the numbers represent. The interpretation of the scale may vary.

Numerical rating scales are useful in recording emerging progress in mathematics. In Figure 6-7, competencies and objectives in math are listed in a checklist format. The student is evaluated three times during the school year. A rating scale is used to make ratings of whether the child needs development (1), is developing as expected (2), or is advanced in development (3).

Graphic Rating Scales

Graphic rating scales function as continuums. A set of categories is described at certain points along the line, but the rater can mark his or her judgment at any location on the line. In addition, a graphic rating scale provides a visual continuum that helps locate the correct position. Commonly used descriptors for graphic rating scales are as follows:

Never

Seldom

Occasionally

Frequently

Always

The classroom behaviors described earlier would be evaluated on a graphic rating scale as follows:

1. To what extent does the student complete assigned work?

   Never   Seldom   Occasionally   Frequently   Always

2. To what extent does the student cooperate with group activities?

   Never   Seldom   Occasionally   Frequently   Always

The behavioral descriptions on graphic rating scales are used more easily than numerical descriptors. Because the descriptors are more specific, raters can be more objective and accurate when judging student behaviors; nevertheless, graphic rating scales are subject to bias because of disagreement about the meaning of the descriptors.

Combination checklist and rating scale

Child's Name: _____   Teacher's Name: _____

School/Center Name: _____   Year: _____

Code: 1 = Needs Development   2 = Developing as Expected   3 = Advanced Development

Competencies and Objectives	Observations		
	Fall	Mid-Year	Spring
1. Develops an awareness of and uses number sense, numbers, and operations			
1.1 Develops number sense and awareness of numbers in the environment			
1.2 Applies one-to-one correspondence by counting concrete objects by ones to 10, 20, 25			
1.3 Matches quantities and numerals for 1-5, then 6-9			
1.4 Counts with understanding and recognizes *how many* in sets of objects			
1.5 Begins to compare numbers of concrete objects using language (e.g., *same, more than, less than*)			
1.6 Begins to identify concepts of a fraction *whole and half by* using real objects			
1.7 Begins to identify the position of objects in a series (e.g., *first, second, third, middle, next, last*)			
1.8 Begins to develop the ability to combine, separate, and name *how many* objects			
2. Develops an awareness of relations and patterns			
2.1 Begins to recognize, describe, reproduce, and extend simple patterns			
2.2 Matches, sorts, and classifies objects based on their similarities and differences			
3. Develops an awareness of and uses geometry and spatial reasoning			
3.1 Recognizes, names, describes, and compares two-dimensional shapes (e.g., *circle, square, rectangle, triangle*)			
3.2 Begins to recognize, name, and compare three-dimensional shapes (e.g., *cylinder, cube, cone, sphere*)			
3.3 Identifies positions of objects in space using language (e.g., *under, over, beside, behind, inside*) to describe and compare their relative positions			
4. Develops an awareness of and uses measurement			
4.1 Sorts and compares objects by size, length, weight, area, and temperature (e.g., *bigger/smaller, hotter/colder, longer/shorter, more than/less than*)			
4.2 Uses nonstandard measurement units (e.g., *unit blocks, paper clips, hand span*)			
4.3 Uses common measuring instruments (e.g., *measuring cups, simple balance scales*)			
4.4 Begins to use time-related words (e.g., *day/night, yesterday/today/tomorrow*)			

FIGURE 6-7 Review of portfolio reading materials

Source: Integrated Assessment System. Copyright © 1990 by Harcourt Assessment, Inc. Reproduced by permission. All rights reserved.

Uses of Rating Scales

One of the most familiar uses of rating scales is report cards. Schools often use rating scales to report characteristics of personal and social development on a report card. Such attributes as work habits, classroom conduct, neatness, and citizenship commonly

---

Inadequate		Minimal		Good		Excellent
1	2	3	4	5	6	7

23. Sand/water*

| 1.1 No provision† for sand *or* water play, outdoors *or* indoors.
1.2 No toys to use for sand *or* water play. | 3.1 Some provision‡ for sand *or* water play accessible either outdoors *or* indoors.
3.2 Some sand toys accessible. | 5.1 Provision for sand *and* water play (either outdoors *or* indoors).
5.2 Variety of toys accessible for play (Ex. containers, spoons, funnels, scoops, shovels, pots and pans, molds, toy people, animals, and trucks).
5.3 Sand *or* water play available to children for at least 1 hour daily. | 7.1 Provision for sand *and* water play, *both* indoors *and* outdoors (weather permitting).
7.2 Different activities done with sand and water (Ex. bubbles added to water, material in sand table changed, i.e. rice substituted for sand). |

Notes for Clarification
*Materials that can easily be poured, such as rice, lentils, bird seed, and cornmeal may be substituted for sand. Sand or sand substitute must be available in sufficient quantity so children can dig in it, fill containers, and pour.

†"Provision" for sand and water requires action on the part of staff to provide appropriate materials for such play. Allowing children to play in puddles or dig in the dirt on the playground does not meet the requirements of this item.
‡Each room does not have to have its own sand and water table, but must be able to use a sand and water table regularly if it is shared with another room.

Questions
(3.1) Do you use sand or water with the children? How is that handled? About how often? Where is this available?

(3.2) Are there any toys for children to use with sand or water play? Please describe them.
(7.2) Do you change the activities children do with sand and water?

FIGURE 6-8 Examples from the *Early Childhood Environment Scale–Revised Edition*

Source: From Thelma Harms, Richard M. Clifford & Debby Cryer, *Early Childhood Environment Rating Scale–Revised Edition.* New York: Teachers College Press © 2005 by Thelma Harms, Richard M. Clifford, and Debby Cryer. All rights reserved.

Inadequate		Minimal		Good		Excellent
1	2	3	4	5	6	7

24. Dramatic play*

1.1 No materials or equipment accessible for dress up or dramatic play.

3.1 Some dramatic play materials and furniture accessible, so children can act out family roles themselves (Ex. dress-up clothes, housekeeping props, dolls).
3.2 Materials are accessible for at least 1 hour daily.
3.3 Separate storage for dramatic play material.

5.1 Many dramatic play materials accessible, including dress-up clothes.[†]
5.2 Materials accessible for a substantial portion of the day.
5.3 Props for at least two different themes accessible daily (Ex. housekeeping and work).
5.4 Dramatic play area clearly defined, with space to play and organized storage.

7.1 Materials rotated for a variety of themes (Ex. prop boxes for work, fantasy, and leisure themes).
7.2 Props provided to represent diversity (Ex. props representing various cultures; equipment used by people with disabilities).
7.3 Props provided for active dramatic play outdoors.[‡]
7.4 Pictures, stories, and trips used to enrich dramatic play.

Notes for Clarification

*Dramatic play is pretending or making believe. This type of play occurs when children act out roles themselves and when they manipulate figures such as small toy people in a doll house. Dramatic play is enhanced by props that encourage a variety of themes including *housekeeping* (Ex. dolls, child-sized furniture, dress-up, kitchen utensils); *different kinds of work* (Ex. office, construction, farm, store, fire fighting, transportation); *fantasy* (Ex. animals, dinosaurs, storybook characters); and *leisure* (Ex. camping, sports).

[†]Dress-up clothes should include more than the high heeled shoes, dresses, purses, and women's hats commonly found in a playhouse area. Clothing worn by both men and women at work such as hardhats, transportation worker caps, and cowboy hats, as well as running shoes, clip-on ties, and jackets should be included.
[‡]The intent of this indicator is that children are provided a large enough space so that their dramatic play can be very active and noisy without disrupting other activities. A large indoor space such as a gymnasium or multipurpose room may be substituted for the outdoor space. Structures (such as small houses, cars, or boats) and props for camping, cooking, work, transportation, or dress-up clothes may be available to the children.

Questions

(7.1) Are there any other dramatic play props children can use? Please describe them.
(7.3) Are props for dramatic play ever used outside or in a larger indoor space?

(7.4) Is there anything you do to extend children's dramatic play?

FIGURE 6-8 (*Continued*)

appear on elementary school report cards. Students and parents often believe that such ratings are particularly subject to teacher bias and feelings about the student.

An example of a rating scale is given in Figure 6-8. Taken from the *Early Childhood Environment Rating Scale—Revised* (Harms, Clifford, & Cryer, 1998), the page pictured shows a numerical scale for rating how the early childhood teacher provides for sand/water play and dramatic play, as well as the quality of the daily schedule. This type of scale is intended to be used to evaluate early childhood centers and to plan for improvements in the program (Harms, 2010).

Advantages and Disadvantages of Rating Scales

Rating scales are a unique form of evaluation. They serve a function not provided by other measurement strategies. Although some of the limitations of rating scales have already been discussed, it is useful to review their strengths and weaknesses.

Advantages of Using Rating Scales

Rating scales can be used for behaviors not easily measured by other means. In the area of social development, for example, a scale might have indicators of coopera-tive behavior. When the teacher is trying to determine the child's ability to work with children and adults in the classroom, the scale of indicators is more usable than a yes/no response category on a checklist. Unlike an observation, which might be completely open ended, the rating scale indicators have clues to behaviors that describe the child's level of cooperation.

Rating scales are quick and easy to complete. Because the rater is provided with the descriptors of the child's behavior, it is possible to complete the scale with

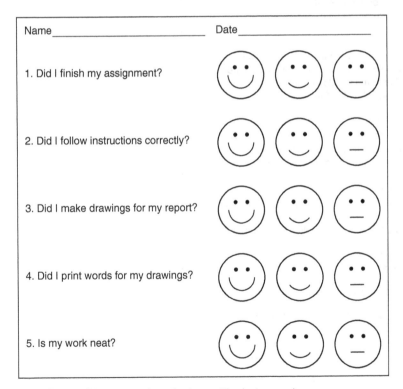

FIGURE 6-9 Observation form for tens with playing cards

Source: Kamii, C., & Rosenblum, V. (1990). An approach to assessment in mathematics. In C. Kamii (Ed.), *Achievement testing in the early grades: The games grown-ups play* (pp. 146–162). Washington, DC: NAEYC. Reprinted with permission from the National Association for the Education of Young Children, p. 151.

minimum effort. The descriptors also make it possible to complete the scale some time after an observation (Jablon, Dombro, & Dichtelmiller, 2007). The user can apply knowledge about the child after an observation or as a result of working with the child on a daily basis and will not always need a separate time period to acquire the needed information.

Minimum training is required to use rating scales. The successful rating scale is easy to understand and use. Paraprofessionals and students can often complete some rating scales. The scale's indicators offer the information needed to complete the scale.

Rating scales are easy to develop and use. Because descriptors remain consistent on some rating scales, teachers find them easy to design. When using rating indicators such as *always, sometimes, rarely,* and *never,* the teacher can add the statements for rating without having to think of rating categories for each one. Figures 6-9 and 6-10

CLASSROOM ASSESSMENT LIST
DATA TABLE, ELEMENTARY SCHOOL

1. Heading
   T: I put my name and the date on my work.
   O: I left my name or the date off.
   W: I did not include my name or date.

2. Title
   T: My title says exactly what the data are about.
   O: My title gives some idea of what the data are about.
   W: I have no title or my title does not
      tell much about what the data are about.

3. Organizing The Data
   T: My data are organized into very neat rows and columns.
   O: Some of my data are organized.
   W: I need to organize my data much better.

4. Naming The Data
   T: The rows and columns have titles and all the data have
      units.
   O: Some rows and columns have titles and some data
      have units.
   W: I need to give the rows and columns titles and/or I
      need to give the data units.

Did I do my best work?

| Terrific | OK | Needs Work |

FIGURE 6-10   Rating scale for data tables (elementary school)

Source: Hibbard, M. K. (1996). Self-assessment *using* performance task assessment lists. In R. E. Blum & J. A. Arter (Eds.), *A handbook for student performance assessment in an era of restructuring* (pp. VI–6:1 to VI–6:19). Portland, OR: Northwest Regional Educational Laboratory. Used by permission of NWREL.

are scales with three indicators that students can use for self-assessment in mathematics. In Figure 6-9, a beginning reader can select a smiling face to evaluate his or her own work. In Figure 6-10, the same type of evaluation can be conducted by a student with more advanced reading and self-assessment skills. These examples are very similar to checklists, but permit the student to make a qualitative assessment on some items.

Finally, rating scales are a useful strategy for assessing progress in the child's journey into understanding the world or in reconstructing knowledge. A rating scale permits the teacher to describe the child's steps toward understanding or mastery, instead of whether the child has achieved a predetermined level, as is the case in the use of checklists.

Disadvantages of Using Rating Scales

Rating scales are highly subjective; therefore, rater error and bias are common problems. Teachers and other raters may rate a child on the basis of their previous interactions or on an emotional rather than an objective basis. The subsequent rating will reflect the teacher's attitude toward the child (Linn & Miller, 2005).

Ambiguous terms cause rating scales to be unreliable sources of information. Raters disagree on the descriptors of characteristics. Therefore, raters are likely to

Quick Check Rating Scales for Self-Assessment

*I*nformation on children using rating scales for self-assessment in this chapter has included examples using faces for children to rate themselves and their work. A second-grade teacher decided to avoid frustrations children experienced when they had to mark a "sad" face. The teacher devised a simple scale with four ratings and indicators. The children used different colors to fill in the circles attached to numerical ratings. Called a "quick check" the scale could be used several times with children progressing to higher ratings. The teacher also developed four desired teaching behaviors that complemented the use of the quick checks:

1. Helping children set or accept and record individualized goals
2. Teaching, modeling, and planning ways the children may progress toward goals
3. Showing the children evidence of their progress with carefully kept records
4. Helping the children celebrate goal achievement and attributing positive feelings to their own efforts

Source: Brown, W. (2008). Young children assess their learning. The power of the quick check strategy. *Young Children, 63*, 14–20.

174
....

CHAPTER 6

*Checklists, Rating
Scales, and
Rubrics*

mark characteristics by using different interpretations. For example, it is easy to have different interpretations of the indicator *sometimes or rarely.*

Rating scales tell little about the causes of behavior. Like checklists that indicate whether the behavior is present or absent, rating scales provide no additional information to clarify the circumstances in which the behavior occurred. Unlike observations that result in more comprehensive information about the context surrounding behaviors, rating scales provide a different type of information from checklists, but include no causal clues for the observer unless notes are taken beyond the rating scale itself.

Rubrics

Like rating scales, rubrics are qualitative instruments that can be used for assessing student progress or scoring student work. Perhaps this purpose for scoring student work distinguishes rubrics from other types of assessment instruments such as checklists and rating scales. Wiggins (1996a) defines a rubric as follows:

> A rubric is a printed set of guidelines that distinguishes performances or products of different quality. . . . A rubric has descriptors that define what to look for at each level of performance. . . . Rubrics also often have indicators providing specific examples or tell-tale signs of things to look for in work. (p. VI–5:1)

It is clear from the definition just cited that rubrics are related to performance assessments. They provide guidelines to distinguish performance from one level to another. Although rubrics are used most frequently with students in later elementary grades and secondary schools, they can also be useful for students in kindergarten and the primary grades.

Indicators of performance can also be called the criteria for scoring. That is, they set the criteria for the score at each level. Indicators can also describe dimensions of performance—different categories of indicators leading to the desired score. In Figure 6-11, six categories of reading comprehension rubric for first and second grade are listed and rated at four levels, Beginning Comprehension, 1 point; Some comprehension, 2 points; Adequate Comprehension, 3 points; and Advanced Comprehension, 4 points. Each child is rated on the six elements with a total score at the bottom of the rubric.

Types of Rubrics

There are generally three types of rubrics: **holistic**, **analytic**, and **developmental**. Each type has characteristics that distinguish it from the others.

Beginning Comprehension 1 point	Some Comprehension 2 points	Adequate Comprehension 3 points	Advanced Comprehension 4 points
1. Tells 1 or 2 events or little detail	Tells some key events or facts	Tells many events (Sequences correctly)	Tells most or all key events and facts
2. Retells a story with very little detail	Retells story with some important details	Retells story with many important details	Retells story accurately and sequentially in own words (elaborates)
3. Does not differentiate between real and make-believe	Differentiates between real and make-believe	Differentiates between real and make-believe in some types of content	Differentiates between real and make-believe in all types of content
4. Responds to questions incorrectly	Responds to questions with some errors	Responds to questions with correct interpretation	Responds to questions with elaboration and higher-level thinking
5. Does not connect to experiences in life	Connects some story events to life experiences	Connects many story events to own life experience	Connects story events to experiences in own life and elaborates
6. Cannot identify any characters in story	Identifies some characters by name	Identifies characters and tells about them	Identifies all characters and tells details about them
Total _____	_____	_____	_____

FIGURE 6-11 Reading rubric

Source: Cohen, J. H., & Wiener, R. B. *Literacy portfolios: Improving assessment, teaching and learning*, 2nd ed., © 2003, p. 141, reprinted by permission of Pearson Education, Inc., Upper Saddle River, NJ.

Holistic Rubric

This type of rubric assigns a single score to a student's overall performance. These rubrics usually have competency labels that define the level of performance. A number of indicators describe the quality of work or performance at each level (Cohen & Wiener, 2003; Payne, 1997; Wiggins, 1996b). Figure 6-12 is an

---

1. *Inexperienced Writer*
Uses scribble writing or letter-like marks. Uses pictures. May dictate a sentence to the teacher.

2. *Beginning Writer*
Attempts to write words on paper, but is very limited. May copy words or sentences. Can write familiar words from memory.

3. *Developing Writer*
May show understanding of conventions of print. Uses spacing for word boundaries. Attempts to sequence thoughts. Uses inventive spelling.

4. *Mature Writer*
Writing is on topic; confident, developing fluency. May write multiple sentences. There is a beginning, middle, and end. Shows some accuracy in punctualization and capitalization. Still makes errors.

FIGURE 6-12   Holistic rubric

Source: Winbury, J., & Evans, C. S. (1996). Poway portfolio project. In R. E. Blum & J. A. Arter (Eds.), *A handbook for student performance assessment in an era of restructuring* (pp. VII–2:1 to VII–2:6). Portland, OR: Northwest Regional Educational Laboratory. Used by permission of NWREL, p. VII–2:5.

example of a simple holistic rubric in emergent writing. It has four levels of competence. The student's work is assessed using the descriptors under each level of competence.

Analytic Rubric

"An analytic rubric describes and scores each of the task attributes separately, uses limited descriptors for each attribute, uses a scale that can be both narrow and broad, and allows for specific diagnostic feedback" (Wiener & Cohen, 1997, p. 249). Analytic rubrics are more specific than holistic rubrics, can be used for diagnostic purposes, and can be more efficient for grading purposes. Figure 6-13 is an example of an analytic rubric for problem solving. It has three dimensions: understanding the problem, solving the problem, and answering the problem. The descriptors for each are listed with a numerical scale. This particular rubric is useful for students in the latter stages of early childhood when reading and writing skills are well developed.

Developmental Rubric

A developmental rubric is designed to serve a multiage group of students or to span several grade levels. The intention is to abandon mastery of skills at a particular grade level; rather, the student is assessed on a continuum that shows developmental progress. Figure 6-14 shows the progression in speaking skills across elementary grade levels.

```
Analytic Scale for Problem Solving

Understanding the problem

0—No attempt
1—Completely misinterprets the problem
2—Misinterprets major part of the problem
3—Misinterprets minor part of the problem
4—Complete understanding of the problem

Solving the problem

0—No attempt
1—Totally inappropriate plan
2—Partially correct procedure but with major fault
3—Substantially correct procedure with major omission or procedural error
4—A plan that could lead to a correct solution with no arithmetic errors

Answering the problem

0—No answer or wrong answer based upon an inappropriate plan
1—Copying error, computational error, partial answer for problem with multiple answers; no
    answer statement; answer labeled incorrectly
2—Correct solution
```

FIGURE 6-13   Analytic rubric

Source: Kubiszyn, T., & Borich, G. (1996). *Educational testing and measurement: Classroom application and practice* (5th ed.). Copyright © 1996 by John Wiley & Sons. Reprinted by permission of John Wiley & Sons, Inc.

How Rubrics Are Designed and Used

Rubrics are frequently discussed as part of performance assessment and the use of portfolios. This is because they are used to assess a performance task. When an overall, general judgment is made about the performance, a holistic rubric is used. An analytic rubric applies a detailed set of criteria, usually after a holistic evaluation has been made. A developmental rubric is designed to measure evolving competencies over a span of grade levels. Each type of rubric is designed for a different type of application, but the design process is similar (McMillan, 2007).

Selecting Rubric Type

There are two major steps in designing a rubric. The first step is to decide what type of rubric is to be used and then design the type of rubric selected. If an overall rating is needed, then a holistic rubric scale is indicated. An analytic rubric is designed if each part of a task needs to be assessed separately, as in Figure 6-14. The three tasks to be assessed in that rubric are (1) understanding the problem, (2) solving the problem, and (3) answering the problem. Each category of the problem has different dimensions. Figure 6-13, in contrast, is holistic. The descriptors support levels of competence, but the focus is on overall proficiency at each level.

SPEAKING RUBRIC
Assessment Scale
(Grades 1–5)

Secure Speaker
- Confident speaker
- Speaks loudly, clearly, and with expression
- Expresses ideas with elaboration and support
- Consistently makes relevant contributions to class discussions

Developing Speaker
- Competent speaker
- Speaks loudly and clearly
- Expresses ideas in complete sentences
- Takes part in class discussions and stays on topic

Beginning Speaker
- May be a reluctant speaker
- Needs to work on speaking skills (volume, clarity, eye contact)
- Rarely contributes to class discussions in a meaningful way

FIGURE 6-14 Developmental rubric

Source: Winbury, J., & Evans, C. S. (1996). Poway portfolio project. In R. E. Blum & J. A. Arter (Eds.), *A handbook for student performance assessment in an era of restructuring* (pp. VII–2:1 to VII–2:6). Portland, OR: Northwest Regional Educational Laboratory. Used by permission of NWREL, p. VII–2:3. Used by permission.

A developmental rubric is designed when the scale covers more than one grade level or developmental level. Figure 6-14 describes levels of competency that are relevant throughout the elementary school experience. The student's progress is assessed by broad levels of achievement in speaking rather than by grade level.

Developing Scoring Criteria

Teachers who are beginners at rubric design might find a generalized rubric useful as a guide to start their own rubric. The rubric can first be divided into levels of performance common to many rubrics:

No attempt

Inadequate response

Satisfactory response

Demonstrated competence

Each level has descriptions of the scoring criteria for that level of competence. This particular rubric also has a numerical rating for each level. Herman, Aschbacher, and Winters (1992) describe four common elements that characterize rubric scoring criteria:

- One or more traits or dimensions that serve as the basis for the student response.
- Definitions and examples to clarify the meaning of each trait or dimension.
- A scale of values (or a counting system) on which to rate each dimension.
- Standards of excellence for specified performance levels accompanied by models or examples of each level. (p. 55)

Unlike the objectives on checklists and descriptors on rating scales, levels of performance or dimensions cannot always be predetermined when the rubric is designed. The dimensions of performance must be based on reasonable expectations of the students to be assessed using existing samples of student work and revised as necessary (McMillan, 2007; Wiggins, 1996b).

Rubrics have many uses and purposes. They can be created to assess processes such as cooperative learning and other group strategies. They are most commonly used with student work or products. Examples are individual and group projects, exhibits, and artistic products. They are also used to evaluate performances of all types. In the classroom, they can be used for oral presentations and discussions. As can be seen from the examples presented in this section of the chapter, in early childhood classrooms, rubrics are commonly used to evaluate progress in development and learning.

Advantages and Disadvantages of Using Rubrics

Advantages of Using Rubrics

One of the many advantages of using rubrics is that they provide guidelines for quality student work or performance. Given this characteristic, other advantages can be added.

Rubrics are flexible. They can be designed for many uses and ability levels. Although teachers conduct most of the assessments using rubrics with very young children, student self-assessment increases as students mature.

Rubrics are adaptable. They are dynamic and subject to revision and refinement. Because they are easily modified and changed, they can meet changing classroom and student needs.

Rubrics can be used by both teacher and student to guide the student's efforts before completing a task or product. The teacher and student can review the expectations for quality during the process of an assignment or project so that the student is clear about what needs to be done to improve work.

Rubrics can be translated into grades if needed. If grades are not used, the rubrics can be used to discuss student work with parents and students. Periodic review of student efforts and comparison with a rubric such as a developmental rubric adds to the understanding of the student's progress.

Disadvantages of Using Rubrics

Despite the strengths of rubrics, rubric design and use are not without difficulty. One difficulty is that teachers just beginning to develop rubrics may have difficulty determining assessment or scoring criteria.

Teachers may focus on excessively general or inappropriate criteria for a rubric. In a similar fashion, a teacher may use predetermined criteria for rubric design rather than basing rubrics on examples of student work or modifying them as needed.

180
....

CHAPTER 6

*Checklists, Rating
Scales, and
Rubrics*

A common mistake in designing and using rubrics is to inappropriately focus on the quantity of characteristics found, rather than the indicators of quality work. The teacher focuses on the wrong characteristics of student work.

Holistic rubrics may lack validity and reliability. The teacher is forced to analyze the criteria for quality when designing an analytic rubric. The descriptors for the holistic rubric can be too general and lack specificity.

Developing Quality Checklists, Rating Scales, and Rubrics

In each section of the chapter, information has been provided on how to design informal instruments for assessment. To ensure that checklists, rating scales, and rubrics are quality measures, guidelines for avoiding inappropriate design are now reviewed.

Checklists

A checklist is used when a student behavior or skill can be indicated with a *yes* or *no* or some other indicator of the presence or absence of the characteristic. Linn and Miller (2005) summarize the steps in appropriate development of checklists:

1. Identify each of the specific actions desired in the performance.
2. Add to the list those actions that represent common errors (if they are useful in the assessment, are limited in number, and can be clearly stated).
3. Arrange the desired actions (and likely errors, if used) in the appropriate order in which they are expected to occur.
4. Provide a simple procedure for checking each action as it occurs (or for numbering the actions in sequence, if appropriate. (p. 284)

Rating Scales

The quality of rating scales also depends on specificity in the description of the rating. When designing a rating scale, the following steps are recommended:

1. Identify the learning outcomes that the task is intended to assess.
2. Determine what characteristics of the learning outcomes are most significant for assessment on the scale. Characteristics should be directly observable and points on the scale clearly defined.
3. Select the type of scale that is most appropriate for the purposes of the assessment.
4. Provide between three and seven rating positions on the scale. The number of points on the scale will depend on how many clear differentiations in level of accomplishment are needed for assessment.

Rubrics

When rubric design has been completed, the rubric should be evaluated for the appropriateness of the scoring criteria. McMillan (1997) has developed a checklist for evaluating scoring criteria for rubrics as follows:

1. Do descriptions focus on important aspects of the performance?
2. Is the type of rating matched with the purpose?
3. Are the traits directly observable?
4. Are the criteria understandable?
5. Are the traits clearly defined?
6. Is scoring error minimized?
7. Is the scoring system feasible? (p. 223)

Consistency in Conducting and Scoring Assessments

Steps can be taken to improve reliability in using checklists, rating scales, and rubrics. If several teachers are going to use the same instrument, the following guidelines can assist in developing consistency:

1. Before using an instrument, the teachers should review the items and indicators and agree on what each is intended to measure.
2. The instrument should be piloted by the individual teacher or group of teachers to determine whether any items are unclear or difficult to assess.
3. Scoring instructions should be reviewed prior to conducting the assessment.
4. Scoring instructions should be made according to the purposes of the assessment. If a score or grade is desired, the score will be numerical. If the assessment is to be used for student and/or parent feedback, more written information on the student's performance may be needed.

Herman and colleagues (1992) provided a checklist for ensuring reliability in using a rating instrument with a group of teachers:

- documented, field-tested scoring guide
- clear, concrete criteria
- annotated examples of all score points
- ample practice and feedback for raters
- multiple raters with demonstrated agreement prior to scoring
- periodic reliability checks throughout
- retraining when necessary
- arrangements for collection of suitable reliability data (pp. 93–94)

Summary

Informal evaluation measures are useful for teachers who need specific information about their students to use when planning instruction. Checklists and rating scales are informal instruments that can be designed and used by teachers to obtain specific diagnostic and assessment data that will help them develop learning experiences for their children.

Checklists are used for more than assessment or evaluation. They are a form of curriculum outline or a framework of curriculum objectives. With checklists, teachers can plan instruction, develop learning-center activities, and evaluate children's progress and achievement on specific objectives.

Rating scales allow teachers to evaluate behaviors qualitatively. Raters can indicate the extent to which the child exhibits certain behaviors.

Checklists and rating scales are practical and easy to use. Teachers can develop them to fit the curriculum and administer them at their convenience. Unlike standardized tests, checklists and rating scales are current and provide the teacher with immediate feedback on student progress.

Using checklists and rating scales also has disadvantages. Because they are not standardized, they are subject to error and teacher bias. Checklists do not include the level or quality of performance on the objectives measured. Rating scales in particular are subject to rater bias. Rating-scale descriptors are ambiguous in definition. Differing interpretations of descriptors by raters lead to different responses and interpretations of children's behaviors.

Rating scales provide a multidimensional format for assessing student products and performances. They include the most complex format for assessing quality in student work. They are particularly useful in helping students understand the expectations for quality in an assignment and to review quality indicators while a project or learning assignment is in progress. Rating scales are also useful in helping parents understand the nature of student assignments and the criteria for quality that were developed for that assignment.

Rating scales can have drawbacks. One possible weakness occurs when teachers predetermine characteristics of quality, rather than using examples of typical student work to determine the indicators. Likewise, teachers can focus on less appropriate indicators of quality work or look at quantity rather than quality of work.

All three of these assessment instruments can be weakened by teacher bias and subjective judgment. Reliability in conducting an assessment with these instruments can be improved if teachers work to achieve consistency in conducting and scoring the assessments.

REVIEW QUESTIONS

1. Describe the different functions of checklists. How can checklists be used by teachers for purposes other than evaluation or assessment?
2. Why is it important to use developmental checklists in early childhood programs?
3. How do developmental checklists serve as a guide for the sequence of development and curriculum?
4. Explain the different strategies that teachers can use to measure progress with checklist objectives.
5. How does the design of a checklist affect its use as an evaluation instrument?
6. What is sequenced organization in checklist design?
7. What methods can be used to record assessment results on checklists? Which form is best?
8. Why do some teachers have difficulty in using checklists? Do you see any solution to their problems?
9. How do rating scales differ from checklists?
10. Why are rating scales vulnerable to rater error and bias?
11. Is it better to use numerical rating scales or graphic rating scales? Why?
12. Which type of rubric is more specific, a holistic rubric or an analytic rubric? Explain how they are different.
13. How do scoring criteria provide indicators of quality of student work on a rubric?

SUGGESTED ACTIVITIES

1. Collect five samples of checklists used in preschool and primary-grade classrooms. Compare the checklists in terms of objectives, evaluation strategies, and record keeping. Under the headings 1. Objectives, 2. Evaluation strategies, and 3. Record keeping, provide an example from each checklist and discuss similarities and differences. Complete the checklist.
2. Develop a checklist for the first 6 weeks of school for behavior you wish to see demonstrated in a classroom or a learning center. First list the behaviors that need to be developed. Next put them into categories and sequence them if appropriate. Design the checklist and determine how the behaviors will be assessed and recorded. Finally, determine how checklist items will be recorded. Complete the checklist.
3. Design a rating scale to measure appropriate study behaviors in the primary-grade classroom. Include five characteristics and at least three points on the scale with descriptors. First list the five study behaviors and characteristics. Below each characteristic, determine three points on the scale with descriptors of the characteristic. Complete the rating scale.
4. Design a developmental rubric for emerging reading skills in kindergarten and first-grade students. Find objectives for beginning readers to develop the characteristics for different stages of development. First study beginning reading curriculum objectives from your state standards. List five characteristics of the beginning reader for the categories of pre-reader, beginning reader, and fluent reader. Organize the rubric into three levels. Next, determine what the child will be able to do to accomplish each level of the rubric.

KEY TERMS

analytic rubric
developmental checklist
developmental rubric

graphic rating scale
holistic rubric
numerical rating scale

SELECTED WEB SITES

About.com Special Education
http://specialed.about.com/od/readingchecklists

Teach-nology.com
http://www.teach-nology.com/

RCampus.com
http://www.rcampus.com

REFERENCES

Bickart, T. (1998). *Summary report of preventing reading difficulties in young children.* U.S. Department of Education Reading Summit. Washington, DC: Teaching Strategies.

Brown, W. (2008, November). Young children assess their learning. The power of the quick check strategy. *Young Children, 63,* 14–20.

Cohen, J. H., & Wiener, R. B. (2003). *Literacy portfolios: Improving assessment, teaching and learning* (2nd ed.). Upper Saddle River, NJ: Merrill/Prentice Hall.

Harms, T. (2010, January/February). Making long-lasting changes with the *Environment Rating Scales. Exchange,* 12–15.

Harms, T., Clifford, R. M., & Cryer, D. (2005). *Early Childhood Environment Rating Scale—Revised Edition.* New York: Teachers College Press.

Herman, J. L., Aschbacher, P. R., & Winters, L. (1992). *A practical guide to alternative assessment.* Alexandria, VA: Association for Supervision and Curriculum Development.

Hibbard, M. K. (1996). Self-assessment using performance task assessment lists. In R. E. Blum & J. A. Arter (Eds.), *A handbook for student performance assessment in an era of restructuring* (pp. VI–6:1 to VI–6:19). Alexandria, VA: Association for Supervision and Curriculum Development.

Irwin, D. M., & Bushnell, M. M. (1980). *Observational strategies for child study.* New York: Holt, Rinehart & Winston.

Jablon, J. R., Dombro, A. L., & Dichtelmiller, M. L. (2007). *The power of observation for birth through eight* (2nd ed.). Washington, DC: National Association for the Education of Young Children and Teaching Strategies, Inc.

Kubiszyn, T., & Borich, G. (1996). *Educational testing and measurement: Classroom application and practice* (5th ed.). Hoboken, NJ: John Wiley & Sons.

Linn, R. L., & Miller, M. D. (2005). *Measurement and assessment in teaching* (9th ed.). Upper Saddle River, NJ: Merrill/Prentice Hall.

Marsden, D. B., Meisels, S. J., Jablon, J. R., & Dichtelmiller, M. L. (2001). *The work sampling system: Preschool–4 developmental guidelines.* Upper Saddle River, NJ: Pearson Education.

McMillan, J. H. (2007). *Classroom assessment: Principles and practice for effective instruction* (4th ed.). Upper Saddle River, NJ: Pearson.

Meisels, S. J. (1996). Charting the continuum of assessment and intervention. In S. J. Meisels & E. Fenichel (Eds.), *New visions for the developmental assessment of infants and young children* (pp. 27–52). Washington, DC: Zero to Three: National Center for Infants, Toddlers, and Families.

Mississippi Department of Education (2006). *Mississippi early learning guidelines for four-year-olds.* Jackson, MS: Author.

Payne, D. A. (1997). *Applied educational assessment.* Belmont, CA: Wadsworth.

Polakowski, C. (1993). Literacy portfolios in the early childhood classroom. In *Student portfolios* (pp. 47–66). Washington, DC: National Education Association.

Ratcliff, N. J. (2001/2002). Using authentic assessment to document the emerging literacy skills of young children. *Childhood Education, 78,* 66–69.

Spodek, B., & Saracho, O. N. (1994). *Dealing with individual differences in the early childhood classroom.* New York: Longman.

Wetherby, A. M., & Prizant, B. M. (2002). *Communication and Symbolic Behavior Scales Developmental Profile (CSBS DP), First Normed Edition.* Baltimore: Brookes.

Weiner, R. B., & Cohen, J. H. (1997). *Literacy portfolios. Using assessment to guide instruction.* Upper Saddle River, NJ: Merrill/Prentice Hall.

Wiggins, G. (1996a). Creating tests worth taking. In R. E. Blum & J. A. Arter (Eds.), *A handbook for student performance assessment in an era of restructuring* (pp. V–6:2 to V–6:9). Alexandria, VA: Association for Supervision and Curriculum Development.

Wiggins, G. (1996b). What is a rubric? A dialogue on design and use. In R. E. Blum & J. A. Arter (Eds.), *A handbook for student performance assessment in an era of restructuring* (pp. VI–5:1 to VI–5:13). Alexandria, VA: Association for Supervision and Curriculum Development.

Winbury, J., & Evans, C. S. (1996). Poway portfolio project. In R. E. Blum & J. A. Arter (Eds.), *A handbook for student performance assessment in an era of restructuring* (pp. VII–2:1 to VII–2:6). Alexandria, VA: Association for Supervision and Curriculum Development.

Wortham, S. C. (1984). *Organizing instruction in early childhood.* Boston: Allyn & Bacon.

Wortham, S. C. (2010). *Early childhood curriculum: Developmental bases for learning and teaching* (5th ed.). Upper Saddle River, NJ: Merrill/Prentice Hall.

CHAPTER 7

Teacher-Designed Strategies

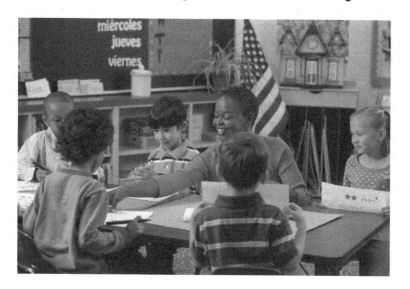

Chapter Objectives

As a result of reading this chapter, you will be able to

1. Describe why teacher-designed assessments and tests are used
2. Understand the relationship between teacher-designed assessments and curriculum and instruction
3. Design assessments for preschool and primary-grade students
4. Understand the process of mastery learning
5. Write an instructional or behavioral objective
6. Develop formative and summative tests and learning, enrichment, and corrective activities for learning objectives

Another type of classroom evaluation to be discussed is teacher-designed assessments. In assessing and evaluating children from birth through the primary grades, measures other than paper-and-pencil tests are generally more appropriate. As children progress through the primary grades, however, they develop skills in reading and writing that will make it possible for them to demonstrate learning on a written test. In this chapter, we discuss how teachers design their own assessments of classroom instruction and use commercially designed classroom tests.

Purposes of Teacher-Designed Assessments and Tests

Although all types of evaluation, both formal and informal, are used to measure and evaluate children's behavior and learning, there are circumstances under which teacher-designed assessments or written classroom tests are especially useful for the teacher. Paper-and-pencil tests, when given to students who are able to use them, can supplement other types of evaluation and provide teachers with information that the other types lack. These purposes include providing objective data on student learning and accountability and providing additional information for making instructional decisions.

Teacher-designed assessments support other evaluation measures, enabling the teacher to make more accurate decisions for the instruction of individual students. The teacher uses observation, tasks during group instruction, and manipulative activities to determine a child's progress in learning. A written test used with older children can reinforce or support the teacher's evaluation with an objective assessment. Objective testing complements the teacher's more subjective, personal evaluation, which can be subject to individual impressions or biases.

Classroom assessments can also support teachers' decisions that may be questioned by parents or school staff members. The teacher may understand, from ongoing work with a child, that the child needs to be instructed at a different level or requires extended experiences with a concept that other children have mastered. Although the teacher is confident in making the decision, a task or paper-and-pencil assessment can support it and, at the same time, help the parents understand the nature of the problem. The teacher-designed assessment thus can increase the teacher's accountability for decisions that affect students' learning.

Teachers must make instructional decisions, both immediate and long term. As they teach, they must decide how long to spend on a particular science unit or math concept. In addition to using informal evaluation strategies, such as individual tasks and ongoing observations of class progress, they can use written tests to provide more information that will help them decide whether to include more experiences, use review activities, skip planned activities, or conclude the current topic and move on to a new one.

Unfortunately, at present, there is increased emphasis on grading young children. Although kindergarten children may be exempt, primary-grade students are being given letter or numerical grades in many schools, and the practice has expanded with the recent emphasis on higher instructional and grading standards.

Teachers find it difficult to assign letter grades to primary-grade children. Whether the practice should continue is debatable; nevertheless, testing can help the teacher make decisions about student achievement. To use only written evaluations for grading would be inappropriate for all the reasons discussed throughout this book; however, when combined with other developmentally appropriate evaluation strategies, paper-and-pencil tests add supporting information on which grades can be based.

In the same fashion, tests can be used to support diagnostic decisions about student needs. The classroom teacher can supplement information from standardized tests and informal evaluations to determine student strengths and weaknesses in content areas. Assessments can be designed that correspond to local instructional objectives and that provide specific information on student accomplishment and instructional needs. Once diagnostic information has been analyzed, the teacher can place students more accurately into instructional groups and regroup periodically as students move through the program at different rates.

Finally, teacher-designed assessments allow evaluation of the local instructional program. Unlike standardized tests, which reflect general objectives suitable for a broad range of school programs at a state, regional, or national level, the teacher-designed test assesses specific or local learning objectives. These objective-based tests evaluate more closely the effectiveness of the local educational program. Without evaluation measures designed for the classroom, there is no ready method to assess local curriculum objectives.

Types of Tests Used With Preschool and Primary-Grade Children

Teacher-designed assessments for preschool children must match the way these children learn—through active interaction with concrete materials. Children who do not yet read cannot demonstrate their learning effectively with a paper-and-pencil test. The teacher constructs assessment activities that allow the child to manipulate materials, explain understanding orally, or point to the correct response if expressive language is limited.

Teacher assessments using tasks or oral responses can be conducted during a teaching activity, as part of a learning-center experience, or as a separate assessment or series of assessments (Wortham, 1984). For example, to determine whether children can recognize uppercase and lowercase letters, the teacher can select letters from concrete classroom materials or cards with the five letters and ask the child to match the upper- and lowercase. Figure 7-1 pictures an array of cards that can be used for this purpose.

To demonstrate an understanding of counting, the preschool child is given objects to count. The teacher can conduct the assessment in two ways. He or she may either select five objects and ask the child to count them or ask the child to group five of the objects. To assess knowledge of shapes, an array of basic shapes could be used. If the objective is to identify shapes, the teacher can ask the child to

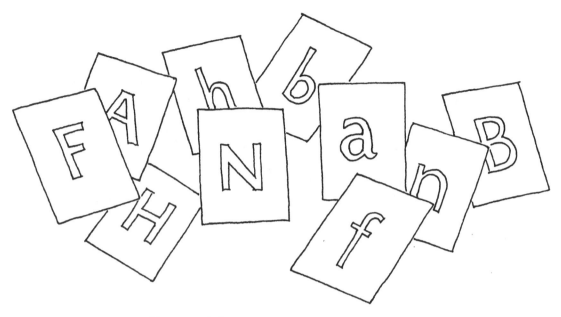

FIGURE 7-1 Uppercase and lowercase letters

find a given shape by saying, "Show me a triangle." The teacher can also point to the shape and ask the child to name it if the objective is to be able to name shapes. Figure 7-2 shows an array of shapes that can be used to identify circles, squares, triangles, and rectangles (Wortham, 1984).

For some preschool assessments, an oral response may be most appropriate. For example, a common preschool objective is for the child to know his or her first and last name. The teacher would ask the child to give this information.

For the objective of sequencing events in a story, the teacher shows the child a set of three to five pictures that have a logical sequence and asks the child to put them in order. The child then is asked to tell the story. Figure 7-3 shows a series of pictures that can be used for sequencing the cards and providing a verbal description.

As children learn to read, the teacher's assessments begin to include printed test activities with pictures and some written words. Instead of a physical response using concrete materials or an oral response, the child uses a pencil with a printed test. The best option is for teachers to design their own assessments to complement the curriculum being used in the classroom. Teachers must be able to design their own tests to evaluate their own or individual learning objectives most effectively. Commercially produced materials designed to be used with student textbooks are also frequently used.

Paper-and-pencil tests must be adapted to the child's limited reading and writing skills. Therefore, tests designed for children in the primary grades use a format that provides pictorial or visual clues to help the student select or write the correct response. To prepare beginning readers and writers for written tests, the teacher

FIGURE 7-2 Array of basic shapes

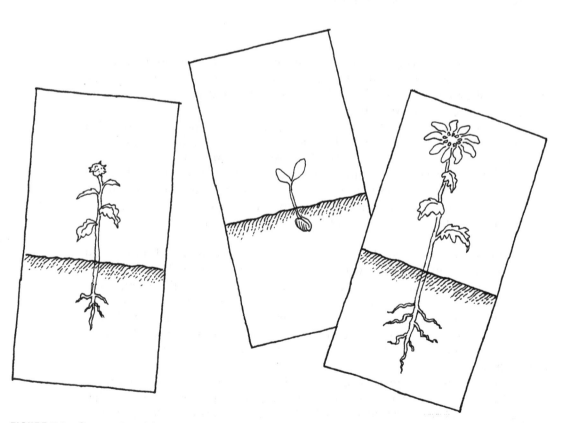

FIGURE 7-3 Sequencing pictures

introduces key words such as *circle* or *draw* that are commonly used in paper-and-pencil assessments. More words are taught until the child is able to read written instructions. Throughout the primary grades, the teacher introduces the assessment page to the children before asking them to complete the page independently.

The most common beginning written tasks include *marking or circling a response, drawing a line to a response, marking a response with an X,* and *writing simple numeral or word answers.*

Children can circle pictures in response to questions before they have learned to read and write. This type of response is continued in the grades where beginning reading skills are acquired. Figure 7-4 presents a page from a commercially designed test in which the child is asked to circle the correct responses and to draw a line to match pictures. On the left-hand side of this figure, the child is asked to circle the correct pictures as the teacher says the name of each. On the right-hand side of the figure, lines are drawn to match animals with their food and habitat. The example is for first-grade students. Although the instructions are printed on the page, the teacher, rather than the student, would provide the information needed to complete the tasks.

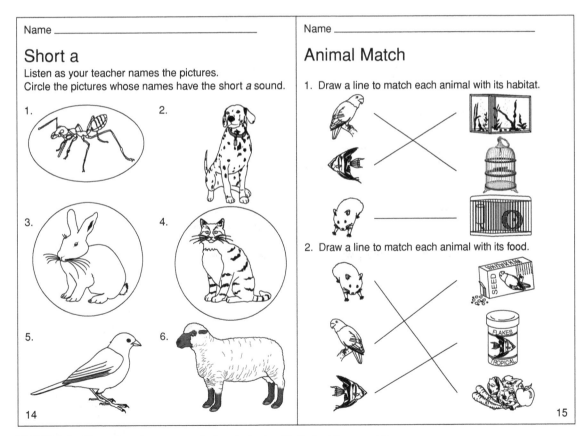

FIGURE 7-4 Examples of assessments for students with limited literacy skills

Source: Scott Foresman ESL Language Activity Book Grade 2. Copyright © 1997 by Scott, Foresman and Company. Reprinted by permission of Pearson Education, Inc.

As reading and writing progress, words can be selected or written for assessment tasks. In Figure 7-5, the student circles the word that fits the blank in a sentence, using a multiple-choice format. In Figure 7-6, a teacher-designed assessment for reading vocabulary, the student must determine whether to write each word under the People category or the Places category.

All the examples of written assessments for the primary grades follow the same guidelines. Not only must the child have visual clues to be able to respond but also an example is usually given to help the child understand the task. Also, although there are written instructions for the child to read, the teacher may need to read and discuss the instructions with the students to ensure that they understand what is required. In the following section, we discuss the design of teacher-constructed assessments and tests.

Growing Flowers

Circle the word that fits in the blank for each sentence.

1. Planting a _____ is the first step in growing flowers.
   Seed   nut   leaf

2. The flower plant next grows a stem and _____.
   Trunk   leaves   bud

3. The _____ carries water for the plant.
   Flower   leaves   stem

FIGURE 7-5   Assessment in which a student selects a word for a sentence

---

PEOPLE AND PLACES

Write each vocabulary word under People or Places below.

People	Places	Words
		bank
		firefighter
		friend
		grocery store
		neighbor
		park
		police officer
		post office
		school
		sister

FIGURE 7-6   Teacher-designed assessment for reading vocabulary

How Tests Are Designed and Used

Classroom tests are closely matched to curriculum objectives and content. Whether designed by the teacher or obtained from a textbook or other commercial source, they are used to measure the student's ability to benefit from classroom instruction.

Unlike standardized tests that provide general information about student achievement, classroom tests measure student accomplishment and learning needs in relation to specific classroom objectives. Classroom tests can be used for placement and diagnosis, formative testing, and summative testing (Linn & Miller, 2005).

Placement and diagnostic testing have a similar function. In placement testing, the student is assessed to determine the instructional group into which he or she should be placed. Tests are given to determine what the student already knows and is ready to learn. Diagnostic testing is used to determine student weaknesses that need to be corrected. The school diagnostician or psychologist can use the same tests for both purposes unless learning difficulties are persistent and need more extensive diagnosis. Placement and diagnostic testing in the classroom are similar to criterion-referenced testing using standardized tests; however, the tests may assess selected learning objectives, rather than objectives for an entire grade level.

Formative and summative tests are related to mastery learning (Bloom, Madaus, & Hastings, 1981). **Formative tests** are given periodically while teaching specific objectives to monitor student progress. These tests measure a limited number of objectives at a time so that the teacher can identify which objectives have been mastered and which call for additional work or activities. They provide feedback and are not used for grading purposes.

The **summative test**, in contrast, is the final test given on completion of a unit of work. The unit of work may be organized for a single objective or for a small group of objectives. The summative test is given after instruction and formative testing reveal that the material has been mastered. It is administered as the final step to verify the student's achievement on the material covered in the unit or by a group of objectives.

The information gained from diagnostic, placement, formative, and summative testing provides the teacher with current, relevant information for instructional planning. It allows the teacher not only to group students for instruction effectively but also to determine how long the class needs to continue working on objectives and whether alternative types of experiences are needed to correct learning weaknesses in particular students. Unlike standardized tests that are administered once a year, classroom tests provide ongoing, criterion-related information about student progress on objectives being covered in a particular classroom. To use classroom testing effectively, the teacher must know how to design appropriate tasks that match the students' ability to use paper-and-pencil tests. The teacher must also know what kinds of tests will accurately measure the students' progress or mastery of each learning objective.

Steps in Test Design

Teacher-designed classroom assessments, although less rigorously constructed than standardized tests, must accurately measure objectives for classroom instruction. Whether the teacher is organizing assessment strategies for preschool or primary-grade students, tests are carefully designed to fit the learning objectives. Although in this section of the chapter we discuss teacher assessment in terms of test design, we refer to evaluation strategies for preschool students who are nonreaders, as well as for students in the primary grades who are beginning to read and write.

Several steps in test design must be followed if a test is to measure student learning accurately. Based on Bloom's model of mastery learning (Block, 1971), the process includes the following:

1. Determining instructional objectives
2. Constructing a table of specifications
3. Designing formative and summative evaluations
4. Designing learning experiences
5. Designing correctives and enrichment activities

Determining Instructional Objectives

In chapter 5, we discussed objectives relative to skills continuums and checklists. The same types of sources are used to develop instructional objectives that will be used to design classroom tests. Although the term *learning outcomes* has replaced *instructional objectives* in many states and school districts, they have the same purpose. School districts have various sources to draw from when determining curriculum objectives for each grade level.

During the 20th century, the common source of curriculum objectives was basal textbook series used in the classroom. Most textbooks in reading, mathematics, social studies, and science were based on learning objectives appropriate for that grade level in school districts in many states. A commonly accepted pool of learning objectives could be found in the content areas for each grade level; however, objectives could vary markedly among different basal series. Textbooks were organized around these objectives, and teacher's editions of the textbooks contained activities to implement instruction for the objectives and tests to evaluate student learning on the objectives.

National and state standards are the current framework for curriculum and instruction. The discussions of NCLB in earlier chapters included the introduction of national standards introduced by professional organizations as well as standards developed by state education agencies. The standards were implemented to clarify educational objectives and raise the learning achievement of students in public schools. More recently, standards have also been developed for early childhood education. (See chapter 1.) Standards have become the primary source for educational objectives (Seefeldt, 2005). Currently a large number of states are developing common standards. Instead of individual states designing their own goals and desired outcomes, there will be a single set of standards that will become national standards.

Today, commercial curriculum publications and other textbook materials are based on national and/or state curriculum standards. Individual school districts establish their own learning objectives following the state-mandated standards. The overall goal is to improve learning for all students. Teacher assessments are one strategy available to provide accountability of learning through the documentation of mastery of skills. They are supplemented with commercial assessments as well as the range of assessment possibilities presented in this text.

Writing Behavioral Objectives. **Behavioral objectives**, or **instructional objectives**, provide the framework for curriculum and instruction and the measurement of the effectiveness of instruction and learning. Many states and school districts require that behavioral objectives that specify the measurement of the effectiveness of instruction and learning be included in instructional planning. The objective is stated in observable, behavioral terms to include the following:

An observable behavior (action verb specifying the learning outcome)

Any special conditions under which the behaviors must by displayed

A performance level considered sufficient to demonstrate mastery (Kubiszyn & Borich, 1996)

Another approach to understanding the elements of a behavioral objective would be to use an ABCD acronym:

A is the audience

B is the behavior

C is the condition

D is the degree or level of mastery

For example, a common objective for preschool children is to be able to sort objects into two groups by using some type of criterion. An instructional or behavioral objective could be written as follows:

Given an array of nuts, the student will be able to sort the nuts correctly into two groups: nuts with smooth shells and nuts with rough shells.

An analysis of the objective would identify the components of an instructional objective as follows:

Given an array of nuts (condition, C), the student (A) will be able to sort the nuts correctly (100% performance standard implied, D) into two groups: nuts with smooth shells and nuts with rough shells (behavior, B).

An objective for physical development might include the ability to catch a ball with both hands. Stated behaviorally, the objective might be worded as follows:

Following a series of activities throwing and catching large rubber balls, the child will be able to catch the ball with both hands in four out of six tries.

To analyze the parts of this objective, it would be described as follows:

Following a series of activities throwing and catching large rubber balls (C), the child (A) will be able to catch the ball with both hands (B) in four out of six tries (D).

Before a learning objective or outcome can be measured, then, it must be stated clearly in terms of its content and the desired behavior. The *content* refers to the knowledge or skill to be learned. The *behavior* is what the student does to demonstrate that the knowledge or skill has been attained.

Analyzing Objectives to Determine Prerequisite Skills. The teacher must not only develop the learning objective but also determine what must be taught to the student to master it. Part of planning for instruction involves studying the learning objective to decide what prior knowledge or skill the student must have to be able to learn the new information. For the objective "Recall addition facts through sums to 5," the teacher plans instruction to help students to learn to combine all possible groups of numbers that equal 5. In addition, the teacher determines what the student must already know to understand and use addition skills. Prior skills to be considered include the following:

1. Knowledge of numbers through 5
2. Identification of numerals through 5
3. Understanding that small groups can be combined to make a larger group

The teacher must decide whether the students have the prerequisite skills to be able to master the targeted learning objective. If not, the prior skills will have to be taught, or retaught if necessary, before the new objective is introduced. A pretest or a diagnostic test may be used to determine student readiness for the learning objective.

Setting a Standard for Mastery. The final step in determining the instructional objectives is to set the level of mastery that will be expected for the student to learn the objective. In the section on writing behavioral objectives, information was included on how to include the performance level for the objective. In this context, the process for determining the level of performance desired or required is discussed. The teacher, the school district, or the state department of education may set the level of accomplishment. This is the minimum standard required to pass the objective. The learning objective can reflect the established standard for mastery. If 80% is established as the minimum standard for mastery, the learning objective can be stated to reflect the standard.

Constructing a Table of Specifications

After the learning objectives for a unit of study or the content of an entire course has been described behaviorally, the teacher or curriculum developer is ready to outline the course content. Before a test can be organized to measure the curriculum objectives, it is necessary to understand more accurately what concepts or skills are to be measured and to what extent the student will be expected to perform to demonstrate mastery of the objective. Will the student be expected to remember information, use the information to solve problems, or evaluate the information? The test items will reflect the level of understanding that is required to master the objective.

Analysis of objectives to determine the level of understanding is commonly done by constructing a **table of specifications** (Linn & Miller, 2005). Here learning objectives are charted by using Bloom's *Taxonomy of Educational Objectives* (Bloom, 1956). This work describes levels of understanding in the cognitive domain, ranging from the ability to recall information (the knowledge level) to the highest level of understanding (evaluation). Figure 7-7 explains the levels of Bloom's taxonomy, with examples of terms that characterize each level. In Figure 7-8,

Level of Understanding	Descriptive Terms	
Knowledge Recognition and recall The ability to remember or recognize information	Tell List Name	Define Identify Locate
Comprehension The ability to translate information in your own words Show that you understand	Restate Discuss Explain Review	Describe Summarize Interpret
Application The ability to use information or apply learning to new situations and real-life circumstances	Demonstrate Construct Imply	Dramatize Practice Illustrate
Analysis The ability to break down information into parts To identify parts of information and its relationship to the whole	Organize Differentiate Compare Distinguish	Solve Experiment Relate

Synthesis
The ability to assemble separate parts into a new
  whole
The ability to take information from various sources
  and present it in a created form
	Design
	Plan
	Develop
		Compile
		Create
		Compose

Evaluation The ability to make judgments about information To be able to evaluate based on criteria or standards	Decide Conclude Appraise Choose	Judge Assess Select

FIGURE 7-7   Explanation of Bloom's taxonomy

Sums to 5	Know	Comprehend	Apply	Analyze	Synthesize	Evaluate
2.1 Recall addition facts through sums to 5	X	X	X			
2.2 Solve problems using cumulative computational skills	X	X	X	X		

FIGURE 7-8   Table of specifications for a unit on sums to 5

an adaptation of the taxonomy is used to make a table of specifications for the mathematics unit covering addition sums to 5. The two objectives for the unit are listed to the left of the figure. The columns to the right describe how the objectives are charted on the taxonomy. The first objective requires that the student be able

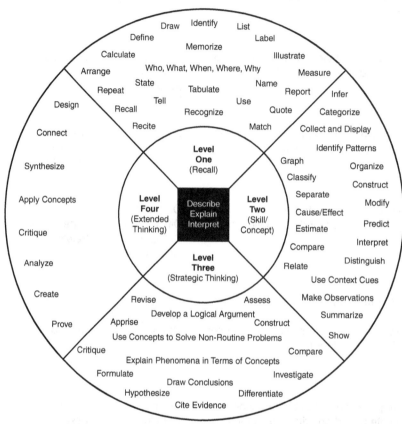

Level One Activities	Level Two Activities	Level Three Activities	Level Four Activities
Recall elements and details of story structure, such as sequence of events, character, plot, and setting.	Identify and summarize the major events in a narrative.	Support ideas with details and examples.	Conduct a project that requires specifying a problem, designing and conducting an experiment, analyzing its data, and reporting results/solutions.
Conduct basic mathematical calculations.	Use context cues to identify the meaning of unfamiliar words.	Use voice appropriate to the purpose and audience.	
Label locations on a map.	Solve routine multiple-step problems.	Identify research questions and design investigations for a scientific problem.	Apply mathematical model to illuminate a problem or situation.
Represent in words or diagrams a scientific concept or relationship.	Describe the cause/effect of a particular event.	Develop a scientific model for a complex situation.	Analyze and synthesize information from multiple sources.
Perform routine procedures like measuring length or using punctuation marks correctly.	Identify patterns in events or behavior.	Determine the author's purpose and describe how it affects the interpretation of a reading selection.	Describe and illustrate how common themes are found across texts from different cultures.
Describe the features of a place or people.	Formulate a routine problem given data and conditions.		Design a mathematical model to inform and solve a practical or abstract situation.
	Organize, represent, and interpret data.	Apply a concept in other contexts.	

FIGURE 7-9   Depth of Knowledge (DOK) levels

to recall addition facts and problems, understand the facts and problems, and apply that understanding. The second objective also requires that the student be able to analyze or solve problems. When designing test or assessment items, the teacher must know the type and level of understanding that test items will reflect and must organize the test so that the described levels of understanding are adequately sampled.

NCLB brought higher expectations of how teachers understand student learning. Teachers were now expected to understand and be able to teach to different levels of knowledge. A system called Depth of Knowledge (DOK) was developed to provide a guide to teachers as they supported children's learning to higher levels (Webb, 2002). Soon state departments of education were using DOK in their curriculum and instruction standards (Webb et al., 2005; Wyoming School Health and Physical Education Network, 2001).

The DOK is very similar to Bloom's taxonomy. Instead of Bloom's five levels of understanding, DOK has four. Level 1 is titled recall; Level 2, skill and concept; Level 3, strategic thinking; and Level 4, extended thinking. In addition, the four levels have many more descriptors of student behaviors for each level. Figure 7-9 provides a chart of the DOK levels and descriptors. At the bottom of the figure, suggested activities are matched with the four levels. Figure 7-10 compares Bloom's taxonomy and Webb's Depth of Knowledge levels.

Designing Formative and Summative Evaluations

After the teacher has determined what is to be measured by designing a table of specifications for the learning objectives to be taught, it is time to design the formative and summative evaluations. Both types of evaluations are derived from the table of specifications. Assessment items will be designed to measure the student's achievement at the levels of Bloom's taxonomy, as described in the table

Bloom's Taxonomy	Depths of Knowledge
KNOWLEDGE Recalls facts, retells events COMPREHENSION Shows understanding, can Explain information	RECALL Recall of a fact, information, or procedure
APPLICATION Is able to use information or apply to new situations	SKILL/CONCEPT Use of information, conceptual knowledge or procedures
ANALYSIS Can break down a situation or information into parts or components	STRATEGIC THINKING Develops a plan or sequence of steps; uses more than one possible answer
SYNTHESIS AND EVALUATION Can assemble parts into a whole and make value judgements about the process	EXTENDED THINKING Uses time to think and process multiple conditions; investigates

FIGURE 7-10 Comparison of Bloom's taxonomy and Webb's Depth of Knowledge levels

of specifications. The assessment items on the two forms are equivalent, but the evaluation purposes differ. The formative evaluation is not a test; it is a checkup or progress report on the student. The teacher uses the formative evaluation to decide whether the student needs further work with the objective.

If the student needs additional experiences, more activities, known as **correctives**, are implemented. Correctives are learning resources designed to approach the objective differently from the original instruction. The intent is to provide various kinds of activities to meet individual students' needs.

If the student's responses indicate mastery on the formative evaluation, the teacher provides **enrichment activities**. The student engages in activities that are at a higher level on Bloom's taxonomy than are required for mastery. Thus, if the mastery level in the table of specifications is at the application level, students who master the information after an initial period of instruction may benefit from activities at the analysis, synthesis, or evaluation levels (Bloom et al., 1981).

The summative evaluation is the final assessment or test of what the student has learned or accomplished. It is given after all instruction has been concluded. Although formative and summative evaluations are interchangeable in content, only the summative form is used as a test. The decisions to be made about both assessments include the format, selection of assessment items, determination of length, and assembly of the assessment.

Test Formats and Assessment Items.   Earlier in the chapter, we talked about test formats for use with children in preschool and primary grades. When the teacher is ready to design classroom assessments, the appropriate format will have to be determined. Most preschool children respond best to concrete tasks and oral questions. Assessment items reflect the table of specifications and use appropriate concrete strategies used with preschool children. Figure 7-11 shows a table of specifications for a preschool unit on classification. Objective B specifies that the student will be able to remove the object that is different from a set of four objects. Figure 7-12 pictures a group of objects that may be used to evaluate the child's performance on the objective. The child chooses or points to the object that does not belong to the group.

Concrete tasks should also be used with children in the primary grades along with activities using reading and writing. When a teacher moves to a written test for first graders, the teacher should limit student responses to tasks that require little or no reading or writing, such as circling, pictures, marking the correct response, and drawing lines to correct responses as introduced earlier in the chapter. In the unit on coins described in Figure 7-13, children will have a variety of experiences using real coins to learn the objectives. More writing and reading can be incorporated into the test format. If several different tasks are to be used, more than one format can be included on a test. Figure 7-13 shows the table of specifications for the unit on coins. The teacher must develop test items that reflect the objectives to be tested. Figures 7-14 and 7-15 are examples of an assessment that includes reading and writing. In Figure 7-14, the student is asked to draw a line from each coin to its letter names as well as writing the value of each coin. In Figure 7-15, the student adds the value of collections of coins and writes the total value of the collections.

Behavioral Objectives	Knowledge	Comprehension	Application	Analysis	Synthesis	Evaluation
A. Classifying						
1. The student will describe the object by naming one of its attributes.	X	X				
2. The student will construct a set from various objects by classifying together those with common attributes.	X	X	X			
B. Noting Differences						
1. From a set of four objects, the student will remove the one object that is different from the others.	X	X	X	X		
C. Classifying by Name						
1. The student will classify a group of pictures into two categories, using class names.	X	X	X			
D. Classifying by Design						
1. The student will classify objects into sets according to design, such as stripes, dots, etc.	X	X	X			

FIGURE 7-11 Unit objective: Classifying objects by common attributes in a table of specifications

Test Length. After determining the format and developing a pool of items to provide the levels of understanding expected from the table of specifications, the test developer must determine how many test items or tasks will be included in the test. For young children, a balance is reached between the number of items needed to demonstrate the child's responses to determine understanding and a reasonable length that will not overtax the child's ability to attend to the task. For preschool and primary grades, the test length should not exceed the time normally needed to complete classroom activities and assignments. A maximum of 20 to 30 minutes is

FIGURE 7-12   Unit on classification: Array of objects

reasonable in testing primary-grade students. Commercial tests designed to evaluate these students are commonly one page long.

Assembly.   The final step in test design is to assemble test items into both a formative and a summative form. The teacher should construct enough items so that both forms of the test can be put together at the same time. The formative evaluation, conducted after the students have had some work with the objective, will enable the teacher to assess how well the students are learning the information. After the formative assessment has been examined, the teacher can reteach, provide different types of experiences or practice for some students, or move on to the summative test if the students show adequate progress. The teacher should have enough items to obtain the feedback needed to monitor student learning and mastery. The formative and summative assessments should be equivalent in terms of the level of understanding required and the types of items used.

When assembling the tests, the teacher must decide how instructions will be given to the students. If written instructions requiring reading skills will be used, they must be simply stated to match the students' reading ability. Pictures used must be clear and easily interpreted. Poorly drawn or inappropriate pictures will hamper the child's ability to respond correctly and distort the child's performance on the test. If the teacher is unable to draw simple pictures, he or she should obtain them from another source or ask a colleague for help.

Designing Learning Experiences

After the table of specifications and the formative and summative evaluations have been constructed, the teacher collects and prepares the activities and instruction that will enable the student to learn the information designed in the objective. Instruction also matches the level given in the table of specifications.

OBJECTIVES	KNOWLEDGE	COMPREHENSION	APPLICATION	ANALYSIS	SYNTHESIS	EVALUATION
1. The student will be able to identify the five coins (half-dollar, quarter, dime, nickel, penny) by sight with 100% accuracy.	X					
2. The student will be able to match the five coins with their letter names with 100% accuracy.	X					
3. The student will be able to match the five coins to their number value using a cent sign (¢) with 100% accuracy.	X	X				
4. The student will be able to classify like coins by counting: pennies by ones, nickels by fives, dimes by tens, and quarters by twenty-fives, with 80% accuracy.	X	X	X	X		
5. The student will be able to differentiate like/unlike coins by switch counting from twenty-fives to tens to fives to ones in necessary order to count collections of coins up to 99¢ with 80% accuracy.	X	X	X	X		
6. The student will be able to analyze and solve story problems by counting coins with 80% accuracy.	X	X	X	X		

FIGURE 7-13   Unit on coins: Table of specifications

Instruction to introduce and work with the objectives includes teacher instruction and other resources normally used by the teacher to help children practice and master new concepts and skills.

The instructional objective contains the structure for the learning experiences that will be provided for the students to interact with and master concepts. The teacher-directed lessons and child-centered activities enable the child to work with information and skills. When planning the activities, the teacher establishes some type of format to describe each activity and how it will be used. The activity description includes the objective, the materials needed, and any other relevant information.

For example, one objective of the unit on classifying objects discussed earlier could be used to describe appropriate activities. Figure 7-11 had the objective under "B. Noting Differences" as follows: From a set of four objects, the student will remove

Name._____   Summative Evaluation

Draw a line to match the coins with their names.

1.

quarter   nickel   half-dollar   penny   dime

2. Write the value of each coin on the line.

1¢

_____   _____   _____   _____   _____

FIGURE 7-14   Teacher-designed test on coins

the one object that is different from the others. Figure 7-12 shows an assessment task that uses an array of objects to permit the child to demonstrate understanding of the objective. Figure 7-16 describes an activity that can be used for young children to experience the same concepts, first as a teacher-directed activity and later in a learning center.

Designing Correctives and Enrichment Activities

Corrective activities for students who need additional work after initial instruction and formative evaluation provide learning alternatives. These include audiovisual

Name _____

Count the value of the coins.
Write the total on the line.

3.

31¢

4.

_____

5.

_____

6.

_____

7.

_____

8.

_____

FIGURE 7-15 Test on coins

resources, games, workbooks, peer tutoring, student–teacher discussions, and other opportunities that are different from the original instruction and activities. The purpose is to provide different or alternative ways for the student to learn the information in the learning objective.

Objective
From a set of four objects, the student will remove the one object that is different from the others.

Materials Needed
A group of 2-inch blocks, 5 of one color, 1 of a different color
Several socks of different types and sizes, 1 shoe
An array of leaves of one type, 1 leaf of a different shape and size

Type of Activity
Teacher-directed, to be placed later in the math–science center. Small group.

Activity Description
The teacher will introduce the concept by using the group of blocks. The words *alike* and *different* will be modeled to describe the blocks.

Next, the socks and the shoe will be explored, with children encouraged to identify the one that is different. The leaves will then be used for the same activity.

As a final step, the teacher will ask each child to find examples in the classroom that are alike and different and to make a group similar to the examples that have been used: three things that are identical and one that is different. Each child is encouraged to describe his or her collection.

FIGURE 7-16 Example of a learning activity

Examples of corrective activities and enrichment activities may use the objective cited previously: From a set of four objects, the student will remove the one object that is different from the others. A child who needs additional activities to internalize the concept would benefit from opportunities to practice, but with alternative types of experiences. If the teacher-directed activities have focused on concrete objects, a corrective activity might consist of a card game of several sets of four cards that could be played by two children. Another corrective might use a flannel board and have the child remove the item that is different from an array of four items.

Children who are English language learners (ELLs) would benefit from opportunities to use the vocabulary associated with the concept. The terms *alike* and *different* would be basic to understanding the concept. Then if colors, shoes, blocks, leaves, and so on were used in lessons, those words would also be used so that they could become part of the child's vocabulary. A similar process would be important for children with special needs. Children with mental delay will need many extra experiences on a one-to-one basis with the concept, while children with visual difficulties may need to have the lesson adapted with items that can be differentiated by touch. Teachers and support staff for children with special needs must plan ahead how the concept could be presented for individual children.

Enrichment activities provide opportunities for higher-level thinking. If additional complexity is desired, the number of items may be increased to five, with two items that are different, rather than one. Another way to increase complexity is to make the difference in the item more difficult to identify. Only a slight difference is evident between the three identical items and the one that is different. For example,

Phyllis and Amy

*P*hyllis and Amy are both in the first grade. Phyllis is an accelerated learner who grasps classroom information with little effort. Amy has mental retardation. She works at a much simpler cognitive level than the other children in the classroom. During the mastery learning process used in the classroom, Amy often works with a teacher's aide who has activities designed for her learning needs. When the class works on the concept of *alike* and *different,* Amy has activities that concentrate on two colors. She and the aide have large discs that are red and blue. After many lessons, Amy is able to say which disc is different in an array of three red discs and one blue disc.

When the class is working on correctives and enrichment activities, Phyllis often asks to work with Amy. Phyllis is given classroom objects that Amy is familiar with and can name. They practice together with *alike* and *different* with pairs of objects. Phyllis alternates using like objects and different objects with Amy as if they are playing a game. Amy loves having Phyllis work with her, and Phyllis enjoys helping Amy feel that she is part of the class.

if the four pictured items are gift-wrapped boxes, the ribbon on one of the boxes is different or part of the ribbon is missing.

Enrichment activities also allow students who easily mastered the objective initially to engage in challenging and more creative activities. The students can work on individual projects that allow them to problem-solve and apply their own ideas in various types of activities that emerge from their own efforts (Block, 1977). Students may develop pictures of items that are alike and different or write a story in which each page has a different category of items with one that is different.

Advantages and Disadvantages of Using Teacher-Designed Assessments

Teacher-designed assessments in the classroom have several advantages over commercially produced tests developed for the same purpose. The advantages are related to the flexibility of the tests constructed for the teacher's own classroom.

When a teacher plans an assessment activity or test, the objective or objectives to be tested may be selected to suit individual class needs. Unlike commercial tests, which may be programmed to fit student progress in a grade-level textbook, the teacher-designed test can vary from the structure or plan of the book. A teacher may be concerned about an objective outside the textbook sequence and feel compelled to conduct an evaluation. Because he or she is developing tests to fit classroom needs, the targeted objective can be tested within the teacher's assessment plans whenever needed.

In addition, teacher-constructed assessments can be designed for a particular class. If the children are nonreaders but have advanced concepts that are normally introduced to children who have reading skills, the teacher can write the test to accommodate their abilities. If the students are advanced readers, the test can be designed to take advantage of their reading skills. The most common difficulty with commercial classroom tests is that they are set for a certain reading level or penalize the child for being unable to perform well because pencil-and-paper skills are required. The teacher can modify test tasks to include manipulative activities, oral

Assessments for Instructional Objectives: How Useful Are They?

Norris teaches kindergarten. He and the other kindergarten teachers have been sent to a training session on designing assessments for instructional objectives using mastery learning. In the session, the teachers have reviewed how to write behavioral objectives and how to construct a table of specifications based on Bloom's taxonomy of educational objectives. Working with the table of specifications prepares them to design assessment strategies for the objectives.

On the way home after the training session, Norris and the other teachers voice skepticism. How can this kind of testing be used with kindergarten children? Norris comments, "I can see how some areas, such as math, can be organized and assessed by behavioral objectives, but how do you decide what 80% accuracy is on learning the Pledge of Allegiance, or what they learn from art or using concepts in science?" Norris finally decides that it is a matter of common sense. The teacher can apply the strategies with some parts of the curriculum in kindergarten but not others. The question is whether the school's principal and the kindergarten coordinator will share Norris's perspective. He and the other kindergarten teachers decide to talk to teachers at other grade levels to determine how they are implementing the assessment strategies. Afterward, they want to study their curriculum and decide where they can use assessments based on a table of specifications. They want to meet with the principal and the coordinator to discuss where the process will work and which parts of the curriculum do not lend themselves to that type of assessment.

When Norris and the other teachers meet with the principal and the kindergarten coordinator, they present tables of specifications and assessments for mathematics and units in science. After they explain their reluctance to use the process with their reading program and other curriculum components, the kindergarten coordinator supports their position. The principal is more reluctant but decides to let the coordinator work with the teachers to determine how and where the assessment strategies will be implemented at the kindergarten level.

responses, and assessment within instructional periods if the child understands concepts but cannot yet respond on a written test.

Teacher-designed assessments can be improved whenever needed. Each time the teacher administers a test, student responses provide feedback on its effectiveness. The test can be changed and improved whenever students' responses indicate problems with the format or test items.

Teacher-designed tests also have disadvantages; potential weaknesses generally focus on the teacher's skill in designing classroom assessments. Because teachers do not generally have extensive experience in developing their own tests, the evaluations they design may not be effective in evaluating student learning.

Because of the abundance of commercially designed tests that accompany curriculum texts and kits, teachers are not always required to construct their own tests. Teachers become dependent on commercial tests and do not consider the necessity of designing their own. As a result, the teacher may not clearly understand the purpose of the tests or the levels of knowledge that are tested.

Teachers may lack the training in test design that affects both understanding of the purpose of the commercial tests and the skills needed to construct tests. For example, teachers may not have learned how to use a table of specifications for curriculum objectives. When they design tests, they are not aware of the levels of knowledge in the curriculum that need to be part of the evaluation process. This lack of awareness may be more true of early childhood teachers than of teachers in intermediate grades and secondary schools. Teachers of preschool and primary-grade children need to be aware of the various levels of cognitive understanding as well as alternative methods of evaluation that are developmentally suited to young students.

Finally, the process of developing good classroom tests, especially for younger students, is time consuming. Because test items must be developed to accommodate emerging reading and writing skills, each item must be carefully considered for both content and method or format. This consideration takes more time than developing items for students who have good reading and writing skills. The method of presentation is as important as the concepts and skills being tested.

Young children benefit from assessments that use real objects.

A discussion of the weaknesses of teacher-designed assessments must include mention of the issues surrounding the use of mastery learning in early childhood education. Because mastery learning requires that the teacher analyze learning objectives and determine the level of mastery to be achieved, it would seem to conflict with the philosophy that early childhood educators should provide developmentally appropriate classroom experiences; that is, the teacher is encouraged to provide learning experiences that are consistent with the child's level of development, rather than to ask the child to fit into a predetermined style of learning that requires specific types of responses to achieve mastery.

The interest in providing developmentally appropriate practices also extends to the use of behavioral or instructional objectives specifically. One criticism of the objectives is the division of learning into small, skill-based objectives, rather than more global constructivist learning. The performance standard or level of mastery seems limiting when compared to the emphasis on child-centered learning that emerges from the child's interests and previous experiences.

Although these issues first applied to preschool classrooms, they are also a concern with primary-grade teachers. Constructivist learning or a "thinking curriculum" (Linn & Miller, 2005) focuses on the student's active involvement in constructing meaning, rather than mastery of specific skills. Thus, students should be engaged in more divergent types of learning and more complex types of outcomes. Performance assessment, discussed in chapter 8, addresses this issue.

Certain components of the preschool classroom curriculum lend themselves to the mastery learning approach. Concept development, particularly in mathematics, has sequential objectives that can be taught within the mastery learning format. Nevertheless, many early childhood educators object to attempts to limit early childhood programs to this approach. The need for exploratory and inquiry-based experiences, originating from the child's opportunity to initiate activities both indoors and outdoors and using self-directed learning, is essential in early childhood classrooms. In fact, these experiences are essential for both preschool and primary-grade levels.

Teachers must ultimately be able to understand and use their own assessments appropriately to match the curriculum and their students' development. Mastery learning must also be used appropriately in early childhood programs.

Despite their weaknesses, teacher-designed evaluations have an important place in early childhood classrooms. An answer to the difficulties in using these assessments may be to help teachers understand the process of test design and to support their efforts to develop tests.

Developing Quality Teacher-Designed Assessments

The steps in test design described in this chapter provide a guide to developing quality assessments that are directly linked to the learning process. Test items and learning activities are linked to the same learning objectives so that teachers are teaching and testing to the same levels of knowledge on Bloom's taxonomy. Similar steps can be taken for all teacher-designed assessments. Following are some suggestions for teachers to consider when designing assessment tasks and tests.

Concrete Tasks for Preschool

- Be sure that the task is at the same level of difficulty as the learning activities designed for the learning objective.
- Have a variety of objects and/or concrete materials so that the assessment task can be administered several times.
- When possible, administer tasks for a number of learning objectives. Have materials for a number of tasks organized and available.

Tests for Primary-Grade Children

- Be sure that test items match the child's reading level. (Use the lowest possible reading level.)
- Use clear directions, even if they will be read by the teacher.
- Ensure that response items for multiple-choice-type assessments have one correct answer.
- Ensure that response options for multiple-choice-type assessments are the same length and are brief.
- Keep the list of items brief for matching exercises.
- Be sure that the list of items for matching exercises is homogeneous.
- Ensure that the length of blanks is the same for completion test items.
- Use only one blank for each completion item.

Summary

Although written tests are the least commonly used method of evaluating the learning of young students, there is a place for these tests once children have mastered some reading and writing skills. Teachers and parents can use written tests as sources of objective information of student progress.

Like standardized tests, teacher-designed and commercially produced classroom assessments are developed through the use of procedures that ensure they are correct in content and method of evaluation. Test design begins with careful analysis and description of learning objectives for the curriculum. The objectives are examined for the prerequisite skills that must be mastered prior to their use and for how the content and skills must be taught. In addition to determining the level of mastery for the learning objectives, the test developer must use a developmentally appropriate test format that will maximize the performance of students who are learning to read and write.

Before test items are constructed, the test designer must describe the level at which the student must demonstrate the new knowledge. A table of specifications organized for the learning objectives is used for this purpose. While constructing the formative and summative evaluations, the teacher must consider length, equivalent items for both evaluations, and what types of test instructions are most appropriate.

Because paper-and-pencil tests may not be the most effective way to evaluate or assess children through the primary grades, teachers must understand when and how such tests are appropriate. Teacher must have acquired the skills to develop such tests if they are to measure learning accurately and appropriately. Teachers of young students must also understand the limitations of written tests and become skilled in combining them with alternative evaluation methods to ensure that each student is tested with procedures that are most appropriate for his or her own level of development and ability to respond.

REVIEW QUESTIONS

1. How do written tests serve a purpose different from other types of tests and evaluation methods?
2. Why should teachers be careful when using written tests with students in the primary grades?
3. How do written tests provide records of student learning that facilitate teaching accountability?
4. Why is the description of content and student behavior important in using learning objectives for assessment design?
5. How does the standard of mastery affect both the learning objective and the test developed to measure achievement of the objective?
6. What is a table of specifications? How is it used with learning objectives?
7. Why do teachers need to understand the levels of knowledge used to chart objectives on a table of specifications?
8. Describe different formats used in written tests developed for beginning readers.
9. What kinds of guidelines should the teacher consider when determining the length of a test for primary-grade children?
10. Can more than one format be used in an assessment?
11. How are formative and summative tests alike? Different?
12. Why are written tests for primary-grade children difficult to design?
13. Why do classroom teachers tend not to develop their own tests?
14. How can teacher-designed tests be more effective than commercially designed tests that evaluate the same objectives?
15. When should teachers use written tests? When should they not use written tests?

SUGGESTED ACTIVITIES

1. Write behavioral objectives for the following: (a) The child will be able to match uppercase and lowercase letters; (b) the child will be able to sort objects by color; and (c) the child will be able to match sets of objects with the correct numeral.
2. Develop a teacher-designed assessment for a learning center in a preschool classroom. First, determine what preschool objective will be assessed and which learning center is appropriate. Next, review appropriate concrete strategies that can be used to assess the objective.

Then, collect or make an assessment that can be used by at least five children at a time. Finally, determine what the teacher will observe as the children engage in the activity.

3. Following the example provided in the chapter, develop a mastery learning unit based on three objectives. The unit should include a table of specifications, two learning activities for each objective, two correctives for each objective, and two enrichment activities for each objective. Construct six activities, two for each category.

KEY TERMS

behavioral objective
corrective
enrichment activity
formative test

instructional objective
summative test
table of specifications

SELECTED WEB SITES

Classroom Assessments
http://fcit.usf.edu/assessment/

Educational Testing Service
http://www.ets.org

National Institute for Early Education Research (NIEER)
http://www.Nieer.org/resources/policybriefs/7.pdf

Assessment in the Early Childhood Classroom
http://www.uen.org/k-2educator/assessment.shtml

REFERENCES

Block, J. H. (1971). Introduction. In J. H. Block (Ed.), *Mastery learning: Theory and practice* (pp. 2–12). New York: Holt, Rinehart & Winston.

Block, J. H. (1977). Individualized instruction: A mastery learning perspective. *Educational Leadership, 34,* 337–341.

Bloom, B. S. (Ed.). (1956). *Taxonomy of educational objectives: The classification of educational goals. Handbook I: Cognitive domain.* New York: McKay.

Bloom, B. S., Madaus, G. E., & Hastings, J. T. (1981). *Evaluation to improve learning.* New York: McGraw-Hill.

Kubiszyn, T., & Borich, G. (1996). *Educational testing and measurement: Classroom application and practice* (5th ed.). Hoboken, NJ: John Wiley & Sons.

Linn, R. L., & Miller, M. D. (2005). *Measurement and assessment in teaching* (9th ed.). Upper Saddle River, NJ: Merrill/Prentice Hall.

Scott Foresman Science Tearcher's Assessment Package, Grade 1. (2000). Glenview, IL: Addison-Wesley Educational Publishers.

Seefeldt, C. (2005). *How to work with standards in the early childhood classroom.* (7th ed.). New York: Teachers College Press.

Webb, N. L. (2002, March 28). *Depth-of-knowledge levels for four content areas.* Madison, WI: University of Wisconsin Center for Educational Resources.

Webb, N. L., Alt, M., Ely, R., Cormier, M., & Vesperman, B. (2005). *Web alignment tool.* Madison, WI: University of Wisconsin Center for Educational Resources.

Wortham, S. C. (1984). *Organizing instruction in early childhood.* Boston: Allyn & Bacon.

Wyoming School Health and Physical Education Network. (2001). Standards, assessment, and beyond. Retrieved Marsh 16, 2010, from http://www.uwyo.edu/wyhpenet

CHAPTER 8

Performance-Based Strategies

Chapter Objectives

As a result of reading this chapter, you will be able to

1. Understand the relationship between authentic learning and authentic assessment
2. Understand the definition and the purposes for performance-based assessment
3. Describe several types of performance-based assessments and how they are used
4. Understand the advantages and disadvantages of using performance-based evaluation tools
5. Discuss how performance assessments can be used to address state standards

In chapters 5, 6, and 7, we discussed the types of classroom evaluations such as observation, checklists and rating scales, and teacher-designed assessments. In this chapter, we discuss how these classroom evaluations contribute to a broader strategy—performance-based assessment. Each classroom assessment discussed in previous chapters contributes to the collection of assessment information that is part of performance-based assessment. The strategies used to conduct these assessments permit the teacher to measure a child's performance.

Before proceeding further, I should explain what is meant by performance-based assessment and how it is seen as a positive alternative to the use of standardized tests to measure children's development and learning. Traditional formal methods of measuring learning have focused on assessing what the child knows. Achievement tests are accurately labeled in that they measure what the child has achieved. Performance assessment is advocated as a contrast to high-stakes testing. Meisels (2000) deplores the current situation in which tests determine what teachers teach, what children learn, and whether children fail or are promoted. Rather than depend on tests that are a single indicator of what a child has learned, Meisels proposes that the teacher should have a generative or transformed role with children. The teacher–learner process permits the learner to use his or her own skills to learn new skills.

Performance assessments require more in that they measure what the child can do or apply, in addition to what the child knows (Herman, Aschbacher, & Winters, 1992; Pierson & Beck, 1993; Wiggins, 1993, 1998). Moreover, performance assessment includes completion of a task in a realistic context. Another term frequently used for this type of assessment is **authentic assessment**, or **authentic performance assessment**. Bergen (1994) proposes that a good authentic performance assessment must have some connection to the real world and be an application of learning. Furthermore, says Bergen, it possesses the following qualities: (1) It is integrative, measuring many facets simultaneously; (2) it is applied, having the complexity of real-world roles; and (3) it may be individual, but is often group based, and the performance of every group member is essential for success as both individual and group performance effectiveness is evaluated. An important element in authentic assessment is that it is linked directly to authentic learning (Baldwin, Adams, & Kelly, 2009). State and national standards for early childhood and elementary school are also significant when considering performance assessments.

Authentic Learning and Authentic Assessment

Advocates of authentic assessment propose that **authentic achievement** must accompany authentic assessment. As described by Neill (1997):

> Assessment to enhance student learning must be integrated with, not separate from curriculum and instruction. . . . Schools need to ensure the development of "authentic instruction," which involves modes of teaching that foster understanding of rich content and encourage students' positive engagement with the world. (p. 35)

If we are to use authentic or performance assessment to understand how children can apply or use what they have learned, the learning experiences they are provided must also be authentic or meaningful. Meaningful learning includes intellectual accomplishments that are similar to those undertaken by successful adults and involve tasks and objectives that engage the mind (Checkley, 1997; Jones & Fennimore, 1996; Newmann, 1996). When children are engaged in authentic learning, they are given opportunities to link new information to prior knowledge and engage in problem solving.

Authentic learning is based on construction of knowledge and focuses on higher-order thinking. The purpose is to move beyond the knowledge level and to construct new knowledge (Wehlage, Newmann, & Secada, 1996). This type of learning includes communication of their construction of knowledge and application of knowledge in meaningful contexts, such as some type of performance (Kulm, 1994; Wehlage et al., 1996).

Like authentic learning, authentic assessment is meaningful. It is "designed to present a broader, more genuine picture of student learning" (Zessoules & Gardner, 1991, p. 49). It requires a different role for the teacher in that there is continual interaction with student work. The teacher engages in dialogues, questioning, suggesting, observing, and guiding to encourage students (Palmer, 1996). The purpose of this approach is to enable students to demonstrate how they can use what they understand and to represent that learning in some type of product or performance. Teachers not only use performance assessments to reflect authentic learning but the results of these assessments are used as resources to extend and deepen student learning (Kleinert, Green, & Harte, 2002).

The teacher also considers the children in the class, their families, their culture, their language, and their life experiences. Children come from diverse backgrounds, even when they are of the same ethnicity. As a result, there will be variations in what families consider meaningful and authentic to their lives and background. The teacher needs to be familiar with each family represented in the classroom when planning for authentic learning and meaningful assessment.

Performance-based assessment is considered particularly useful with young children because it measures progress as well as achievement. Children in the early childhood years are proceeding through rapid changes in development that are described as complex because of the interaction between maturation, experience, and learning (Hills, 1993). Performance assessments provide a vehicle for measuring developmental progress in addition to progress in learning new concepts. Performance assessments permit teachers to understand the processes children use to learn and how they actively construct meaning through analysis, synthesis, and evaluation (Brown, 1989; Harrington, Meisels, McMahon, Dichtelmiller, & Jablon, 1997; Meisels, 1993).

Purposes for Performance-Based Assessment

What, then, are the purposes of using **performance-based assessment** with young children? First, the importance of measuring young children appropriately has been an ongoing theme in this text. Contrary to many of the standardized tests and more formal strategies that have been criticized as inappropriate to the young child's development, performance assessments can be good tools for evaluating progress in development. Because they are designed to measure a child's performance of a real or designed task or activity relevant to the desired learning, performance observations are directly related to the child's development and achievement (Harrington et al., 1997).

Second, performance assessments are integrally related to instruction. The performance activity is a natural outcome of ongoing curriculum and instruction and not a separate, unrelated type of experience that is unfamiliar to the child. Krechevsky (1991, p. 45) characterizes the close relationship as "blurring the line between curriculum and assessment." When using performance-based evaluation, the classroom teacher needs to know how to design appropriate, related assessment tools, interpret assessment results to understand the child's progress and plan for further instruction, and interpret performance assessment results to parents and administrators (Hills, 1993).

Finally, performance assessments are used to evaluate whether preschool programs are meeting the needs of the young students. Good performance assessment tools help clarify the goals of preschool programs to provide developmental curriculum. Progress assessment reflects both individual developmental progress and accomplishment of developmental program goals (Harrington et al., 1997; Schweinhart, 1993). The teacher then has the responsibility to report program accomplishments in a meaningful way to administrators (Hills, 1993).

In the next sections, we discuss the types of evaluation strategies that use performance assessments. Although most of the tools are selected or created by the teacher, others use examples of the child's work. Both the teacher and the child plan some, while others occur spontaneously when the teacher takes advantage of an ongoing activity or event to conduct an assessment.

All of the evaluation strategies discussed are adapted to the individual differences in children. Children who are ELLs may be assessed differently according to their progress in learning English. The child who cannot hear may be interviewed using sign language, while a child without vision may have many sensory materials included in the assessments. Directed assignments would be modified for the needs and abilities of children. Likewise, contracts would reflect individual learning abilities, and games would be adapted to make it possible for children with special needs, including second-language needs, to participate.

Types of Performance-Based Assessment

Many strategies can be used to conduct performance-based assessments. Like checklists and observations, performance-based evaluation has been used for many decades; however, in this context, it may have a broadened purpose or a more comprehensive role as part of a system of evaluation. The assessment strategies appropriate for use with young children are interviews, contracts, directed assignments, games, work samples, projects, and portfolios.

Interviews

Teachers use **interviews** to find out what children understand about concepts. Interviews are especially appropriate for young children who are just beginning to develop literacy skills and cannot yet express themselves with a paper-and-pencil activity. The strategies followed in interviews complement the techniques used by Piaget to understand children's thinking. By questioning and asking more questions based on children's responses, Piaget determined not only what the child understood but also the thinking processes used to organize responses to the questions (Seefeldt, 2005).

Interviews can be described as **unstructured**, **structured**, or **diagnostic**. An *unstructured interview* can occur when children are playing, working in centers, or otherwise engaged in classroom activities. The teacher becomes aware that it is an opportune time to engage the child in an interview and takes a few minutes to question the child.

Structured interviews are planned by the teacher and conducted to acquire specific understandings about the child. For example, the teacher might want to determine the beginning reader's understanding of a story. After a reading of the story, the teacher asks probing questions to elicit the child's thoughts about the meaning of the story (Engel, 1990). Likewise, concepts in mathematics can be assessed through a structured interview when the teacher asks oral questions about a concept or process and explores the child's responses with further questions. Kamii and Rosenblum (1990) described an activity to determine the kindergarten child's understanding of small addends by dropping beads into two glasses. The child was interviewed about the sum of the two groups of beads to assess the child's progress in mental arithmetic.

Diagnostic interviews serve an additional purpose: to determine the child's instructional needs. The interview may be informal or structured. The teacher's questioning is directed more at understanding what kind of help the child needs through responses to questions. If the teacher notices that the child is confused or making errors, the diagnostic interview can reveal the difficulty the child is experiencing in thinking about the concept or skill.

Teachers can use several techniques to enhance the effectiveness of interviewing for assessment. In addition to taking notes when conducting an interview, teachers can make an audiotape of the child's responses for later review. Seefeldt (2005) suggests that when interviewing children about a social studies concept, responses need not be limited to talking. The child could act out a concept, find an example of the concept in pictures, or draw the things he or she knows about the concept. These possibilities would be helpful for children who are native speakers of another language or otherwise have difficulty expressing themselves verbally.

Interviews with young children should be short. Engel (1990) suggests that 10 minutes is an appropriate length of time. Other tips are (1) to continue questions after the child's initial responses to find out more than whether the child's response is correct and (2) to give the child plenty of time to think about and respond to the teacher's questions. The child needs to feel comfortable with the process if pertinent responses are to be elicited.

Contracts

Contracts serve a dual purpose. They provide a plan between the teacher and the child and a record of the child's progress. Contracts of activities the child will engage in are designed for a period during a day, for the whole day, or for several days. Preschool

A Structured Interview to Assess Classification Skills

*N*ykesha Hillmon's kindergarten class has been studying classification skills. Over a period of weeks, Nykesha has conducted lessons on sorting objects into two groups by using the physical characteristics the objects have in common. The children have worked with the classification of nuts, rocks, and classroom plants. Today, Nykesha has placed an assortment of beans in the science center. She is interviewing Tyrone, who has been asked to make two groups of beans. As Tyrone is in the process of forming the groups, Nykesha begins the interview with questions she has planned earlier:

NYKESHA: Tyrone, can you explain how you decided to make the two groups of beans?

TYRONE: Well, one group of beans is round. They are all round.

NYKESHA: And the other group?

TYRONE: They are all the same as this one (lima bean). I don't know what to call them.

NYKESHA: Good. You have one group of beans that are round and another group of beans that have the same shape. You have made your groups by using their shape. Can you think of another way you could make two groups?

TYRONE: (After some hesitation) I could make groups of big ones and little ones.

NYKESHA: Could you think of another way?

TYRONE: I don't think so.

NYKESHA: How about using their color?

TYRONE: Oh, yes. I could put the ones that have brown together, and the rest that don't have brown together.

---

children need pictures or other visual representations of activities to be completed. Primary-grade children can follow simple written instructions. After the child has completed an activity, some type of check-off system can be used to record the accomplishment.

Contracts can also be used to record accomplishment of skills and concepts. The teacher and the child can use the contract as a guide for conferences and interviews or as a recording system for the teacher to indicate when the child has completed an objective or needs more opportunities to interact with a concept. Over a period of time, completed contracts can provide information on progress and accomplishments.

Directed Assignments

Directed assignments are an extension of teacher-designed assessments, discussed in chapter 7. They are also similar to interviews, except that a specific task is involved in acquiring the child's understanding, rather than an interview. Children

Using Contracts to Assess Performance

Graciela, a second-grade student, is discussing her mathematics contract with her teacher, Luis Garza. Luis plans contracts with the students on Monday of each week and conducts conferences with the students throughout the week to monitor their progress. Graciela has worked on her contract for two days. Her contract on Monday and Tuesday included the following:

Monday:

1. Small-group lesson on subtraction
2. Center activity solving subtraction problems
3. Worksheet of subtraction problems

Tuesday:

1. Game with a partner solving subtraction problems
2. Subtraction worksheet
3. Conference with Mr. Garza

Luis discusses Graciela's work to date. They review her work, which includes the worksheets and problems solved in the math center. Luis notices that Graciela has made several subtraction errors. He questions Graciela and then gives her blocks to help her to work out the subtraction problem. After she has described how she arrived at her answer, he tells her to work out the problem with the blocks again. After the conference, Luis makes a note to observe Graciela the following day to determine whether she needs further help with the subtraction process.

who are beginning to read independently might be asked to read a story and discuss it. Preschool children might be asked to use concrete objects to solve a problem in mathematical thinking. The important point is that the teacher makes a specific assignment or task for the purposes of assessment. Discussion and questioning may be a part of the process, but the child's ability to carry out the assignment is the focus of the assessment process (Hills, 1992).

Games

Games can be used to understand children's progress with a skill or a concept. Although more than one child will be playing the game at one time, the teacher can use observation to assess the child's abilities and thinking. Kamii and Rosenblum (1990) suggest that the teacher use games for systematic observation of an entire class. Two children or a slightly larger group play the game until all the children have been assessed. The ability to make 10 with two numbers is one example of a

Teachers can design games to be used to teach concepts and for assessment.

skill that can be assessed through the child's performance in a game. Cards from one to nine are arranged in groups of nine at one time. The child shows all the pairs that can be combined to make 10. In addition to determining whether the child has mastered the skill, the teacher can observe the process the child uses to solve the problem. If the child arranges combinations quickly, a higher level of progress of mental addition has been achieved than that of a child who must count up from the first card to get the sum with the second card. Figure 6-9 shows a form for recording levels of understanding for this concept.

Games may be used for concepts and skills in other content areas. Over many decades, games have been developed for reading skills. Card games to identify letter knowledge are one ready example. Board games can be adapted or developed for language arts, mathematics, and social studies. A game similar to Trivial Pursuit, in which children must respond to an oral or a written question related to a topic being studied, is an example of how games can be used to test the child's ability to perform a task or solve a problem as an assessment activity.

Work Samples

Teachers and students are equal participants in the use of **work samples** for performance assessment. Work samples are examples of all types of children's work that can demonstrate the child's developmental progress or accomplishments. For preschool children, work samples may be clay models of animals that reflect the child's understanding of concepts in a thematic study related to animals. Other work samples include paintings, emergent writing, and dictated interpretations of wordless books (Ratcliff, 2001/2002). Primary-grade children might have samples of book reports, creative writing that has been illustrated, and work pages of computation problems. Grace and Shores (1991) suggest using other visual media, such as photographs, videotapes, and tape recordings or audiotapes.

Digital cameras are especially useful for this purpose. They can be used to document children's work as well as serving as a mechanism for transferring work into an

*J*oan Harrison, a first-grade teacher, is using a board game to assess reading words. The purpose of the game is to assess children's knowledge of words that have been used in reading activities. Each student has an individual bank of words from books he or she has read. Kim Soo and Martha are playing the game. The children take turns drawing a word card. If they name the word correctly, they can advance one square on the board. The first child to reach the end wins the game. Words that are missed are put in a separate pile, and Joan notes them in her notebook so that she can work with the words in small-group activities.

electronic form. When classes engage in project work, photographic samples can be made of the project's progress from beginning to the end of the topic being studied.

Work samples are often included in discussions about portfolios because portfolios become the means through which work samples and other types of information related to performance assessment are stored. A system for selecting and organizing work samples is important if the collection is to serve appropriately for performance assessment (Meisels, 1993).

Projects

A **project** is an activity conducted by a student or a group of students that is lengthier than a classroom activity conducted during a single class period. The project can be part of a unit of study, such as a science or social studies unit, or part of a theme that is studied by a class. A product of some type results from the project. For example, a second-grade class may study spring wildflowers. A group of students may gather samples of the flowers, identify them, and describe their characteristics. Each flower is dried and attached to the completed information. The completed booklet of wildflowers becomes the product of the project that could be evaluated.

Projects are flexible in terms of meeting student needs. Children with limited English skills engage in projects that expand language as well as work with new concepts. Student interests are a part of the project; therefore, different groups may vary in how they conduct a project.

Portfolios

The **portfolio** was one of the most popular methods of documenting authentic assessment in the 1990s. In looking for alternatives to standardized tests, drill worksheets, and other assessment measures that reflect skills development rather than developmental progress evolving from the student's own demonstrations of performance, school districts across the United States have implemented portfolios as a preferred type of reporting performance-based evaluation. Some states have initiated performance assessment to replace standardized tests (Givens, 1997).

Portfolios are a process or method whereby student performance information can be stored and interpreted. Portfolios may be a folder very similar to collections of student work that many teachers have used for decades for reporting to parents. They may contain examples of papers that students have completed, as well as checklists, anecdotal records, summary reports for a grading period, and any other materials that students and teachers think are relevant to demonstrate the student's performance.

Portfolios may also be the vehicle used for assessing and reporting the student's progress and accomplishments to parents and administrators. How portfolios are designed and used will be discussed in chapter 9.

Understanding the Interrelated Nature of Performance Assessments

Different types of informal and performance-based assessments have been discussed in both this chapter and earlier chapters. At this point, it is important to describe how these assessments are used in an interrelated manner to understand the characteristics of a child's performance. For example, observation can be the basis for assessing a child's performance on a directed assignment, whereas a checklist might be used to record the child's progress on the same assignment. In the following sections, we explore the characteristics of performance assessments and how the teacher uses them to evaluate the development and achievement of the whole child.

The Role of the Teacher

The teacher has the primary role in selecting the types of performance assessments to be used and how they will be used. Because teachers assess and use the assessment information, they also have the responsibility to decide which strategies will be most effective for their purposes.

Performance assessment occurs continually in the early childhood classroom. Information is collected throughout the day when children are working in centers, playing outdoors, participating in small-group instruction, and performing whole-group activities. The teacher observes and participates in these activities to acquire the information about each child's progress and the child's own thinking about what and how he or she is learning.

Collecting information is only a part of the teacher's role. Interpreting and using the data are another responsibility. First, the teacher must obtain enough information to know the child's abilities and needs so that appropriate planning can further growth and development. Second, the teacher must collect comprehensive information about each child so that all areas of development and learning are addressed (Harrington et al., 1997). The teacher's goal is to design and implement a program that is appropriate for the child's physical, intellectual, and social development. Likewise, the program should be developmentally appropriate for all the children. In summary, Hills (1992) describes the teacher's role and responsibilities for assessment:

1. To integrate instruction and assessment fully in planning and carrying out the program
2. To use knowledge of young children to choose or design assessment processes
3. To analyze the results to find their meaning for the program and the children
4. To apply what has been learned to planning next steps and improving the program
5. To communicate with parents and involve them in an exchange of information about their child's learning and development (p. 46)

Meisels (2000) adds another dimension to the teaching role. The teacher's role has transformed in that the teacher's approach to teaching is different in authentic learning and assessment. The teacher provides meaningful learning experiences that children would have never experienced otherwise. At the same time, the teacher empowers the children to learn more independently and spontaneously.

Assessments that are consistent with a relationship of trust and authority between teachers and children also have a different approach. Early childhood educators should be aware of the following (Meisels, 2000):

- In an early childhood setting it is essential to address yourself to the personal and unique attributes of the children in your care.
- You need to learn to listen, diagnose, examine, hypothesize, intervene, evaluate, and then reflect and redesign.
- Your goal should be to try to create a relationship of trust with children—one upon which learning is based. (p. 18)

Thus, in performance assessment, teaching, learning, and evaluation result from a partnership relationship between teacher and child. Moreover, the teacher uses performance assessment strategies to collaborate with children on the nature of their accomplishments and the next steps in their learning.

The teacher in the classroom described in the box on p. 225 is focusing on emerging literacy skills. The strategies that are being used for performance assessment are checklists, observations, videotapes, audiotapes, and work samples.

The teacher uses checklists to document reading and writing skills. Children drawing an illustration for a big book demonstrate their understanding between pictures and text. As children write menus for the "Pizza Hut," the teacher can observe and document left-to-right skills in their writing skills or their use of uppercase and lowercase letters.

Observations with anecdotal notes can provide more detail about the process a child uses in reading or writing. A videotape or audiotape can record an entire episode. This type of documentation provides information on various children engaged in an activity which can be analyzed for assessment of what children can do.

A Teacher's Assessment Role in a Kindergarten Classroom

Upon entering the classroom of 5-year-olds, a buzz of activity captures the visitor's attention. Children working in small groups are busily pursuing a number of activities. One group is drawing illustrations for the big book that the class wrote describing their trip to Pizza Hut. Another group is creating menus for the restaurant they are setting up in the dramatic play area. "Don't forget to put 'We have pepperoni' on your menu," one child says. The other children nod their heads and continue drawing and writing on their papers. One child is bent over a large sheet of construction paper, with marker in hand. He is carefully copying the words "Pizza Hut" from the word wall the children have created. When finished, he tapes the paper to two chairs he has placed in front of the dramatic area. "Here's the sign," he tells the others. Three other children are looking at a recipe book and discussing the "gredients" they will need to make the pizzas. Another group is looking at books about restaurants in the literacy corner.

Source: Ratcliff, N. J. (2001/2002). Using authentic assessment to document the emerging literacy skills of young children. *Childhood Education, 78,* 66–69.

Finally, work samples provide the teacher with specific evidence of accomplishment. In the classroom activities described in the scenario, the teacher would have work samples of big-book illustrations, menus, and a Pizza Hut sign for documentation of performance.

Classification and Organization of Performance Assessments

Although all performance assessments are considered informal measures, they can be categorized as structured or unstructured and direct or indirect. These organizational patterns are similar to structured and unstructured interviews but are more comprehensive in the types of assessments that are included.

One approach to categorizing assessments is by the type of activity used for assessment. Lee (1992) describes **unstructured** (or nonstructured) **performance assessments** as those that are part of regular classroom learning activities, such as writing samples, projects, checklists, and teacher-designed tasks and tests. **Structured performance assessments** are predetermined or designed to include questions or tasks that require problem solving, synthesis, and analysis. Questions are open ended, and all students are administered the questions through similar test administration procedures.

Another perspective of the two classifications is as spontaneous or structured. Similar to Lee's definition, spontaneous assessments evolve from the teacher's natural day-to-day interactions and observations in the classroom. Structured performance assessment is not only planned but also must meet the standards for reliability and validity required of standardized measurement instruments. Such assessments are carefully designed and have specified scoring criteria, as well as well-defined behaviors that are to be measured.

Performance assessments can also be classified as direct or indirect. On the one hand, **direct performance measures** require students to use knowledge in some type of application. On the other hand, **indirect performance measures** measure what students know about a topic. An example of an indirect measure is a paper-and-pencil test. An example of a direct measure is taking measurements of a table to determine how large to make a tablecloth to fit the table. The distinction between these performance measures is assessing knowledge versus assessing application of knowledge (Pierson & Beck, 1993).

The Role of Observation

Strategies for observation were discussed in chapter 5, and the importance of using observation to evaluate the development of young children was emphasized. A discussion of the role of observation within performance assessments reinforces that importance. When considering the measurement of the young child's performance, observation is the most effective strategy (Harrington et al., 1997; Hills, 1992; Segal & Webber, 1996). Observation behaviors such as attending, examining, heeding, considering, investigating, monitoring, studying, and watching enable the teacher to understand and know the child and what the child can do in real-life circumstances and common learning situations (Hills, 1993).

Observation should occur throughout the day in all types of classroom activities. Strategies for observation, including anecdotal records, running records, observation with checklists and rating scales, and time and event sampling, can all have a role in performance assessment. To ensure that the desired performance is observed and recorded, Hills (1993) recommends that the following components be determined prior to conducting the observation:

- **Purpose**—What do we want to know?
- **Focus**—Who or what is being observed? Exhibits what behaviors? When? Where?
- **Record/documentation**—What information is needed? How will it be recorded? How frequently?
- **Use of the observation**—What does the observed event mean for the child's progress and needs? What next steps would we take to further the child's development? (p. 27)

Gathering and documenting information through observation is not enough. Analysis and use of assessment data must also be facilitated as a result of the observation. Therefore, the child should be observed at different times and places and using different materials before determining whether new knowledge has been developed (Bergan & Feld, 1993; Segal & Webber, 1996). In addition, teachers should spend time reflecting on the information that has been gathered. The purpose of this reflection is so that teachers will use assessment in an intentional manner to plan for children's future learning opportunities. To properly collect and reflect on observation data, teachers might include the following steps (Hills, 1992): (1) Establish purpose and focus; (2) observe and record; (3) compile what was recorded, both for individual children and for the group; and (4) reflect on the records and refocus teaching and learning activities.

Observation is the foundation of performance assessment. It is used with interviews when the teacher observes the child's responses and behaviors. It is integral to directed assignments as the teacher observes the child completing the assignment or task. Observation enables the teacher to understand the child's thinking and knowledge when engaging in assessment games. Observation complements other strategies used for unstructured and structured and direct and indirect performance assessments. Finally, checklists and rating scales and teacher-designed assessments of various types incorporate observation as part of or all of the process of understanding the child's performance (Baldwin et al., 2009).

The Role of Documentation

The term *documentation* has been used throughout this text to mean a method of recording a child's progress or accomplishments. Thus, observation, checklists, rating scales, and rubrics can document development and learning, as can assessments related to mastery learning.

Portfolios can be used to share a child's performance with parents.

Documenting Infant Development

*S*ugar is 6 months old. She is in the infant room in a corporate-sponsored child-care center near a large insurance company. Her parents both work for the company.

Caregivers at the center observe the children daily. They are tracing the infant's development toward developmental milestones. Sugar recently learned to roll over. She is now enjoying rolling over frequently during her periods of play. Now she is developing the skills to be able to sit up by herself. She is in the process of using her arms to lift her upper body to an upright position. Each day, the caregiver notes what actions Sugar uses to learn to sit. These will be reported to the parents at the end of the day. When Sugar is consistent in being able to move to a sitting position, she will have reached another physical milestone. The caregivers and parents will have a chronological documentation of this stage of Sugar's development.

In the context of performance assessment, documentation can take a broader meaning, particularly when it is linked to an early childhood program and child-centered or constructivist learning experiences. In Reggio Emilia schools (Wurm, 2005) and early childhood programs using the Project Approach (Helm & Beneke, 2003), the curriculum is child initiated. Although teachers have a major role in preparing curriculum, what is to be learned is not predetermined. Rather, as projects proceed in both programs, children's ideas and questions for exploration take the work in more than one direction or are expanded from the original plan. Documentation in these curriculum approaches is a process of documenting the progress of the activities and to better understand the children's interests, thinking, and problem solving within their activities. A major purpose of observation and videotapes, digital photographs, and children's work is to note how children reacted to experiences and to record the chronological progress of a period of work (Wurm, 2005). The displays and sharing of work at the end of a project is a culminating activity. Displays of the work accomplished serve as documentation of what was accomplished that can be shared with parents, other teachers, and students in the school or preschool program (Helm & Beneke, 2003; Wurm, 2005).

The Role of Rubrics

In chapter 6, rubrics were described as being essential to performance assessment. Different types of rubrics were defined and the process used to develop rubrics was discussed. Examples of different kinds of rubrics were provided to demonstrate their flexibility and adaptability to different developmental stages and content areas in preschool and primary grades.

In this section, it might be helpful to reemphasize why rubrics are essential for performance assessment. Checklists, rating scales, and teacher-designed assessments tend to focus on whether a developmental milestone or skill has been achieved or how well it has been achieved. Performance assessments, on the contrary, focus on process and progress in development and learning. Teachers must be grounded in how children develop as well as how children use emerging mental processes to acquire knowledge and new concepts. Rubrics provide the framework to assess processes of learning that focus on child-initiated accomplishments. The assessment strategies discussed earlier in the chapter—interviews, contracts, directed assignments, games, work samples, portfolios, and projects—can be used with rubrics. (See chapter 6 for examples of rubrics.)

For example, Figure 6-12 can be used in structured interviews. The teacher may read a story to the class and then interview children individually to discuss the story. By asking questions such as "What happened (to a character) in the story?" or "Can you tell me the story in your own words?" the teacher can assess comprehension of text in an emerging reader.

Likewise, a kindergarten teacher can use Figure 6-13 for a developmental assessment using work samples or a directed assignment. The teacher can use children's writing efforts to assess progress in the emerging ability to write.

When working with children who engage in thematic projects, the teacher may use the following range of four points or levels to establish the structure of a rubric to evaluate the projects:

- Begin again
- Revision needed
- Acceptable
- Well done

For example, a kindergarten class may study the topic of "homes." After investigating different types of homes in the surrounding neighborhood, small groups select a type of home to study. Construction of a model of a type of home is the task of small groups to represent what they have learned. The teacher designs the following rubric to establish performance standards:

1. *Begin again*

   Group is unable to initiate task.
   Teacher redirection is needed to initiate an appropriate approach.
   Initial efforts show little evidence of understanding the task.

2. *Revision needed*

   Project work is incomplete; needs elaboration.
   Project does not reflect the information learned.
   Additional planning is needed to achieve the desired results.

3. *Acceptable*

   Project is completed.
   Project reflects the purpose of the task, although details and elements are missing.
   Information about the project could be expressed more clearly.

4. *Well done*

    Project shows clear understanding of the concepts learned.

    Project fully accomplishes the purposes of the task.

    Project includes details and elements essential to communicate learned information.

This rubric is generic in that it can be applied to different types of thematic studies. Although it can be applied to projects reflecting the study of homes, it can also be adapted to other projects and topics. It can be simplified or made more detailed as circumstances indicate.

Standards and Performance-Based Assessment

How do state standards for early childhood affect authentic learning and performance-based strategies? Because standards for learning achievement are linked to mandated standardized tests for accountability in public education and Head Start programs, many educators may assume that authentic learning and authentic assessment are not compatible with mastering state standards. There has been much information on documenting achievement and accountability through such testing, but performance assessment should not be overlooked as the major tool in verifying what children have learned. Performance assessment is particularly important when understanding development in the early childhood years.

    To link standards and performance-based assessments teachers must understand how standards are integrated into the curriculum and how assessment emerges from the implementation of learning experiences. Meeting standards is accomplished by making them a part of best practices rather than as a separate part of the curriculum.

Connecting Standards to Authentic Learning

The first step in linking standards with performance assessments is to connect standards to the curriculum. The task is to develop a relationship between the standards and best practices for young children in quality early childhood programs. Processes such as child-centered learning, active learning with an environment rich with opportunities for a variety of activities, projects or units of learning, and play, both indoors and outdoors (Baldwin et al., 2009; Drew, Christie, Johnson, Meckley, & Nell, 2008).

    One approach is to relate state standards to content areas in the curriculum. Teachers study the standards and match them to the instructional activities planned for the children. The content areas of the curriculum and the standards are organized so that the relationship is mapped out for the teachers.

    If curriculum is planned within projects or study or the study of topics, the state standards are analyzed matched to the topic being planned (Jacobs & Crowley,

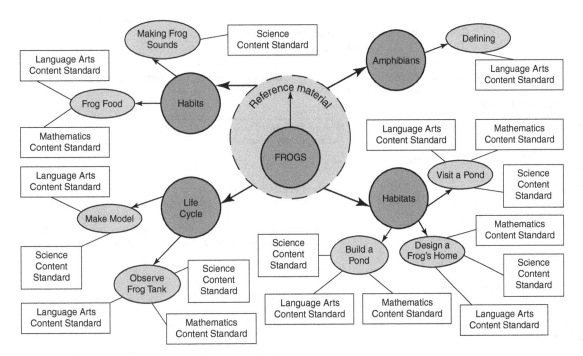

FIGURE 8-1 Planning web correlated with standards

Source: Baldwin, J. L., Adams, S. M., & Kelly, M. K. (2009). Science at the center: An emergent standards-based, child-centered framework for early learners. *Early Childhood Education Journal, 37,* 71–77. Reprinted with permission of Springer, p. 75.

2010). One way to chart the relationship is to use a curriculum web for a topic or project. Figure 8-1 shows a planning web for a study of frogs with the content standards to be addressed (Baldwin et al., 2009).

Teachers can even connect standards with curriculum within play activities. A group of educators were able to match Arizona's Early Learning Standards with research on constructive play (Drew et al., 2008). Figure 8-2 shows the relationship between standards and research on play activities.

Connecting Standards to Performance Assessment

Assessment related to standards incorporates all of the strategies that have been discussed in this book and especially in this chapter. Whatever type of assessment is used is matched to a standard or several standards. Evidence of a child's accomplishments in activities planned for a project are also evaluated on applicable state standards. Figure 8-3 shows an example of assessment of a child's performance based on the teacher's observation, the child's explanation, and the standards in science that were addressed. The teacher maintains a child-centered, developmentally appropriate classroom, an integrated curriculum, and performance assessment that has a direct a direct relationship with state standards (Baldwin et al., 2009).

Connections between Arizona Early Learning Standards and Constructive Play

Early Learning Standards (Arizona)	Constructive Play, Research Supported
Language and Literacy	
Strand 2: Pre-Reading Processes, **Concept 5:** Vocabulary Development— The child understands and uses increasingly complex vocabulary.	Research by Cohen (2006) shows that children learn new vocabulary words as they socially interact with partners and in groups during constructive play.
Strand 2: Pre-Reading Processes. **Concept 1:** Print Awareness—The child knows that print carries meaning.	Literacy-enriched play centers contain theme-related reading and writing materials. For example, a block center might contain pencils, pens, materials for making signs, storage labels (for large blocks, Legos), and so on. Research indicates that when children play in print-enriched settings, they often learn to read play-related print (Neuman & Roskos 1993; Vukelich 1994).
Strand 3: Pre-Writing Processes, **Concept 1:** Written Expression—The child uses writing materials to communicate ideas.	Research by Pickett (1998) shows that adding writing materials to block centers results in a large increase in emergent writing, including making signs to identify function and ownership, regulate behavior, and communicate messages.
Mathematics	
Strand 4: Geometry and Measurement, **Concept 1:** Spatial Relationships and Geometry— The child demonstrates an understanding of spatial relationships and recognizes attributes of common shapes.	Recent research by Miyakawa, Kamii, and Nagahiro (2005) confirms that block building can help children learn important spatial relationships.
Social-Emotional	
Strand 2: Social Interactions with Others, **Concept 2:** Cooperation—The child demonstrates the ability to give and take during social interactions.	Creasey, Jarvis, and Berk (1998) contend that a two-way relationship exists between group play and social development: the social environment influences children's play, and play acts as an important context in which children acquire social skills and social knowledge needed to engage in group play. Children learn attitudes and skills needed for this play from their parents, teachers, and other children. At the same time, play with others has a key role in social development by providing a context in which children can acquire many important social skills, such as turn taking, sharing, and cooperation, as well as the ability to understand other people's thoughts, perceptions, and emotions.
Strand 4: Approaches to Learning, **Concept 5:** Problem-solving—The child demonstrates the ability to seek solutions to problems.	Bruner (1972) proposes that play contributes to children's ability to solve problems by increasing their behavioral options and suggests that block play encourages inventive thinking and logical reasoning while constructing three-dimensional patterns. Copely and Oto (2006) find that young children demonstrate considerable problem-solving knowledge during block play.

FIGURE 8-2 Learning standards and play research

Source: Drew, W. F. et al. (2008, July). Constructive play. A value-added strategy for meeting early learning standards. *Young Children, 63,* 38–44. Reprinted with permission of the National Association for the Education of Young Children, p. 41.

Standards Covered:

___Explore and identify parts and wholes of familiar objects

X Explore and compare materials that provide many different sensory experiences

___Explore ways of moving objects in different ways

___Explore musical instruments and objects and manipulate one's own voice to recognize the changes in sound

X Identify the intended purpose of familiar tools

X Use familiar objects to accomplish a purpose, complete a task, or solve a problem

X Demonstrate the safe use of tools

___Ask questions about objects, organisms, pictures, letters, signs, and events

X Show interest in investigating unfamiliar objects, organisms, and phenomena during shared stories, conversations, and play

___Participate in simple, spontaneous scientific explorations with others

Science
Physical Science, Science and Technology, and Scientific Inquiry

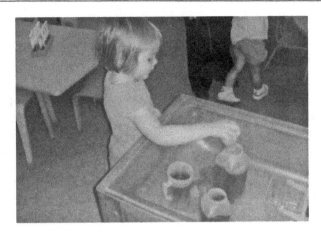

This one holds the most water because it is bigger. - Grace S.

6-20-07

Teacher Reflection:

Grace is able to change the amount of water in the containers using the tools provided. She understands vocabulary related to size and comparison. She is ready to learn more about measuring and ordering.

FIGURE 8-3 Standards correlated to anecdotal observation

Source: Baldwin, J. L., Adams, S. M., & Kelly, M. K. (2009). Science at the center: An emergent standards-based, child-centered framework for early learners. *Early Childhood Education Journal, 37,* 71–77. Reprinted with permission of Springer, p. 76.

Learning is a process, and children experience many learning activities before they accomplish a standard. Authentic performance assessments conducted over a period of time demonstrate the child's path to learning (Gronlund, 2006). Moreover, because advances in development are of primary importance in the early years, performance assessments are the best indicators of progress toward meeting early childhood standards.

Advantages and Disadvantages of Using Performance-Based Assessment

Advantages of Using Performance-Based Assessment

Performance-based evaluation for assessment of young children has definite advantages. Although performance assessment is recommended for children of all ages, it is particularly suitable for children in preoperational and concrete operational stages of development. Because young children learn best by acting on the environment, it logically follows that assessment that permits the child to demonstrate ability by performing some action is most compatible with developmental capabilities. Performance assessments, then, are fitting for the development of children in the early childhood years. Some arguments for using performance assessments for evaluation are the following:

1. Performance assessments are conducted in the context of what children are experiencing, rather than in isolation from classroom curriculum. In addition, they are conducted within the teacher's knowledge of families and what is authentic to them. Assessments are adapted to differences in language, culture, and ability. Earlier in the chapter, it was recommended that assessment be an integral part of curriculum and instruction. Whenever possible, performance assessments are conducted as part of a lesson, during center activities, or serendipitously when the teacher observes desired learning demonstrated spontaneously. Performance assessments are meaningful and timely.

2. Performance assessments take advantage of the premise that children construct their own understanding. Early childhood educators today prepare curriculum activities with the comprehension that the teacher does not transmit knowledge; instead, the child gradually forms or produces new knowledge through repeated encounters with concepts and information. Performance assessment provides the teacher with tools to observe and document the child's progress. This provision means that assessment goes beyond assessing whether the child has mastered the teacher's learning objectives. The child's progress toward mastery using Vygotsky's (1983) zone of proximal development can also be evaluated. The zone described by Vygotsky refers to the variability between what the child can currently do and what the child can master potentially in the future. The teacher can determine whether the child is unable to demonstrate an ability or understanding, whether the child can show some of the desired behaviors with assistance, or whether the child can perform independently (Hills, 1992). Also, the focus of the assessment is on the child, and not on the child's responding to the teacher. The teacher still plays a major role in the assessment, but the child's performance is the key and the teacher responds to what the child is doing.

3. Performance assessments provide a variety of means whereby the child can demonstrate what he or she understands or can do. The child's ongoing work examples, art products, play, conversation, emergent writing, and dictated stories are a few examples of ways that children can perform. Some of the performances can be recorded as a result of the teacher's observation or interviews, whereas others can be documented by work samples. Because assessment is integrated with instruction and daily activities, the possibilities for observing and interpreting accomplishments are almost unlimited.

4. Performance assessment is continuous or ongoing. Unlike more formal assessments such as tests, end-of-chapter assessments, and reporting-period evaluations, performance assessments reflect daily opportunities to be aware of the child's thinking and work.

5. Performance assessments provide meaningful information for parents to understand their child's progress and accomplishments. They also enable parents to contribute to and participate in the assessment process. Teachers can use performance assessments of all types in parent conferences. Because teachers have visited the homes and are familiar with the parent (see chapter 10), they can adapt the conferences to be most meaningful for the parents. Likewise, parents can become more aware of behaviors their child is using at home that demonstrate developmental advancement and share their observations with the teacher. Once parents understand the significance of the child's activities and their relationship to development and learning, they can be partners with the teacher and child in facilitating opportunities for the child (Kleinert et al., 2002).

Disadvantages of Using Performance-Based Assessment

Performance assessments have disadvantages or limitations. Like all other informal assessments, they are subjective; teacher bias and interpretation are part of the process. Teachers must be constantly alert to the need for objectivity when evaluating young children. Also, performance assessments increase the responsibility and accountability of the teacher in administering and interpreting evaluations. This opportunity for more meaningful assessments is accompanied by the need for teachers to be skilled in the assessment process.

Although some of the strategies used to evaluate children in performance assessments are not new, the approach as the primary means to assess and give grades to students is considered an innovation. Like any educational innovation, problems and difficulties can cause teachers and administrators to become disenchanted with the process and to doubt the effectiveness of the practice. Therefore, it is important to be aware of and understand the implications and limitations of performance assessment, as well as the benefits. Following are some of the concerns that measurement specialists propose about the use of performance assessments:

1. Performance assessments are time consuming. Teachers need time to conduct observations, record data, and interpret information in planning future instruction. All performance assessments require extensive involvement of the teacher. Record keeping adds to paperwork responsibilities; moreover, teachers must consider how to fit assessment into otherwise busy days. Teachers must develop the ability to do several things at once and to keep up with reflection on information and ideas they gain from studying the child's performance activities. For example,

the teacher can keep a notepad handy to jot down notes during the course of the day. Assessments can be made using observation in the course of teaching lessons to note which children are consistently accurate and which students are struggling with a concept. During project work, the teacher can observe children's actions and note advances in physical and language development. All of these methods are integrated into the school day, making specific assessment activities needed less often.

2. Authentic assessment can be more complex than more traditional types of assessment. Because assessment is integrated into instruction, teachers must clearly understand what they are looking for in assessment. Assessment with young children might be interdisciplinary or measure more than one type of development when it is a part of integrated curriculum and child-centered activities. The teacher must determine explicit standards of performance for development and learning objectives, no matter how incidental or integrated the assessment process is. The more complex and integrated the curriculum is, the more difficult the performance assessment process will be in terms of interpreting the implications of the child's performance (Bergen, 1994). A related issue is in scoring performance assessments. A common concern is who will determine the quality of performance assessments when they are used for grading or state-level evaluations (Givens, 1997).

3. More traditional forms of assessment have had the goal of evaluating the child's achievement. Performance assessment has the goal of evaluating progress as well as achievement. Teachers may have difficulty incorporating this new role of understanding the child's progress and implications for curriculum planning for that child. Teachers must not only develop new competencies in acquiring assessment information but also become more competent in using progress information to further the child's development. Teachers may find this requirement very confusing and be uncertain about how skillfully and appropriately they are using performance assessments (Bergen, 1994).

4. There are also concerns about the validity and reliability of performance assessments. Schweinhart (1993) proposes that early childhood assessment tools must be developmentally appropriate, valid, reliable, and user friendly. As described in the previous section, the difficulty of using performance assessments would raise doubts about how user friendly they are. To be valid, the tools must correlate with concurrent measures being used to assess young children. Likewise, assessments should be internally consistent and assessed similarly by various assessors. Informal procedures used in performance assessments must provide evidence of validity, reliability, objectivity, and freedom from bias if they are to be considered feasible (Goodwin & Goodwin, 1993). The probability that public school systems will understand this necessity and undertake the extensive work needed to ensure quality seems doubtful (Givens, 1997).

5. Parental involvement and education are a requirement when implementing performance-based evaluation. Parents are familiar with traditional evaluation and reporting practices. School districts must plan to educate and prepare parents before moving into performance assessments. Parents need to be knowledgeable and comfortable with how the innovative assessment process is used before they encounter it in their child's grade report or in a parent–teacher conference. Unfamiliar terminology and assessment procedures can cause a lack of confidence in and support for the school and teachers.

Most of the disadvantages and limitations discussed previously seem to be related to proper preparation and training for performance assessments. Too often in the past, schools have embraced and implemented curriculum and instruction innovations without training teachers and administrators properly. Some of the authors cited in this chapter consistently discuss the need for extensive training and preparation prior to using new performance assessments. As with any other change or new approach to curriculum or assessment, adequate training and knowledge about performance assessments can do much to ensure that they will be a successful and appropriate alternative for assessment of young children. Because performance assessments inherently have the potential to measure young children's development and learning in a realistic and meaningful way, the limitations can become either difficult obstacles or perceptive cautions that can be used to facilitate appropriate and skilled use of new tools.

Developing Quality Performance Assessments

An important step in developing quality performance assessments is to use rubrics both to describe the performance and to serve as evaluation tools. Suggestions for developing quality rubrics were given in chapter 6. Additional suggestions can be listed for performance assessments as a whole. Following are a few guidelines:

- Base assessments on instructional goals and state standards.
- Use fully developed task descriptions for performance assessments.
- Review assessment criteria against instructional goals and state standards.
- Score systematically and recheck scoring strategies periodically.
- Compare rubric and other performance scoring with other informal assessments when appropriate.
- Use more than one assessment in making important decisions.
- Conduct assessments that are consistent for all students to eliminate bias. (Herman et al., 1992)

Summary

This chapter has discussed the merits of performance assessment as a process that deepens understanding of the child's learning. In this chapter, we have discussed performance-based evaluation as an alternative or authentic method of assessing young children. Meisels believes that this approach to assessment makes teachers more powerful and in control of the learning-evaluation process:

Performance assessments document activities in which children engage on a daily basis. They provide a means for evaluating the quality of children's work in an integrated manner. They are flexible enough to reflect an individualized approach to academic achievement. They are also designed to evaluate many elements of learning and development that standardized tests do not capture well. As active constructors of meaning, children analyze, synthesize, evaluate, and interpret facts and ideas (Brown, 1989). Performance assessment allows teachers the opportunity to learn about these processes by documenting children's interactions with materials and peers in the classroom environment. In short, performance assessment puts assessment back where it belongs: in the hands of teachers and children, and in the classrooms that they inhabit. (Meisels, 1993, p. 36)

A number of methods or strategies can be used to evaluate a child's development or learning through performance of what he or she understands and can do. Interviews, contracts, directed assignments, games, work samples, projects, and portfolios are among the assessment activities that permit young children to demonstrate their ability to understand and apply new skills and information.

Performance assessments complement each other in how they focus on the child's progress and accomplishments. In addition, informal assessment methods, such as observation, checklists and rating scales, and teacher-designed assessments, are used in the process of assessing through performance.

Performance assessment transfers responsibility to teachers for the instructional and assessment process. This empowerment of the teacher facilitates the teacher's opportunity to design assessment that includes all areas of development and that is appropriate for the level of development of each child. It also allows the teacher to make a close connection between curriculum and evaluation. It also permits the teacher to consider learning and assessment within the family backgrounds of the children. Knowing that performance assessment should be meaningful, the teacher interacts with the family and home frequently to understand what type of performance is suitable for individual students.

Although performance assessment is more relevant and appropriate than traditional formal methods of measuring learning, it can also be more difficult. Teachers must accept the time that is needed to organize and conduct this type of evaluation; moreover, they must overcome limitations related to validity, reliability, and accountability. Care must be exercised in planning and implementing performance assessment if it is not to become an educational fad that fades after a few years.

*R*EVIEW QUESTIONS

1. Explain the definition of *performance assessments* or *performance-based assessments.*
2. Why is performance assessment suited for children in the early childhood years?
3. Why do measurement specialists describe performance and instruction as closely related?
4. Interviews can be used for evaluation in several ways. Discuss three types of interviews and when they are appropriate.
5. How are interviews helpful for understanding children's thinking processes?
6. Why can it be said that directed assignments are designed by the teacher, but contracts are designed by the teacher and child?
7. How is assessment through games different from assessment through an interview?
8. Explain the role of observation in performance assessments.

9. What is meant by interrelated assessments? Describe two assessments that can be interrelated.
10. Explain the difference between direct performance measures and indirect performance measures.
11. How do you believe performance assessments will be advantageous to you as a teacher of young children?
12. Explain how performance assessments can be difficult to interpret.
13. How can teachers ensure that performance assessments are accurate?
14. Why is it possible that performance assessments can lack validity and reliability?
15. What role should parents have in using performance assessments? Explain.

$\mathcal{S}$UGGESTED ACTIVITIES

1. Visit a classroom where performance assessments are used. Identify the assessments used that demonstrate what the child *knows* and those that demonstrate what the child *can do* or *can apply*. Discuss at least three different types of assessments.
2. Select a learning objective suitable for a child in first grade. Design assessments that use observation, an interview, and a game. Describe how you would conduct the observation and interview and analyze the results. Construct the game that would be suitable for the objective.
3. Your school is now using performance assessments as one assessment strategy to measure children's progress. You are preparing for a school–family meeting to discuss the new type of assessment. Study carefully the advantages and disadvantages of using performance assessments. Be prepared to discuss these with the parents. Identify three different performance assessments you use in the classroom and be prepared to demonstrate how you can ensure that they are valid and reliable.

$\mathcal{K}$EY TERMS

authentic achievement
authentic assessment
authentic performance assessment
contract
diagnostic interview
directed assignment
direct performance measure
game
indirect performance measure

interview
performance-based assessment
portfolio
project
structured interview
structured performance assessment
unstructured interview
unstructured performance assessment
work sample

$\mathcal{S}$ELECTED WEB SITES

Springer Link (Springer)
http://www.springerlink.com

National Association for the Education of Young Children
http://www.naeyc.org

Association for Childhood Education International
http://www.acei.org

REFERENCES

Baldwin, J. L., Adams, S. M., & Kelly, K. M. (2009). Science at the center: An emergent, standards-based, child-centered framework for early learners. *Early Childhood Education Journal, 37*, 71–77.

Barbour, A., & Desjean-Perrotta, B. (1998). The basics of portfolio assessment. In S. C. Wortham, A. Barbour, & B. Desjean-Perrotta (Eds.), *Portfolio assessment: A handbook for preschool and elementary educators* (pp. 15–30). Olney, MD: Association for Childhood Education International.

Bergan, J. R., & Feld, J. K. (1993). Developmental assessment: New directions. *Young Children, 48*, 41–47.

Bergen, D. (1994). Authentic performance assessments. *Childhood Education, 70*, 99, 102.

Drew, W. F., Christie, J., Johnson, J. E., Meckley, A. M., & Nell, M. L. (2008). Constructive play: A value-added strategy for meeting early learning standards. *Young Children, 63*, 38–44.

Brown, R. (1989). Testing and thoughtfulness. *Educational Leadership, 7*, 31–33.

Checkley, K. (1997). Assessment that serves instruction. *Education Update, 39*, 1, 4–6.

Engel, B. (1990). An approach to assessment in early literacy. In C. Kamii (Ed.), *Achievement testing in the early grades: The games grown-ups play* (pp. 119–134). Washington, DC: National Association for the Education of Young Children.

Givens, K. (1997). Performance assessment tests: A problematic panacea. *Contemporary Education, 69*, 27–29.

Goodwin, W. L., & Goodwin, L. D. (1993). Young children and measurement: Standardized and nonstandardized instruments in early childhood education. In B. Spodek (Ed.), *Handbook of research on the education of young children* (pp. 441–463). New York: Macmillan.

Grace, C., & Shores, E. F. (1991). *The portfolio and its use.* Little Rock, AR: Southern Association on Children Under Six.

Gronlund, G. (2006). *Make early learning standards come alive: Connecting your practice and curriculum to state guidelines.* St. Paul, MN: Redleaf Press.

Harrington, H. L., Meisels, S. J., McMahon, P., Dichtelmiller, M. L., & Jablon, J. R. (1997). *Observing, documenting, and assessing learning: The work sampling system handbook for teacher educators.* Ann Arbor, MI: Rebus.

Helm, J. H., & Beneke, S. (2003). *The power of projects: Meeting contemporary challenges in early childhood classrooms—Strategies and solutions.* New York: Teachers College Press.

Herman, J. L., Aschbacher, P. R., & Winters, L. (1992). *A practical guide to alternative assessment.* Alexandria, VA: Association for Supervision and Curriculum Development.

Hills, T. W. (1992). Reaching potentials through appropriate assessment. In S. Bredekamp & T. Rosegrant (Eds.), *Reaching potentials: Appropriate curriculum and assessment for young children* (pp. 43–64). Washington, DC: National Association for the Education of Young Children.

Hills, T. W. (1993). Assessment in context: Teachers and children at work. *Young Children, 48*, 20–28.

Jacobs, G., & Crowley, K. (2010). *Reading standards and beyond in kindergarten.* Washington, DC: National Association for the Education of Young Children and Thousand Oaks, CA: Corwin, a Sage Company.

Jones, B. F., & Fennimore, T. (1996). The new definition of learning: The first step for school reform. In R. E. Blum & J. A. Arter (Eds.), *A handbook for student performance assessment in an era of restructuring* (pp. III–7:1 to III–7:11). Alexandria, VA: Association for Supervision and Curriculum Development.

Kamii, C., & Rosenblum, V. (1990). An approach to assessment in mathematics. In C. Kamii (Ed.), *Achievement testing in the early grades: The games grown-ups play* (pp. 146–162). Washington, DC: National Association for the Education of Young Children.

Kleinert, H., Greene, P., & Harte, M. (2002). Creating and using meaningful alternative assessments. *Teaching Exceptional Children, 34*, 40–47.

Krechevsky, M. (1991). Project Spectrum: An innovative assessment alternative. *Educational Leadership, 48*, 43–48.

Kulm, G. (1994). *Mathematics assessment: What works in the classroom.* San Francisco: Jossey-Bass.

Lee, F. Y. (1992). Alternative assessments. *Childhood Education, 69,* 72–73.

Meisels, S. J. (1993). Remaking classroom assessment with the Work Sampling System. *Young Children, 48,* 34–40.

Meisels, S. J. (2000). On the side of the child. *Young Children, 55,* 16–19.

Neill, M. (1997). Transforming student assessment. *Phi Delta Kappan, 79,* 34–40.

Newmann, F. M. (1996). Introduction: The school restructuring study. In F. M. Newmann & Associates, *Authentic achievement: Restructuring schools for intellectual quality* (pp. 1–16). San Francisco: Jossey-Bass.

Palmer, J. (1996). Integrating assessment and instruction: Continuous monitoring. In R. E. Blum & J. A. Arter (Eds.), *A handbook for student performance assessment in an era of restructuring* (pp. IV–6:1 to IV–6:12). Alexandria, VA: Association for Supervision and Curriculum Development.

Pierson, C. A., & Beck, S. S. (1993). Performance assessment. The realities that will influence the rewards. *Childhood Education, 70,* 29–32.

Ratcliff, N. J. (2001/2002). Using authentic assessment to document the emerging literacy skills of young children. *Childhood Education, 78,* 66–69.

Schweinhart, L. J. (1993). Observing young children in action: The key to early childhood assessment. *Young Children, 48,* 29–33.

Seefeldt, C. (2005). *Social studies for the preschool-primary child* (7th ed.). Upper Saddle River, NJ: Merrill/Prentice Hall.

Segal, M., & Webber, N. T. (1996). Nonstructured play observations: Guidelines, benefits, and caveats. In S. J. Meisels & E. Fenichel (Eds.), *New visions for the developmental assessment of infants and young children* (pp. 207–230). Washington, DC: Zero to Three: National Center for Infants, Toddlers, and Families.

Vygotsky, L. (1983). School instruction and mental development. In M. Donaldson, R. Grieve, & C. Pratt (Eds.), *Early childhood development and education: Readings in psychology* (pp. 263–269). New York: Guilford.

Wehlage, G. G., Newmann, F. M., & Secada, W. G. (1996). Standards for authentic achievement and pedagogy. In F. M. Newmann & Associates, *Authentic achievement: Restructuring schools for intellectual quality* (pp. 21–48). San Francisco: Jossey-Bass.

Wiggins, G. P. (1993). *Assessing student performance.* San Francisco: Jossey-Bass.

Wiggins, G. P. (1998). *Educative assessment.* San Francisco: Jossey-Bass.

Wurm, J. P. (2005). *Working in the Reggio way.* St. Paul, MN: Redleaf Press.

Zessoules, R., & Gardner, H. (1991). Authentic assessment: Beyond the buzzword and into the classroom. In V. Perrone (Ed.), *Expanding student assessment* (pp. 47–91). Alexandria, VA: Association for Supervision and Curriculum Development.

CHAPTER 9

Portfolio Assessment

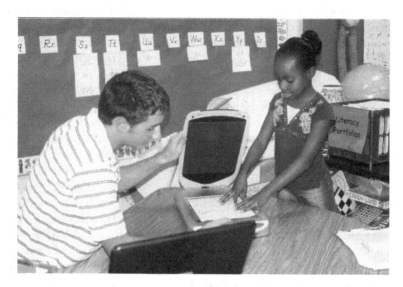

Chapter Objectives

As a result of reading this chapter, you will be able to

1. Understand the limitations of report cards for reporting student progress
2. Understand the importance of developing alternative reporting systems
3. Design and use portfolios for assessing and reporting student progress
4. Understand how narrative reports are used for reporting progress
5. Become familiar with model reporting systems used with young children

What is the best way to assess a young child's progress and develop an evaluative report for that child? In early chapters of this text, we discussed standardized measures, how they are developed and used, and when they are not appropriate for evaluating young children. We also discussed some strategies for conducting informal assessments. In chapter 8, we described performance assessments and how informal strategies are part of or complement performance assessments.

In this chapter and the next, we address how to take the data we collect by using informal or performance assessments and construct a holistic picture of a child's progress that can be reported to parents and school district administrators periodically throughout the school year. These alternative types of reporting are suggested as more suitable for communicating the development and learning of children in the early childhood years. They are equally important for children in elementary schools. First, we will discuss why we need alternative types of reporting, particularly report cards. Then the majority of the chapter will be devoted to one type of assessment and reporting system: portfolios.

Understanding the Need for Alternative Assessment and Reporting Systems

We are in a period of new trends in curriculum and instruction that have implications for assessment. As the work of Piaget (1936/1952, 1945/1962, 1963) and Vygotsky (1978) has resulted in a more constructivist approach to student learning, early childhood teachers have been reinforced in using child-centered learning. An emphasis on constructivism is reflected in whole language, emergent reading and writing, the use of manipulatives, and attention to individual learning styles (Lescher, 1995). Teachers are more aware of the cultural, linguistic, and ability diversity in their students and are designing activities that complement the strengths that accompany this diversity. Alternative informal and performance assessments (discussed in chapters 5 through 8) and strategies to report performance (addressed in this chapter) are partly in response to the limitations and concerns about standardized tests and partly to fulfill the need for more appropriate methods of measuring the new trends in curriculum and instruction (Glazer, 1994). At the same time teachers are working with new expectations for achievement and accountability that cause tension between (1) constructivist approaches to teaching and (2) testing that includes inappropriate strategies for assessing young children.

Using Alternative Assessments Appropriately

In this period of transition in curriculum and instruction and assessment, particularly with children in the preschool and primary years, the fundamental task for educators is to make a knowledgeable shift from more traditional forms of assessment and reporting to alternative strategies. Basic to any transition is first determining what method of reporting achievement and progress to parents is to be used. If the traditional report card is to be maintained, assessment records will have to be compatible with that type of report. That is, if grades or some type of scale to compare progress among students is the profile to be reported, teachers must be accountable for how they determined the child's grade. If an alternative process such as a portfolio, rather than a report card, is to be used to present the child's profile of progress, there must be understanding and consensus as to what the report means and how parents can share in the communication of the child's development and achievement.

Administrators and teachers must be clear about the purposes of and methods of assessment. School districts that are moving toward a constructivist approach and integrated curriculum in elementary classrooms, but are expecting teachers to be accountable for letter grades, particularly in primary-grade classrooms, must understand the incompatibility of methodology and assessment and reporting. In sum, the trend toward holistic, developmental, and integrated learning must be accompanied by sensible assessment and evaluation strategies provided in the alternative assessments defined as authentic and performance based.

Limitations of Letter Grades and Report Cards

Currently, teachers in school districts all over the United States are reviewing and redesigning report cards. A primary motive for this endeavor is the difficulty teachers have in following new trends in curriculum and instruction and in trying to report the child's progress in terms of isolated skills or letter grades based on teaching methods affected by NCLB.

During the last half of the 20th century, curriculum and instruction for children in the early childhood years in quality programs was shifting from an academic approach, in which children are expected to learn the same information at the same time, to a developmental approach. The developmental approach reflects the understanding of development and learning as a continuum along which each child progresses via an internal clock and an individual cognitive process that depends on maturation and previous experiences. Each child's understanding of new knowledge is based on the cognitive information stored from previous encounters in the environment. A basic incompatibility exists between (1) constructivist programs that include child-initiated learning and (2) instruction that is teacher-directed and assessed for letter grades on a report card. Seidel et al. (1997) describe student work as disposable under conditions that result in grades on report cards. Student work is graded and returned with no further value to the teacher or the student. Now in the 21st century, teachers have to rethink how they assess children and shift again to meet the expectations for accountability and the expanded use of standardized tests. Although letter grades still have limitations, they are still in use.

Letter grades can reward students for correct answers and discourage risk taking and experimentation. Newer trends in curriculum and instruction stress the student's willingness to use ideas and develop problem-solving strategies as part of the process of learning. Grading undermines these instructional practices because students are unwilling to take the chance of making errors and possibly receiving low grades.

Letter grades are also limited because they measure only achievement. They do not reflect a student's strengths and weaknesses or the effort made to earn the grade. Critics believe that grades tend to limit how many students can do well. The system tends to sort students into categories; in addition, slower students lose their motivation to learn as a result of continuing negative feedback. In addition, they get labeled as poor students, and teacher expectations are lower for them than for students who make higher grades (Willis, 1993).

Alternative systems of reporting that use authentic or performance assessments provide more than letter grades. They can include (1) a continuum of development and learning, (2) information about the whole child, not just about skills that have been mastered, (3) diagnostic information that allows the teacher to adjust instruction and activities, and, most important, (4) examples of what the child has done to demonstrate understanding. Alternative assessment systems can provide both accountability and a comprehensive understanding of achievement.

Report cards are changing as teachers and administrators find more flexible and meaningful types of reporting. Figure 9-1 shows a continuum or hierarchy of skills for language arts, math, science, and social studies. The report is used as an ongoing tool to report progress. The continuum begins at the bottom of the page, and the complexity or difficulty increases as the indicators or objectives move up the page. After the child has mastered a concept or a skill, it is checked off. Progress is the important factor, rather than a letter grade given if mastery is demonstrated during a reporting period. Likewise, the child can progress along the hierarchy of objectives above or below grade level. As teachers and administrators become more knowledgeable and skilled, more indicators of development may be included, along with refinements in the objectives presently listed.

Once school district policy makers, administrators, and teachers determine that performance assessments are to be included in the evaluation process, decisions are then made on how to use performance assessments and develop a comprehensive picture of the child's progress. Collection and interpretation of data relevant to the child's performance require organization of an evaluation system that permits the teacher to describe growth in a meaningful manner. Portfolios are one such assessment.

Portfolio Assessment

Portfolios are a collection of a child's work and teacher data from informal and performance assessments to evaluate development and learning. A portfolio may be kept just by and for the child, with samples of work over a period of time. It may also be organized by the teacher and contain observation reports, checklists, work samples, records of directed assignments, interviews, or other evidence of achievement. There are child portfolios, teacher portfolios, and combinations that include entries made by both the child and teacher.

Purposes for Portfolio Assessment

How the contents of a portfolio are used depends on the purpose. Portfolios can be used for assessment and evaluation, for self-assessment and reflection, and for reporting progress.

Using Portfolios for Assessment and Evaluation

A portfolio collection is used to develop a holistic picture of activities the student has engaged in over a period of time. The portfolio should include many examples of a student's work that will provide multiple assessments of concepts, skills, and projects that result in an accurate picture of what the student understands and is able to use in a meaningful context (Micklo, 1997; Valencia, 1990). In addition to the child and the teacher assessing the child's achievement, the portfolio can be

FIRST GRADE

	Language Arts	Math	Science	Social Studies
6.0	☐ Recognizes vowels ☐ Reads primer-level simple sentences ☐ Understands antonyms ☐ Writes phrases ☐ Arranges events in sequential order ☐ Alphabetizes according to initial letter ☐ Acquires basic sight vocabulary ☐ Engages in creative dramatic activities and nonverbal communication ☐ Responds to nonverbal cues	☐ Knows greater than/less than ☐ Writes numerals 1–20 ☐ Recognizes simple color and size patterns ☐ Recognizes and sorts plane figures ☐ Finds differences by separating and comparing objects ☐ Solves problems involving addition and subtraction with manipulatives ☐ Uses numeral sentences	☐ Acquires data through the use of senses ☐ Identifies careers related to theme (mayor, construction workers, business people) ☐ Identifies internal organs and their functions (brain, heart, lungs) ☐ Identifies skeletal parts (skull, ribs, pelvis, spine) ☐ Classifies food into pyramid levels ☐ Classifies events in a consistent, organized fashion while making observations (plant growth)	☐ Is aware of others' needs ☐ Identifies kinds of work of school personnel and family members ☐ Knows birth date ☐ Knows geography of school campus ☐ Identifies name of school ☐ Knows geographical location of home in relation to school/community ☐ Identifies and accepts one's classroom responsibilities ☐ Completes assigned tasks ☐ Identifies positive traits of self and others
6.3	☐ Selects topics of interest to self and others ☐ Understands opposites ☐ Understands naming words (people, places, things, animals) ☐ Recognizes a sentence ☐ Understands action words ☐ Identifies the main idea in speaker's words ☐ Uses basic phonics: media/message/final consonants ☐ Uses pronouns properly ☐ Contributes ideas and information in group discussion	☐ Finds sums by combining groups and counting ☐ Finds differences by separating and comparing objects ☐ Estimates and predicts quantities ☐ Identifies lines of symmetry ☐ Measures/estimates mass using standard units ☐ Develops concept of conservation (measuring capacity using containers) ☐ Constructs picture graphs	☐ Creates an order of events in a logical continuum while making observations ☐ Collects information to make reasonable interpretations ☐ Makes accurate measurements and uses them appropriately as descriptors ☐ Manipulates laboratory materials and equipment ☐ Uses information and observations to make reasonable interpretations	☐ Contributes to group activities ☐ Understands food processing ☐ Discusses visuals (pictures, charts) ☐ Knows how animals are used for clothing, food, etc. ☐ Understands and distinguishes animal habitats ☐ Uses terms concerning time (today, tomorrow, yesterday) ☐ Knows months of the year ☐ Knows the days of the week ☐ Knows N, S, E, W ☐ Knows the four seasons

FIGURE 9-1 A first-grade reporting system

used to evaluate the teacher. The child is given an opportunity to provide feedback to the teacher.

Using Portfolios for Self-Assessment and Reflection

Portfolios, particularly those that are used over a period of several years, make it possible for the student to observe growth and progress by comparing work samples and drawings longitudinally (Hebert & Schultz, 1996). Many teachers in kindergarten and primary grades have students make a drawing of themselves at the beginning of a school year. At the beginning of each subsequent reporting period, another drawing is made. Students can look back and see how their efforts have improved. Samples of writing provide the same type of comparison. Students at the end of second or third grade may not even recognize their earlier efforts at the beginning of the year.

Using Portfolios for Reporting Progress

At the beginning of the chapter, we discussed how alternative reporting methods to report cards are needed to report student progress to parents. Portfolios are a comprehensive alternative approach. When parents are engaged with their child and teacher in selecting and reviewing what has been completed during a grading period, they are able to see the work and assessment examples that have been used (Gilkerson & Hanson, 2000). If grades are required, the work in the portfolio can document the assessments used to determine the grade. More about communicating with parents about student progress will be discussed in chapter 10.

Organizing Portfolios

Portfolios have become a popular trend in elementary schools in the last few years, particularly in the language arts. Although abundant literature is available on how to use the portfolio for assessment in language arts, particularly for the whole-language and emergent literacy approaches, less has been offered for other developmental or content-area categories. More recently, portfolios have been used for many content areas in the curriculum. It is just as appropriate to use portfolios for social studies, science, and mathematics as it is to use alternative or authentic strategies for assessment for all types of curriculum and instruction.

Types of Portfolios

As teachers and students use portfolios to fulfill the three purposes of portfolio assessment described earlier, they make decisions about the type of portfolio that best serves their purposes. Among these possibilities are working portfolios, evaluative portfolios, showcase portfolios, and archival portfolios. The portfolios can be organized by the teacher, by the teacher and child, and by the child alone.

Decisions must be made about who will determine portfolio contents and purpose. Will the portfolio be maintained and used by the teacher alone? Will the teacher and child make choices for the portfolio together? What role will parents play in the process? Will parents be encouraged to make selections for a portfolio and bring samples of work done at home to be included? These considerations can be included for each of the types of portfolios described next.

Working Portfolios

A working portfolio is used to collect examples of student work for future evaluation. During an interval of a reporting period, the work is collected without making final decisions as to what will be kept and what will be discarded. Samples are collected by both the teacher and the child. Progress notes and planning for subsequent work are important components (Gronlund, 1998). The items in the working portfolio later can become part of another type of portfolio.

Evaluative Portfolios

This is the most commonly understood type of portfolio. An evaluative portfolio permits the teacher to make an assessment of the student's progress, both formative and summative. The teacher uses the materials included to evaluate the student's developmental advances and needs for future growth and learning. The evaluative portfolio is used for reporting to parents and administrators and for planning for curriculum and instruction (Barbour & Desjean-Perrotta, 1998).

Showcase Portfolios

A showcase portfolio is used to exhibit the child's best work. Showcase portfolios are most frequently used to share the child's accomplishments with his or her parents. They can also be used for school open-house events or occasions when children from different classrooms and grade levels share what they are learning and doing. Showcase portfolio contents are frequently chosen by the child (Barbour & Desjean-Perrotta, 1998; Gronlund, 1998).

Archival Portfolios

In some preschools and elementary schools, student portfolios follow students from one year to another. This type of portfolio is sometimes called an *archival* or *pass-along portfolio* because it can provide information to the child's next teacher and/or other future teachers (Puckett & Black, 2000; Seidel et al., 1997).

Portfolios can be organized by developmental category, by content area, or by topics or themes if an integrated curriculum is followed. As is true for curriculum design, the goals of the program and objectives for development and learning serve as the foundation for instruction and assessment. As teachers understand more about the emergent nature of cognition and development, their task is to become comfortable with using characteristics of emerging development and how that is reflected in the work they and the children can collect for assessment. In this respect, understanding the principles and characteristics of development become essential if the teacher is to comprehend how to assess the child's developmental progress. In the following sections, examples of organization of a developmental portfolio and content-area portfolio are provided.

Examples of children's work can be used in portfolio assessment.

Organizing Portfolios Using a Developmental Approach

A sensible approach to organizing portfolios for preschool and primary-grade children is by developmental category. Thus, the teacher might provide dividers in the portfolio for motor development, concept development, language development, and social and emotional development. Grace and Shores (1991), citing Meisels and Steele (1991), make the following suggestions for organizing such a portfolio:

1. *Art Activities (Fine-Motor Development)*

   Drawings of events, persons, and animals. The child may dictate descriptions or explanations of the drawings to the teacher or a parent or classroom volunteer. Or the child may write such explanations. (The teacher may need to make notes if the child writes his or her own picture caption.)

   Photos of unusual block constructions or projects, labeled and dated.

   Collages and other examples of the child's use of various media when designing a picture.

   Samples of the child's manuscript printing. (The appearance and placement of the letters on the page are evaluated in the context of a developmental continuum.)

2. *Movement (Gross-Motor Development)*

   Notes recorded by the teacher or videotapes of the child's movement activities in the classroom or on the playground, which reflect the child's developing skills.

   Notes, photographs, videotapes, and anecdotal records that demonstrate the child's skills and progress in music activities and finger plays.

   Notes from teacher interviews with the child about his or her favorite active games at school.

3. *Math and Science Activities (Concept Development)*

Photographs of the child measuring or counting specific ingredients as part of a cooking activity.

Charts on which the child has recorded the planting, care, watering schedule, periods of sunlight, and so on, of plants in the classroom or on the school grounds.

Work samples demonstrating the child's understanding of number concepts. An example is the numeral 4 formed with beans glued to a sheet of paper and the appropriate number of beans glued beside the numeral.

Work samples, teacher notes, and taped pupil interviews illustrating, in a progressive fashion, the child's understanding of mathematical concepts.

Photographs and data gathered from checklists and taped pupil interviews that document the child's conceptual understanding, exploring, hypothesizing, and problem solving. (The documentation will depend on the child's developmental stages during the life of the portfolio.)

4. *Language and Literacy*

Tape recordings of a child rereading stories that he or she "wrote" or dictated to a parent, teacher, or classroom volunteer.

Examples of the child's journal entries.

Copies of signs or labels the child constructed.

A log of book titles actually read by the child or read to the child by a teacher, parent, or other adult.

Copies of stories, poems, or songs the child wrote or dictated.

Taped pupil interviews that reveal the child's increase, over time, in vocabulary and skill in using the language. (These strategies are also appropriate for students in ELL and bilingual programs.)

5. *Personal and Social Development*

Teacher notes and anecdotal records that document interactions between the child and his or her peers. Such interactions can indicate the child's ability to make choices, solve problems, and cooperate with others.

Teacher notes, anecdotal records, and video recordings that document events that occurred on field trips. Such incidents may illustrate the child's social awareness.

Notes from teacher–parent conferences. (pp. 21–25)

Organizing Portfolios Using a Subject-Area Approach

The teacher may prefer to organize portfolios using a subject-area approach. If so, the teacher must choose whether to include all subject areas or to dedicate a portfolio to a single content area. If a comprehensive collection of the child's work, teacher assessments, and other evaluation data is desired, Batzle (1992) recommends the following contents for the portfolio:

1. Required Tests and Accountability Measures
   Standardized tests
   Minimum competency tests

    Criterion-referenced tests
    Chapter or unit tests

2. Samples Across the Curriculum
    Language arts
    Reading responses
    Reading logs
    Home reading logs
    Oral reading tapes
    Writing folders
    Writing samples
    Spelling work
    Math
    Fine arts
    Content areas

3. Teacher Observations and Measures
    Kid watching and anecdotal records
    Running records
    Retellings
    Progress checks
    Teacher-made tests
    Rubrics
    Conference records
    Summary of findings

4. Inventories and Other Forms
    Reading inventory
    Informal reading inventory
    Writing inventory
    Parent surveys, comments, and evaluations

5. Additional Items
    Cassette or photo of drama presentations
    Oral presentation, book talk
    Oral language inventory
    Oral "publishing" (p. 35)

This example includes possibilities for several subject areas to be included; nevertheless, some subjects, such as social studies, are omitted. Moreover, the predominant categories suggested are related to language arts. Note that inclusion of results of standardized tests is recommended.

The pamphlet "Portfolio Assessment: A Worthwhile Testing Alternative," published by Teaching for Excellence (1992), has more complete ideas for a portfolio that include all subject areas. The ideas proposed could focus on specific subjects or integrated subject areas. Possibilities suggested are the following:

- Self-evaluation through an "All About Me" portfolio in which students choose items to express themselves, such as their likes, dislikes, hobbies, personality, and family.
- Written literacy portfolios, with works such as timed writing samples, best notes, log and journal entries, essays, critiques, and short stories.

- Math portfolios, with such items as statistical studies, graphic representations, diagrams of problem-solving steps, written descriptions of math investigations, and responses to open-ended questions and problems.
- Creative expressions such as art, music, dance, and photography.
- Projects such as science and social studies investigations. A fun way to teach and test applications is to assign job role simulations, such as an archaeologist who must find the culture or time period of an artifact, or a policy analyst who must predict the future in a country being studied.
- Videotapes and written analysis of progress for physical skills such as soccer, gymnastics, and volleyball.

Organization of student portfolios can focus on a single content area, and there are options for how to organize the contents. Farr (1993) suggests some organization patterns for student portfolios for a reading and writing system as follows:

1. *Organization by topic.* Students might put reading and writing materials on sports in one section, school topics in another, and mysteries in another.

2. *Organization by genre.* Students might arrange materials according to whether they are stories, letters, articles, songs, and other genres for reading and writing.

3. *Organization by difficulty.* One section might include those things that were easy to do; in another those that were more difficult; and in a third those that were very difficult.

4. *Chronological organization.* Students use weeks or some other time period as the organizational pattern.

5. *Organization by preference.* Students use one section for reading and writing activities they liked a great deal, another for those they felt neutral about, and a third for those they disliked.

6. *Multiple-level organization.* Students arrange materials first by topics and then within topics by genre, preference, or difficulty. (p. 13)

Setting Up Portfolios

The decision to initiate the use of portfolio assessment should be approached thoughtfully. If the process of implementing portfolio assessment is to succeed, the early childhood center or school must have a good climate that will support the change (Seidel et al., 1997). The purposes of portfolio assessment and how they are associated with a philosophy of learning and instruction need to be understood and accepted by the teachers before embarking on a new and complex assessment approach (Harris, 2009; Seitz & Bartholomew, 2008).

Steps in Getting Started

Once the decision has been made to use portfolio assessment and the teacher understands the implications of undertaking the changes, several decisions must be made prior to beginning the process. The first steps are to select the purpose, format, and storage system for portfolios. Then the teacher must determine what will go into the portfolio by selecting portfolio contents and decide how student work will be collected, organized, and reviewed. Finally, the teacher must decide how assessment of student progress will be reported.

What Is the Purpose?

The purpose of the portfolio is determined by the teacher's objectives for assessment. If the purpose is to assess development for a reporting period, an evaluative portfolio with a developmental format is chosen. If the purpose is for the student to initiate learning objectives and engage in reflection and self-evaluation, a working portfolio may be the obvious choice. If portfolios are implemented for parent conferences and are not the major sources of assessment, a showcase portfolio might be indicated.

The teacher may determine multiple purposes for a portfolio. The portfolio may be used both for assessment and as a showcase. For this type of portfolio, both the teacher and the student may have sections of student work. As an alternative, there may be a section for assessment and another for showcase entries. There are all kinds of possibilities. The teacher will want to consider what purpose or purposes will best serve his or her objectives for assessment.

How Will It Be Organized?

After the teacher has decided why and how the portfolio is to be used for assessment, some decisions will be made as to how to organize the contents. For an evaluative portfolio in preschool, a chronological organization may be the best choice to display student progress in developmental domains. If the teacher uses a thematic curriculum, the materials placed in the portfolio may be organized by thematic topic. If a portfolio is to serve as the assessment system for a single content area, the genre approach to organization permits division of the contents into reading, writing, skills practice, and so forth. Organization by difficulty may be preferred for a mathematics portfolio.

Once the format has been determined, it can be further organized using a table of contents. The following can be used for various formats:

- A table of contents
- A title page that identifies the student and explains what can be found in the collection and the purpose of the portfolio
- Dividers with labels that identify contents of each section
- Dates on all entries
- A review or assessment section that includes both teacher and child assessments to include teacher comments (Seidel et al., 1997; Wortham, 1998)

Where Will It Be Stored?

An important decision is how to store portfolios. The purposes for the portfolio and types of materials to be stored influence the type of storage containers to be used. A writing portfolio composed primarily of student writing samples can be housed in a file folder; in contrast, a portfolio that contains project work or video- and audiotapes may require a box. Some suggested storage containers include the following (Barbour & Desjean-Perrotta, 1998; Grace & Shores, 1991):

- Expandable file folders
- X-ray folders
- Pizza boxes
- Grocery bags stapled inside each other
- Large mailing envelopes
- Office supply boxes
- Paper briefcases
- Shoeboxes containing file folders
- Plastic crates
- CD-ROM

What Will Go in the Portfolio?

Based on the purposes and format of the portfolio, decisions must now be made about portfolio contents. Will the portfolio for 4-year-olds include all developmental domains or just literacy? Will the content-area portfolio be for math and science or language arts? Will the portfolio include only student work, or will teacher assessments be included? There are many possibilities for determining what will go into the portfolio that will vary according to the developmental level of the child and the purposes of the portfolio. As the use of portfolios evolves, teachers will modify the components portfolios include. In some cases, they may find that they are collecting too many types of materials. In other cases, they may find that they need to expand the examples that are to be included.

Teachers may find it useful to develop a checklist for reviewing the steps they have taken in getting started in using portfolio assessment. Lescher (1995) provides one model for such a checklist as pictured in Figure 9-2.

Collecting and Organizing Work

When the portfolio process is getting underway, the teacher and children decide how they will collect and organize entries for the portfolio. Periodically, during a grading period or another designated time, pieces are selected for the portfolio. The teacher can likewise select samples for the portfolio from assessment activities or tests that have been administered, checklists, rating scales, essays, and other evidence of work. Rubrics for individual and group work are included in the assignments. When it is time to finalize the portfolio, the teacher, child, or teacher and child make final choices for the portfolio.

Over the duration of the school year, more decisions are made as to which materials will remain for the entire year and which will be replaced by better or more advanced work. If a longitudinal review is desired at the end of the year, work completed at intervals throughout the year is retained for comparison over time. If the portfolio is for archival purposes, decisions are made about what will be passed on to the next teacher and what will be eliminated. Size and amount

```
┌─────────────────────────────────────────────────────────────────┐
│                   PORTFOLIO DESIGN WORKSHEET                       │
│  ───────────────────────────────────────────────────────────      │
│                                                                    │
│  1. What will be included in your portfolio?                       │
│       ☐ Work samples                                               │
│       ☐ Journal                                                    │
│       ☐ Teacher assessment                                         │
│       ☐ Self-assessment                                            │
│       ☐ Examples of your best work                                 │
│       ☐ Assessment progress reports                                │
│                                                                    │
│  2. How will your portfolio be organized?                          │
│  ───────────────────────────────────────────────────────────      │
│                                                                    │
│  ───────────────────────────────────────────────────────────      │
│                                                                    │
│  3. How will portfolio entries be collected?                       │
│  ───────────────────────────────────────────────────────────      │
│                                                                    │
│  ───────────────────────────────────────────────────────────      │
│                                                                    │
│  4. Who will be included in assessment of your portfolio?          │
│  ───────────────────────────────────────────────────────────      │
│                                                                    │
│  ───────────────────────────────────────────────────────────      │
│                                                                    │
│  5. How will your portfolio be shared? How will assessment         │
│     results be reported?                                           │
│  ───────────────────────────────────────────────────────────      │
│                                                                    │
│  ───────────────────────────────────────────────────────────      │
│                                                                    │
│  ───────────────────────────────────────────────────────────      │
└─────────────────────────────────────────────────────────────────┘
```

FIGURE 9-2 Checklist for portfolio design

become important factors in all portfolio collections, but archival portfolios require careful selection (Seitz & Bartholomew, 2008).

Selecting Portfolio Assessments

A major task for the teacher is to determine which assessments will be included in the portfolio, depending on the purpose of the portfolio. Barbour and Desjean-Perrotta (1998) suggest that there should be a balance between process and product. Process work will be the work that reflects the student's progress toward a developmental goal or cognitive skill. Product is the final step in the process where the child has achieved success. Therefore, there should be a balance between examples of both types of assessments. The portfolio contents should include traditional assessment measures, performance assessments, and observation results. The assessments that are chosen should correspond to the possibilities or purposes of their use. At this

PURPOSES OF PORTFOLIO ASSESSMENTS

Work Samples
To assess and evaluate
To make a diagnosis
To assess longitudinal progress
To conduct student self-evaluation
To understand student thinking processes
For self-selection of important work

Diaries
For student reflection
To trace progress
To express understanding
For problem solving
For self-evaluation
For self-expression

Interviews
For specific feedback
To evaluate conceptual understanding
To observe thinking processes
To assess skills
To assess progress

Interactive Journals
For communication and feedback
For peer editing
For building support
To stimulate creativity
For problem solving

Checklists and Rating Scales
To assess and report progress and mastery
To assess and report development
To record task list results
For instructional planning
To assess teaching processes

**Teacher-Designed Tests, Tasks,
  and Observations**
To assess skills
To assess cognitive processes
To document progress
To determine eligibility for special programs
For screening
To establish zone of proximal development (ZPD)

Contracts
For behavior management
To conduct student self-assessment
To assess student work habits
To conduct student self-initiated planning
For student management of learning activities
For feedback on student activities
For feedback on student interests
For recordkeeping

**Audio/Video/Photographs/Computer
  Assessments**
For assessment through observation
To determine progress
To assess learning processes
For self-assessment
For reporting to parents
To demonstrate skills
To maintain an electronic portfolio

Performance/Criterion-Related Tasks
To conduct a demonstration or exhibit
To conduct application of learning in context

Group Assessments
To assess group performance
To evaluate instruction
To evaluate program progress
To assess skills
To assess student progress in learning how to learn
To assess student progress in cooperative group
  learning

Narrative Summary
For teacher reflection on student progress
For summative assessment
For reporting to parents
To screen for special programs

FIGURE 9-3 Portfolio assessment purposes

point, all the assessment possibilities that have been included in this text can be analyzed and considered for the portfolio. Although most of the assessment types are performance based, teacher-designed tests and tasks and other assessment instruments are included in the total range of possibilities. Figure 9-3 shows a range of assessments and the purposes they can serve for portfolio assessment.

A kindergarten teacher selecting assessments for a comprehensive preschool or kindergarten portfolio may consider several types. For example, the pattern of emergence in writing and reading can be organized into a checklist, rubric, or other record-keeping form to determine the child's progress in emergent literacy (Farr, 1993; Sulzby, 1993; Wortham, 1998). Figure 9-4 is a form for keeping a record of a

Student:	
BOOKS THE CHILD HAS READ INDEPENDENTLY	
Title	Date Read
BOOKS THE CHILD HAS READ WITH ASSISTANCE	
Title	Date Read
Comments/Instruction needed:	

FIGURE 9-4 Teacher's record of child's reading

LEARNING CENTER DEVELOPMENT GUIDE SHEET

Objective(s): _The student will use descriptive language_

Materials: _paper, pencils, markers, pens_

Duration: _1 week_

Addressing different levels and assessment:

Level	Activity/Expectation	Assessment
Pre-writer	The student will describe a picture using words	Rubric uses pictures May copy letters or words Can write some familiar words
Developing Writer	The student will describe a picture using sentences. • Upper and lower case letters • Some punctuation	Understands sound-symbol relationship uses invented spelling Can read own writing
Experienced Writer	The student will describe a picture using sentences in a paragraph • Capitals used correctly • Correct punctuation	Using conventions of print in spelling Demonstrates sentence sense Can use correct punctuation and use of upper and lower case letters

LEARNING CENTER DEVELOPMENT GUIDE SHEET

Objective(s): _____

Materials: _____

Duration: _____

Addressing different levels and assessment:

Level	Activity/Expectation	Assessment

FIGURE 9-5   Learning center writing rubric

child's emergent and conventional reading (Sulzby, 1993), and Figure 9-5 is a rubric that can be used to select materials for a learning center and assess emergent writing. Figure 9-6 is an example of an interview form that might be used with a child in kindergarten or first grade.

A teacher wishing to track the acquisition of skills development and project work in science may develop a checklist to assess accomplishments and participation in projects. Figure 9-7 shows two different checklists that evaluate both developmental skills and performance work in group projects (Cliatt & Shaw, 1992). Figure 9-8 provides for self-assessment by the child.

Reading Interview with *name* _____ *Date* _____

1. What kinds of books do you like?

_____

_____

2. What is your favorite book?

_____

_____

3. Do you have books to read at home?

_____

_____

4. Does someone read to you at home?

_____

_____

5. Do others read at home? What do they like to read?

_____

_____

_____

_____

FIGURE 9-6 Teacher interview form

Analyzing Portfolio Assessments

Periodically, the teacher, child, and parents review portfolio contents to determine the child's progress and how appropriate experiences should be planned for further growth and development. To prepare for discussions, the teacher first conducts an analysis based on established learning objectives, indicators of developmental progress, and other criteria that demonstrate learning accomplishment. Work samples, interview results, checklists, rating scales, rubrics, teacher-designed assessments, and performance tasks are studied to determine what the child has learned. The child's work as presented in the portfolio is evaluated in terms of developmental domains, sequences of skills,

	Children												
Behaviors													
Makes groups consistently when given a basis for classification.													
Names basis for classifying.													
Devises basis for classifying.													
Makes subclassifications.													
Other													

A checklist for classifying skills.

	Children												
Qualities													
Applies information.													
Conveys information clearly.													
Represents creative work.													
Neatly made.													
Clearly explained (as applicable).													
For group projects, was project work shared?													
Was work cooperative?													
Other													

A checklist for evaluating projects.

FIGURE 9-7 Science assessment checklists

Source: Cliatt, M. J. P., & Shaw, J. M. (1992). *Helping children explore science: A sourcebook for teachers of young children*, © 1992, p. 59. Reprinted by permission of Pearson Education, Inc., Upper Saddle River, NJ.

Reviewing My Portfolio

name _____

date _____

teacher _____

1. The work I like best in my portfolio is _____

I will draw or write about it here

```


```

2. I have the most work in _____

I will draw or write about it here

```


```

3. I would like to have more of this kind of work in my portfolio.

I will draw or write about it here

```


```

FIGURE 9-8 Reviewing my portfolio

and objectives established by the teachers and school. Using such established criteria, the teacher develops a profile of the child's strengths and weaknesses, as well as the interests and creative expressions revealed in various types of work samples.

The teacher and child can then use the portfolio as a vehicle for the child to reflect on progress and interests. Parents can also interact with the teacher and child on accomplishments and discuss future plans and goals together (Smith, 2000). More about analysis and summarization of child development and learning will be discussed in chapter 10.

Strategies for Developing Successful Portfolios

Teachers who have used portfolios in their classrooms offer suggestions from their experience in getting started with portfolio assessment. Larry Buschman, a second-grade teacher in Jefferson, Oregon, uses portfolios. He uses student conferences at the end of every quarter to assess how his students are doing. His students help create and maintain their portfolios and choose most of the work samples that are included in their portfolios. Buschman (1993) makes the following suggestions to teachers who are beginning the process:

- Start small and emphasize quality, not quantity.
- Use photographs, drawings, and reflective descriptions to document projects that don't fit inside the portfolio.
- Make sure each portfolio has a table of contents.
- Be sure students date their work.
- Select a few work samples yourself.
- Give parents the opportunity to review their child's portfolio. (p. 24)

Advantages and Disadvantages of Using Portfolios to Report Student Progress

The advantages of using portfolios for assessment and reporting were discussed earlier. Portfolios permit a wide range of assessment methods and a variety of ways that children can demonstrate mastery and growth in development. They allow for flexibility in how the teacher documents student progress; at the same time, they provide parents with extensive information about their child's experiences in school that facilitate learning and accomplishments.

Portfolios provide evaluation above and beyond letter grades on a report card. Children can be tracked on a continuum of development. In addition, assessment can be used for diagnostic purposes, as well as to document learning. Teachers can meet the individual needs of each child by examining portfolio contents and discussing progress and problems with the child through interviews and conferences (Harris, 2009).

Portfolios include input from the child, making the child an active partner in the evaluation process. The child not only makes selections for portfolio contents but also participates in the assessment process. This participation includes discussing progress with parents during parent–teacher conferences.

The most obvious difficulty in organizing and maintaining portfolios is the issue of time. Both the teacher and the children need time to implement and maintain portfolios. It is important for the teacher and the children to work regularly with portfolios, review contents, discuss progress, and make changes in what is to be kept in the portfolio. If the portfolios are to be effective, they must be kept organized and current. Time is needed to work with portfolios, and teachers who are enthusiastic about the benefits of portfolios may also be concerned about the time needed to use portfolios appropriately.

Teachers are also concerned about accountability and grading portfolios. If a school district combines the use of portfolios with evaluation of the child's longitudinal progress, and if the evaluation of that progress is the primary purpose of reporting, teachers can become very comfortable with using portfolios. If, however, portfolios are used to assess and assign grades, the evaluation process is much more difficult when using portfolios. Teachers can be much more anxious about using portfolio assessment when they have to use them to compare the achievement of students with each other. The issue of assigning grades can be one of the biggest challenges teachers face when initiating portfolio assessment.

A major concern when using portfolios for assessment and reporting is validity of the assessment strategies used. Earlier in the chapter, we discussed the need to predetermine standards and procedures that would be used to assess portfolio contents. In addition, steps must be taken to ensure that the assessment strategies have been checked for validity (Goodwin & Goodwin, 1993). Teachers are particularly concerned about their own accountability for the evaluation process. They may be insecure about using portfolio assessment because they are uncertain whether they will be able to grade the child's work appropriately.

The statewide use of portfolios in Vermont (O'Neil, 1993) gives some information about the possible difficulties in establishing reliability. Low reliability coefficients in the 1991–1992 statewide assessment process led Vermont to improve the portfolio assessment process to overcome these technical limitations. Teachers who are individually trying to be accountable for the quality of their assessments are rightfully concerned about the ability to be accountable to parents and administrators about the evaluation process they use in the classroom.

Developing Quality Portfolio Assessments

Ensuring the quality of the assessments that are placed in portfolios was discussed in earlier chapters. The development of quality in performance assessments through the use of rubrics and other strategies was discussed in chapter 8. But how is the quality of the portfolio as a whole to be developed? The portfolio is one type of assessment system and must have quality as a system. Six suggestions have been provided to help teachers to establish quality in portfolio assessment (Arter & Spandel, 1992, as cited by Herman, Aschbacher, & Winters, 1992):

- How representative is the work included in the portfolio of what students can really do?
- Do the portfolio pieces represent coached work? Independent work? Group work? Are they identified as to the amount of support students received?
- Do the evaluation criteria for each piece and the portfolio as a whole represent the most relevant or useful dimensions of student work?
- How well do portfolio pieces match important instructional targets or authentic tasks?
- Do tasks or some parts of them require extraneous abilities?
- Is there a method for ensuring that portfolios are reviewed consistently and criteria applied accurately? (pp. 120–121)

Another consideration in developing portfolios that include quality assessments is relevance. *They must be purposeful.* Hanson and Gilkerson (1999) propose that a meaningful portfolio must meet the following criteria:

- Be clearly linked with instructional objectives.
- Be an ongoing assessment system.
- Avoid becoming a teacher-manufactured document.
- Be performance based; emphasize purposeful learning; be ongoing in all cultural contexts of home, school, and community. (p. 81)

Strategies for Reporting Student Progress

Using Portfolios to Report Student Progress

Although portfolio assessment is a valuable system to report student progress, parents must be involved, particularly when teachers are transitioning from traditional reporting, such as report cards, to portfolios. Although parents have typically been left out when portfolios are initiated (Hill & Ruptic, 1994), in a partnership relationship, parents are invited to learn about portfolios at the beginning of the transition process. Parent training sessions can be held to explain the purposes and goals of portfolio assessment, followed by opportunities to understand how portfolio entries are selected, how the format is designed, and how entries will be evaluated (Seitz & Bartholomew, 2008; Weldin & Tumarkin, 1998/1999).

Using Narrative Reports to Report Student Progress

Purposes of Narrative Reports

Narrative or summary reports are another alternative to report cards for communicating a child's progress to parents. A *summary report* is an evaluation written by the teacher to describe the child's development and learning. A narrative report can stand alone as the periodic evaluation of progress or be combined with other assessment and reporting strategies. A narrative report can be part of a portfolio assessment or another system of assessment and reporting. Purposes of the report are to describe a review of the child's growth over a period of time and to describe that growth in a meaningful way for parents.

A summary report can describe the child's strengths, using developmental categories or subject areas. It (1) can be organized to include projects and integrated curriculum topics, (2) is a profile of development and change over time, and (3) is written with terminology that parents can understand to draw a picture of their child. Using the results of observations, checklists, performance assessments, and other performance strategies, the teacher translates the information so that parents can comprehend what their child has accomplished (Horm-Wingerd, 1992; Krechevsky, 1991; Meisels, 1993).

Writing a Narrative Report

A narrative report as described by Horm-Wingerd (1992) includes the following:

1. Descriptions of examples of the child's behaviors
2. Examples of what the child can do
3. Concerns the teacher may have about the child's progress
4. Goals and plans for the child in the future

Advocates of written summaries to report child progress express concern that teachers write reports in such a manner that parents appreciate their child and value his or her progress. Strengths, rather than weaknesses, should be stressed. When the child's weaknesses are described or concerns are expressed, the teacher should be careful not to assess blame and to use a positive tone in the report. The goal is to develop reports that promote a positive home–school relationships (Horm-Wingerd, 1992). Project Spectrum, described in more detail later, suggests that any home activities described for the parents for use with their child require inexpensive, readily available materials (Krechevsky, 1991).

It is important for teachers to write the narrative report carefully and accurately. It should inform the parents about the child's progress and educate them about appropriate instruction and assessment practices. Horm-Wingerd (1992) suggests the following procedure when writing narratives:

1. Open with an overall statement describing a child's progress in a broad developmental area since the last report or conference.
2. Give a specific example of behavior to serve as evidence for your global description of change and to help parents understand exactly what you are describing.
3. State your plans.
4. If appropriate, note what the parents can do at home to facilitate their child's development. (p. 14)

Horm-Wingerd also provides guidelines for writing narrative reports to ensure that complete and appropriate information is shared with the parents. Figure 9-9 includes specifications, suggestions, and cautions that, if followed, help the teacher write a quality report to share with parents.

Teachers frequently have difficulty in reporting objectively about some children in their classroom. It is easy to write a very positive report about an attractive child who is cooperative and eager to please the teacher. The teacher may not be aware that the child's progress is being overestimated and reported because the teacher has very positive personal feelings about the child. On the other hand, teachers may have great difficulty in evaluating and reporting objectively on children who pose problems in the classroom. Children who are disruptive, rude to their peers and the teacher, or physically unattractive can have their progress underestimated. The teacher may put too much negative emphasis in the report, rather than stressing the child's accomplishments. The guidelines in Figure 9-9 have strong suggestions for

Format

- Are organizing categories congruent with philosophy, goals, and curriculum?
- Does it reflect the "whole" child?
- Does it honestly encourage and facilitate parent–teacher communication?

General Content

- Does it blame the child?
- Does it blame the parent?
- How will it make the child feel?
- How will it make the parent feel?
- How will it impact parent–teacher relations?
- How will it affect parent–child relations?

Specific Content

- Does it contain information about the essential areas of development and learning?
- Does it describe patterns of typical classroom behavior over time?
- Does it describe individual growth and progress?
- Does it focus on strengths rather than weaknesses?
- Does it contain specific examples of what the child can do?
- Does it communicate real, authentic, and meaningful information?
- Does it let the parents know your plans?
- Does it let the parents know that you are "on the child's side"?
- Does it educate parents about developmentally appropriate practices?

Preparation

- Is the tone conversational, personal, and positive?
- Is it clear and easy to understand?
- Does it contain educational jargon?
- Is it professionally prepared? (Grammar, spelling, handwriting)
- Has it been proofread?

FIGURE 9-9 Guiding questions for designing, writing, and critiquing narrative reports

Source: Horm-Wingerd, D. M. (1992). Reporting children's development: The narrative report. *Dimensions of Early Childhood, 21,* 15. Reprinted with permission from *Dimensions of Early Childhood,* Southern Early Childhood Association, 8500 West Markham St., Suite 105, Little Rock, AR 72205. 1-800-305-7322.

writing positive reports; however, teachers can be unaware that they have subjective perceptions of some of their students. Additional questions a teacher might ask are these: Am I being objective about this child's progress? Are my personal feelings about this child affecting how I write the narrative report? The narrative report should stress positive information about the child first, but even negative information should be discussed accurately and fairly.

Example of a Narrative Report

Montessori/Kindergarten Classroom
Emmanuel Felane
November 17, 2009

Overall Report

Emmanuel has adjusted very well in kindergarten during the first quarter of school. He participates well with other children, both during indoor class time and during outdoor play periods. He is particularly interested in working in the block center and focuses on complex constructions for an extended period of time. He is comfortable with the structured nature of the Montessori materials and responds well to individual lessons. Although he is a fairly quiet child, he has several good friends and has little difficulty when working in small groups.

Personal and Social Development

At the beginning of school, Emmanuel was very shy and hesitant about some of the class activities. He had some difficulties in replacing materials in an orderly manner after using them. He is working on being more responsible with these activities and others in the classroom. He tends to interact in small groups or by himself during outdoor play.

Language and Literacy

Emmanuel has a large vocabulary and a well-developed level of oral communication. These abilities are demonstrated in classroom discussions and during play activities.

His fine motor skills are developing more slowly; he finds emergent writing activities a bit difficult. He is encouraged to spend time engaged in fine motor Montessori activities during self-selected work periods.

He participates in emergent literacy activities and Montessori phonetic activities and can recognize about 20 words from class storybook reading activities.

Mathematical Thinking

Emmanuel is advanced in understanding mathematical concepts. He is well-advanced in mathematical lessons and activities beyond the preschool/kindergarten level. He enjoys these activities and particularly likes the sequenced nature of the Montessori materials.

Science and Social Studies

Science and social studies are integrated within study topics and projects. During the first quarter of school, we have studied occupations near the school and weather in the fall season. Emmanuel has contributed to a mural about local jobs and engaged in individual art work demonstrating how leaves change in the fall. (Photos of Emmanuel's contributions are attached to this report.) Emmanuel has also contributed to the construction of neighborhood buildings made of cardboard boxes. They can be viewed in the project corner of the classroom.

Physical Development and Health

It was mentioned earlier that Emmanuel's fine motor skills are still emerging slowly. However, his large motor skills are progressing normally. He loves outdoor activities and enjoys group games that require running.

His health is good, although he has trouble with allergies. He is receiving medication that is reducing the severity of this problem. He has good eating habits and enjoys all kinds of food. He is more slender than some of his classmates, but his weight is within the normal range.

Summary and Recommendations

Emmanuel is particularly well-suited for the Montessori activities in the classroom. He likes working by himself and usually completes activities without any problems. He seems to enjoy school. Emmanuel can be helped at home by guidance in keeping his things in order. Drawing and other activities requiring him to use his fingers will help with his fine motor development. He likes art activities such as working with clay and painting. Similar activities at home will be enjoyable for him.

Reading and enjoying books will extend his language and literacy skills.

Advantages and Disadvantages of Using Narrative Reports to Report Student Progress

Many of the advantages and disadvantages of using performance assessments in general and strategies for reporting the child's performance and development discussed in terms of portfolios are true for narrative reports. Advantages are that they permit the teacher to report the child's broad range of developmental characteristics over a period of time. They can incorporate information from various sources and assessment and record-keeping strategies when the child's evaluation is reported. A unique aspect of the narrative report is that the teacher can describe in writing what the child has accomplished. Unlike the portfolio, which may be the focus of verbal exchange between the parents and the teacher, the narrative report requires the teacher to think through what is desired in the report and to write it down prior to a conference. If a face-to-face conference is not possible, the narrative report contains the essential information and interpretation the teacher wishes to communicate.

The obvious disadvantage of the narrative report is the time needed to write, edit, and finalize a narrative report in professional form. The teacher must not only collect pertinent information and organize it to reflect the advances made in all developmental or subject areas of the curriculum, but also translate these data into a coherent, comprehensive, concise narrative. The ideal is to combine the written summary with the portfolio so that contents of the report can be supported with contents of the portfolio; however, each additional component of an evaluation also adds time to the teacher's overall evaluation tasks. Perhaps if the written report is completed at the end of the school year or, at most, twice a year, the teacher will have the opportunity to write down thoughts and descriptions about the child.

Model Assessment
and Reporting Systems

Attempts have been made in recent years to develop models of assessment and reporting systems that reflect the strengths of authentic or performance assessments. Educational leaders and measurement specialists for young children have worked toward designing and piloting methods of assessing and reporting children's evaluations logically and coherently. The goal is to guide teachers in connecting curriculum, instruction, assessment, and reporting via natural and meaningful strategies. Three examples of these models are Project Spectrum, the Work Sampling System, and the Child Observation Record. Each of these systems seeks to correct the mistakes in assessment that are currently being made with young children. They also focus on strategies for informal and performance assessments differently, but with the same goal of evaluating and reporting child development and learning in a meaningful and constructive manner.

Project Spectrum

Project Spectrum was initiated in 1984 at Harvard and Tufts Universities to better understand the linguistic and logical bases of intelligence. A major goal of the project was to produce a developmentally appropriate approach to assessment in early childhood. In addition to studying the child's individual cognitive style, the project emphasized the child's areas of strengths often not included in Piagetian approaches to education. The areas of cognitive ability examined in the project included numbers, science, music, language, visual arts, movement, and social development. The assumption was that when educators evaluated the young child's strengths in many domains, all children would exhibit performance in some domains.

Assessment is integrated into curriculum and instruction in Project Spectrum. A variety of activities are offered to the children; assessment is conducted through the child's involvement in the activities. Thus, assessment is performance based within both structured and unstructured tasks and teacher observation. Assessment is interfaced with meaningful activities provided in the classroom environment. Assessment is conducted throughout the year and documented through observation checklists, score sheets, portfolios, and tape recordings. Activities used for curriculum and assessment include games, puzzles, and other activities in learning areas such as obstacle courses for movement assessment, a child's activity in reporting for language assessment, and a bus game designed to evaluate the child's ability to make mental calculations and to organize numbers.

Assessment data collected during the year are reported through a Spectrum Profile, a summary of the child's participation in project activities during the year in the form of a narrative report. The child's areas of strength are described, along with suggestions for follow-up activities the parents can conduct with the child.

The child's active involvement in the assessment process and the wide range of developmental domains incorporated into the curriculum are considered strengths of Project Spectrum. A concern is that parents may focus only on the child's strengths described in project assessments and focus on these strengths prematurely, thus neglecting the development of other areas (Krechevsky, 1991).

The Work Sampling System

The Work Sampling System was designed as an alternative to the use of standardized tests for the assessment of young children. The system is based on the philosophy that performance assessments are appropriate because they (1) document the child's daily activities, (2) reflect an individualized approach to assessment, (3) integrate assessment with curriculum and instruction, (4) assess many elements of learning, and (5) allow teachers to learn how children reconstruct knowledge through interacting with materials and peers.

The first component of the Work Sampling System is teacher observation by means of developmental checklists. Because learning and instruction are integrated with assessment, the documentation of development and learning also provides information on the curriculum. Checklists cover seven domains: (1) personal and social development, (2) language and literacy, (3) mathematical thinking, (4) scientific thinking, (5) social studies, (6) art and music, and (7) physical development. Guidelines are provided for understanding the process of observation with the checklist indicators.

A second component is portfolios, which provide an assessment process that actively involves the teacher and child. Both the teacher and child select portfolio contents. The activity of organizing the portfolio permits the teacher and child to review progress and plan future activities, thus integrating the teaching–learning process. Items are selected that represent the seven domains covered by the checklist. Essential or core items of work samples are selected several times during the year, in addition to other items selected that represent all domains. The portfolio becomes a tool for documenting, analyzing, and summarizing the child's learning and development through the year (Harrington, Meisels, McMahon, Dichtelmiller, & Jablon, 1997; Meisels, 1993).

A third component of the Work Sampling System is the summary report completed for each child three times a year. The report summarizes the child's performance by means of specific criteria for the evaluation. Information from the checklists and the portfolios is used to communicate the child's progress to the parents. The child's overall progress is reported, as well as whether the child is making appropriate progress in each developmental category. Figure 9-10 is a diagram of the components of the Work Sampling System and how domains of development serve as the foundation for the assessment and reporting process.

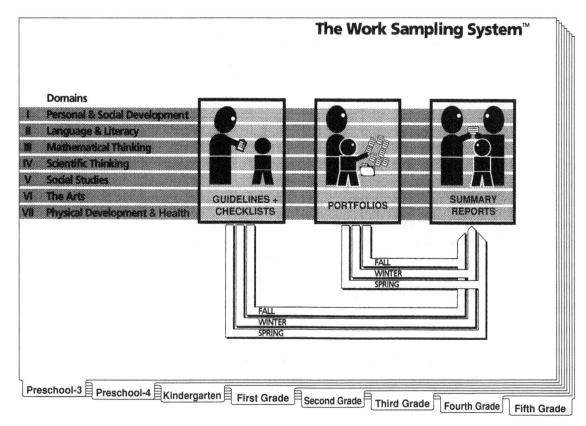

FIGURE 9-10 The Work Sampling System

Source: The Work Sampling System® Work sampling in the classroom: A teacher's manual by Samuel J. Meisels. © 2001 by Pearson Education, Inc., publishing as Pearson Early Learning. Used by permission.

The Preschool Child Observation Record

The Preschool Child Observation Record is based on observation as the core of the assessment project with young children. The system was developed as an answer to the misassessment of young children, including those in caregiving settings during the preschool years. The goal was to produce an assessment process that is developmentally appropriate, reliable, valid, and user friendly. Also, the purpose of the system is to observe and assess children conducting child-initiated tasks for some of the activities. Because child-centered activities integrate all categories of development, children can be assessed during natural daily activities. Developmental checklists combined with anecdotal recordings of observations from the activities are used by the teacher in the assessment process.

The Preschool Child Observation system was developed by the High/Scope Educational Research Foundation for use in all developmentally appropriate programs. The system was studied for 2 years to establish validity and reliability. It assesses six areas of development: (1) initiative, (2) creative representation, (3) social relations, (4) music and movement, (5) language and literacy, and (6) logic and

271

The Work Sampling System and the Ounce Scale: Early Childhood Accountability in Pennsylvania

*T*he *Ounce scale* was first introduced in chapter 3 as an infant/toddler scale that measures domains of development from infancy through 3 years. When paired with the Work Sampling System, children's development can be followed from infancy through the fifth grade. The combination of the two tests has been found to be useful for measuring children's progress on early learning standards. An example is the Office of Child Development and Early Learning in Pennsylvania. In 2007 the Office and the Bureau of Early Intervention Services issued an announcement that the two scales were to be used to measure child progress on the Early Childhood Accountability in Pennsylvania or ECAP system. The two measures were later to be used as a data collection system for early intervention programs (Department of Public Welfare commonwealth of Pennsylvania, July 13, 2007).

mathematics. The teacher rates the child several times a year on thirty items that have five levels of indicators. Anecdotal notes taken on an ongoing basis through observations are used to complete the ratings (High/Scope Educational Research Foundation, 2003; Schweinhart, 1993).

Teacher-Designed Systems

The examples of assessment and reporting systems just described provide some clues as to how teachers can design and organize their own systems. The Work Sampling System provides a sample framework for a system. First the Work Sampling System provides the categories to be included in the curriculum. In this case, the developmental approach is being used and all domains are being represented. Three basic strategies are included in the system: checklists and guidelines, portfolios, and summary reports. When the teacher designs a system, state or national standards may be the framework used to determine categories. Thus standards in mathematics, language, arts, and science, may be the categories. Strategies such as checklists, commercial and teacher-designed tests, inventories, and other assessment activities may be included in the system.

How will the portfolio support standards and objectives for learning? What will the teacher include in the portfolio for reporting periods? Will it include work samples, group reports, teacher interviews, photo documentation, and cassette tapes? The teacher does not need to include all options included in this chapter, but can be selective using strategies that provide a variety of indicators of a child's progress and achievements and are suitable for the purposes of the portfolio.

How much material should be included in the portfolio for each reporting session? Teachers can become overwhelmed by the amount of material they have gathered and the prospect of keeping it manageable. A good possibility is for the teacher to remember the difference between a working portfolio and an evaluative portfolio. Materials can be gathered in a working portfolio and reduced to significant samples for the portfolio that will be used for reporting. Much of the material can be sent home after this process has taken place.

How often should reporting be done? This will largely be controlled by how the school system or preschool center has determined reporting periods. In the Work Sampling System, reporting is done three times a year. Some schools report every 6 weeks, every 9 weeks, or twice a year. The system will be organized accordingly.

Finally, how will the child's progress and accomplishments be reported to parents? Will there be a written summary such as is used in the Work Sampling System? Will a report card be involved? Will there be a conference with the parents? Will the child be included in the conference? Will the parents have opportunities to provide input into the evaluation? Will the child be an active participant in the process? Some of these questions will be addressed in chapter 10.

Summary

Education in the United States reflects a history of embracing innovations only to discard them within a few years. Some instructional changes lack the research that can prove or question effectiveness. The introduction of portfolio assessment may suffer from this pattern. As with other innovations, teachers in some schools are asked to implement portfolios without the training needed to make the process successful. Likewise, when training is provided, only the positive characteristics of portfolio assessment may be stressed, without adequate information about difficulties and cautions that should be observed and followed. A major limitation of portfolio assessment may be this lack of competence and confidence that teachers need to implement the process successfully. Implementation of portfolio assessment and reporting must be accompanied by training, decision making, and preparation that are required for any type of assessment to be a quality method of assessing and evaluating student progress and achievement.

In this chapter, we have explored some strategies for reporting student progress to parents through performance or authentic assessments. We discussed the inherent limitations in traditional report cards that report only what the child knows. In contrast, performance assessments demonstrate what the child knows and how the child applies that knowledge in a realistic context.

A major focus of the chapter was to describe some alternative methods of constructing an evaluative profile of the child's development and learning that permits the teacher and the child to communicate to the parents broad information about what the child has accomplished. Portfolios can contain many types of informal and performance assessment results to support what the child has learned.

The teacher will need to design some type of system for assessing and reporting the child's accomplishments. The system will include a portfolio, but may not be limited to the child's work. It can include tests, teacher assessments, checklists, and other strategies for documenting and summarizing the learning objectives for the instructional period.

REVIEW QUESTIONS

1. What are the concerns about using report cards with young children?
2. How do authentic assessments and reporting provide a broad picture of children's progress?
3. Describe why curriculum and instruction and reports of performance need to complement each other.
4. How are report cards being revised to be more compatible with current trends in curriculum and instruction?
5. How do portfolios meet the criteria for appropriate performance assessment and reporting?
6. Outline the possible components of a portfolio and briefly describe each.
7. What types of teacher assessments can be included in the portfolio?
8. How can teachers overcome concerns they might have about initiating the portfolio process?
9. How are children actively involved in the assessment process when portfolios are used? How are they a part of the process of reporting to parents?

SUGGESTED ACTIVITIES

1. Design a portfolio to be used with preschool children. Include (1) sections or dividers for the portfolio, (2) the types of teacher assessments you would use, and (3) a description of how you would report the child's progress to parents. Put in hypothetical contents in each section for an imaginary child. Write a narrative report to summarize the child's progress based on entries in the portfolio.
2. Design a portfolio to document your preparation to become a early childhood teacher.

First, determine what types of information a personnel director would want to know about you. Make a divider for each type of information. Review the courses you have taken and examples of work that you have done to fulfill each category. Organize the portfolio and enter the examples. Use photographs if needed for examples of performance activities you have completed. In the last section write a narrative report on yourself summarizing your preparation and why you want to be a teacher.

SELECTED WEB SITES

High/Scope Educational Research Foundation
http://www.Highscope.org

North Central Regional Educational Laboratory
http://www.ncrel.org/sdrs

REFERENCES

Arter, J., & Spandel, V. (Spring 1992). Using portfolios of student work in instruction and assessment. *Educational measurement: Issues and practice, 11,* 36–44.

Barbour, A., & Desjean-Perrotta, B. (1998). The basics of portfolio assessment. In S. C. Wortham, A. Barbour, and B. Desjean-Perrotta (Eds.), *Portfolio assessment: A handbook for preschool and elementary educators* (pp. 15–30). Olney, MD: Association for Childhood Education International.

Batzle, J. (1992). *Portfolio assessment and evaluation: Developing and using portfolios in the K–6 classroom.* Cypress, CA: Creative Teaching.

Buschman, L. (1993). Windows on learning: Taking an integrated approach. *Learning, 21,* 22–25.

Cliatt, M. J. P., & Shaw, J. M. (1992). *Helping children explore science.* Upper Saddle River, NJ: Merrill/ Prentice Hall.

Department of Public Welfare, Commonwealth of Pennsylvania. (2007, July 13). *Announcement: ELS/EI-07 #9.* Office of Child Development and Learning, Bureau of Early Intervention Services. Retrieved April 13, 2010, from http://www. portal.state.pa.us

Farr, R. C. (1993). *Portfolio assessment teacher's guide grades K–8.* Orlando, FL: Harcourt Brace Jovanovich.

Gilkerson, D., & Hanson, M. F. (2000). Family portfolios: Involving families in portfolio documentation. *Early Childhood Education Journal, 27,* 197–201.

Glazer, S. M. (1994, January). Assessment in the classroom: Where we are, where we're going. *Teaching K–8,* 68–71.

Goodwin, W. L., & Goodwin, L. D. (1993). Young children and measurement: Standardized and nonstandardized instruments in early childhood education. In B. Spodek (Ed.), *Handbook of research on the education of young children* (pp. 441–463). New York: Macmillan.

Grace, C., & Shores, E. F. (1991). *The portfolio and its use.* Little Rock, AR: Southern Association on Children Under Six.

Gronlund, N. E. (1998). Portfolios as an assessment tool: Is collection of work enough? *Young Children, 53,* 4–10.

Hanson, M. F., & Gilkerson, D. (1999). Portfolio assessment: More than ABCs and 123s. *Early Childhood Education Journal, 27,* 81–86.

Harrington, H. L., Meisels, S. J., McMahon, P., Dichtelmiller, M. L., & Jablon, J. R. (1997). *Observing, documenting, and assessing learning: The work sampling system handbook for teacher educators.* Ann Arbor, MI: Rebus.

Harris, M. E. (2009, May). Implementing portfolio assessment. *Young Children, 64,* 82–85.

Hebert, E. A., & Schultz, L. (1996). The power of portfolios. *Educational Leadership, 53,* 70–71.

Herman, J. L., Aschbacher, P. R., & Winters, L. (1992). *A practical guide to alternative assessment.* Alexandria, VA: Association for Supervision and Curriculum Development.

High/Scope Educational Research Foundation. (2003). *Preschool Child Observation Record.* Ypsilanti, MI: Author.

Hill, B., & Ruptic, C. (1994). *Practical aspects of authentic assessment: Putting the pieces together.* Norwood, MA: Gordon.

Horm-Wingerd, D. M. (1992). Reporting children's development: The narrative report. *Dimensions of Early Childhood, 21,* 11–15.

Krechevsky, M. (1991). Project Spectrum: An innovative assessment alternative. *Educational Leadership, 48,* 43–48.

Lescher, M. L. (1995). *Portfolios: Assessing learning in the primary grades.* Washington, DC: National Education Association.

Meisels, S. J. (1993). Remaking classroom assessment with the Work Sampling System. *Young Children, 48,* 34–40.

Meisels, S. J. (2001). *Work sampling in the classroom: A teacher's manual.* New York: Pearson Education.

Meisels, S. J., & Steele, D. (1991). *The early childhood portfolio collection process.* Ann Arbor: University of Michigan, Center for Human Growth and Development.

Micklo, S. K. (1997). Math portfolios in the primary grades. *Childhood Education, 73,* 194–199.

O'Neil, J. (1993). The promise of portfolios. *ASCD Update, 35,* 1, 5.

Piaget, J. (1952). *The origins of intelligence in children.* New York: Basic Books. (Original work published 1936.)

Piaget, J. (1962). *Play, dreams, and imitation in childhood.* New York: Norton. (Original work published 1945.)

Piaget, J. (1963). *The origins of intelligence in children* (M. Cook, Trans.). New York: Norton.

Polakowski, C. (1993). Literacy portfolios in the early childhood classroom. In L. Grosvenor et al., *Student portfolios* (pp. 47–66). Washington, DC: National Education Association.

Puckett, M. B., & Black, J. K. (2000). *Authentic assessment of the young child: Celebrating development and learning* (2nd ed.). Upper Saddle River, NJ: Merrill/Prentice Hall.

Schweinhart, L. J. (1993). Observing young children in action: The key to early childhood assessment. *Young Children, 48,* 29–33.

Seidel, S., Walters, J., Kirby, E., Olff, N., Powell, K., Scripp, L., et al. (1997). *Portfolio practices: Thinking through the assessment of children's work.* Washington, DC: National Education Association.

Seitz, H., & Bartholomew, C. (2008). Powerful portfolios for young children. *Early Childhood Education Journal, 36,* 82–85.

Smith, A. F. (2000). Reflective portfolios: Preschool possibilities. *Childhood Education, 76,* 204–208.

Sulzby, E. (1993). *Teacher's guide to evaluation: Assessment handbook.* Glenview, IL: Scott, Foresman.

Teaching for Excellence. (1992). Portfolio assessment: A worthwhile testing alternative. *Teaching for Excellence,* 12.

Valencia, S. (1990). A portfolio approach to classroom reading assessment. *Reading Teacher, 43,* 338–340.

Vygotsky, L. S. (1978). *Mind and society: The development of higher mental processes.* Cambridge, MA: Harvard University Press.

Weldin, D. J., & Tumarkin, S. R. (1998/1999). Parent involvement: More power in the portfolio process. *Childhood Education, 75,* 90–95.

Willis, S. (1993). Are letter grades obsolete? *ASCD Update, 35,* 1, 4, 8.

Wortham, S. C. (1998). Introduction. In S. C. Wortham, A. Barbour, & B. Desjean-Perrotta (Eds.), *Portfolio assessment: A handbook for preschool and elementary educators* (pp. 7–13). Olney, MD: Association for Childhood Education International.

Chapter 10

Communicating With Families

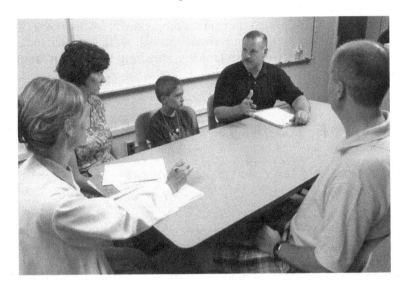

Chapter Objectives

As a result of reading this chapter, you will be able to

1. Understand how schools can develop partnerships with families to benefit the child
2. Understand how communication between schools and families is a two-way process
3. Discuss the importance of family conferences and how they can be conducted
4. Describe strategies for communicating student progress with families

Parents have an important role in their child's development and learning. Teachers and administrators in early childhood programs and schools have learned that the child's success as a learner depends on parents as well as teachers. As early childhood education continues in a new century, the importance of having parents as partners with early childhood settings is a goal for quality education. However, children today experience all types of family relationships. Some children might live with a single parent or with a grandparent or grandparents. Children live in blended families where both parents have had previous marriages and children from those marriages who now live together as one family. Therefore, the term *families* is added to the concept of parents to acknowledge the expanded roles of parenting. Throughout this book, information related to keeping families informed and helping families understand assessment results has been discussed. In chapter 4, explanations of different types of test scores described how teachers can help families understand the results of standardized testing. Chapter 9 included information on how portfolios provide families with a more comprehensive understanding of student progress.

A major part of this chapter will be devoted to how families should play a major role in the child's school experience and how schools can develop partnership relationships with adults who serve a parenting role for children. Then strategies for communicating with families about student progress will be discussed, including planning and conducting family conferences. Throughout the chapter, the emphasis will be on sharing information with families, soliciting input from families, and including families in planning for the child.

Developing School–Family Partnerships

Roles of Families in the Child's Development and Learning

Parents have always been active in the schools. When my father was an elementary school student in the early 20th century in Austin, Texas, mothers took turns going to the school to prepare lunch for the children. Parents have traditionally helped with school parties and volunteered in the classroom. Parent–teacher organizations have raised money to provide needed books, equipment, and other materials that are not in the school budget. The idea of a partnership with parents goes beyond helping with school programs. The National Association of Elementary School Principals has developed standards for early childhood education that denote the relationship with parents as a partnership. The indicators for this partnership describe new dimensions of parent–school relationships. In the standards, the following statement is made (National Association of Elementary School Principals, 1998, p. 22): "Parent involvement is of basic importance to the success of all elementary school programs. For an early childhood program, it is crucial and should be a high priority for the principal." Standards descriptors for the partnership include the following (National Association of Elementary School Principals, 1998):

- Parents share development of the school's educational program, and so understand and support it. In meetings, newsletters, conversations, and other ways, the principal and staff provide information about the developmental philosophy of the program and its goals.
- Parents are helped to increase their effectiveness in working with their children, both at school and in the home, through their involvement in the school's work and their participation in classrooms, meetings, and conferences.
- Parent concerns regarding parenting and their individual performance as parents are addressed both formally and informally—through conferences, newsletters, and workshops, and in personal conversations.

Building Bridges With Families of Infants and Toddlers

For many families, the partnership between school and home begins when their children are infants and toddlers. A large percentage of children under three are in some type of care while parents are at work. The development of relationships between the home and the center are initiated when the child is transitioned from home to a center or other caregiving setting. The reliability, development of trust, and positive consistent caregiving are important in developing bonds between the caregiver and the child and the caregiver and the parents. Each day the child and family adults go through separation when the child is left in the caregiving setting and then another adjustment when they are united at the end of the day. Caregivers and other center personnel who show sensitivity and understanding of cultural differences can facilitate the daily transitions and ongoing interactions with the child and family. Families of babies have the same needs for support and communication regarding their child as families of older children in school settings; however, the needs for daily communication and exchange of information about the child are even more important for positive home and center relationships.

- Parents are actively involved in the school site council, making decisions about the program.
- A reciprocal relationship is formed and nurtured. Teachers recognize that parents have valuable information to share about their children. All parties seek to make both school and home places where young children feel secure and enjoy success. (p. 22)

The last descriptor declares that parents have valuable information to share about their children. This includes active involvement in the assessment of children's progress in development and learning. Communication with families is not only limited to reporting to them but also includes them in the information-gathering process when children are assessed.

Establishing Relationships With Families

The importance of a partnership becomes more evident as we learn more about how children benefit from a strong teacher–parent relationship. All parties in the partnership have an equal role. School staff members are not inviting families to be participants and provide input, but rather they have a vital role as true partners. The quality of the partnership affects the child's security and maximizes the child's potential for learning. This quality partnership includes frequent two-way communications, interest, and acceptance of the views of the other partner. The partnership grows through mutual consultation on important decisions, and working through differences with mutual respect (Keyser, 2006; Lightfoot, 2003).

The expanded nature of parenting that includes other family members also includes an understanding of diversity. The school–family partnership includes people from many different cultures, ethnicities, family structures, and levels of income. Different languages may be spoken, and families might have different views on how children should be raised. This means that all parties to the school–family partnership must learn about others both at school and at home. Families need to learn about the school culture and how their child fits into a group of diverse children. Likewise, school staff must understand the possible areas of diversity in each child (Keyser, 2006).

Parents and teachers are not the only beneficiaries of a partnership. Children also benefit. When their parents and other significant adults in their life have a positive relationship with the teacher, children feel that they and their family are honored and respected. The better the relationship, the more the children feel that they, too, can have a trusting relationship with the teacher. They learn how to conduct social relationships by watching adult relationships. They notice all the nuances of language, body language, and tone of voice that the adults use. They use these positive models to develop their own relationships with others (Keyser, 2006).

Home Visits

One of the most effective ways to establish a relationship with a child and the family is to make a home visit prior to the beginning of school. When the teacher visits the home environment, a context for understanding the child and family is established. When I was a young teacher, I made home visits at the beginning of every school year. It was very educational for me to learn how and where the children in my classroom lived. I taught in a bilingual program; as a result, most of the children in the classroom were Hispanic. Many of them were children of migrant workers. A majority of families I visited had a very low income. One family lived out of two cars several miles from the school bus route. The children were dressed and ready to leave by 5 a.m. so that they could walk with their older siblings to the bus stop. In the afternoons, it was almost dark before they reached home again. Another family lived very near the school, but in a very old wood frame house with bare wood floors. The mother had to get water from the tap outside for cooking and cleaning. She had a history of being abused and beaten by her husband. When I visited, the house was very clean, and the mother proudly showed me the room where three of the girls shared a double bed. Later in the year, when the child from that family in my classroom appeared at school with a broken arm, I was able to notify the school nurse to work with child welfare authorities to investigate and assist the mother if needed. The families I visited were pleased that the teacher would come to their home and visit. The children were always dressed in their best clothes and on their best behavior. We discussed family pictures, the children's toys, and often the plants in the yard. Because I spoke Spanish, those initial visits were vital to the parents' feeling comfortable with me, and they were able to overcome their hesitations to come to the school for meetings and conferences. Many times parent conferences were conducted at a parent's place of work because they couldn't leave their job or didn't have transportation to the school. Home visits continued in some situations when the family or I needed support from the other.

Continuing conversations and other forms of communications are a second step in establishing a partnership. Again, it is important to maintain communications as a reciprocal process. At times the teacher initiates the communication, but at other times the parent initiates the contact. Families have different ways to engage in the partnership. The continuum from relationship to partnership is different from family to family. The teacher needs to be sensitive to how best to communicate with families. Written newsletters to parents are not effective if the parents speak another language. They may also be very intimidated by requests for them to give information through written notes. My years as a teacher of children from families in which Spanish was the home language provides another example of how we must be sensitive to the parents. The principal decided that all our newsletters and information sheets would be communicated in both English and Spanish. It took some reflection and awkward interactions before we understood that the Spanish-speaking families in our school community could not read in Spanish either. Patience and goodwill are necessary for both families and teachers as the partnership develops during the school year.

Today school–family communications can take advantage of computer and cell phone technology. The teacher can establish a classroom Web site where information can be shared and ideas exchanged. Photographs and videos of class work can be posted and opportunities for family comments provided. E-mails to individual families can replace notes with families who have access to a computer. Other families without computers can continue to exchange written notes with the teacher. Cell phone calls can include photographs of the child at school and possibly text messages to keep families informed. The messages can include anecdotes about the child's experiences at school, new accomplishments, or newly developed social skills (Mitchell, Foulger, & Wetzel, 2009).

Using Professional Ethics in School–Family Partnerships

Teachers are responsible for maintaining professionalism in their relationships with parents. Guidelines for teachers are provided by professional education organizations. The Code of Ethical Conduct was first published by the National Association for the Education of Young Children in 1989. The most recent edition was developed in 2005. The code provides guidelines for professional behavior for teachers and caregivers of young children. It describes categories of ethics that provide a framework for how teachers interact in their positions in early childhood. Throughout the discussion of the code it is stressed that professional ethics includes responsibilities for children, families, communities, and society. The descriptions discuss that professional ethical judgments guide educators as to what they should do and not do as professionals. The code of ethics is a document that permits the profession to speak as a group. The hope for the future is that the code can not only be used as a basis for advocacy addressing the needs of young children and their families, but also to help early childhood educators to focus on what is best for all young children and their families (Feeney, 2010).

Assessment Roles of Families of Children With Disabilities

When parents discover that their infant or toddler has a delay or disability, they soon find out the importance of assessment of the child. They experience conflicting emotions about what the assessment will reveal. One mother described her reaction (Rocco, 1996):

> When assessments emphasize deficits and diminished expectations for future success, we parents generally begin to look for a way to thwart these negative prognostications. At the very best, we want a miracle cure. At the least, we want professionals to "fix" our children. . . . We believe that professionals have all the answers, and therefore, all the power. (p. 56)

After parents experience the first stages of screening and diagnosis, they find they have a major role in assessing what the child needs and participate in planning for the child. Once the child has been evaluated and determined eligible for services, the ongoing assessment and intervention process centers on parents and the family. The extent of the family's involvement affects the child's performance and the relevance of the child's assessment in guiding intervention services (Berman & Shaw, 1996; Ray, Pewitt-Kinder, & George, 2009). Berman and Shaw describe the assessment process as family directed or family centered, with the child's and family's priorities and values the most important in planning for the child. The Individuals with Disabilities Education Act (IDEA) requires that families be involved in assessment, decision making, and activities planned for helping the child. Conferences with families who have a child with a disability is more complex than the common understanding of parent–teacher conferences. An Individualized Family Service Plan (IFSP) is developed specifically for the affected child and family. A team of intervention providers that might include therapists, early intervention specialists, teachers, and family members are involved in both planning for the family and child's needs and later assessing progress on the IFSP with the family (Ray, Pewitt-Kinder, & George, 2009).

Involving All Parents in the Assessment Process

Practices established for parents of children with disabilities involve parents in the assessment process used with all children. Home visits with parents before the beginning of school can initiate the process of gathering information about the child. Thereafter, parents can participate in the assessment process through the teacher's ongoing efforts to solicit information from parents, participating in conferences when the child's progress is reported, and contributing information about the child's progress within the conference, through written responses submitted to the teacher and by telephone or e-mail messages (Gilkerson & Hanson, 2000).

All the assessment strategies discussed in this text apply to children with disabilities. Some types of assessments may have to be modified, especially for children who have a cognitive delay or physical disability. Nevertheless, children with disabilities should not be excluded from performance assessments and portfolios. These children should have opportunities to demonstrate what they understand and can use. Teachers and parents will need to be creative in finding ways for children to engage in their own assessment if they are unable to participate in the same manner as children without disabilities. Computers and other types of assistive technologies can be used, as well as photographs, videotapes, and audiotapes. The important point is that children with disabilities should be included in the assessment and planning process to the best of their abilities. Bridging their disabilities with alternative assessment strategies will complete their inclusion as full members of the classroom.

Parent Partnership in Portfolio Assessment

The principal, teachers, and parents at Thomas Jefferson Kindergarten and Primary School discussed portfolio assessment at school council meetings for several months. Teachers and a principal from a school in a nearby community were invited to attend the council meeting and talk about their experiences in starting portfolio assessment. In April, the council decided to implement portfolios the following year. As training sessions were held for the teachers at the end of the school year, newsletters were sent to parents informing them of the change in reporting using portfolios and of evening sessions that would be held to share how the teachers were preparing for using portfolios.

During the summer months, teacher training continued. At the beginning of the school year, an open house was held to further explain how the portfolio process would be used and the rationale for moving to this type of assessment and reporting. Following a general meeting in the multipurpose room of the school, parents visited their child's classroom, where the teacher showed a model of the portfolio that would be used in the classroom and how parents could contribute to the information that would be included in the portfolio. Questions about the portfolio assessment process were answered.

At the first parent–teacher conferences, portfolio assessment to report student progress was used for the first time. Parents were invited to reflect on what the child had accomplished. In some classrooms, the child participated in the conference and discussed why some entries were important. Following review of the portfolios, both the parents and teacher discussed how to plan for the child's learning experiences based on the progress made during the first part of the school year.

Some teachers found the move to the portfolio process easier than others. Likewise, some parents understood and supported portfolio assessment more quickly than others. The principal provided troubleshooting sessions for teachers, and the school council discussed how to continue to improve the process.

Communicating With Families About Children's Progress

Whatever approaches a teacher uses to assess children, a report is made to communicate with the parents about the child's developmental advances and learning accomplishments. The assessments that have been made are evaluated to determine what will be in the report. Families are given the opportunity to share their ideas about the child's growth and progress and to respond to the report that the teacher has developed. Although written reports and portfolios are helpful assessment systems to use when sharing information with families, conferences permit families and teachers to interact directly. In the following sections, parent conferences will be discussed, including how to prepare for and conduct conferences.

Types of Parent Conferences

In chapter 9 different types of portfolios were discussed. One type would be for work in progress, another to showcase student work, and a third to serve as a student's evaluation. In this chapter we can discuss types of parent conferences. In addition to more traditional teacher-led conferences, we can consider three-way conferences, student-led conferences, and parent group meeting conferences.

Three-Way Conferences

In the three-way conference, the student, parent, and teachers all participate. The student has an opportunity to present and discuss his or her work through a portfolio, the parent has an opportunity to introduce relevant information about the child's progress, and the teacher has the opportunity to summarize what has been accomplished during the time period. All participants plan together for future goals, projects, and general learning. All participants discuss how the home and the school can work together to accomplish the child's learning goals.

Student-Led Conferences

Students can be taught to conduct a conference with the family. Using a showcase or evaluative portfolio, the student and parent study portfolio contents and discuss the student's work. The teacher can join the conference later and answer questions the parent might have or elicit the family's ideas for the child's further progress (Stiggins, 2005). Regardless of the approach to be used for the parent conference, the conference should follow the assumption that families are partners in the process:

> The inclusion of families in the overall assessment is critically important. They need to be involved in more than just the final stage of the process if they are to see all the skills and strategies that their children are developing and to assist their children along the way.

Family involvement with portfolios can take many forms, including holding three-way conferences that include students, teachers, and parents. Parents may also respond in writing to the work in the portfolio. They can complete a questionnaire about their perceptions of the student's work and provide examples that the parent thinks are indicative of growth. (Lescher, 1995, p. 28)

Parent Group Meeting Conferences

When circumstances do not permit conferences with individual families, a group conference for all parents might be considered. In this type of conference, the teacher spends time explaining to all the parents the assessments that have been used, the nature of those assessments, and information on projects or thematic study topics. Classroom documentation in various forms is explained and parents are invited to spend time looking at them. Individual student portfolios or reports are also made available and explained before the parents share them with their child. The teacher makes opportunities for individual questions and for parents with concerns to stay after the group meeting to discuss these with the teacher. Arrangements might be made for individual phone calls or other communications when needed to discuss future questions or issues.

Preparing for Family Conferences

The teacher must prepare the information that is to be shared prior to conducting a conference with a family. Some of the information should involve input from parents and the student. As part of the preparation, the teacher selects the assessments that will be used for reporting progress and develops a profile or some type of encapsulation that summarizes the child's evidence of development and learning.

Selecting Options for Reporting Progress

If the teacher uses portfolio assessment, the process of preparing the portfolio contents for the child's evaluation becomes the vehicle for reporting. If a portfolio is not used, the teacher gathers and organizes examples of the child's work, assessments that have been conducted, and some type of report on the child's evaluation that has been determined by the teacher.

Developing a Profile for the Child Using Assessment Results

Portfolios include the assessments and evidence of the child's work that permit an evaluation to take place. Materials in the portfolio, when combined with a narrative report, provide a profile of progress. A profile can also be developed using checklist assessments, samples of the child's work, and a summary report as in the Work Sampling System (Harrington, Meisels, MacMahon, Dichtelmitter, & Jablon, 1997) and the checklist and anecdotal records used in the Preschool Child Observation Record (Schweinhart, 1993). Given the many types of assessments and record-keeping strategies described in earlier chapters, the teacher has a variety of ways to organize assessment and evaluation into a comprehensive profile of the child to share with parents. This may also include the results of standardized tests in the primary grades.

Considering Individual Family Backgrounds and Needs

As the teacher prepares for the conference with the parents, the backgrounds and needs of parents are considered. Parents must feel comfortable and relaxed when they come for the conference. A translator should be provided for parents who speak another language. The environment for the conference should be welcoming. Some teachers provide refreshments and decorate the area with flowers and student work.

When preparing for a conference, the teacher must consider the diverse backgrounds of the children. The children may come from different religions, cultures, languages, and family practices. For example, in some cultures the father takes the lead in participating in the conference with the mother taking a secondary role. In other cultures, especially traditional American groups, both parents participate equally, or the mother takes the lead.

If language is an issue, provisions should be made for someone to translate if the teacher does not speak that home language. In the event of families speaking several different languages, volunteers who speak both languages might facilitate the conference conversations.

Sometimes parents are intimidated by the teacher and the school and are uncomfortable attending a conference at the school. Parents may feel inadequate or have bad memories from their own school experiences. Teachers need to be very sensitive to hesitant parents and be ready to help these parents feel welcome and appreciated (Kersey & Masterson, 2009).

Another factor to consider is parental awareness of how assessments are conducted and interpreted, particularly in the case of standardized test results. Some families may be very familiar and comfortable in understanding the meaning of different terms used in standardized test reports. Others may be totally bewildered when a child's test profile is discussed. The teacher will want to vary how these tests are discussed and what explanations might be necessary. Standardized tests and test reports were discussed in chapters 3 and 4. The teacher will want to understand test reports and how to interpret them to parents from diverse backgrounds.

Conducting Family Conferences

Once the parents or other family representatives have arrived and the conference is ready to begin, the teacher keeps three guidelines in mind when conducting a successful experience for the parents and the child, if the child is to participate: (1) helping parents understand evaluation information, (2) helping parents interpret evaluation information accurately, and (3) soliciting parental and child input for assessment and planning for the child. If standardized test results are used, these guidelines are especially important.

The teacher can also think through best strategies that will ensure a positive conference result. Following are some measures teachers take to conduct successful conferences:

- *Start and end on a positive note.* It was mentioned earlier that parents should feel welcomed by the teacher. This positive beginning can be extended by starting the conference on a positive note. The teacher shares the child's strengths and good experiences at school to include class activities that the child has enjoyed.
- *Encourage parents to share information about their child.* Early in the conference, parents are asked about their child. The teacher may ask questions about how the child and family interact at home. The objective is to have the parents take the lead in the discussion about their child.
- *Discuss relevant information about the child's progress.* Important information about the child's accomplishments is discussed with the parents, using portfolio examples, various assessments, and standardized test results, when appropriate. Parents are included in the discussion throughout this part of the conference. Their questions are answered, and the teacher asks questions to extend the information.
- *Discuss the child's needs or issues about progress.* Difficulties the child might be experiencing at school are discussed objectively. The teacher focuses on the most important difficulties that a child might be experiencing. The teacher asks the parents for help in addressing the child's needs. The parents and teacher discuss how they might help the child. The teacher asks the parents for suggestions about how the child might be better helped in school. If possible, the parents and teacher set a plan for the child to be addressed in a follow-up conference or other communication (Kersey & Masterson, 2009).
- *End the conference on a positive note.* The teacher closes the conference by again focusing on the child's positive attributes. The teacher thanks the parents for attending and being helpful in providing needed information. The teacher stresses that the school–family relationship is a partnership to further positive feelings with parents or family representatives.

Helping Parents Interpret Evaluation Information

When parents encounter a collection of student work and teacher assessments that form the basis for the child's evaluation, they may feel a bit overwhelmed when they compare this type of reporting with a report card. If the teacher and school have prepared the parents for the use of portfolios and performance assessments, they will appreciate understanding how the materials they are seeing form a picture of what the child has learned; nevertheless, they are likely to have questions about assessments and the meaning of the child's work. The teacher needs to be prepared to volunteer information about the assessment strategies used and why the collection of the child's work provides evidence of learning. Parents may have questions such as the following: How are checklist

Parents need to engage in the assessment process.

assessments conducted? What kinds of things does the teacher do to acquire checklist information? Why are observation reports important? What does the teacher learn about the child by doing observations? What do the summaries of the child's advances and accomplishments mean when compared with a traditional report card? How does a rubric work? How does the teacher design written tests for primary-grade children? The teacher should be able to explain during the conference how and why assessments are used so that parents understand the assessment process. Parents will vary in how they understand technical information. The teacher needs to be prepared to help interpret assessment results with individual families.

The same is true of assessment materials shared at the parent–teacher conference. One method of summarizing the child's progress and overall evaluation is to have a summary report or narrative report for the parents. The teacher goes over the report with the parents, helping them understand the relationship between the assessment resources and the child's overall evaluation. If a summary report is not used, the teacher must have an overall evaluation ready to share with the parents. The assessments and work samples must be explained, with their implications for the child's progress and future needs for instructional experiences.

Soliciting Parental Input for Assessment and Planning

Opportunities for parental input into assessment and planning should be built into the conference. If parents do not voluntarily reflect on the child's progress and make suggestions, the teacher should be ready to solicit input. As the teacher completes the evaluation report, parents can give their own views about progress and concerns they might have about the child. The child also discusses progress and how learning might be improved. As the teacher discusses the next steps in planning for the child, parents can give their suggestions of what might be helpful for the child. Also, the teacher and parents can discuss what the parents might do to help the child at home. The important point is that parents and children need to feel that they are a vital part of the evaluation process and not mere recipients of

A Group Conference for a Child with ADHD

Miles Clark is a third-grade child who was identified as having ADHD in the first grade. He was evaluated and received special education classification at that time. He has received the help of a resource teacher for the past 2 years. The purpose of the conference is to determine how Miles should be served as he moves to fourth grade. The conference includes Miles's parents, his grandmother, the regular classroom teacher, the school counselor, the resource teacher, and the principal. The conference has been called at the request of Miles's mother, who is concerned about the possible end of services by the resource teacher.

Each member of the teaching and support staff presents an assessment of Miles's progress. At the end of each presentation, the parents and other members of the group are invited to comment or ask questions. The classroom teacher and resource teacher present examples of work that Miles has been able to complete on his own, without assistance. Each member of the group is asked about Miles's ability to work independently, without a resource teacher to assist with assignments. School staff members believe that their plan to transition Miles to working without assistance is showing good progress. Miles's mother is not convinced and insists that Miles is entitled to the continued services of the resource teacher because of his designation as having ADHD.

At the end of the conference, each member of the conference group summarizes his or her current assessment of Miles and what future planning is appropriate for his continued progress. The school counselor summarizes the events of the conference and asks the parents for their assessment. Miles's mother strongly supports the continuation of assistance for Miles. The school staff reluctantly agree to continue the use of the resource teacher during the next school year.

the evaluation report. Although the teacher may need to discuss improvements that the child needs to make, parents should also be encouraged to look at problems and suggest solutions. If a true partnership has been established, parents will be able to address the child's needs and help plan ways to guide the child without feeling that they are being judged.

Summary: Looking to the Future

Assessment in early childhood in the 21st century includes opportunities and challenges. Many of the issues that developed during the latter decades of the 20th century persist at the beginning of a new century. The implementation of the No Child Left Behind Act has presented its own challenges.

Assessment of young children that evolved during the 20th century has broadened and intensified over the decades, as more has been learned about how young children develop and learn and how variances in development and culture may cause young children to encounter difficulties when they enter school. Tests and measures to assess young children have been developed for children who need intervention services and preschool programs to enhance their academic success when they enter the primary grades.

The development and use of a variety of approaches to assessment of children in the early childhood years are not without problems. Because of the nature and rapidity of development of young children, it is difficult to design measures that are dependable and that accurately measure personal characteristics and other needed information. Each kind of measure designed for use with young children has pluses and minuses. Users of each type of assessment must be informed about the strengths and limitations of the strategies they plan to use. With young children especially, a combination of assessment approaches, rather than a single instrument or method, is indicated.

As school reform decisions increase the use of testing of preschool and primary-grade children for placement, promotion, and retention, teachers increasingly believe that they are accountable for their role in the decisions made about their students. If they disagree with the grading procedures they are required to use, for example, do they have a responsibility to voice their concern? When they have research-based information that an instrument is being used for the wrong purpose or lacks reliability, should they inform the personnel who selected the tests? Should teachers press for alternative methods of assessment that include informal strategies and performance assessments? Do school policies prohibit any variation in how children are assessed? Parents want teachers to explain the use of performance assessments and changes in student progress reports that accompany the use of these assessments. Teachers want parents to have input when the decision is made to move to this type of assessment and the use of portfolios, rather than report cards. In addition, teachers want to be confident that they have the skills to use and interpret assessment results with parents.

No crystal ball reveals future trends in measuring the young children. Demands for accountability and increases in learning achievement currently drive curriculum and assessment. School reform, which is a national phenomenon, will continue to affect early childhood education. As the importance of the early years is again being emphasized, the school reform movement continues to force restrictive parameters on the education of young children. The push for quality early childhood programs conflicts with efforts to raise academic standards. And, as the makeup of early childhood classrooms changes to reflect the presence of more children with disabilities and diverse backgrounds and languages, competence in selecting and using appropriate types of assessments assumes even more importance. Decisions about educational practices are often political rather than educational. As different forces affect representation in Congress, policies can change.

The issues that surround the assessment of young children will not be resolved soon. If present trends continue, improvement in methods of assessment of young children will continue in the effort to improve their potential for optimal development and learning. The ongoing improvement in assessment methods should have a positive effect on the quality of early childhood programs and services as well.

REVIEW QUESTIONS

1. How is a parent–teacher partnership different from roles parents had as school volunteers in the past?
2. How does the concept of parents as partners affect the assessment of the child?
3. Why is assessment especially difficult for parents of children with disabilities?
4. How do portfolios and narrative reports support an active role for parents in contributing to the overall evaluation of their child?
5. What does a narrative report contribute to assessment and evaluation that is lacking in portfolios?
6. How does planning or lack of planning affect a parent–teacher conference?
7. Should the child be a part of the conference with parents? Why or why not?
8. Why is it important that parents understand how assessments are used and the implications of the information gained from assessments?
9. Why do parents need to be involved in planning for the child based on the progress report?

SUGGESTED ACTIVITIES

1. Arrange to sit in on a parent–teacher conference in a school that uses portfolios. Observe the strategies the teacher uses to make the parents welcome and comfortable at the beginning of the conference. Note the strategies the teacher uses when sharing portfolio assessment information with the parents. What method is used to summarize the student's progress? What role do the parents have in the conference?
2. Assume that you are a second grade teacher in a multicultural school setting. Your students speak four different home languages. The families of your children are immigrants who have lived in this country for at most 2 years. As you prepare to hold conferences with the families, make a list of what you will need to consider when communicating with diverse families speaking different languages. Using the steps to conducting a parent–teacher conference, determine how you will conduct the conference with two imaginary families and how you will relate differently with them. First, describe the situations of each family. Then use that information to prepare for the conference.

SELECTED WEB SITES

U.S. Department of Education
http://idea.ed.gov

TeacherVision
http://www.teachervision.fen.com/ teacher-parentconferences/resource/3713.html

PTA
http://www.pta.org/2532.htm/

REFERENCES

Berman, C., & Shaw, E. (1996). Family directed child evaluation and assessment under the Individuals with Disabilities Education Act (IDEA). In S. J. Meisels & E. Fenichel (Eds.), *New visions for the developmental assessment of infants and young children* (pp. 361–390). Washington, DC: Zero to Three: National Center for Infants, Toddlers, and Families.

Feeney, S. (2010, March). Ethics today in early care and education. *Young Children, 65,* 72–77.

Gilkerson, D., & Hanson, M. F. (2000). Family portfolios: Involving families in portfolio documentation. *Early Childhood Education Journal, 27,* 197–201.

Harrington, H. L., Meisels, S. J., MacMahon, P., Dichtelmitter, M. L., & Jablon, J. R. (1997). *Observing, documenting, and assessing learning: The work sampling system handbook for teacher education.* Ann Arbor, MI: Rebus.

Keyser, J. (2006). *From parents to partners.* St. Paul, MN: Redleaf Press.

Lescher, M. L. (1995). *Portfolios: Assessing learning in the primary grades.* Washington, DC: National Education Association.

Lightfoot, L. S. (2003). *The essential conversation: What parents and teachers can learn from each other.* New York: Ballantine Books.

Mitchell, S., Foulger, T. S., & Wetzel, K. (2009, September). Ten tips for involving families through Internet-based communication. *Young Children, 65,* 46–49.

National Association of Elementary School Principals. (1998). *Early childhood education and the elementary school principal* (2nd ed.). Alexandria, VA: Author.

Ray, J. A., Pewitt-Kinder, J., 7 George, S. (2009, September). Partnering with families of children with special needs. *Young Children, 64,* 16–22.

Rocco, S. (1996). Toward shared commitment and shared responsibility: A parent's vision of developmental assessment. In S. J. Meisels & E. Fenichel (Eds.), *New visions for the developmental assessment of infants and young children* (pp. 55–58). Washington, DC: Zero to Three: National Center for Infants, Toddlers, and Families.

Schweinhart, L. J. (1993). Observing young children in action: The key to early childhood assessment. *Young Children, 48,* 29–33.

Stiggins, R. J. (2005). *Student-involved assessment for learning* (4th ed.). Upper Saddle River, NJ: Merrill Prentice Hall.

Glossary

achievement test   A test that measures the extent to which a person has acquired information or mastered certain skills, usually as a result of instruction or training.

alternative assessment   An assessment that is different from traditional written or multiple-choice tests. Usually related to authentic and performance assessments.

alternative-form reliability   The correlation between results on alternative forms of a test. Reliability is the extent to which the two forms are consistent in measuring the same attributes.

analytic rubric   A rubric that provides diagnostic feedback and is more specific than a holistic rubric.

anecdotal record   A written description of an incident in a child's behavior that can be significant in understanding the child.

aptitude test   A test designed to predict future learning or performance on some task if appropriate education or training is provided.

arena assessment   An assessment process whereby a group of specialists in developmental disabilities observes a child in natural play and working situations. A profile of the child is developed by the group, comparing their individual observations of some facet of the child's behaviors.

assessment software   Software that has been developed to enable children to be assessed using a computer. Textbook publishers and developers of early childhood assessment tools make assessment software available as an option alongside traditional assessment tools.

attitude measure   An instrument that measures how an individual is predisposed to feel or think about something (a referent). A teacher can design a scale to measure students' attitudes toward reading or mathematics.

authentic achievement   Learning that is real and meaningful. Achievement that is worthwhile.

authentic assessment   An assessment that uses some type of performance by a child to demonstrate understanding.

authentic performance assessment   *See* authentic assessment.

behavioral objective   An educational or instructional statement that includes the behavior to be exhibited, the conditions under which the behavior will be exhibited, and the level of performance required for mastery.

checklist   A sequence or hierarchy of concepts and/or skills organized in a format that can be used to plan instruction and keep records.

concurrent validity   The extent to which test scores on two forms of a test measure are correlated when they are given at the same time.

construct validity   The extent to which a test measures a psychological trait or construct. Tests of personality, verbal ability, and critical thinking are examples of tests with construct validity.

content validity The extent to which the content of a test such as an achievement test represents the objectives of the instructional program it is designed to measure.

contract An agreement between teacher and child about activities the child will complete to achieve a specific objective or purpose.

correctives Instructional materials and methods used with mastery learning that are implemented after formative evaluation to provide alternative learning strategies and resources.

criterion-referenced test A test designed to provide information on specific knowledge or skills possessed by a student. The test measures specific skills or instructional objectives.

criterion-related validity To establish validity of a test, scores are correlated with an external criterion, such as another established test of the same type.

developmental checklist A checklist that emphasizes areas and levels of development in early childhood.

developmental rubric A rubric that is organized using domains of development.

developmental screening Evaluation of the young child to determine whether development is proceeding normally. It is used to identify children whose development is delayed.

diagnostic evaluation An evaluation to analyze an individual's areas of weaknesses or strengths and to determine the nature and causes of the weaknesses.

diagnostic interview An interview to determine a child's learning needs or assess weaknesses. May be part of a diagnostic evaluation.

directed assignment A specific assignment to assess a child's performance on a learning objective or skill.

direct performance measure A performance measure that requires the student to apply knowledge in an activity specified by the teacher.

documentation A process of documenting information about progress of project activities and recording information about children's interests, ideas, thinking, and problem solving within their activities.

electronic management of learning (EML) Resources available to early childhood programs for instructional experiences using the computer. The materials can include creative, skill development, and assessment software.

enrichment activity In the context of mastery learning, a challenging activity at a higher cognitive level on Bloom's taxonomy than the instructional objective described on a table of specifications.

equivalent forms Alternative forms of a test that are parallel. The forms of the test measure the same domain or objectives, have the same format, and are of equal difficulty.

event sampling An observation strategy used to determine when a particular behavior is likely to occur. The setting in which the behavior occurs is more important than the time it is likely to occur.

formative assessment An assessment designed to measure progress on an objective rather than to give a qualitative result.

formative evaluation Evaluation conducted during instruction to provide the teacher with information on the learning progress of the student and the effectiveness of instructional methods and materials.

formative test A test designed to evaluate progress on specific learning objectives or a unit of study.

game In the context of authentic assessment, a structured assessment whereby the student's performance progress is evaluated through engagement with the game.

grade equivalent The grade level for which a given score on a standardized test is the estimated average. Grade-equivalent scores, commonly used for elementary achievement tests, are expressed in terms of the grade and month.

grade norms Norms on standardized tests based on the performance of students in given grades.

graphic rating scale A rating scale that can be used as a continuum. The rater marks characteristics by descriptors on the scale at any point along the continuum.

group test A test that can be administered to more than one person at a time.

holistic rubric A rubric with competency levels that indicate levels of performance. It assigns a single score to a student's performance.

inclusion The process of including children with disabilities into a classroom where they would have been placed if they had not experienced a disability.

indirect performance measure A measure that assesses what a student knows about a topic. The teacher's assessment is accomplished by observing a student activity or examining a written test.

individualized instruction Instruction based on the learning needs of individual students. It may be based on criterion-related evaluation or diagnosis.

individual test A test that can be administered to only one person at a time. Many early childhood tests are individual tests because of the low maturity level of the examinees.

informal test A test that has not been standardized. Teacher-designed tests are an example.

instructional objective *See* behavioral objective.

integration Facilitating the participation of children with disabilities into the classroom with peers who do not have disabilities. The child is integrated with other children, and the needs of all children are met without treating some children as "special."

intelligence quotient (IQ) An index of intelligence expressed as the ratio of mental age to chronological age. It is derived from an individual's performance on an intelligence test as compared with that of others of the same age.

intelligence test A test measuring developed abilities that are considered signs of intelligence. Intelligence is general potential independent of prior learning.

interest inventory A measure used to determine interest in an occupation or vocation. Students' interest in reading may be determined by such an inventory.

internal consistency The degree of relationship among items on a test. A type of reliability that indicates whether items on the test are positively correlated and measure the same trait or characteristic.

interview A discussion that the teacher conducts with a child to make an assessment.

item analysis The analysis of single test items to determine their difficulty value and discriminating power. Item analysis is conducted in the process of developing a standardized test.

learning disability A developmental difference or delay in a young or school-age child that interferes with the individual's ability to learn through regular methods of instruction.

mainstreaming A process of placing children with disabilities into regular classrooms for part of the school day with children who do not have disabilities. Mainstreaming is being replaced by inclusion or integration, in which the child with disabilities is not singled out as being different.

mastery testing Evaluation to determine the extent to which a test taker has mastered particular skills or learning objectives. Performance is compared to a predetermined standard of proficiency.

mean The arithmetic average of a set of test scores.

minimum-competency testing Evaluation to measure whether test takers have achieved a minimum level of proficiency in a given academic area.

multiple choice A type of test question in which the test taker must choose the best answer from among several options.

narrative report An alternative to report cards for reporting a child's progress. The teacher writes a narrative to describe the child's growth and accomplishments.

neonatologist A physician who specializes in babies less than 1 month old.

normal distribution The hypothetical distribution of scores that has a bell-shaped appearance. This distribution is used as a model for many scoring systems and test statistics.

norm-referenced test A test in which the test taker's performance is compared with the performance of people in a norm group.

norms Statistics that supply a frame of reference based on the actual performance of test takers in a norm group. A set of scores that represents the distribution of test performance in the norm group.

numerical rating scale A series of numerals, such as 1 to 5, that allows an observer to indicate the degree to which an individual possesses a particular characteristic.

obstetrician A physician who specializes in pregnancy and childbirth.

pediatrician A physician who specializes in the development, care, and diseases of young children.

percentile A point or score in a distribution at or below which falls the percentage of cases indicated by the percentile. The score scale on a normal distribution is divided into 100 segments, each containing the same number of scores.

percentile rank The test taker's test score, as expressed in terms of its position within a group of 100 scores. The percentile rank is the percentage of scores equal to or lower than the test taker's score.

performance assessment An assessment in which the child demonstrates knowledge by applying it to a task or a problem-solving activity.

performance-based assessment An assessment of development and/or learning that is based on the child's natural performance, rather than on contrived tests or tasks.

personality test A test designed to obtain information on the affective characteristics of an individual (emotional, motivational, or attitudinal). The test measures psychological makeup rather than intellectual abilities.

play-based assessment Assessment often used for children with disabilities that is conducted through observation in play environments. Play activities can be spontaneous or planned. Play-based assessment can be conducted by an individual or through arena assessment.

portfolio A format for conducting an evaluation of a child. Portfolios are a collection of a child's work, teacher assessments, and other information that contribute to a picture of the child's progress.

preassessment An assessment conducted before the beginning of the school year or prior to any instruction at the beginning of the school year.

project An authentic learning activity that can also be used to demonstrate student achievement.

rating scale A scale using categories that allow the observer to indicate the degree of a characteristic that the person possesses.

raw score The number of right answers a test taker obtains on a test.

reliability The extent to which a test is consistent in measuring over time what it is designed to measure.

rubric An instrument developed to measure authentic and performance assessments. Descriptions are given for qualitative characteristics on a scale.

running record A description of a sequence of events in a child's behavior that includes all behaviors observed over a period of time.

scope (sequence of skills) A list of learning objectives established for areas of learning and development at a particular age, grade level, or content area.

specimen record Detailed observational reports of children's behavior over a period of time that are used for research purposes.

split-half reliability A measure of reliability whereby scores on equivalent sections of a single test are correlated for internal consistency.

standard deviation A measure of the variability of a distribution of scores around the mean.

standard error of measurement   An estimate of the possible magnitude of error present in test scores.

standardized test   A test that has specified content, procedures for administration and scoring, and normative data for interpreting scores.

standard score   A transformed score that reports performance in terms of the number of standard deviation units the raw score is from the mean.

stanine   A scale on the normal curve divided into nine sections, with all divisions except the first and the last being 0.5 standard deviation wide.

structured interview   A planned interview conducted by the teacher for assessment purposes.

structured performance assessment   A performance assessment that has been planned by the teacher to include specific tasks or activities.

summative assessment   A final assessment to assign a grade or determine mastery of an objective. Similar to summative evaluation.

summative evaluation   An evaluation obtained at the end of a cycle of instruction to determine whether students have mastered the objectives and whether the instruction has been effective.

summative test   A test to determine mastery of learning objectives administered for grading purposes.

T score   A standard score scale with a mean of 50 and a standard deviation of 10.

table of specifications   A table of curriculum objectives that have been analyzed to determine to what level of Bloom's taxonomy of educational objectives the student must demonstrate mastery.

test–retest reliability   A type of reliability obtained by administering the same test a second time after a short interval and then correlating the two sets of scores.

time sampling   Observation to determine the frequency of a behavior. The observer records how many times the behavior occurs during uniform time periods.

true score   A hypothetical score on a test that is free of error. Because no standardized test is free of measurement error, a true score can never be obtained.

unstructured interview   An assessment interview conducted by the teacher as the result of a naturally occurring performance by a child. The interview is not planned.

unstructured performance assessment   An assessment that is part of regular classroom activities.

validity   The degree to which a test serves the purpose for which it is to be used.

work sample   An example of a child's work. Work samples include products of all types of activities that can be used to evaluate the child's progress.

Z score   A standard score that expresses performance in terms of the number of standard deviations from the mean.

Index